What Happened to the
USMNT
The Ugly Truth about
the Beautiful Game

Steven G. Mandis and Sarah Parsons Wolter

TRIUMPH
B O O K S

Library of Congress Cataloging-in-Publication Data

Names: Mandis, Steven G., author. | Parsons Wolter, Sarah, author.
Title: What happened to the USMNT : the ugly truth about the beautiful game / Steven G. Mandis and Sarah Parsons Wolter.
Other titles: What happened to the United States Men's National Team
Description: Chicago : Triumph Books, 2021.
Identifiers: LCCN 2021000005 | ISBN 9781629378572 (hardcover) | ISBN 9781641256131 (epub)
Subjects: LCSH: United States Mens National Soccer Team—History. | Soccer—United States—History.
Classification: LCC GV944.U5 M36 2021 | DDC 796.334/630973—dc23
LC record available at https://lccn.loc.gov/2021000005

This book is available in quantity at special discounts for your group or organization. For further information, contact:

Triumph Books LLC
814 North Franklin Street
Chicago, Illinois 60610
(312) 337-0747
www.triumphbooks.com

Printed in U.S.A.
ISBN: 978-1-62937-857-2
Design by Nord Compo
Page production by Patricia Frey

*This book is dedicated to the former, current, and future members
of the U.S. national men's and women's soccer teams*

*In recognition of you and our thanks, author proceeds
from sales of this book are donated to charity*

Contents

Preface

In 2004, after advancing out of the group stage, Greece beat France (with Zinedine Zidane and Thierry Henry) in the quarterfinals, the Czech Republic (with Pavel Nedvěd and Petr Čech) in the semifinals, and heavily favored Portugal (with Luís Figo and Cristiano Ronaldo) in Portugal in the Finals to win the 2004 UEFA European Championship. When Greece qualified for the tournament (the only other time they qualified was in 1980), their goal was to win a single game—after all, the bookmakers had them at 80–1 odds to win the tournament. In a 2016 interview with Rory Smith of ESPN, Vasilis Tsiartas, a Greece midfielder during the tournament, said, "Just one game. It was something none of the [Greece] national teams had been able to do [at a major tournament]. Even the [Greece] side who had gone to the World Cup in 1994 had not managed to beat anyone. That would have counted as a success: winning just once."

Actually, Greece didn't even score a goal in the 1994 World Cup, while allowing 10 goals in three group stage matches. Greece's left back Takis Fyssas added, "We only had the weapons we had been given. We did not have a Zidane…or Cristiano Ronaldo. We only had hard work, sacrifice, determination, and that family spirit. What we did is the same as how Atlético Madrid play now."

Atlético Madrid reached the Champions League Final in 2014 and 2016 and are a perennial contender to win the tournament even though they don't have the budget and talent of many of their competitors. They are a club many of the favorites fear. Atlético Madrid have an identity centered around *grinta* (literally: grit)—an extraordinary determination difficult to describe and find in players, a warrior mentality. Their players are willing to abandon caution and throw their heads where most players wouldn't extend their cleats. Their fans, players, and coach prioritize *grinta* even over results—it's their identity. After being criticized for their reliance on grit and a counter-attacking style combined with superb goalkeeping, defense, and set pieces, Atlético Madrid's coach Diego Simeone responded, "Everyone has their own style of play. You may like it or not, but football is beautiful because you can win in different ways."

And maybe that is an ugly truth about the beautiful game.

Introduction

In the 2002 FIFA World Cup jointly hosted by South Korea and Japan, the U.S. men's national soccer team (USMNT) had a memorable run. The USMNT beat Portugal 3–2 in the group stage. Portugal had three players nominated for the 2001 Ballon d'Or, including Luís Figo, who finished sixth and played for Real Madrid.[1] With the win, the USMNT advanced out of the group stage and defeated Mexico 2–0 in the Round of 16. In the quarterfinals, the USMNT lost to soccer power Germany 0–1. Germany had three players in the top 15 voting for the 2002 Ballon d'Or, including goalkeeper Oliver Kahn, who finished third. Nearly the entire team played in the Bundesliga, the top German professional league.

The USMNT certainly were not outplayed by Germany—the USMNT had more time of possession, shots on goal, and shots on target. The match included a controversial no-call of a handball by a German defender on his goal line that prevented what would have been a match-tying USMNT goal. After a dismal performance at the 1998 World Cup, where they finished 32nd out of 32 teams, the USMNT had shown they deserved to

---

1. The Ballon d'Or is an award for best soccer player from any origin who had been active at a European club. In 1995, the Ballon d'Or was expanded to include all players from any origin that have been active at European clubs. George Weah (father of USMNT player Tim Weah) was the first non-European to win.

be on the world stage in 2002. With the crowd chanting "USA! USA!," the players walked off the field in South Korea with their heads held high.

The USMNT didn't have any players even close to being nominated for the Ballon d'Or. Most experts said that the players' athleticism exceeded their technical ability. The USMNT utilized hard work, energy, hustle, speed, and teamwork. They took advantage of set pieces, luck, and opponents' mistakes. The USMNT played counter-attacking soccer. If the Italians have their *catenaccio*, the Spanish their *tiki-taka*, the Dutch their *totaalvoetball*, the Germans their *kampfgeist*, and the Brazilians their *ginga*, then the American style was, for lack of a better word or phrase, "Spirit of '76."[2] The Americans compressed space, worked in groups defensively, and looked to counter-attack. It wasn't beautiful, inspired soccer in a European or South American sense, but it was the uniquely "American way" to play, reflecting parts of U.S. culture, history with the sport, and skill level. Many USMNT fans played the American style in youth leagues or high school. The USMNT style of soccer was authentically "American." Many U.S. fans were extraordinarily passionate about and loyal to the USMNT precisely because they identified with their American style and values. In addition, the fans identified with the values and personalities of the players, who seemed to work together, sacrificed for the greater good, and embraced being underdogs. This emergent fan base was contributing to the growing popularity of the sport of soccer. Many fans felt that with more resources, player development, experience, and luck, the USMNT could be a regular contender to reach the later stages of the World Cup. With surprise sensations Landon Donovan and DaMarcus Beasley, both just 20 years old at the 2002 World Cup, the future looked bright.[3]

While extraordinary progress has been made in the last few decades— the USMNT reached the Final of the 2009 FIFA Confederations Cup and advanced to the Round of 16 in the 2010 and 2014 World Cups—the

---

2. Later we will explain why we give this American style the nickname "Spirit of '76."

3. Also, 18-year-old Eddie Johnson, 19-year-old Clint Dempsey, and 23-year-old Tim Howard were coming up the ranks.

USMNT never seemed to fully live up to increasing expectations and the 2002 World Cup quarterfinal comparison.

In 2017, the USMNT failed to qualify for the 2018 World Cup. After several disappointing results, all the team needed to do to qualify was to defeat or tie Trinidad & Tobago (T&T), an opponent that had won only one of its previous nine matches. The USMNT lost 1–2.

When we looked up the starting lineups for the match, we were surprised. None of the T&T starters played in Major League Soccer (MLS). Most played in the TT Pro League, T&T's top soccer division. Three starters played internationally, one in the highest Dutch professional league, one in the second-level Belgian professional league, and one in the third-level Mexican professional league. The USMNT had six starters who played in MLS, three in the Top Five Leagues in Europe (England's Premier League, Spain's La Liga, Germany's Bundesliga, Italy's Serie A, and France's Ligue 1), and two in Mexico's Liga MX.

In a passionate rant to ESPN *SportsCenter* anchor Max Bretos that went viral, Taylor Twellman, a retired USMNT player who works as a television analyst for ESPN, called the loss and failure to qualify a "complete embarrassment." Most, if not all, of the players felt the same way, expressing their collective disappointment, sadness, and frustration after the match. Omar Gonzalez, who scored an unfortunate own goal at the 17-minute mark, said, "It's the worst day of my career. I am extremely sad right now. What was supposed to be a celebration is now…I, I don't even know what to say. It's terrible. We let down an entire nation today."

A little more than two years after the Americans lost to T&T, the USMNT saw their 34-year, 17-match unbeaten streak against Canada come to an end, suffering a 0–2 defeat.

In an interview with ESPN host and reporter Sebastian Salazar, Taylor Twellman expressed that he was "just real apathetic about the entire thing. It's almost like I have no emotion, which actually scares the living crap out of me."

What Happened to the U.S. Men's National Soccer Team?

When the USMNT qualified for the 1990 World Cup, their first qualification since 1950, they, the United States Soccer Federation (USSF), and most media members and fans had one common mission (the reason they were so passionate)—to prove the legitimacy of soccer in the United States. The USMNT's goal was to qualify for the World Cup to prove they (and therefore soccer in the U.S.) belonged amongst the world's best. The USSF, the USMNT, and most fans also wanted to prove that the U.S. legitimately deserved to host the 1994 World Cup, then build off that success to grow the sport of soccer in the U.S.[4] The *why*— prove the legitimacy of soccer in the U.S.—led to a *how*—an American soccer culture and style of play. The "American style" of play was a "counter-attacking style" with a reliance on superb goalkeeping, defense, and set pieces.[5] The *how* also led to the players—the *who*—willing to sacrifice themselves and, with a common purpose, work together to prove U.S. Soccer legitimately belonged. While their style of play was counter-attacking, their identity was grit. We label the identity and style coming out of the 1994 World Cup as the "Spirit of '76," embracing an underdog status or mentality similar to the American Patriots in 1776. Also, the USMNT seemed to be a group of loveable characters.

---

4. Brazil and Morocco were also competing for a chance to host the 1994 World Cup. The final vote was U.S. 10, Morocco seven, and Brazil two. The USSF had tried to host the 1986 World Cup, which was awarded to Mexico. At the time, the FIFA president said, "Mexico is a real soccer country. The United States and Canada are not ready for such a competition." The USMNT didn't advance to the final CONCACAF round to try to qualify for the 1986 World Cup. In 1984 the U.S. hosted the Summer Olympics and the numbers overall were staggering. Most surprisingly, soccer, of all sports, led attendance. An average of almost 45,000 people attended 32 games. Rick Davis scored two goals. Even though the U.S. didn't advance out of the first round, attendance continued to rise. This was surprising because the North American Soccer League went bankrupt in 1984.

5. A counter-attacking style involves a team withdrawing players into their own half but ensuring that one or two players are committed to the attack. The style requires a strong defensive foundation that is able to sit back and hold strong against almost constant pressure. If the opponent has the lead, the style doesn't work as well, as the leading team will not advance the ball but instead possess the ball in its half of the field. In addition, if a counter-attacking team favored to win plays a team that doesn't attack, it must have the patience and skill to capitalize on few opportunities, which increases the risk of losses to non-favored teams. The execution of the counter-attacking style of play is fairly simple and therefore is often viewed as "inferior" to or "less exciting" than attacking styles.

In preparation for the 1994 World Cup and without a major domestic professional league, USMNT players were paid to train year-round together at a national team training center in Mission Viejo, California, south of Los Angeles. Most of those at the USMNT training center were not considered skilled or experienced enough to get good opportunities to play in European leagues—they were underdogs.

Many Americans think of themselves as, or have a particular affinity for, underdogs. There is something in the American psyche to want to cheer for loveable people who seem to be up against the odds, like the 1980 U.S. Olympic Hockey Team's "Miracle on Ice." In many ways, that team was the last memorable U.S. national team to be a true underdog in a major sport. In 1986, the International Olympic Committee (IOC) granted professional athletes the ability to compete in the Olympic Games so long as they were deemed eligible by their respective international federations, and in 1992 USA Basketball sent the "Dream Team" to compete in the Olympic Games. In the movie *Miracle*, Kurt Russell as Coach Herb Brooks said, "I always found that term [Dream Team] ironic because now that we have Dream Teams, we seldom ever get to dream. But on one weekend, as America and the world watched, a group of remarkable young men gave the nation what it needed most—a chance, for one night, not only to dream, but a chance to believe."

By the 1994 World Cup, many U.S. sports fans, no longer having a national "underdog," were curious if the USMNT could pull off a "Miracle on Grass" against soccer powers—they wanted to dream and believe. Hosting the 1994 World Cup and advancing to the Round of 16 gave the USMNT a platform to showcase their *why*, *how*, and *who*. Stadium attendances and TV ratings exceeded all expectations. The USMNT games gave fans an opportunity to get to know and passionately root for the loveable underdogs fighting for the legitimacy of soccer in the U.S.

Over the next two decades, soccer became more popular in the U.S., and the USMNT often overachieved. The USMNT improved and had some good results on the field, which fueled American ambition, competitiveness, and impatience. Increasingly, the USSF and USMNT felt various pressures to show progress on and off the field in an upward-trending straight line, year after year. They, the media, the sponsors, and the fans started to develop and rely upon flawed comparisons and unrealistic expectations—and didn't fully recognize the overachievement. For example, many compare recent results to the 2002 World Cup quarterfinals, like we were just guilty of earlier in the introduction. While that was a remarkable and well-deserved accomplishment, we discovered any comparison to 2002 is flawed for a number of reasons, including the luck that was involved. Each result needs context.

The *why*—prove the legitimacy of soccer in the U.S.—may have stayed the same, but the meaning of legitimacy gradually shifted from just demonstrating U.S. Soccer belonged on a world stage to winning the World Cup while playing like European teams.[6] This change was not deliberate; rather, the drift happened so slowly that the modification in meaning of the *why* became normalized by the USSF, USMNT, the fans, sponsors, and the media.

Around the same time, European soccer was becoming more commercialized and growing quickly. Attracted by the money and level of competition, more of the best players from around the world went to Europe to play at earlier and earlier ages, including Americans. A European team (in most recent order: France 2018, Germany 2014, Spain 2010, and Italy 2006) has won the last four World Cups. Before

---

6. Chancellor of the German Empire Otto Von Bismarck said, "Whoever speaks of Europe is wrong: it is a geographical expression." He said this in the 19th century, but it is still valid today. There is no concrete European identity or culture, and there likely never will be. *European* is simply an adjective used to describe the fact that someone was born in, or resides in, Europe. Using the phrase *European style* is always difficult because European soccer style encompasses many countries and styles and even within those countries there are different styles. To simplify what we mean when we use the term *European style*, we are referring to a style that is distinct from a traditionally American counter-attacking style and reliance on grit, goalkeeping, defense, and set pieces and from a typical Latin and South American style. This is not to say that certain European teams and clubs don't play a counter-attacking style. To simplify what we mean when we use the phrase *Latin and South American style*, we are referring to an open style of soccer that requires more individual creativity, technical skills, and proactive attacks. This is not to say that certain South American and Latin teams and clubs don't play a different style. In fact, we found that even in Brazil there are multiple styles, primarily due to where most immigrants came from, proximity to other countries, and weather. In all of our interviews no one ever mentioned that the USMNT should play more like any Latin or South American country or club or any other region—people referred to either a country or club in Europe. In addition, in all of our interviews no one mentioned that the USMNT needed to play more like any regional style within the United States.

2002, South American teams had only once failed to win two World Cups in a row, back in the 1930s. The 2018 World Cup saw all four semifinalists come from Europe, and six of the eight quarterfinalists also came from the continent. Europe's dominance is only continuing to grow in the international game. Prior to 2010, no European team had ever won a World Cup that was hosted outside of Europe—before back-to-back triumphs in 2010 in South Africa and in Brazil in 2014. In terms of prestige, the UEFA European Championship is considered the second-best (in terms of highest level of competition) national soccer tournament after the World Cup.

In 2009, Simon Kuper and Stefan Szymanski published their influential book *Soccernomics*. In a 2009 interview with Jack Bell of the *New York Times*, Kuper declared, "The best coaching week in and week out is in Western Europe, and the U.S. needs to adopt the best practices. And if you want to win, send all your best players to play in Europe and hire all your coaches from Europe." The lead TV announcers for the 1990–2010 World Cups were American. Starting in 2010, things changed. Martin Tyler, an English soccer commentator, led ESPN's coverage of the 2010 FIFA World Cup. Many factors created a subconscious bias toward or deference to Europe and an inferiority complex about soccer in the United States.

As their mission drifted, the USMNT slowly shifted from having an underdog mentality America loved, identified with, and rooted for to being more and more, for lack of a better word, arrogant. Americans are used to being dominant in many of the other major sports, from those in the Olympics (where the U.S. has more than twice as many gold and total medals as any other country) to American football, baseball, and basketball (where Americans generally accept that the champions of the NFL, MLB, NBA, and NHL are "World Champions"). Given the United States' resources and large population, the USMNT's relatively lower skill level and "sophistication in style" in soccer compared to Europe presented a serious conundrum—and one that Americans grew less willing to accept. Losing to countries not historically considered "soccer powers" was incomprehensible.

The drift to wanting to be and play "more European" resulted in Jürgen Klinsmann being hired as coach in the summer of 2011, though it had begun long before that event.[7] Klinsmann's hiring just accelerated the belief that the USMNT needed to act and play more like Europeans and not be underdogs in order to progress and be more successful. The result of the drift was the USMNT's mission, identity, and style of play became less clear. No one person or group or organization is to blame. Even the USMNT fans wanted to be and act "more European." The first USMNT supporters' club, Sam's Army, was started in 1995 and was inspired by the supporters' clubs of European professional clubs.[8] A European-style supporters' club was adding "legitimacy" to soccer in the U.S., as was hiring a German coach with World Cup credentials (or MLS clubs increasingly incorporating words such as "United" or "FC" or "Real" or "Inter" while the NASL [1968–1984] with the New York Cosmos did not). In a 2014 *Wall Street Journal* article titled "The Problem with American Soccer Fans: It All Feels Like an Elaborate Affectation," Jonathan Clegg warned, "The great regret about all this is that mimicking the customs of [soccer] fans from everywhere else could hinder the development of your own American soccer identity."

Regardless of your thoughts on Clegg's warning, he touched on an important point—having a distinct and authentic identity. The USMNT seemed to have a clearer identity and style of play that was working—especially considering the team's relative skill level—up until the 2010 World Cup. The USMNT reached the 2009 FIFA Confederations Cup Final and won their group at the 2010 World Cup.[9] And while it is in theory possible to mimic a certain style of play with enough talent and time, it is impossible (not to mention counterproductive) to copy a style of play that evolved through a distinctive culture, history, values, and even

---

7. Pia Sundhage, who won the 1984 UEFA Women's Championship with Sweden, was hired to be the USWNT coach in 2008, after the USWNT finished in third place in the Women's World Cup for the second consecutive time.

8. The name of the group derives from Uncle Sam, a national personification of the United States, and Scottish supporters' group the Tartan Army.

9. The USMNT tied England in the group stage and won the group on the tiebreaker of scoring more goals; England also lost in the Round of 16.

physical environment, and reflects a certain level of skill. Not advancing to at least the quarterfinals in 2010, like in 2002, made it appear that progress had stagnated and provided another reason why a European approach seemed necessary.

Once again, we want to emphasize that significant progress was made with soccer in the U.S. and that recent disappointments on the field should not overshadow a lot of good work done by many unheralded people. All countries go through cycles and have bad luck. After the 2014 World Cup, the U.S. were one of only eight countries—along with Argentina (who have won the World Cup two times in history), Brazil (5), England (1), Germany (4), Mexico (0), the Netherlands (0), and Spain (1)—to advance to the knockout round at three of the previous four World Cups. Notably absent from the list are Belgium (0 World Cup titles), Croatia (0), Czech Republic (0), France (2), Italy (4), Portugal (0), Serbia/Yugoslavia (0), and Uruguay (2). While it may be easier for the USMNT to qualify for a World Cup from the CONCACAF region, for this statistic they still have to advance out of the group stage.

Two issues often surrounding disappointments are flawed comparisons and unrealistic expectations. While in hindsight many things could have been done better, taking a step back to reflect on the data, the results are pretty good—especially considering the history and skill level of soccer in the U.S. However, it is clear that the drift from the original *why, how,* and *who* is constraining progress.

The story of drift is messy and complex. Many seemingly unrelated pressures, results, events, and decisions over time, as well as their independent, unintended, and compounding consequences, slowly changed the USMNT's mission, culture, and style of play. Different elements of the USMNT's mission, culture, and style of play changed at different times, at different speeds, and at different levels of significance. Evolution and innovation are necessary to improve, but the USMNT shouldn't try to be something they are not. Drift is not the only reason the team did not qualify for the 2018 World Cup. There are many factors involved, including luck. However, the changes to their *why, how,* and *who* were major contributors and have hindered progress and development.

Lastly, when making comparisons to previous performances and results (both by the USMNT as well as other countries' national teams), the USSF, USMNT, media, sponsors, and fans need to add context—which should help set more realistic expectations.

What Are Realistic Expectations for the U.S. Men's National Soccer Team?

Even for the best of the best soccer powers, progress does not chart a straight line and dominance comes and goes, especially in a tournament that takes place every four years. Only eight countries have won the World Cup since it was first held in 1930. Frenchman Jules Rimet, the president of FIFA from 1921 to 1954, is credited with having created the competition now called the World Cup. It took almost seven decades for his country to win a World Cup Final in 1998.

Germany, who won in 2014 and are arguably the best and most consistent country in modern times, didn't make it past the group stage in 2018, having scored only two goals in the tournament. The only realistic expectation by any federation, team, media member, sponsor, or fan is to be a consistent contender and to recognize that there are ups and downs and cycles for various reasons. And the narrative is impacted by the slimmest of margins. Therefore, the focus needs to be on what can be controlled—*why*, *how*, and *who*.

Putting aside *winning* the World Cup—*it is very difficult to even reach the semifinals*. As evidence, soccer power Spain—with all of their great players over the years, with the clubs Barcelona and Real Madrid, and with their Top Five League—have reached the semifinals *once* since 1950. In 2010, Spain reached the semifinals on their way to winning their one and only World Cup—and since, in 2014 and 2018, they finished 23rd and 10th, respectively. Spain won the 2010 World Cup as well as the 2008 and 2012 European Championships. Many experts credited Spain's dominance to their *tiki-taka* style, which is a Spanish style of play characterized by collective short passing and movement, working the ball through various channels, and maintaining possession. German soccer journalist and author Raphael Honigstein explained that *tiki-taka* evolved from Spain deciding "they weren't physical and tough enough to outmuscle opponents, so instead wanted to concentrate on monopolizing the ball." Many experts considered *tiki-taka*, which requires skillfully technical players at every position, "sophisticated" and "romantic." FIFA TV even has a video titled "How Tiki-Taka Took Spain to the Top of the World." We examined how Spain won the 2010 World Cup and their subsequent performance to provide some of the context that is necessary to analyze the USMNT.

The Ugly Truth about How Spain Won the 2010 World Cup

In 2010, Spain had *seven* players from Barcelona (*plus two* other players who attended the Barcelona youth academy not playing for Barcelona) familiar with the *tiki-taka* system that the national team adopted plus *five* players from Real Madrid (as well as *four* from Valencia), who had played against Barcelona many times and were familiar with the *tiki-taka* system. In comparison, as it relates to familiarity, the most players the USMNT had from one domestic professional team in 2010 was two, from the LA Galaxy.[10] Twenty of the 23 players on the Spanish team were playing in Spain's La Liga (the other three played in the English Premier League—two for Liverpool and one for Arsenal). In comparison, the 23 USMNT players were playing in nine different leagues. In reality, Spain's national identification and development program was essentially Barcelona's youth training academy, La Masia, as well as a few other Spanish club academies. Similarly, when Germany and Italy won World Cups they had a core group of players from Bayern Munich and Juventus, respectively, who utilized the styles of their respective teams. Unlike Major League Soccer, there are no salary caps in the Top Five European Soccer Leagues. The domestic clubs with the largest revenues can afford to hoard the best domestic talent, allowing them to train together in a familiar style. (The storytelling of great European national federations or teams is actually a story about the youth academies of European clubs.) Spain also had talent—*six* players finished in the top 15 votes for the 2010 Ballon d'Or.

---

10. However, six players played in the U-17 Residency Program at IMG Academy in Bradenton, Florida, and three players attended UCLA.

Even with all of that talent and familiarity with each other and a system, Spain only scored *eight goals in seven matches* at the 2010 World Cup. In four knockout round matches, including the Final, which went into extra time, Spain won 1–0. In Spain's first knockout round match, replays later showed their goal scorer was offside.[11] In the quarterfinal match, Spain's goalkeeper saved a penalty kick, and Spain scored on a penalty kick. In the semifinals, Spain scored on a header from a corner kick. In the Final, the Spanish goalkeeper saved two one-on-one breakaways in regulation, and Spain scored on a quick counter-attack after their opponent received a red card and were a man short in extra time. In summary, in the knockout rounds, two of Spain's goals (50 percent) were from set pieces (penalty kick and corner kick), one goal was offside, and one goal was on counter-attack when they had a man advantage—after those numbers, *tiki-taka* may be different from how it is often portrayed. While Spain were very deserving champions, it is important to understand the context of how they won.[12]

An ugly truth about Spain's 2010 World Cup and *tiki-taka* is that in the knockout rounds, Spain had 27 shots on target over 400 minutes played (one shot every 15 minutes!) and only managed four goals (one goal every 100 minutes played—and two were from set pieces) from the 27 shots on target (15 percent success), which was one of the lowest success rates in the tournament. We recognize that part of the strategy of *tiki-taka* is to keep the ball away from the opponent to limit their opportunities, and their opponents "parked the bus" to try to win against an outstanding team. However, even with all the accolades of *tiki-taka*, there was a lively debate in the international press about whether Spain's style of play in the

---

11. The video assistant referee (VAR) was implemented in the 2018 World Cup.

12. It's also important to note that Spain's *tiki-taka* is not necessarily Barcelona's *tiki-taka* because national team and World Cup soccer have many different characteristics and challenges from club and league soccer—not to mention Barcelona had Lionel Messi. Barcelona scored 98 goals in 38 matches played in the 2009–10 La Liga season (2.6 goals per game), and Lionel Messi won his first Ballon d'Or, with 34 goals and 13 assists in 35 matches played. In addition, 2009–10 Barcelona, coached by Pep Guardiola, lost 2–3 on aggregate to Inter Milan, coached by Jose Mourinho, in the Champions League semifinals. Mourinho used a compact, disciplined defense and fast counter-attacks—and he got his players to play with a chip on their shoulders. In the semifinals, over two games, Barcelona had over 70 percent of possession. Barcelona also completed 1,076 passes, with 86 percent passing success, compared to 225 completed passes, with 66 percent passing success, for Inter.

2010 World Cup was beautiful or boring to watch. (Some commentators pleaded, "Would somebody please just shoot?")

Before winning in 2010, Spain were eliminated in the 2002 and 2006 World Cups in the quarterfinals and the Round of 16, respectively— the same as the USMNT in 2002 and 2010! After winning in 2010, in the subsequent 2014 World Cup, the players who were the engine of Spain's *tiki-taka*, such as Barcelona's Andres Iniesta and Xavi, were over 30 years old (past peak age for performance). Spain were eliminated in the group stage with one win and two losses. The USMNT reached the Round of 16!

For the 2018 World Cup, Spain were one of the top three favorites to win, according to sports bettors. Just one day before the start of the 2018 World Cup, the Spanish coach was fired amid controversy. The new coach, Fernando Hierro, one of the best defenders in the world during his playing days at Real Madrid, said, "the key will be to change as little as possible." However, he never really settled on a starting lineup through the group stage and modified the tactics and personnel to be slightly more cautious than usual. The changes caused Spain to doubt themselves. The self-doubt festered inside Spain, a team for whom identity is so fundamentally important, infecting their play and eventually proving fatal.

In 2018, Spain lost to the hosts, Russia, the lowest-seeded team in the competition, in a penalty shootout in the Round of 16, demonstrating more factors than talent alone have an impact on performance. With their *tiki-taka*, possession-based passing style, Spain attempted 1,137 passes and completed 1,029 (91 percent accuracy), the most ever in a game at the World Cup, and had 75 percent possession. In contrast, Russia completed the same number of passes—1,029—in *four* matches at the World Cup. Russia beat Spain completing 202 of 285 passes (71 percent accuracy). Russia used a five-man defensive back line for the first time in the 2018 World Cup. When Russia's coach was asked why, he thought back to the 2008 European Championship, where Russia lost to Spain 1–4 in their opener and 0–3 in the semifinals. He replied, "Let us say this openly, they are better than us in many ways. So, I don't believe that we should risk going forward."

In 2010, Spain won their four knockout round matches 1–0, relatively slim margins. Against Russia, they were winning 1–0 due to a Russia own goal, but then Spain conceded the equalizer off of the sequence of corner kick, handball, and penalty kick. Gerard Piqué's left arm was raised with his back to a Russia defender when the ball struck his hand—a clear penalty, and clearly bad luck, as was the own goal that gave Spain their goal. The game would go to a penalty shootout. Against all odds, Russia beat Spain on penalties 5–3.[13]

The margins between winning and losing in soccer are so small. Spain's exit was eerily similar to 2002, when host country South Korea ousted them on penalty kicks in the quarterfinals. In 2018, Spain joined Argentina, Germany, and Portugal on early flights home. Spain, a country that is seen as a soccer power with the talent and strong domestic league to back it up, certainly hasn't had progress in an upward-trending straight line. While we choose to single out Spain here, what is most important is that they are not unique.

At the conclusion of this book, we'll revisit the ugly truth about how Spain won the 2010 World Cup.

What Is the Relative Talent of the USMNT?

In the last four World Cups, the winning team have had an average of *six* players in the top 15 votes for the Ballon d'Or. In comparison, the USMNT has never had a player receive one vote for the Ballon d'Or. The USMNT have had two players, DaMarcus Beasley, playing for Dutch club PSV in 2005, and Tyler Adams, playing for German club RB Leipzig in 2020, play in the semifinals of the Champions League.[14] In comparison, since the first

---

13. Spain would go first, and they converted. Teams that go first in a penalty shootout and convert win 60 percent of the time because, in theory, shooting second, and thus from behind, puts players under greater psychological pressure.

14. PSV lost to AC Milan in the semifinals. Beasley played for 61 minutes in the first leg. He could not play the second leg because of an injury. Leipzig lost to Paris Saint-Germain. Adams came on in the 64th minute. There was only one match due to the COVID-19 shortened tournament. Adams scored the winning goal against Atlético Madrid in the quarterfinal.

Champions League Final in 1956, 1,112 players representing 65 nations have been to the Final, including Canada—Alphonso Davies with Bayern Munich in 2020—and 42 nations have had at least two players appear in the Champions League Final, including Mexico—Rafael Márquez with Barcelona in 2006 and 2009 and Javier "Chicharito" Hernández with Manchester United in 2011.[15]

We did investigate the USMNT's talent over time. This is highly subjective and there is no one universally accepted or agreed-upon metric. To measure talent on the USMNT (and putting Ballon d'Or voting or Champions League Final appearances aside), we analyzed both the number of players and their minutes in the Top Five Leagues for the season preceding the World Cup. Some commentators focus on the number of players in the Top Five Leagues, but that can be misleading because players can be selected for a team for a variety of reasons or not regularly play. The number of minutes on the field, actually playing, would be a better indicator of talent. We also examined the minutes including and excluding goalies because the USMNT have traditionally had a lot of talent at the goalkeeper position, and they play a lot of minutes.

The number and minutes played of USMNT players (including and excluding goalies) in the Top Five Leagues increased gradually over the course of the 1990s and early 2000s from not a single player, and therefore zero minutes, at the 1990 World Cup, to six players and 12,312 minutes in 2006. Those figures then almost doubled in 2010 to 12 players and 23,265 minutes, leveled off in 2014 with 10 players and just over 23,000 minutes, then dropped sharply in 2017, with only four players playing a total of 9,156 minutes. The decline surprised us. We discovered there was a talent boom resulting from the 1994 World Cup reaching a peak

---

15. Midfielder-forward Jovan Kirovski is the only American with a Champions League medal. He played for the U.S. in the 1996 Olympics and made 62 appearances for the USMNT beginning at age 18. He is often forgotten because he played in Europe for 10 years and never was on a World Cup squad. Kirovski, the son of Macedonian immigrants, joined Manchester United's youth academy in 1992 when he was 16 years old, but was not able to play for the first team because of work permit regulations. When he was 20 years old, he played in Borussia Dortmund's 1996–97 campaign when they won the Champions League. He was a substitute in two group stage games and was on the bench in the other games, including the semifinals against Manchester United. However, he was not on the roster for the Final.

in 2006 to 2010. Still, the decline was steeper than expected. When the USMNT lost to Trinidad & Tobago in 2017, the number and minutes of USMNT players in the Top Five Leagues (four players, 9,156 minutes) had regressed to less than the 1998 USMNT World Cup numbers (five players, 11,025 minutes).

Table: # of Players and Minutes of USMNT in Top Five Leagues

	1990	1994	1998	2002	2006	2010	2014	2017*
WC Finish	Group Stage	Round of 16	Group Stage	Quarterfinals	Group Stage	Round of 16	Round of 16	DNQ
WC Place (#)	23	14	32	8	25	12	15	N/A
Coach	Bob Gansier	Bora Milutinović	Steve Sampson	Bruce Arena	Bruce Arena	Bob Bradley	Jürgen Klinsmann	Bruce Arena
Total Team Caps	454	425	1,156	1,153	1,030	813	820	1,245
# Players Top 5 Leagues	0	1	5	8	6	12	10	4
% Players Top 5 Leagues	0%	5%	23%	35%	26%	52%	43%	17%
Total Minutes Top 5 Leagues	0	1,857	11,025	12,652	12,312	23,265	23,042	9,156
Total Minutes Top 5 (ex. Goalies)	0	1,857	6,975	7,972	8,668	15,285	16,359	9,156
Avg. Minutes/Player Top 5	0	1,857	2,205	1,582	2,052	1,939	2,304	2,289
# Players Europe	4	6	6	12	12	17	12	5
Total Minutes Europe		7,484	13,674	21,548	31,875	32,140	27,457	13,476
% Players Europe	18%	27%	26%	52%	52%	74%	52%	22%
# Players Champions/Europa League Play	0	0	2	0	1	3	2	1
Total Minutes Champions/Europa League Play	0	0	750	0	0	1,152	253	546

* The USMNT did not qualify for the World Cup in 2017; this was the squad from the last game

The decline in minutes can be partially explained by a few players who played in Top Five Leagues moving back to the U.S. to play in MLS.[16] MLS compensation increased over the years, especially for USMNT star players. Earlier MLS clubs had a reputation for underpaying top American players; today, star players on the USMNT can make more money in MLS than a Top Five League in Europe. However, in most instances, the players who moved back to the U.S. were over the age of 30 and past their age of peak performance. The two exceptions are Michael Bradley (27 years old when he came back to the U.S. to play in MLS) and Jozy Altidore (26). Even adding in Bradley and Altidore's expected minutes in 2017 (which would have been around 2,500 minutes each), there still would have been a decline in number of minutes to just above 2002 and 2006 levels.

Table: # of Players and Minutes of USMNT in Top Five Leagues
(including Bradley and Altidore Expected Minutes)

---

16. Most notably, Clint Dempsey in 2013; Michael Bradley, DaMarcus Beasley, and Jermaine Jones in 2014; Jozy Altidore in 2015; and Tim Howard in 2016.

	1990	1994	1998	2002	2006	2010	2014	2017
WC Finish	Group Stage	Round of 16	Group Stage	Quarterfinals	Group Stage	Round of 16	Round of 16	DNQ
WC Place (#)	23	14	32	8	25	12	15	40
Coach	Bob Gansier	Bora Milutinović	Steve Sampson	Bruce Arena	Bruce Arena	Bob Bradley	Jürgen Klinsmann	Bruce Arena
Total Team Caps	454	425	1,156	1,153	1,030	813	820	1,245
# Players Top 5 Leagues	0	1	5	8	6	12	10	6
% Players Top 5 Leagues	0%	5%	23%	35%	26%	52%	43%	26%
Total Minutes Top 5 Leagues	0	1,857	11,025	12,652	12,312	23,265	23,042	14,656
Total Minutes Top 5 (ex. Goalies)	0	1,857	6,975	7,972	8,668	15,285	16,359	14,656
Avg. Minutes/Player Top 5	0	1,857	2,205	1,582	2,052	1,939	2,304	2,443
# Players Europe	4	6	6	12	12	17	12	7
Total Minutes Europe		7,484	13,674	21,548	31,875	32,140	27,457	18,976
% Players Europe	18%	27%	26%	52%	52%	74%	52%	30%
# Players Champions/Europa League Play	0	0	2	0	1	3	2	1
Total Minutes Champions/Europa League Play	0	0	750	0	0	1,152	253	546

On a relative basis, the USMNT's overall skill level had at the very least stagnated, if not actually declined. The number of USMNT players in the Top Five Leagues was declining in part because more players from the around the world were getting identified and developed. This matters because most players will improve more by playing against better competition—and the best competition is in the Top Five Leagues and even more so in the European club tournaments. The peak in minutes in the Top Five Leagues in 2010 also coincided with a peak in the number of players and minutes in the Champions League or Europa League (three players and 1,152 minutes).

The stagnation and decline on a relative basis can be put into context when comparing the USMNT with rival Mexico. From early 2000 to the 2010 World Cup, the USMNT had a 5–4 record versus Mexico. During this time, the USMNT had more players and more minutes in the Top Five Leagues. The same was true at the 2014 World Cup. However, the USMNT that lost to Trinidad & Tobago in 2017 had fewer players playing in Europe and fewer players in the Top Five Leagues than Mexico—but, in fairness, the USMNT players had more minutes in the Top Five Leagues. Since the 2010 World Cup, the USMNT have a 1–4–2 record versus Mexico. We are not arguing stagnating or declining relative talent is the sole reason for the worse record, but it certainly is a factor.

Table: # of Players and Minutes of Mexico in Europe

	1994	1998	2002	2006	2010	2014	2018
WC Finish	Round of 16	Round of 16	Round of 16	Round of 16	Round of 16	Round of 16	Round of 16
WC Place (#)	13	13	11	15	14	10	12
Coach	Manuel Mejia Baron	Manuel Lapuente	Javier Aguirre	Ricardo Lavolpe	Javier Aguirre	Miguel Herrera	Juan Carlos Osorio
Total Team Caps	302	972	914	1,018	997	948	1,387
# Players Top 5 Leagues	2	0	4	3	5	6	5
% Players Top 5 Leagues	9%	0%	17%	13%	22%	26%	22%
Total Minutes Top 5 Leagues	4,657	0	4,966	4,997	6,384	14,627	6,766
# Players Europe	2	0	4	3	9	8	11
# Players Champions/Europa League Play	1	0	0	3	3	2	2
# Minutes Champions/Europa League Play	235	0	0	1,229	625	619	185

*Mexico was banned from the 1990 World Cup

In a 2020 article for ESPN.com titled "State of the USMNT," Jeff Carlisle and Noah Davis compared the EA Sports FIFA video game ratings of the 2020 USMNT starting XI to previous USMNT teams.[17] They calculated that the 2020 USMNT starting XI had an average rating of 77, as compared to 77 and 76 for the starting XI versus Ghana on June 16, 2014, and England on June 12, 2010, respectively. The data corresponds with our analysis with minutes in the Top Five Leagues demonstrating that generally the USMNT talent has not relatively improved since 2010. Once again, keep in mind: scores are relative and not absolute.

The data helps explain why issues related to talent identification and development, such as pay-to-play and neglecting Hispanic origin and Black American players, are very important to revisit. However, many of the issues related to talent identification and development existed when the USMNT qualified for the World Cup in 1990, reached the Round of 16 in 1994, reached the quarterfinals in 2002, and won their group in 2010. This leads us to believe that other factors are involved, such as culture and familiarity.

While the absolute skill of the USMNT may have improved from when they first qualified for the 1990 World Cup, some other countries are improving faster, making it look like the USMNT has not progressed—or has even gone backward—in the past several cycles.

In the United States, MLS clubs may be training future USMNT players, but they are also doing the same for other countries. For example,

---

17. EA Sports ratings are often debated. We find them interesting because the ratings are relative—meaning 100 is the highest in any year.

more and more players from other CONCACAF nations are choosing to play and develop in MLS. At the 2011 Gold Cup, MLS was represented by 29 players, 23 of whom played for countries outside of the U.S. In 2015, that figure jumped to 50 MLS players, with 41 coming from outside the United States. And finally, at the Gold Cup in 2019, there were 59 MLS players representing 12 countries total, with 43 coming from outside the United States.

More players from other countries are also playing in the Top Five Leagues (e.g., more players from Asia as well as more and younger South Americans). For example, in the 2002 World Cup, 10 players of the 23-man Brazil squad played in the Brazilian domestic league, with the others playing in the Top Five Leagues. The players who left for Europe were on average 22 years old, down from 24 in 1994. In 2018, 19 players on Brazil played in Europe, and the average age at which they left Brazil was 19. They spent comparatively little time in the professional Brazilian league, where display of skill and joy is as important as winning. While skillful tricks are celebrated in Brazil, they can be considered "unsportsmanlike showboating" and showing a "lack of humility" in Europe, contrary to a pragmatic result with so much on the line. The total number of minutes played by Brazil's national team in the Top Five Leagues more than doubled from 2002 to 2018. The number of players and minutes in the Champions League or Europa League are among the highest at the World Cup.

Table: # of Players and Minutes of Brazil in Europe

	1958	1962	1970	1982	1994	2002	2018
WC Finish	Champions	Champions	Champions	Second Round	Champions	Champions	Quarterfinals
WC Place (#)	1	1	1	5	1	1	6
# Players Top 5 Leagues	0	0	0	2	10	10	17
% Players Top 5 Leagues	0	0	0	9%	43%	43%	74%
Total Minutes Top 5 Leagues	0	0	0	5,696	27,665	29,355	572,46
# Players Europe	0	0	0	2	10	10	19
Avg. Age Leave for Europe	NA	NA	NA	26	24.3	22.3	19.3
# Players Champions/Europa League Play	0	0	0	1	5	9	16
# Minutes Champions/Europa League Play	0	0	0	180	2,114	6,772	10,976

The table above helps answer Pelé's question: "What happened to Brazil's *ginga*?" Our answer: it was "Europeanized."[18]

There is a lot of optimism about the current young group of USMNT players playing in Europe—deservedly so. However, before getting too excited, we wanted to provide a historical comparison for context. As of this publication, the USMNT have not qualified for the 2022 World Cup and a squad hasn't been selected. Therefore, any analysis and comparison is flawed. We took a subset of a list of American players mentioned in www.ussoccerplayers.com/usmnt-players-abroad (based on the most promising young players) and assumed that they were the sole American players playing in Europe who were selected for the USMNT, and that the World Cup was in 2020, to develop an "Imaginary 2020 World Cup USMNT."

---

18. As to familiarity, when examining the years Brazil won the World Cup, typically they had a cluster of players from two or three professional clubs from two or three distinct areas. Brazil need to hope that clusters of their players are at top clubs to have familiarity. In leagues such as La Liga, each club is allowed five non-EU players, but is only allowed to name three non-EU players in each matchday squad. The term "non-EU" refers to a player whose country of citizenship is outside of the European Union. Éder Gabriel Militão, Vinícius Júnior, and Rodrygo are often registered as Real Madrid's three non-EU players. Until Uruguayan midfielder Federico Valverde was granted Spanish nationality, Rodrygo was sent to Madrid's B-team Castilla to gain experience and Japanese international forward Takefusa Kubo was loaned out. Citizenship requires two years of residence in Spain. Real Madrid already have Brazilians Casemiro and Marcelo—both were granted Spanish nationality after two years. With such EU restrictions, Brazil, and other South American countries, will struggle competing against European teams with a core group of talented players at peak age with more familiarity.

Table: Selected American Players in Europe
on an Imaginary 2020 World Cup USMNT[19]

Name	Date of Birth (Age)	Team	Country
Tyler Adams	February 14, 1999 (21)	RB Leipzig	Germany
John Brooks	January 28, 1993 (27)	Wolfsburg	Germany
Sergiño Dest	November 3, 2000 (19)	Ajax	Netherlands
Weston McKennie*	August 28, 1998 (22)	Schalke 04	Germany
Christian Pulisic	September 18, 1998 (21)	Chelsea	England
Gio Reyna	November 13, 2002 (17)	Borussia Dortmund	Germany
Josh Sargent	February 20, 2000 (20)	Werder Bremen	Germany
Zack Steffen*	April 2, 1995 (25)	Fortuna Düsseldorf	Germany
DeAndre Yedlin	July 9, 1993 (27)	Newcastle	England

Of course, there are many other Americans playing in Europe, and they may make the final roster. We fully admit that the methodology is imperfect (and not scientific) and will likely understate the number of players in Europe and playing in the Champions League and Europa League tournaments, if the USMNT qualify for the 2022 World Cup.[20]

Even with all of the American talent in Europe, the Imaginary 2020 World Cup USMNT number of players and minutes in the Top Five Leagues (eight players and 13,507 minutes) would be fewer than 2010 (12

---

19. Note this is for the 2019–20 season. Weston McKennie is on loan to Juventus in Serie A in 2020–21. Zack Steffen was on loan from Manchester City in 2019–20 and returned for 2020–21. In the 2019–20 season, Sergiño Dest, who transferred to Barcelona in October 2020, was at Ajax in the Netherlands, which is not a club in a Top Five League. This list is certainly not exhaustive—the point is to focus on the rising young talent in the United States. In addition to these players, there were three other players who had Champions League/Europa League experience during the 2019–20 season, but with fairly limited minutes: Tyler Boyd (25), Batsikas (Turkey)/Europa League; Tim Chandler (30), Frankfurt/Europa League; and Jordan Siebatcheu (24), Stade Rennais (France)/Europa League. Siebatcheu grew up in France, is a French citizen (although he was born in Washington, D.C.), and has previously played for the France U-21 team. Tim Weah was injured and missed Lille's (Ligue 1) Champions League matches in 2019–20. There are other players in Europe worth noting for the 2020–21 season: Reggie Cannon (Boavista, Portugal), Konrad de la Fuente (Barcelona B), Matthew Hoppe (Schalke), Ethan Horvath (Club Brugge, Belgium), Richard Ledezma (PSV, Netherlands), Ulysses Llanez (Heerenween from Wolfsburg), Matt Miazga (Anderlecht from Chelsea), Chris Richards (Hoffenheim from Bayern Munich), Antonee Robinson (Fulham), Sebastian Soto (Telstar from Norwich City), Luca de la Torre (Heracles Almelo, Netherlands), and Cameron Carter Vickers (Bournemouth from Tottenham). Yunus Musah (18) plays for Valencia (La Liga). He can play for England, Ghana, Italy, or the USA. See appendix for a more up-to-date ESPN Big Board List and estimated minutes.

20. To compensate for the fact that this list is only a subset of eligible players, we also looked at the actual USMNT roster, defined as the players named to the team for the most recent friendly against Costa Rica (which took place on February 1, 2020), and then in addition included all recent call-ups (defined as call-ups that happened in the past 12 months). In that group, there are a total of 15 players on European teams out of 47 players in the pool (32 percent), nine of whom are currently on a team in one of the Top Five Leagues in Europe. This is not dramatically different from what we show above.

and 23,265) and 2014 (10 and 23,042). If we included all U.S. players in the Top Five Leagues, and not just our subset, the minutes would not change meaningfully. These numbers are more comparable to 1998 than to 2006. However, the Imaginary 2020 World Cup USMNT would have five players playing in the Champions and Europa League tournaments, more than the previous high of three in 2010, and the number of minutes would be greater than all the other years as well.

Table: # of Players, Minutes, and Average Age of USMNT in Europe[21]

	1990	1994	1998	2002	2006	2010	2014	2017	2020
# Players Top 5 Leagues	0	1	5	8	6	12	10	4	8
Total Minutes Top 5 Leagues	0	1,857	11,025	12,652	12,312	23,265	23,042	9,156	13,507
Avg. Age Top 5 League Players	NA	30	27	30	30.3	27.3	26.5	26	22.5
# Players Europe	4	6	6	12	12	17	12	5	9
Total Minutes Europe	NA	7,484	13,674	21,548	31,875	32,140	27,457	13,476	16,238
Avg. Age Europe Players	NA	26.5	27.3	29	29.2	27.2	25.9	27	22.1
# Players Champions/Europa League Play	0	0	2	0	1	3	2	1	5
Total Minutes Champions/Europa League Play	0	0	750	0	0	1,152	253	546	1,399
Avg. Age Champions/Europa Players	NA	NA	28.5	NA	27	28.7	25.5	19.0	21.0

What stands out the most is the average age of the players. In 2010, the average age of the 12 USMNT players in the Top Five Leagues was 27.3, while in our Imaginary 2020 squad, eight players average 22.5 years old. In 2010, the average age of the three USMNT players in the Champions League and Europa League tournaments was 28.7, while in our Imaginary 2020 World Cup squad, five players average 21 years old.

To manage expectations and provide a comparison, we also compared the Imaginary 2020 World Cup USMNT squad with France's 2014 World Cup squad (France won the World Cup in 2018) and Germany's 2010 World Cup squad (Germany won the World Cup in 2014). France and Germany both had what were widely considered young teams (25 to 26 years old) in the World Cups prior to the tournament they won. Regardless of how you look at it, the USMNT will not have the same high-level experience. In 2010, Germany had 23 players in the Top Five Leagues (19 players in Champions or Europa League) who played a combined 78,994

---

21. Note 2020 is for the 2019–20 season. The 2020 players in Champions/Europa League Play: Tyler Adams, John Brooks, Sergiño Dest, Gio Reyna, and Christian Pulisic. There are other players in Europe not on the list, including de la Tore, Carter-Vickers, Robinson, Chandler, Giochinni, Green, Holmes, Horvath, Llanez, Miazga, Morales, Ream, Soto, Vassilev, and Weah. There is no scientific way to produce an Imaginary USMNT, and it is highly subjective.

minutes (13,765 minutes in European competitions). In 2014, France had 22 players in the Top Five Leagues (15 players in European competitions) who played a combined 70,999 minutes. In comparison, the Imaginary 2020 USMNT squad has eight players in the Top Five Leagues (five players in European competitions) who played 13,507 minutes (1,399 minutes in European competitions).

**Table: Imaginary 2020 USMNT Comparison
to France 2014 and Germany 2010 Squads[22]**

	USA–2020	France–2014	Germany–2010
World Cup Finish	N/A	7	3
# Players Top 5 Leagues	8	22	23
Total Minutes Top 5 Leagues	13,507	70,999	78,994
Avg. Age Top 5 League Players	22.5	26.5	25.0
# Players Europe	9	23	23
Total Minutes Europe	16,238	74,724	78,994
Avg. Age Europe Players	22.1	26.4	25.0
# Players Champions/Europa League Play	5	15	19
Total Minutes Champions/Europa League Play	1,399	8,747	13,765
Avg. Age Champions/Europa Players	21.0	26.1	25.2

While we wish the USMNT only the best, the only realistic expectations for the 2022 World Cup, assuming the USMNT qualifies, should be that the 2022 World Cup is part of a development process for a young American team and an opportunity to highlight their identity. The 2022 World Cup can give a core group of young players the much-needed international competition experience and familiarity to be a contender at the 2026 World Cup, with home-field advantage, and take advantage of a global platform. Similar to after the 1994 World Cup in the U.S., we expect a talent boom 12 to 18 years after the 2026 World Cup that, combined with new economic incentives to identify and develop players, will help give the USMNT the talent to be a consistent contender, recognizing that there are ups and downs and cycles for various reasons.

What Factor Does Luck Play?

At the outset, it is important to mention that it is actually very frightening how much luck impacts soccer results and the narrative. Around 50 percent of goals in soccer are a result of some sort of lucky incident (e.g.,

---

22. Note the Imaginary 2020 USMNT would be two years older for the 2022 World Cup.

an unheralded player makes a ball redirection or lucky bounce or block to a goal scorer). Goals typically happen in situations that can't easily be replicated, many times even when the players are in exactly the same position (e.g., an unheralded player makes a fluky 1-in-100 shot or a defender slips). The game can be significantly impacted by a refereeing error or judgment (e.g., if the referee sees or judges a handball, or if the referee believes a foul was made in the box or not, or if the referee believes an infraction merits a yellow or red card). Also, referees are human and can be influenced by crowd reaction and noise (i.e., "home-field advantage"). Players can be missed through injury or suspensions for red cards and accumulation of yellow cards or not play at peak performance because of mental and physical fatigue (e.g., the "too-tired-and-old effect"). Lastly, although soccer is a 90-minute game, the ball is usually "active" for only around 60 to 65 minutes per game because of various stoppages.

All of this is magnified by a low average total goals per game in soccer (around 2.7). A lower-ranked team can "park the bus" in front of the goal and limit opportunities for their higher-ranked opponent to score. Then, the lower-ranked team can capitalize on one mistake, score, and win the game. In basketball, there is a shot clock to ensure many opportunities to score and defend. In baseball, there are a minimum number of opportunities to bat. Chris Anderson and David Sally explain in their soccer book *The Numbers Game* that the team favored by bettors wins just half the time in soccer, whereas the favorite wins three-fifths of the time in baseball and two-thirds of the time in basketball.

A team can have a favorable or unfavorable group (e.g., "Group of Death") or Round of 16 opponent in the World Cup. Even when a team plays their toughest match in the group stage of a World Cup can have a significant impact, as teams that lose their first game have a much lower probability of advancing to the knockout rounds.

Sports are supposed to reward determination, skill, and hard work. The existence or acknowledgment of luck undermines merit—luck rewards the undeserving. Paradoxically, luck is both an ugly truth about the game and an essential part of the beauty of the game.

The Problem with Limited Data Points

Add on top of luck the fact that the World Cup is played every four years, so there are limited data points. For example, many USMNT fans compare recent results to the USMNT's quarterfinal result at the 2002 World Cup. As we admitted, we were guilty of this faulty comparison. It has impacted the narrative and expectations of the USMNT ever since. South Korea and Turkey advanced to the semifinals of the 2002 World Cup. If we stopped the narrative in 2002, we could write a fascinating story about how South Korea and Turkey became among the world's best soccer nations. However, since 2002, South Korea have advanced to the Round of 16 once, in the 2010 World Cup. Since 2002, Turkey haven't even qualified for a World Cup.

Each USMNT result needs to be taken into context with relevant facts. When we present the context of what happened as the USMNT reached the quarterfinal in 2002, readers will better understand how the result contributed to unrealistic expectations. As it relates to the USMNT, they have only played in 26 World Cup matches since 1990. Therefore, it is much more challenging, imperfect, and unrealistic to connect all the facts with context, draw straight lines, reach definitive conclusions, and set realistic expectations. We tried to do our best to provide a balanced approach with research, data, and analysis.

Why What Happened to the USMNT Matters

The USMNT and USWNT are much more than national sports teams. If you don't believe us—why do the topics of pay-to-play, overlooked talent, diversity and inclusion, and equal pay generate so much passion and emotion as they relate to soccer in the U.S., as opposed to the other major sports? There is an element of pay-to-play in almost every major sport and entertainment youth activity in America (and around the world). For example, the fees and expenses of elite youth travel basketball are comparable to elite youth travel soccer programs ($400 to $4,000 per season to play, including uniforms). However, there aren't such passionate pleas about pay-to-play negatively impacting youth basketball, baseball, and football, or their national teams, as there are for soccer.

Every major sport and entertainment youth activity in America (and around the world) also fails to identify and develop (overlooks) talent because of race, socioeconomic factors, month of birth, proximity to training and facilities, and values of the community. For example, there are great basketball players in rural or remote areas of America who don't get exposure to major college basketball programs. However, the geographic size of America isn't typically raised as an impediment to USA Basketball.

USA Swimming have won 553 total Olympic medals, 365 more than second-place Australia. However, fewer than 10 Olympic medals have been won by Black American swimmers. On the Women's Olympic Hockey Team that won gold in 2018, there wasn't one Black American—actually, there has never been a Black American on any of the Women's Olympic Hockey teams. However, compared to soccer, there aren't nearly as many articles comparing the breakdown of USA Swimming or USA Women's or Men's Hockey to the nation's overall population or observers commenting that those teams need to do a better job recruiting from wider areas. If you think that is because they win—the USA Men's Hockey Team have not won the Olympics since 1980, and before 1980 the last USA Men's Hockey Olympic gold was 1960. Only one Black American has been on the USA Men's Olympic Hockey Team.[23] Only 2 percent of NHL players are Black Americans—once again, demonstrating that despite the tireless work of a few (including Kim Davis and her commendable efforts at the NHL), progress in many sports has been exceptionally slow, but there isn't nearly the same amount of attention on diversity as there is for the USMNT or USWNT. Unlike soccer, there aren't many people writing articles that USA Hockey needs to recruit Black American athletes from underserved areas to win gold.

USA Women's Basketball have won the last six Olympics, while the Men's team has won the last three.[24] However, while the WNBA and players fight for more equality, there isn't nearly as much attention from the general media and public about their equal pay as there is for the USWNT. For example, after a major tournament win, the fans in the

---

23. Jordan Greenway in 2018, and that was a year when no NHL players competed in the Olympics.
24. The USWNT placed fifth in the 2016 Olympics, after winning the previous three gold medals.

stands are not chanting "equal pay" like they did for the USWNT after the 2019 World Cup.

The answer why has to do with the combination of a few characteristics about soccer itself as well as soccer in America, which will help explain why what happened to the USMNT matters. As to soccer itself, statistically, more Americans fit the physical attributes of a professional soccer player than any other major sport, therefore psychologically more people believe they (or their children) have a chance to be an elite soccer player. Great male soccer players' heights have ranged from 5'6" to 6'2", heights that include more than 80 percent of American adult males. Landon Donovan displayed a typical average height and build at 5'8" and 158 pounds. Lionel Messi is 5'6" and 154 pounds. In contrast, most people don't believe they (or their children) have a chance to be an elite basketball player. A mere 5 percent of American men are 6'3" or taller (around 14 percent are taller than 6'0"), whereas the average height of an NBA player is 6'7"—not to mention NBA players have an extraordinary wingspan. Stephen Curry, who is 6'2", is beloved in part because, as he said, "I'm them. I can't jump the highest. I'm obviously not the biggest, not the strongest. And so they see me out there and I look like a normal person." He does what a "normal person" can do—shoot. He said, "They can sit out there all day shooting. You can't teach them how to tomahawk dunk, but you could probably teach them how to shoot." Soccer doesn't have the equivalent of "tomahawk dunks." As for the women, great female soccer players' heights have ranged from 5'1" to 5'11", heights that include more than 80 percent of American adult women. Forwards Mia Hamm and Tiffeny Milbrett are 5'5" and 5'2", respectively. In contrast, the average height in the WNBA is around 6'0". A mere 1 percent of American women are 6'0" or taller (the equivalent height cutoff for American men at 1 percent is about 6'4"). Therefore, soccer is more of an "equal opportunity" team sport.

Soccer is also the sport of the world—the only team sport that stretches to almost every corner of the globe—because it doesn't require expensive equipment or a designated place to play. To make a game of soccer possible, all that is really necessary is a ball. In some developing countries, children play barefoot in back streets, alleyways, and empty lots, sometimes kicking around soccer balls made from clothes and plastic bags. Therefore, the sport's global nature, even in developing countries, reinforces soccer as an "equal opportunity" team sport.

As to soccer in the U.S., many Americans associate both the men's and women's U.S. national teams in soccer with being an underdog or looking for respect or legitimacy, each for different reasons. As we mentioned, many Americans think of themselves as, or have a particular affinity for, underdogs. After 1986, when the IOC ended its amateurism mandate, there really weren't any U.S. national team underdogs in major sports to root for—no more "Miracle on Ice" opportunities. The 1994 World Cup was perfect timing. The USMNT were portrayed as recent college graduates, essentially amateurs, competing against soccer powers with highly paid professional stars. The USMNT have never been considered a soccer power in the modern era. While the USWNT are a soccer power, having won the Women's World Cup four times, many Americans associate them with being "underdogs," but in a different way than the men—the women are fighting for equality. When the USWNT aren't battling soccer opponents on the field, they are battling the powerful authority of the USSF and the establishment for equal pay and conditions—reinforcing their underdog status and identity.

Generally, Americans have empathy for underdogs primarily because of the backdrop and storytelling of U.S. history—the "underdog" American Patriots could beat the colonial British superpower and Abraham Lincoln could rise from a log cabin to become president. This backdrop and storytelling of U.S. history resonates with Americans and makes them feel that America is the land of equal opportunity. Obviously, there are many complexities and contradictions in U.S. history and the American Dream, but the storytelling supports the belief in, or aspiration for, the ideal.

Storytelling of the American Dream is very important in sports and impacts perceptions. For example, conventional wisdom holds that the typical NBA player is from a lower socioeconomic background and therefore saw basketball as his escape. The story continues that his hardships growing up were what gave him the perseverance and grit necessary to excel. In 2013, Seth Stephens-Davidowitz wrote an article in the *New York Times* titled "In the NBA, Zip Code Matters" that challenges this common thinking with data. He calculated the probability of reaching the NBA by race in every county in the U.S. He discovered "growing up in a wealthier neighborhood is a major, positive predictor of reaching the NBA for both black and white men." Most Black American players in the NBA were born in the richest 20 percent of geographic counties. This is not driven by sons of NBA players like Stephen Curry. Take those players out and the result is similar. The data analysis challenges the stereotype of a Black basketball player being driven by an intense desire to escape poverty. However, the storytelling of the underdog captures an American media audience and gives us a different perception.

Soccer is the only major sport in the U.S. where this belief or aspiration of underdogs fighting is connected to a national team—both the USMNT and USWNT. With qualification and other tournaments throughout the year, rooting for them is relatively frequently experienced together as a nation—not just every four years like many Olympic sports.

More than any other major sport, Americans associate soccer with the idea that everybody has a chance, and if one finds that the underdogs don't have a chance, it undermines that dream, and that makes people extremely passionate about equal opportunity—from pay-to-play to equal pay. America and soccer's relationship to underdogs and equal opportunity provide context to the meanings of *why*, *how*, and *who* for the USMNT and USWNT. *What happened to the USMNT matters because the USMNT (and USWNT) represent much more than a national sports team.*

Barcelona have the motto "more than a club." The USMNT (and USWNT) are "more than a national team." And that is an ugly truth for those who believe just winning on the field is all that matters for the USMNT (and USWNT).

Authors' Note

A Summary of the Book and How the Book Is Organized

The first chapter describes the 1990 and 1994 World Cups. We demonstrate how and why the USMNT's identity and style were established. The style evolved from "kick it at goal" to a counter-attack style we label as the "Spirit of '76," embracing an underdog status or mentality similar to the American Patriots in 1776. In addition, familiarity played a key role in the USMNT's success in the 1994 World Cup. We will demonstrate that familiarity is one of the most important factors for success in the World Cup—yet it is often overlooked and underappreciated.

In the second chapter, we pause from describing World Cup action and explain the importance of clearly answering the *why*, *how*, and *who*. We also describe the significance of expectations and comparisons and how they relate to the USMNT. Lastly, we demonstrate the significance of culture in soccer because of the teamwork required to score and to overcome the "too-much-talent effect."

Generally, the next few chapters of the book go through various World Cups and other tournaments to explain and illustrate how and why the *why*, *how*, and *who* of the USMNT have changed and "drifted" (including meanings, perceptions, expectations, and comparisons) from the early 1990s. We demonstrate that over time, more and more of the USSF, USMNT, fans, sponsors, and media progressively started to assume and believe if the USMNT didn't act and play like Europeans, then they were less legitimate and couldn't progress in an upward-trending straight line and win the World Cup.

Chapters Four and Five go through the 2002 World Cup and detail how each goal was scored. Six of the USMNT's seven total goals (86 percent) were from set pieces, crosses into the box, or an own goal. We explain how the USMNT benefited from an incredible goalkeeper performance and a wide range of luck. We also examine other factors such as speed and youth. The margins between winning and losing are so small that factors such as luck and goalkeeping can have an outsized impact on the narrative—yet their contributions fade from storytelling and context in setting expectations and comparisons. With the context, it becomes clearer why the USMNT's remarkable 2002 World Cup performance can be a flawed comparison and set unrealistic expectations.

In Chapter Seven, we investigate second World Cup cycles for coaches. We explain how the "too-tired-and-old effect" and being blinded by loyalty and experience have negatively impacted coaches in their second World Cup cycles. A study demonstrated if a reigning champion simply brought back its roster from four years before, its mean age would increase by four years, and it would be expected to finish a dismal 17th. While probabilities indicate a coach will have a poor second cycle, we explain why Germany's Joachim Löw and France's Didier Deschamps succeeded.

After describing the various World Cups and other tournaments, including the drift toward wanting to be and play more "European" over time (with the hiring of Klinsmann reflecting this shift), in Chapter 12 we contrast the USMNT's approach versus Trinidad & Tobago in 2017 with the USMNT's approach versus Trinidad & Tobago in 1989—the USMNT's qualification for a World Cup was on the line in both matches. The drift from underdog mentality to arrogance becomes very clear.

In Chapter 13, we turn our attention to the identification and development of elite male soccer players even before they are selected for the USMNT. We focus on pay-to-play, Hispanic origin and Black American players, dual nationals, MLS (including promotion and relegation and calendar), college soccer, and soccer culture in the United States. Our conclusions will surprise many observers and challenge conventional wisdom. While pay-to-play and promotion and relegation get a lot of attention, the three biggest external development factors impacting the USMNT are (1) there are not enough economic incentives for MLS clubs to identify and develop players at their youth academies; (2) there are not a few dominant youth academies in MLS yet to serve as feeders to the USMNT so the players have familiarity, and (3) the salary cap in MLS essentially prohibits a few teams from having a core group of players on one or two club rosters to gain familiarity (e.g., Bayern, Juventus). College soccer is more important than many observers currently believe—but not for the reasons most often cited. College soccer alumni are critical. They bring their passion and knowledge about the sport to their communities and their own children. In addition, many argue that America can't be competitive in soccer because the U.S. "doesn't have a soccer culture." We investigate why Spain, which doesn't have a "basketball culture" but a "soccer culture," are very good in basketball. They took advantage of their own culture and strengths in creating their own identity and style—as well as embracing being underdogs. They didn't drift to wanting to be or play like Americans.

Chapter 14 identifies factors that make a national team player—height, weight, zig-zag shuttle speed, month of birth, family, community (zip code), pickup games, and futsal. We challenge a commonly provided explanation for why the USMNT aren't dominant in soccer—because soccer loses great athletes to other major sports. We also challenge another regular notion—that the USMNT suffer because the U.S. is too geographically large and diverse. Many soccer powers get most of their players from a few areas that place an emphasis on soccer and are close to or have a concentration of professional soccer clubs. In addition, the majority of their players come from a few youth academies within their country.

We also explain when observers argue that great players develop in poor favelas in Rio de Janeiro or alleyways in Buenos Aires because of their drive to escape poverty—they are missing an important element. They are great, in part, because soccer is a part of the fabric of communities' daily lives and so they regularly play informal pickup games. Furthermore, because they live in urban environments, those pickup games are in confined streets and spaces, which improves their technical skills and influences their style of play. Community (zip code) matters. Informal pickup games also matter. The USMNT players are just as athletic as, if not more athletic than, any other national team's players. The issue is players at traditional soccer powers play more informal pickup games as children, which is compounded by the powerful economic incentives to identify the best young players and develop them. And then core groups of those young players play and develop together at a few youth academies and teams.

Lastly, we learn family matters—a lot. Due to history and popularity, soccer powers have more family members who play and have played soccer at elite levels. The U.S. will catch up. Take Gio Reyna, whose father and mother played on U.S. national soccer teams. Christian Pulisic's parents played college soccer; his father was a coach who included Christian in practices as a boy against grown men and helped start a futsal league so his son could play futsal.[25] Michael Bradley's father also played college soccer and was a coach, similar to Pulisic, bringing his son to practices where he would play with older, stronger, and faster players—a distinct development advantage. There is no question the U.S. can develop elite, athletic soccer players. However, for the elite U.S. players to progress, typically (not always) they will have to go to Europe at some point to play against better competition.[26] Historically, the perception was MLS didn't want their top youth academy players to go to Europe. Now, there are economic incentives that provide more motivation. With some notable successes and economic incentives of their own, European club youth academies are also now more aggressively scouting youngsters in America.

Chapter 15 tries to answer a question that we could not escape during our research—why the USWNT win so often. It's not always fair to make comparisons between the two teams for various reasons, but we felt compelled to try to answer the question because of how often they are associated or compared against one another. Contrary to popular belief,

---

25. Many top skill players played futsal or street soccer growing up.

26. Having players play in Europe will influence the USMNT style as well as improved skill will influence style, but we are not suggesting trying to copy a European style.

the USWNT didn't start at the top of the women's soccer mountain; they climbed their way to the top and, with help from a competitive culture established by their 1991 World Cup coach, Anson Dorrance, and Title IX, they fight to stay there every single day. We also discovered the incentives behind pay-to-play have contributed to the USWNT's success. While the parents of American boys can't outspend the professional club youth academies around the world in development, the parents of American girls have collectively outspent the federations around the world with pay-to-play.[27] However, professional clubs in Europe are starting to spend on women's identification and development, which will change women's soccer and competitive dynamics.

In the conclusion, we finish with optimism. Going into 1994, the USMNT were 3–5–23 against rival Mexico, and there wasn't a major U.S. professional soccer league. Since 1994, the USMNT are 16–10–13 against Mexico, and MLS is booming! There has been a lot of good work and progress. The fact that so many people care that the USMNT did not qualify for the 2018 World Cup is progress in and of itself. To put into perspective how much has changed—the 2002 and 2006 World Cups came very close to not being televised in English in the United States. No major networks bid on the rights because there wasn't enough interest.

The USMNT are fortunate to have a great group of young rising stars coming through the system. Some are going to Europe to test and prove themselves—their success will cause more European clubs to scout, and pay more for, U.S. talent. Most importantly, the younger generation also understand the original meaning of *why* and are actually evolving and extending the mission in a positive way—and more in line with the USWNT. In addition, with the U.S., Mexico, and Canada hosting the 2026 World Cup, we expect a USMNT talent boom, similar to after the 1994 World Cup in the U.S., around 12 to 18 years later. Talent-wise, the USMNT will be serious contenders for the 2038 to 2046 World Cups. They need to focus on *why*, *how*, and *who*.

---

27. Generally, European professional soccer clubs didn't spend on girls/women until recently.

Chapter 1

1990 and 1994 World Cups: Identity and Style of Play

Qualifying for the 1990 World Cup: Defend and "Kick It at Goal"

Tony Meola grew up playing boys' high school soccer in New Jersey. He learned his love for the game from his father, Vincenzo, who played for an Italian second division club before immigrating to the United States. Tony was an All-State goalkeeper (1985) and forward (1986). He not only excelled in soccer, he was a three-sport varsity letterman. He was captain of his high school's basketball team and was named an All-State baseball player in 1987. The New York Yankees drafted him out of high school, though he didn't sign a contract with them. Tony attended the University of Virginia with soccer and baseball athletic scholarships. He earned first-team 1988 and 1989 All-American honors as a goalkeeper both his freshman and sophomore years.

Under the hot sun of November 19, 1989, Tony walked onto the field as a member of the USMNT to play Trinidad & Tobago (T&T) in their national stadium in Port of Spain for the right to go to the 1990 World Cup. The USMNT, T&T, Costa Rica, Guatemala, and El Salvador were playing a Confederation of North, Central America and Caribbean Association Football (CONCACAF) regional round-robin tournament where the top two finishing teams would qualify for the 1990 World Cup. Costa Rica had already claimed one spot by winning the tournament with a 5–2–1 record. The other spot would go to either T&T or the USMNT, each with a 3–1–3 record. T&T only needed a tie to qualify because they had a greater goal differential, which is used as the tiebreaker. The most formidable team in the region, Mexico, was disqualified because they had used overaged players in a junior tournament (known as the Cachirules scandal). Even without Mexico participating, the USMNT were given little to no chance of qualifying.

With all of their resources, it is hard to think of America as an underdog. However, in 1989 in soccer the USMNT were clear underdogs. T&T were playing at home, and their government had already declared the following day to be a national holiday for the country's population of 1.2 million because they expected their team to win. The USMNT had not won an away qualifying match in more than 21 years and hadn't scored a goal in their last two games. The team consisted mostly of college kids and recent graduates playing in semipro and Sunday leagues to try to keep fit. For many of the players, this was their last shot to play meaningful soccer. Most of the players were not good enough to play professionally in Europe, and the professional North American Soccer League (NASL) had folded in 1985. Before the match, Mike Windischmann, the captain of the USMNT, told his teammates, "Don't you realize if we lose some of us will have to go out and get jobs?"

Even though soccer had been played in the U.S. for more than a century, it was of only nominal concern to most Americans in 1989.[28] Soccer was the preferred sport of many European and South American immigrants. The sport struggled to find the mainstream acceptance that baseball and football enjoyed. However, there was a lot riding on the USMNT earning a berth to the 1990 World Cup for the first time in 40 years. FIFA guaranteed that every team that qualified would receive at least $1.4 million. In addition, the USMNT looked to prove they belonged on

---

28. Soccer was actually the second major sport, after baseball, to organize professionally in the U.S. In 1894, brothers Fred and Oliver Watson were the earliest documented Black American soccer players in the U.S. See Society For American Soccer History (ussoccerhistory.org).

the world stage. On July 4, 1988, FIFA awarded the United States, in a narrow vote, the hosting rights to the 1994 World Cup, which came with an automatic qualification.[29] If the USMNT didn't qualify on their own for the previous World Cup, the award to America to host over soccer-crazy Brazil, and the accompanying automatic bid, would look more like a charity handout to get access to the large American commercial market.

Three and a half hours before the game, T&T officials had to stop letting people in the stadium because it was at full capacity. In America, ESPN turned down the opportunity to show the match live. When the match kicked off, the atmosphere was electric. Defensively, the USMNT sat back, compressed space, and forced the T&T players to shoot from long range. However, the USMNT needed to win, which meant they needed to score a goal. It seemed the USMNT's offensive strategy was the cliché "kick it at goal."[30] And it worked. In the 31st minute, USMNT defensive midfielder Paul Caligiuri—who would only ever score five goals in 110 appearances for the USMNT—beat one man and 30 yards out kicked the ball toward goal with his left foot. The wishful shot looped in an arc toward the T&T goal, caught the goalkeeper by surprise, and dipped in. The raucous crowd went absolutely silent. It was the USMNT's first goal in almost four hours of match play, and only their fifth in eight matches. The goal was dubbed by the *New York Times* as "the shot heard around the world." Caligiuri later admitted, "There was a lot of luck involved."

Wearing a white baseball cap to protect his eyes from the sun, Meola was put under pressure in goal for the remaining 60 minutes of the game, pulling off two excellent saves in the 85th and 86th minutes while screened by bodies in the box. Unaccustomed to being in the lead, the USMNT managed to hold on to win 1–0. Meola didn't concede a goal in four qualifying matches and was highlighted in *Sports Illustrated*.

Just two minutes before Caligiuri scored, a T&T striker was taken down by USMNT defender John Doyle in the USMNT's box. As the striker

---

29. Many don't know the U.S. Soccer establishment joined FIFA in 1913, Brazil in 1923.

30. This phrase is not meant to be derogatory or disparage the skill level of the USMNT at the time. The team didn't get enough credit for having players with skill. It is more a relative lack of overall understanding of the tactical and other nuances of the game at a professional level.

went to the ground, the USMNT players held their collective breath. Doyle admitted years later, "In today's game, that's a foul, for sure," which would have given T&T a penalty kick. But the Argentine referee waved play on, and two minutes later Caligiuri scored.

Caligiuri's goal would ultimately put around $10 million into the coffers of the USSF, their share of the 1990 World Cup broadcast, attendance, and licensing rights. As for Caligiuri, he was having trouble making payments on his condo in Los Angeles. He refused to sign a two-year exclusive commitment to the USSF to train at the USMNT Mission Viejo camp for the 1994 World Cup because he wanted the option to return to Europe. He played at the USMNT camp as a volunteer, only receiving a $40 per diem for out-of-pocket expenses.

Of the starting XI USMNT players, three players (John Harkes, Tony Meola, and Tab Ramos) grew up playing club soccer together around Kearny (pronounced CAR-nee), New Jersey, a blue-collar immigrant town adjacent to Newark. Kearny has 36,000 residents. Today, visitors are greeted with a sign stating WELCOME TO KEARNY. SOCCER TOWN, USA. The soccer tradition that produced these World Cup players can be traced to the mid-1870s, when thousands of Scottish and Irish immigrants settled in the town after a Scottish thread manufacturing company opened a factory. The immigrants brought soccer with them, and not long after, new soccer clubs were established and flourished. Soccer was part of the everyday fabric of life in Kearny. Eventually places like Thistle SC, Kearny High, Scots Club, and the unrivaled street soccer scene at The Court in Harrison or at Emerson Courts in Kearny served as training centers. Harkes,[31] Meola, and Ramos were all Kearny Thistle SC youth players.[32] In many ways, the road to the 1990 World Cup started in the basement of the Scots-American club, dubbed "the dungeon," where the three players would meet and put on their Thistle jerseys. Sometimes they would play four matches in a single day with their families and neighbors watching.

---

31. Uruguayan-born Tab Ramos' family immigrated to America when he was 10.

32. Sal Rosamilia, a future All-American at Columbia University, and Bill Galka, a future All-American at Southern Connecticut, also played during their era. In addition, Sir Alex Ferguson has family ties with Kearny and has visited Kearny.

Many of the players on the USMNT were familiar with each other. Harkes and Meola would both play together for Coach John Millar at Kearny High School and for Coach Bruce Arena at the University of Virginia.[33],[34] Two players, Paul Caligiuri and Paul Krumpe, grew up in the Los Angeles area and played together for Coach Sigi Schmid at UCLA.[35] Bruce Murray and Eric Eichmann were teammates at Clemson. Jimmy Banks and Desmond Armstrong had met and became friends when they were 15. Brian Bliss, John Harkes, and Mike Windischmann played for the Albany Capitals in the American Soccer League, which had a league salary cap of $50,000 for an entire team. Almost half the USMNT were immigrants or first- or second-generation Americans. John Harkes', Tony Meola's, Tab Ramos', and Peter Vermes' fathers played professional soccer in Scotland, Italy, Uruguay, and the Netherlands, respectively.

Most of the 1990 USMNT players were born in the mid to late 1960s and were young boys watching some of the most famous global soccer stars play professional soccer in America. During the mid to late 1970s, soccer stars Pelé, Franz Beckenbauer, Giorgio Chinaglia, Johan Neeskens, and Carlos Alberto played for the New York Cosmos and Johan Cruyff and George Best played for the Los Angeles Aztecs in the NASL (before it folded in 1985). John Harkes and Tony Meola were ball boys for the New York Cosmos. The U.S. didn't host the World Cup until 1994, but it had some glamour of the World Cup for a few years that inspired a new generation who would start to reach peak soccer age in the early 1990s.

1990 World Cup, Italy: Stay Compact, Force Turnovers, and Quickly Hit on the Counter

In 1989, Bob Gansler was named coach of the USMNT, an appointment notable for the fact that the USSF made it a full-time position. Gansler, a

---

33. Ramos attended Saint Benedict's Preparatory School, the same high school attended by Claudio Reyna and Gregg Berhalter a few years later.

34. For similar reasons to Kearny, St. Louis also features prominently in American soccer history. Four of the starting XI in the famous U.S. victory over England in the 1950 World Cup were born in St. Louis, and one other was on the squad. Every USMNT has had at least one player from St. Louis (if one also includes St. Louis University graduates), and 29 St. Louisans have been inducted into the National Soccer Hall of Fame.

35. Eric Wynalda also grew up in the Los Angeles area.

native of Hungary who then played for the USMNT, had a reputation as a stern taskmaster. Gansler was heavily criticized for his squad selection. During qualifying he used mostly players who were either in college or recently graduated and completely bypassed more experienced players who had to play in indoor leagues after the demise of the NASL. When the team qualified, Gansler was determined to persevere with the players who excelled in qualifying, but it came at a price. Most other national teams consist of a mix of mostly veterans, a few rookies, and then players in the middle. The USMNT were essentially all rookies. His decision to favor youth would help set up the USMNT for the 1994 World Cup.

The USMNT entered the 1990 World Cup in Italy with the youngest roster, with an average age of 23 years old, and included three players who were still on college teams.[36] USMNT head coach Bob Gansler said of the team's tactical philosophy, "Our formula is simple: 11 guys play offense, and 11 guys play defense." The English soccer journalist Brian Glanville dismissed the USMNT as a "galloping side of corn-fed college boys." But David Wangerin, author of *Soccer in a Football World*, noted, "If their university experience and its emphasis on structured, disciplined team play did not lend itself well to creative freedom and ball artistry, it had certainly built a competitive psyche and an indomitable spirit."

1990 FIFA World Cup: Group Stage, Game 1
June 10, 1990, at Stadio Comunale, Florence
USA 1–5 Czechoslovakia
The USMNT's first match was against Czechoslovakia, who would ultimately get to the quarterfinals of the 1990 World Cup. For the first 20 minutes of the game, the Americans held their own. USMNT forward Peter Vermes nearly scored early on. Goalkeeper Tony Meola made a few good saves. As the game went on, it became obvious that the Czechs were better, faster, smarter, and more experienced. The USMNT defenders seemed a half-step slower than the Czech forwards. In the 26th minute, the Czechs scored on a turnover with the USMNT slow to get back, get

36. There wasn't a single player on the team who was over the age of 27.

organized, and defend. In the 38th minute, a USMNT defender tripped a Czech player who quickly and unexpectedly stole the ball from the defender in the USMNT box. The Czechs scored on the resulting penalty kick. The two goals were the result of the Czechs forcing turnovers and their quick reactions. The Czechs' third goal was a near post header off of a corner kick. The Czechs were renowned for their corner kick play, and the USMNT could have been better prepared for it.

A minute later, the USMNT went down to 10 men. The Czech players were experienced professionals who also knew how to unnerve and bait an inexperienced international player into committing a foul. A day after his 21st birthday, fiery American striker Eric Wynalda was given a red card and ejected in the 52nd minute when he shoved a Czech player. The Czech had been deviously stepping on Wynalda's feet with his cleats.

Then something amazing happened that is often overlooked in USMNT history. In the 60th minute, USMNT defensive midfielder Paul Caligiuri intercepted a lazy pass in the midfield on the run and then one-timed a pass to center forward Bruce Murray, who peeled off the back line to act as support. Caligiuri buzzed into space to receive the perfect return ball and, after making a quick run, was past the last defender. The Czech goalkeeper came out to try and defend, but Caligiuri made a quick move to the right and, from about 16 yards out, slotted the ball into the goal to make it 1–3. However, playing a man short for 38 minutes was too much for the USMNT. The Czechs scored two more goals and the USMNT lost 1–5. The *New York Times* said the USMNT had been "humiliated to the point of embarrassment." What was lost on most was that the USMNT showed it could score with a quick counter-attack. If they could score at this level of competition, then it meant they could win matches. It was an important moment.

Caligiuri is most famous for his "shot heard around the world" goal against T&T that qualified the USMNT for the 1990 World Cup. But it is his goal against the Czechs that helped launch and define the American style: stay compact, force turnovers, and quickly hit on the counter. We label the American style "Spirit of '76." It is admittedly more of a mouthful than *total voetball, tiki-taka* (which literally means in Basque "taking quick, light steps"), *ginga* (which literally means "to sway with rhythm"), *catenaccio* (which literally means "door-bolt"), or *kampfgeist* (which literally means "fighting spirit"). Caligiuri's goal at the 1990 World Cup showed the USMNT offensive style had progressed beyond the cliché "kick it at goal" in T&T.

After the loss, the USMNT players were upset, and the training sessions became really intense. At one point, Bruce Murray and Eric Eichmann, who were old teammates at Clemson, ended up tangled up in the net throwing punches at each other after fighting for a ball during a possession game. The incident highlighted that everyone still had spirit and a lot of fight.

1990 FIFA World Cup: Group Stage, Game 2
June 10, 1990, at Stadio Olimpico, Rome
USA 0–1 Italy
The USMNT would show the potential of the American style in their next match against the 1990 World Cup host nation, Italy, in Rome. The seasoned Italians were loaded with stars and were one of the favorites to win the tournament. The entire Italy team played in Italy's Serie A, with five players from Juventus, five from Inter Milan, and four from AC Milan. Serie A was stacked with excellent teams at the time. AC Milan had won back-to-back Champions League trophies in 1989 and 1990, while Juventus won the trophy in 1985. Juventus and Inter Milan won the Europa Cup in 1990 and 1991, respectively. Italy would ultimately get to the semifinals of the 1990 World Cup, losing in a penalty shootout to Diego Maradona's Argentina. At the time, Maradona played for Napoli in Serie A.

There is a caveat to why Italy was so good in the 1980s and 1990s, which we discovered researching our book about Serie A. Regional Italian industrialists financially supported soccer clubs because, besides ego and pride, they considered the financial losses as necessary business expenses for political clout and to entertain their employees. With rich owners who could spend whatever they wanted, there was a large economic incentive to develop young Italian boys into elite players. They sponsored youth programs, built soccer facilities, and hired the best coaches. The owners were willing to pay for player development, keep Italian stars, and import global stars, whom the Italian players would play with and against and improve. With a limit on the number of foreign players, money spent on outside players went primarily to strikers and forwards, which helped develop Italy's defenders. Some of the best talent in Italy migrated to defending to get on the field because the best foreigners were occupying traditionally offensive positions.

When the Italian media tycoon Silvio Berlusconi purchased AC Milan in 1986, he upped the ante. Soccer was now about content for his media business and a tool for politics. Italy's Serie A soccer league dominated European tournaments. Eventually, as players' costs rose, non-Italian European teams and leagues in the 2000s adapted and focused on developing sustainable commercial models to compete. Meanwhile, the Italians didn't adapt and continued to primarily rely on regional owners to keep absorbing the financial losses. This was unsustainable and eventually Serie A clubs had to cut their budgets and sell players to those that had adapted their business models. Because of this and for a variety of other reasons, slowly Italy's Serie A and the level of Italian soccer declined. Eventually, Italy would not qualify for the 2018 World Cup, which hadn't happened since 1958.

At the 1990 World Cup, the Italian media speculated that their team, nicknamed the *Azzuri* (which translates to "the blues") because of their home jersey color, would score more goals on the USMNT than the Czechs. When the USMNT players looked out the windows of their bus on the way to the stadium, they saw Italians put both hands up. The players thought the Italians were being friendly and waving at them, but then quickly figured out that the Italians were signaling "10," as in Italy will score 10 goals if the Czechs could score five.

When Italy scored in the 11th minute with a great give-and-go play in the box, most people watching probably believed the USMNT would be soundly beaten again. However, the USMNT stuck to playing the American style and in front of a packed Stadio Olimpico, the USMNT shocked the tournament and earned respect, even without winning. In the 70th minute, the USMNT nearly equalized when the Italy goalkeeper couldn't hold on to a Bruce Murray free kick from 24 yards out. Peter Vermes quickly charged down the rebound and had a shot from just six yards out. The ball squirted through the goalkeeper's legs and was rolling toward the goal line, where it was cleared away by an Italy defender. The USMNT would lose 0–1.

Italy were clearly better and had a lot more chances. They even missed a penalty kick. Nevertheless, after the match, Italy's coach declared, "The Americans proved they are an excellent team, nothing like the team that lost 5–1." Coach Bob Gansler said, "This is the U.S. team that I know." After the final whistle the Italian crowd were cheering for the USMNT. The Italy team came into the USMNT locker room after the game to talk and trade jerseys. While sitting around and drinking beers with the USMNT, the Italy players told the USMNT they had a good game plan and should be very proud of themselves. The next day, on the way to training, the players noticed Italians giving them thumbs up and clapping over their heads. The "Spirit of '76" almost worked on the field and certainly worked in attracting fans and gaining more respect off the field.

1990 FIFA World Cup: Group Stage, Game 3
June 19, 1990, at Stadio Comunale, Florence
USA 1–2 Austria

With their performance against Italy, the USMNT got the attention of their next opponents, Austria, who came out pushing, shoving, and kicking in the hopes of intimidating a more confident USMNT. In the 33rd minute, an Austria player was sent off with a red card. To that point, the USMNT had played in a disciplined fashion, probing and looking for each other and minimizing the impact of Austria using three forwards, one more than usual. However, after the red card, instead of the USMNT having an advantage, their cohesion dissipated. Austria scored two goals on quick counter-attacks. On both plays the Austrians outraced the Americans, who were also out of position. The USMNT finally scored in the 83rd minute, but it was too little too late. Despite holding a man advantage for 57 minutes, the USMNT allowed two goals, scored only one, and lost 1–2. Their performance highlighted their lack of tactical acumen and experience more than a lack of skill. Overshadowing the USMNT's deficiencies was the nastiness of the game, which seemed to have rattled the inexperienced Americans. Austria picked up five yellow cards and one red, while the USMNT received four yellow cards. The average total yellow and red cards in a World Cup match are 3.4 and 0.06, respectively.

The USMNT lost all three of their games in the 1990 World Cup. However, most people missed the point. The USMNT were starting to form a style—stay compact, force turnovers, and quickly hit on the counter—and an identity—grit and a fighting spirit. Offensively the American style of quickly counter-attacking was demonstrated with a goal against Czechoslovakia and defensively the American style of working together in two blocks of four to compress space was exhibited against Italy. The USMNT's next step was to put both of these things together. It seemed possible with more experience, practice, and familiarity, as well as being faster and smarter. While the USMNT finished next to last in the tournament, spared by the United Arab Emirates' inferior goal difference, the young Americans also got much needed experience. They proved they had the ability to execute a style of play that worked for their skill level and could set them up for success. The 1990 World Cup paved the way for many of the USMNT players to get spots on European clubs' squads. With no domestic league, about 30 Americans ended up on European teams, most of them in leagues in the middle echelons—but MLS didn't exist yet.

West Germany beat Argentina 1–0 in the 1990 World Cup Final, with a late penalty kick the game's only goal. Only 500,000 viewers watched the Final in America.

The 1994 World Cup, USA: "Spirit of '76"
The 1994 World Cup in the U.S. was coming up. The USSF didn't have time for decades of slow, organic development. The USSF needed out-of-the-box solutions to ensure the USMNT would be competitive. Because many of the USMNT players had few professional options, the USSF

offered to pay the players and provide them with housing so they could train full-time together and play a program of friendlies. A permanent national team camp was set up in Mission Viejo, California, just south of Los Angeles, for almost two years leading up to the World Cup.[37] In comparison, the 1980 U.S. Men's Olympic Hockey team trained together for around seven months. Some of the players, like Alexi Lalas and Cobi Jones, had never played professional soccer. Out of necessity at the time, they went from college straight to being full-time international players.

Most national team coaches complain that they don't get enough time with their players. This was a unique opportunity to have the core of the team essentially function as a club team—living and training together on a daily basis and playing international games. The USMNT was basically the players' professional club. They trained twice a day, morning and afternoon, and then the federation scheduled as many friendlies as possible. It was all geared toward preparing the USMNT to compete against the best in the world. In 1993, the USMNT played 29 official international matches and an additional 15 friendlies in the first five months of 1994 leading into the World Cup. The benefit was that players gained the international match experience they lacked in the 1990 World Cup and everyone was more familiar with each other and the style. As a result, the total team caps (number of international appearances) for the 1994 team was 425. To put this in perspective, it was still significantly less than eventual winner Brazil's total caps (653), but greater than second-place finisher Italy's (389). However, the average age for the USMNT was 26.4 years old (compared to 27.4 and 27.5 for Brazil and Italy, respectively). So, in spite of being a relatively young team, the USMNT actually had gained a reasonable amount of international experience. Youth and international experience are a great combination.

After the USMNT lost all three games in the 1990 World Cup, the USSF looked for a new coach. No American coaches had a proven international track record. The USSF wanted to find someone with the reputation of squeezing the last drop of potential out of a team. In this

---

37. Orlando was runner-up in the selection process.

regard, Bora Milutinović's name came up again and again. He has been called a combination of the charismatic, energetic Pete Carroll and the enigmatic Yoda.[38] He led Mexico to the quarterfinals at the 1986 World Cup, their highest finish. In addition, Milutinović took over Costa Rica just 90 days before the 1990 World Cup. He cut the captain and other starters, and, remarkably, managed to get Costa Rica to the knockout Round of 16.

After Milutinović was hired by the USSF he left no doubts of who was in charge, cutting three players, including Bruce Murray, the all-time leading USMNT goal scorer. Milutinović was very focused on if the players knew what they were playing for (their *why*) and how much it meant to them—who would sacrifice and who showed commitment. When Alexi Lalas first showed up at training camp, Milutinović told him to cut his trademark shoulder-length red hair or get off the team. Milutinović was testing Lalas—how much was he willing to sacrifice to play for the USMNT. Milutinović also asked Tony Meola to stay with the national team and not continue pursuing his dream of playing professionally in Europe. Another test in sacrifice. Meola stayed and would captain the 1994 USMNT. Milutinović knew Meola was the guy closest to both the group of players playing in Europe and the group at Mission Viejo and would be the leader to help integrate the two.[39] This would be important because when the group of European players would return to the U.S. after their European seasons, some would be taking the places of players who had to endure months or years of the physical and mental challenges of Milutinović's practices.

Milutinović focused on the *how*. First, he understood that tactics are effective only if players are capable of employing them. He found and trained players who'd succeed in playing in an American style—rugged central defenders and box-to-box defenders and midfielders who refused to get stretched and would work together to defend in groups, and fast

---

38. Milutinović took his video camera almost everywhere he went as if he were a tourist and had enlisted a Mexican named Pablo to assist him with his work at home and the office.

39. This was incredibly insightful. The USMNT always need a captain who can unite those playing in the U.S. and Europe.

attackers who could quickly counter-attack. Milutinović's 4-4-2 produced an American style of play that used "banks of four" to great effect. The style utilized American athleticism and provided defensive balance and support to compensate for less talent, yet gave a chance for fast-attacking players to quickly take advantage on the counter. Defensively, everything was done in groups, and attacking was done either with speed or on set pieces. Turnovers and careless mistakes, such as needless fouls in dangerous areas, were not tolerated.

To Milutinović, chess and soccer were very similar. In chess, one learns to always protect the king, then go for the opponent's king. Opening space around the king makes one vulnerable. To Milutinović, the USMNT needed to play intelligent soccer, know who they were up against, and take advantage of opportunities.

Milutinović proved to be a master at understanding a team's talents and a country's soccer culture to develop a successful style. The American style played to the American players' strengths. He also was willing to pick players who fit the style or opponent over more skillful or famous players.[40] For example, Mike Sorber, a 23-year-old from St. Louis, Missouri, and the son of Pete Sorber (the head soccer coach who led St. Louis Community College-Florissant Valley to 10 junior college national championships), had never been a member of a U.S. national team at any level. At the time, the main path to the national team was through U.S. Youth Soccer's Olympic Development Program, a fragmented system over which U.S. Soccer had no control and little input. It was easy for players to fall through the cracks. Milutinović attended the Final Four match in the NCAA championship soccer tournament between St. Louis University, where Sorber was at the time, and the University of Virginia to see Claudio Reyna play.[41] He spotted Sorber and invited him to the

---

40. Milutinović also selected 31-year old Cle Kooiman, who began his professional career playing in the Major Indoor Soccer League. At the end of 1990, Kooiman moved to Mexico to play soccer. While with Cruz Azul, he became the first U.S. citizen to captain a Mexican soccer team. He would play the full 90 minutes in the U.S.'s opening game against Switzerland. He would only play for the USMNT during 1993–94. In 1996, he moved to the U.S. to play in the newly established MLS.

41. Brian McBride was Sorber's teammate.

pre-World Cup residency camp in Mission Viejo, California. Sorber's role on the team grew in importance when Claudio Reyna tore a hamstring two weeks before the start of the tournament. Even as it became clear that Sorber would play a major role during the World Cup, he himself struggled to explain what made him stand out. When *Sports Illustrated's* Wolff asked Sorber why he was on the team, Sorber responded, "Another Bora mystery."

Not only did Milutinović select him, he started Sorber every game in the 1994 World Cup. Following the tournament, according to *SoccerAmerica*, Milutinović said, "When you analyze the World Cup, Sorber was probably our MVP. It is difficult for me to explain what I feel about him. He is disciplined and intelligent." After the World Cup, Sorber spent two seasons in Mexico, where he was the first American player ever to be named a Mexican League All-Star, and then played a few years in the newly formed MLS. Unlike most of the starters on the USMNT 1994 World Cup team, however, he never went on to play in Europe. In five years in MLS, Sorber scored nine goals and added 17 assists, plus a goal and five assists in the playoffs. Milutinović also selected six players from the 1990 World Cup team to make sure they had a group with some experience.

Milutinović searched for players abroad who would be eligible to play for the USMNT in advance of the 1994 World Cup as well. He discovered defensive midfielder Thomas Dooley, the German son of an American serviceman and German mother. Dooley spoke very little English when he joined the USMNT. He assumed U.S. citizenship in 1992 and made his first international appearance on May 30 of that year. Dooley became a regular for the USMNT almost immediately, being named U.S. Soccer Athlete of the Year in 1993 and then playing every minute at the 1994 World Cup. Dooley was Sorber's roommate. In addition to Dooley, Milutinović added Earnie Stewart, who was the son of a Black American U.S. Air Force airman and his Dutch wife. Stewart grew up in and played professional soccer in the Netherlands.

While Dooley was from Germany and played many years there, he eventually moved his family to Mission Viejo in 1993 to join the domestic players for a full year. All the players could see how hard he tried to acclimate himself with the group by training twice a day and then studying English. Milutinović and the players admired his commitment. Stewart played in the Netherlands but spoke perfect English. Many players felt he was like a brother and brought positive energy to the squad. MLS didn't exist at the time. Harkes and Wegerle played in England, Ramos in Spain, and Klopas in Greece, but all had either grown up in the U.S. or played at some level in the U.S. before heading to Europe.[42] The other players felt they all were grateful and excited for the opportunity to represent the USMNT at the 1994 World Cup. Dooley and Stewart ended up playing in more World Cups and in MLS.

The 1994 World Cup was the last of the 24-team format (in 1998 it was expanded to 32 nations) and the first World Cup in which three points were awarded for a win instead of two under the old format.[43] It was also the first World Cup to eliminate the goalkeeper's ability to pick up a back pass from a teammate. According to a *New York Times* article by Jere Longman, a Harris poll showed that only 20 percent of the American public knew the World Cup was being played in the U.S.[44] Meanwhile, an estimated one billion viewers around the world tuned in at some point to watch its Final. For comparison, an estimated 150 million viewers around the world watched the 1993 Super Bowl. Up to 1994, a European team had never won a World Cup played in the Americas. Brazil was the consensus favorite to break its 24-year drought, which would ensure that streak would continue.

Many feared that if the USMNT lost all three group stage matches like at the 1990 World Cup in Italy, the popularity of soccer in America

---

42. While John Harkes played for Sheffield Wednesday of the English Football League in 1990, he won English football's "Goal of the Year" award for a 35-yard blast against Derby County. Harkes became the second American (after Bill Regan in 1948–49) to play soccer at Wembley Stadium when Sheffield Wednesday reached the 1991 League Cup Final and beat Manchester United 1–0.

43. FIFA instituted this feature to encourage attacking soccer after the defensive display of many teams at Italia 1990.

44. Two weeks before the World Cup, Alexi Lalas was sitting in a middle seat on an airplane and an older woman sat down next to him. They proceeded to have a conversation. She asked him what he did and Lalas said, "I play soccer." She responded, "Well, isn't that nice?" And then she asked, "So, what do you do for money?"

would suffer severely. Therefore, the USMNT needed to advance from the group stage against Switzerland, Colombia, and Romania into the single-elimination Round of 16. However, most outsiders did not think the USMNT had a chance. Romania had beaten the USMNT 2–1 earlier in the year. Colombia, led by their unmistakable captain Carlos Valdererrama, was a popular choice to win it all.[45] Pelé picked them to win. Colombia thrashed Argentina 5–0 in September 1993 in Buenos Aires during qualifying, part of a 28-game unbeaten streak.

There is a caveat to Colombia's soccer success. In the 1980s and early 1990s, Colombian professional soccer clubs began to be supported by drug lords' narcotics money. One drug lord in particular, Pablo Escobar, loved soccer. The various drug lords financially supported soccer clubs for regional pride, ego battles, and allegedly gambling. They also allegedly laundered their dirty money by over-marking gate receipts at stadiums and inflating player transfer fees between clubs. Suddenly, like Italy in the 1980s and 1990s, there was a large economic incentive to develop young Colombian boys into elite players. They sponsored youth programs, built soccer facilities, and hired the best coaches. Also, Colombian clubs had money to hold on to most of their best players and sign incredible talent from across the continent. Colombia returned to the World Cup in 1990, the first time since 1962. In the 1994 World Cup, 18 of the 22 Colombian players on the squad played in Colombia instead of going to Europe. Six played for Atlético Nacional in Medellín (associated with Escobar of the local cartel) and five for American Cali (associated with Miguel Rodriguez Orejuela of the local cartel)—both teams associated with drug money.

In the lead-up to the 1994 World Cup, the USMNT had a few positive results—including a 1–1 draw against Italy in 1992 and a 2–0 win against England in 1993. In early 1994, the USMNT went three months without a win, tying Moldova and losing to Iceland as Milutinović experimented with different players and systems. While the results from the 52 games played in the year and a half before the 1994 World Cup may have been mixed, the experience gained by the team was invaluable. In the course

---

45. Valdererrama was unmistakable, in part, because of his distinctive frizzy blonde hairstyle and wrists adorned with colorful bracelets.

of that full schedule, the USMNT played 13 of the 24 teams that would appear in the 1994 tournament. Their 1–0 win against a good Mexico team at the Rose Bowl on June 4, 1994, (in front of a very pro-Mexico crowd) gave the team confidence.[46] Going into the match the USMNT were 3–5–23 against Mexico (16–10–13 since).

The USMNT had only one player (Roy Wegerle) in the Top Five Leagues which was fewer than Colombia, Romania, and Switzerland.

Table: 1994 World Cup—USA and Opponents (Group Stage)

1994 World Cup—USA & Opponents (Group Stage)					
Team	World Rank (Pre-WC)	Average Age (Team)	Average Age (Starters)	# Players Top 5 League	# Minutes Top 5 League
USA	26	26.4	28.1	1	1,857
Switzerland	13	27.8	27.7	4	11,173
Colombia	19	26.9	27.7	2	5,901
Romania	15	24.6	25.5	4	9,738
Group Total (ex. US)	47			10	26,812

The USMNT wanted to prove they could play soccer, and they had a plan to shock the world and advance. None of the Switzerland players had World Cup experience, and the country's last appearance was 28 years prior. The USMNT thought maybe they could get a win against Switzerland and all three points. Then, they felt like they had a chance of getting a draw with either Colombia or Romania, and with that, a much-needed point. With four points, the USMNT felt they could advance to the knockout round.

1994 FIFA World Cup: Group Stage, Game 1
June 18, 1994, at Pontiac Silverdome, Michigan
USA 1–1 Switzerland
The USMNT wanted to avoid becoming the first host country not to advance to the knockout round, but certain outside factors initially looked to put that in jeopardy. The entire team was tired from having stayed up to watch the O.J. Simpson car chase. Also, Eric Wynalda woke up in the morning covered with hives, apparently suffering an allergic reaction to an ingredient in the electrolyte sports drink he had drunk.

---

46. Mexico would go on to win their group, which included Italy.

The USMNT's opener against Switzerland was played at the Pontiac Silverdome on a temporary grass field, the first match in World Cup history to be played indoors. Many fans were dressed in red, white, and blue or wearing USMNT jerseys. The only problem for the fans and players was that the air circulation was poor, and the temperature inside the stadium reached 106 degrees.

Understandably, the USMNT played a little tentatively to start the game but soon settled in. Then, in the 39th minute, USMNT midfielder Thomas Dooley brought down a Switzerland player from behind just outside the penalty area. A tackle from behind can lead to a red card, an automatic ejection from the game and suspension from the following game, but the referee gave Dooley the benefit of the doubt. The defensive wall had initially aligned itself short of the required 10 yards, and the Americans were forced back by the referee. A Switzerland player put a 19-yard free kick around the American wall and past the screened goalkeeper Tony Meola. As the ball was kicked, Meola took a half step to his right toward the American wall-side, but the ball was kicked to the left corner goalkeeper-side.

When Switzerland scored on the free kick, many Americans feared a repeat of the lopsided score against Czechoslovakia in 1990. However, in the final minute of the first half, after Harkes made a threatening run on the dribble and was tackled, the USMNT won a free kick around 30 yards out from goal. It was a distance that Switzerland never feared. Wynalda, the striker who had been sent off in the 5–1 loss to Czechoslovakia four years earlier and who was suffering from an allergic reaction, launched a laser beam free kick that could not have been more perfectly placed into the top corner of the goal, beyond the outstretched arms of the goalkeeper, nicking off the underside of the crossbar and into the back of the net. Wynalda would later admit, "I was almost in disbelief. It was the greatest goal of my life." The unstoppable free kick was as if the USMNT were saying, *We are legitimate and we are here to prove we have skills too*. Wynalda had also revealed a new important feature of the American style—goals off of set pieces. The USMNT also showed they had more maturity and experience. The game ended 1–1. It wasn't the three points the USMNT had hoped for going into the tournament, but a tie is worth a point, and the last time the USMNT had accumulated a point at the World Cup was 1950. Their hopes were still alive.

From a strategic point of view, every team views the first game as the most important game of the group stage for obvious reasons. If a team gets three points, it is in the driver's seat. A loss and no points, and then the team feels the next game is a must win, and the pressure mounts. The negative media attention of the loss starts to get to players. Players also know the odds of advancing out of the group stage are significantly lower, and they feel like all of their work and sacrifices for the World Cup cycle are lost. A coach is often tempted to tactically push too hard for a win as well, and the added risk-taking can often lead to a disastrous second-game loss—and an exit from the tournament. One point from a draw is not ideal, but not terrible either.

1994 FIFA World Cup: Group Stage, Game 2
June 22, 1994, at the Rose Bowl, California
USA 2–1 Colombia

Four days after their draw with Switzerland, the USMNT faced heavily favored Colombia at the Rose Bowl. In a strategic move, Milutinović inserted defender Fernando Clavijo into the lineup in place of usual starter Cle Kooiman. Clavijo was born in Uruguay and started playing professionally there at the age of 16. In 1979, at the age of 22, he moved to the U.S. and took a job as a busboy at a New Jersey restaurant. Eventually, he would be discovered playing amateur soccer and would make his way to the NASL, Major Indoor Soccer League (MISL), and U.S. national futsal team. In 1994, Clavijo was 38 years old and generally considered well past his prime, but Milutinović wanted him to defend Faustino Asprilla, Colombia's leading goal scorer. Milutinović sensed that Clavijo understood the South American style better than anyone else on the team, was exceptionally fast, even at his age, and would be more effective in defending Asprilla.[47]

June 22 was a beautiful, hot day. When the USMNT bus arrived at the stadium, the players could hear the fans tailgating in the parking lot. The atmosphere was like a big college football game at the Rose Bowl. When the whistle blew to start the game, there was a deafening roar. After their humiliating and unexpected defeat to Romania, Colombia was in a must-win situation and came out to play right out of the gate. They immediately pressured the USMNT and moved the ball quickly around the field. Around 10 minutes into the game, a ball awkwardly deflected off of Mike Sorber and struck the post before Fernando Clavijo cleared it off the line. Colombia controlled play in the early stages of the match.

Momentum changed in the 34th minute when John Harkes, while running down the wing, kicked a low cross intended for Earnie Stewart, who was dashing into the box with a run toward the back post. A sliding Colombia defender Andrés Escobar stretched his leg to block the cross, but when he made contact, the ball was unintentionally redirected toward the goal. The goalkeeper couldn't have anticipated the redirection and couldn't stop his momentum. He helplessly watched the ball go past him into the back of the net. While the USMNT didn't "score it," they created the goal. The USMNT were up 1–0. Against Colombia. In the World Cup. Escobar was lying on his back on the ground, his hands covering his face. The Colombians were shocked. The own goal highlights the importance of luck.

At halftime, the USMNT knew they had played a good half. They discussed how Colombia would push forward, so there would be more opportunities to score another goal. However, the coaches emphasized that it was important to be smart with the ball and defend together as a group. When they got back onto the field to start the second half, they

---

47. He would do so well that he would start the remaining USMNT matches at the tournament. After the game Cle Kooiman was asked about not starting. Kooiman said, "It was Bora's call, and if he [Clavijo] can keep doing it, more power to him," Kooiman continued. "I'm a team guy. Today, I'm just happy to be here, to be on the team. I sat on the bench, but right now, I feel like I played an entire game. I got chills out there. Near the end, I felt like crying."

learned Faustino Asprilla was being substituted. It gave the team a boost of energy and confidence.

In the 49th minute, the USMNT won a free kick. The USMNT had its defenders move up toward Colombia's goal. The free kick was passed to Ramos, who took one touch and then attempted a shot from long range. The ball was deflected twice and bounced through Colombia's line. Alexi Lalas got to the ball first and rifled a long-range shot from the top of the penalty area that glanced off the crossbar and into the upper corner of the goal. The goal was incorrectly called offside, and Lalas received a yellow card (presumably for shooting the ball after the whistle).

In the 52nd minute, Marcello Balboa, whose father, Luis Balboa, played professionally in Argentina and with the Chicago Mustangs of the NASL, collected the ball deep in the USMNT end and passed the ball to Harkes, who one-touched it back to Balboa, who then one-touched it to Sorber. Sorber dribbled around a Colombia player and passed it to Harkes, who one-touched it to Dooley. Dooley received the ball in the middle and passed it to Wynalda. Wynalda then passed the ball to Ramos on the right, who dribbled a couple of touches. Ramos then played a perfectly weighted through pass to Stewart, who was streaking behind the Colombia defense, and met the ball at the top of the penalty area. Stewart one-touched the ball with the inside of his right foot past the rushing goalkeeper, and the ball bounced a few times, glanced off the inside of the post, and went into the net for the USMNT's second goal. USA 2–0 Colombia. The action went from the left side into the middle over to the right side and down the middle. The beautiful display of skill and possession alerted the world that the USMNT had improved a lot since the 1990 World Cup. The crowd started to chant, "U-S-A! U-S-A!"

In the 81st minute, the USMNT won a corner kick. Tab Ramos took the corner kick, and defender Marcelo Balboa tried a daring bicycle kick about 15 yards from goal. It just missed—about a foot wide of the post. The ball was struck so hard and cleanly that the Colombia defender guarding the post didn't even have time to flinch as the ball whizzed passed him. At first the crowd gasped in amazement, and then they roared. If the ball had gone in, it would have been the goal of the tournament, and one of the top goals in World Cup history. The brash attempt alerted the world of soccer—the USMNT had skills.[48]

Colombia scored in the 89th minute, but it was too little too late—the USMNT pulled off a 2–1 upset. When the final whistle blew, the USMNT players and fans all celebrated as if they had just won the championship. Americans were throwing USA flags onto the field. If the draw against Switzerland proved that the USMNT legitimately belonged at the World Cup, this result proved they weren't satisfied with that. Many believe it was the greatest victory in U.S. soccer since 1950.

Many people are unaware that the night before the USMNT had to submit their official roster to the FIFA World Cup officials, Alan Rothenberg, President of the USSF, met with Milutinović. Rothenberg had gotten word that Fernando Clavijo was going to make the USMNT squad. Clavijo was the oldest player on the team and wasn't going to go on to play in Major League Soccer. Supposedly, Milutinović was adding him because Clavijo's wife and Milutinović's wife were friendly, and Milutinović's wife wanted a friend to travel and be with during the World Cup. So, Rothenberg explained, "Look Bora, we're trying to use this as a promotional vehicle for this new soccer league that we're starting and there's this good-looking blond-haired kid from UCLA named Chris Henderson [who was on the 1990 World Cup USMNT and youngest player in the tournament]. Put him [Henderson] as your 22nd guy, and the federation will pay for Clavijo's wife to travel with your wife. We just want to be able to say that when Chris Henderson goes into Major League Soccer that he was on the World Cup team." And Bora supposedly replied, "Oh, yes, Mr. President." Of course, when Milutinović submitted the roster, Clavijo was on it, and not Henderson. After Clavijo's performance in the Colombia game, Rothenberg told Milutinović, "That's the last time I tell you who to play."

Some wondered if the Colombia team were guilty of believing too much of the hype or underestimated the USMNT (i.e., didn't consider soccer in

---

48. In 2000, Balboa scored an astonishing bicycle kick from a cross from Anders Limpar for the Colorado Rapids that won MLS Goal of the Year 2000 and is still one of the greatest, if not the greatest, goals in MLS history.

the U.S. legitimate) until it was too late. Perhaps the 5–0 thumping of Argentina in qualifying gave Colombia unrealistic expectations. However, we discovered necessary context after researching the background. Colombia had a troubled mind-set ahead of the tournament match against the USMNT. Going into the tournament, in December 1993, the Colombian military tracked down and killed Colombian drug lord Pablo Escobar. The nation was in a state of pseudo civil war. In the chaos, players, who are national heroes, were dealing with death threats. Weeks before the tournament, defender Luis "Chonto" Herrera's infant son was kidnapped.

Going into the match against the USMNT, Colombia had lost to Romania in their first game. This caused Colombia to feel intense negative media and pressure to press to win—which made Colombia vulnerable to counter-attacks. After Colombia's loss to Romania, Herrera also got a message from his family that his brother had been killed in a car crash. He decided to still play against the USMNT in service of his nation. Just prior to the match against the USMNT, the Colombia coach allegedly received a phone call or fax threatening that if midfielder Gabriel Gomez wasn't dropped from the starting lineup, Gomez, the coach, and the players' families would be harmed. Gomez was a key cog in the Colombia wheel. No one knew who the threat was from, but many assumed it was gamblers associated with the drug cartels. The coach replaced Gomez in the starting lineup.

As if the Colombia team didn't have enough to concern them, their squad was not built to endure the long days in a team hotel together for four weeks in preparation for and during the tournament—an element of World Cup competition that is often overlooked or underestimated. Many teams self-destruct because of poor team chemistry. How a team gels together in a World Cup camp (which is different from just a night of travel and a hotel before a game) and if and how much they can see their families are factors that are often overlooked when examining World Cup results. Most Colombia players didn't have their families with them. The colorful and talented 33-year-old midfielder Carlos Valderrama's personality did not mesh with temperamental 25-year-old forward Tino Asprilla, who was exhausted after a long season at Parma—which had just lost in the 1994 European Cup Final in May (remember Serie A was at its heights). Valderrama was also coming off of an injury. Two key personalities did not fit together, were tired or injured, and missed their families.

The margins between winning and losing are so small. While the context is very important, it should not take away from the outstanding performance of the USMNT. They displayed they had more skill than most soccer experts had given them credit for.

Once a dark horse to win the tournament, Colombia were eliminated. They were warned to stay in the U.S. while tensions and disappointment subsided in their country. However, the players decided to go home to be with their families, and so were advised to at least stay indoors. Andrés Escobar (no relation to Pablo), who was responsible for the own goal against the USMNT, chose to go out and have a drink on July 2. Tragically, while getting in his car to return home, six bullets were fired into his chest as the killers allegedly shouted, "Gooooooal." More than 120,000 people attended his funeral. Afterward there was a government crackdown on Colombian soccer's nefarious business affairs, and drug money stopped going into soccer. Colombia had another disappointing World Cup performance in 1998 and realized its soccer program had to be rebuilt. Having not qualified for the 2002, 2006, or 2010 World Cups, Colombia would come back and qualify and advance to the 2014 World Cup quarterfinal, led by James Rodríguez, who won the tournament's Golden Boot, before losing to Brazil. In contrast to 1994, when 18 players played in Colombia because of the unsustainable economic incentives generated by drug money, in 2014 only three players on the team played in the Colombian domestic league.

1994 FIFA World Cup: Group Stage, Game 3
June 26, 1994, at the Rose Bowl, California
USA 0–1 Romania
Regardless of the drama surrounding the Colombia game, the USMNT were still alive to advance. They faced Romania next, again in the Rose Bowl, needing only a draw to secure a spot in the Round of 16. It was

over 100 degrees at the start of the game. Romania packed its defense tight and patiently let the Americans advance while lying in wait for a chance to counter-attack on the flanks. The USMNT had the same strategy. The first real chance of the game went to the USMNT. A USMNT corner kick that Romania tried to clear found Harkes at the top of the box. His low shot made it through a crowd and hit the post. In the 17th minute, Romania won a ball in the middle and connected on a series of quick passes and scored. For the rest of the game, Romania played keep-away with their short, quick passes. In the oppressive heat, the USMNT had no answers. The USMNT were undone by Romania's greater experience and tactical discipline, losing 0–1.[49]

After the game, USMNT midfielder Tab Ramos said, "We showed our inexperience. We forgot that we're still the underdog and that our first priority is to defend. We got caught going forward and being too aggressive. I don't think we remembered that we had to be humble.... We are the underdogs all the way. We must remember that." Perhaps the USMNT started to believe they were something other than a team of young men who must always work hard for what they get. Ramos' comment underscores the importance of the USMNT having a certain underdog mentality and how that feeds into approach.

To make matters worse, midfielder John Harkes drew a yellow card from the referee for not lining up the requisite 10 yards from the ball on a free kick by Romania. It was Harkes' second yellow card in the tournament, which meant that he would be declared ineligible if the USMNT advanced to the Round of 16. The Americans were already missing Claudio Reyna for the entire tournament with a hamstring injury and without Harkes, the attack in the midfield would lack some creativity and danger.

Romania and Switzerland automatically advanced to the knockout round as first- and second-place finishers in the group. The USMNT had a chance to advance if their four points proved enough to finish among the top four third-place finishers in the group stage. It took two days

---

49. Romania later lost to Sweden on penalty kicks in the quarterfinals, and could easily have been in the semifinal, which speaks to the quality of the team.

to find out, but four points was enough and, remarkably, the USMNT would next face Brazil in the Round of 16.[50]

1994 FIFA World Cup: Round of 16
July 2, 1994, at Stanford Stadium, California
USA 0–1 Brazil

Under the blazing sun, in front of a sold-out Stanford Stadium crowd of 84,000 and 28 million television viewers, the USMNT walked onto the field to play their first knockout round game of the modern era in a World Cup—against soccer power Brazil. Adding to the moment, it was July 4, Independence Day, and six years to the day since the World Cup was awarded to the U.S. in 1988. The USMNT's red-and-white striped jerseys stood in contrast to Brazil's traditional yellow jerseys. Except this was not a traditional, beloved Brazil that played beautiful, attacking soccer. Brazil had seen Italy's and Germany's success in the previous two World Cups that came from focusing on defensive fundamentals. This Brazil played with pragmatism over artistry, giving in to the pressure to win another World Cup after a 24-year drought. Carlos Alberto Parreira, who coached Brazil, said, "Brazilians love fancy football...[but] if we need to play ugly to win a match, we are going to do that."

The USMNT played well early and did the little things to give them a chance. Milutinović ceded control of the match to Brazil by packing his defense with eight players in the penalty area and crowding the middle passing lanes. Milutinović chose the aging Hugo Perez at forward instead of Wynalda, who would end up replacing Ramos at halftime. Playing in place of suspended John Harkes, Cobi Jones used his speed to disrupt Brazil's attack on the flanks. Balboa and Alexi Lalas smothered Brazil's dangerous forwards, Bebeto and Romário, which was no easy feat. As Paul Caligiuri said, "Romário is the Michael Jordan of soccer and Bebeto is the Magic Johnson."

---

50. The ranking of the third-place teams to advance to the Round of 16 was Argentina, Belgium, USA, and Italy. The USA and Italy were tied in points, but the USA were ranked higher because of goals scored. If Lalas' goal against Colombia had counted, it would not have mattered. Belgium had won two matches, and the USMNT had won only one. If the USMNT had one fewer goal, the USMNT would have been ranked behind Italy and played Nigeria instead of Brazil.

The USMNT forced Brazil into mostly shots from the outside. However, within a three-minute span midway through the first half, Brazil had three or four excellent chances to score, even hitting the post twice. It appeared that the soccer gods were looking out for the USMNT. Two minutes before halftime, American midfielder Tab Ramos tried to get the ball past Brazil defender Leonardo. As they were scrambling for the ball near the sideline, Ramos stepped out of bounds. When Ramos re-entered the field, Leonardo was holding Ramos' arm and Ramos was tugging on Leonardo's shirt, and the frustrated Brazilian retaliated with a vicious right elbow to Ramos' head. Leonardo was ejected, leaving Brazil with only 10 men for the final 46 minutes. Ramos was taken to the hospital and diagnosed with a fractured skull. Later, Leonardo, who didn't have a reputation for being a dirty player, visited Ramos in the hospital and apologized. Leonardo received a four-match suspension "for violence against another player."

The USMNT couldn't capitalize on the man advantage. Brazil controlled play for the entire match. Without Ramos, John Harkes (suspended), and Claudio Reyna (injured), even with a man advantage, the USMNT attack seldom threatened and the midfield were unable to control the ball or generate quick counter-attacks. Ironically, with a man down Brazil's Romário seemed to find more space to operate. In the 74th minute, Romário dribbled past both Dooley and Balboa, then perfectly played the ball to Bebeto on his right, who dribbled past Lalas and beat Meola to the far post with a precise shot. In the 85th minute, the USMNT went down to 10 men after Fernando Clavijo was ejected after receiving his second yellow card. The USMNT would lose 0–1 to Brazil. The USMNT had only four shots (none on goal) to Brazil's 16.

Two weeks later, Brazil defeated Italy on penalty kicks in the Rose Bowl to win the 1994 World Cup, their fourth trophy. After a 24-year drought, Brazil were once again on top of the world, but the sentiment of the Brazilian media and fans was that the 1994 Brazil team, with their relatively pragmatic and defensive-minded performances, didn't belong in the same prestigious club as previous Brazil World Cup winners (or even the teams in the 1980s that didn't win).

Once Brazil captain Dunga was handed the trophy, he turned to the photographers, lifted the trophy above his head, and shouted: "This is for you, you treacherous b-----ds! What do you say now? C'mon, take the pictures, you bunch of treacherous motherf-----s! It's for you!" The 1994 Brazil team thought they gave their country what they wanted (the trophy), but didn't appreciate why they wanted it (to be entertained and showcase Brazilian joy, beauty, art, and culture) and how they wanted it (*ginga*; *jogo bonito* [beautiful game]; positive exiting, attacking artistic style that had characterized their previous teams and culture). The Brazilian fans and media often disdainfully refer to the era of Brazil's "ugly" soccer in the 1990s (champions in 1994 and second place in 1998). In contrast, the era of Brazil's creative audacity in the 1980s, which never advanced beyond a quarterfinal and was led by Zico, is revered.[51,52]

The USMNT accomplished more than most expected. They gained international respect. Mike Sorber said, "As a group we had a lot of talented players, and we proved that we could play. Were we better? No, we weren't necessarily better, but on any given day we could compete, and we could get results. I think a lot of people watched it and it gave people a lot of hope for the future.... I know the hard work and the effort that I put into trying to help the team and be a part of that group." A few players, like wild-haired defenders Alexi Lalas and Marcelo Balboa, were suddenly counter-culture stars. Forward Eric Wynalda and goalkeeper Tony Meola became household names. While many players were extremely popular, most never played in the Top Five Leagues at some point. Of the 22 players on the 1994 USMNT World Cup team, only 10 played in the Top Five Leagues, which had almost 100 teams in the 1990s and only four played more than 200 games (about five seasons). In comparison, of the

---

51. Zico played on a local futsal street team run by his older brothers growing up; three of his brothers would play professionally like their father.

52. The Brazil team at the 1982 World Cup captured the hearts and minds of soccer fans all over the world. To emphasize their contempt for traditional formations and rigid playing structures, their formation was presented as a 2-7-1, with two center-halves staying back. Zico, Sócrates, Falcão, Cerezo, and Éder were considered artistic geniuses. Their philosophy, imagination, style, courage, grace, instinct, passion, and love of the beautiful game, all played to a soundtrack of samba drums and rhythmic dancing. The memories, emotions, and art those five exceptional players produced will be treasured through the rest of time.

20 players on the 1980 Men's U.S. Olympic Hockey Team, 13 would go on to play in the NHL, which had more than 20 teams in the 1980s, and five played more than 400 games (about five seasons).

In the U.S., there was an electric atmosphere for about a month during the tournament. The surprising success of the USMNT would launch the dreams of many American children. Graham Zusi was eight when the World Cup happened and was one of thousands of children taking part in the opening ceremony. Michael Bradley, then an impressionable six-year-old living in New Jersey, recalls going to watch the Norway and Italy players train. Chris Wondolowski watched Brazil practice in Santa Clara, where he would later play professionally. Omar Gonzalez took part in pregame festivities at the Cotton Bowl in Dallas.

The total attendance and average attendance per game at the 1994 World Cup set records that still hold today, higher than the 2006 World Cup in Germany and the 2014 World Cup in Brazil. The 1994 World Cup was a springboard for the USMNT and the sport in America. The USSF was left with a $50 million surplus after the tournament. Approximately $5 million would be used as seed money for MLS. The 1994 World Cup solidified the USMNT as loveable underdogs, changed how Americans viewed the game, and increased the amount of money going into the sport (from sponsors for the USMNT to pay-to-play youth leagues). A 10-team league (Major League Soccer) was launched in 1996, with deep-pocketed investors such as Phillip Anschutz, Lamar Hunt, and Robert Kraft operating teams. But it was still just the beginning.

As Hank Steinbrecher, secretary general of the USSF, and Alan Rothenberg, president of the USSF and director of the organizing committee of the World Cup, left the Rose Bowl after the Brazil–Italy Final, a lady in the parking lot asked them to take a photo. Delighted with their success, they politely stopped and posed with big smiles. The puzzled mother explained they had misunderstood—she wanted one of them to take a picture of her and her family. Soccer in the U.S. wasn't completely legitimate. The story is a poignant reminder to soccer in the U.S. to never be content and to always be fighting to prove legitimacy.

The "Spirit of '76"

During the 1990 and 1994 World Cups, the USMNT solidified a culture, style, and identity. We labeled the American style "Spirit of '76." In 2012, Matthew Doyle, MLSsoccer.com Armchair Analyst, watched more than 50 hours of USMNT tape going all the way back to 1990 to discern for *Howler* magazine what, if anything, characterizes the American style of play. He concluded, "A neutral observer of the last 22 years could be forgiven for assuming that the American style—to the extent one exists at all—is 'try hard, run fast,' and don't spend too much time thinking about tactics. That's what happens when you have players whose athleticism (with rare exceptions) exceeds their technical ability. But as unsexy as it sounds compared to, say, 'Total Football,' U.S. national team players did (and do) habitually try hard and run fast. They eagerly compress space. They work in groups defensively and love to break forward. It's a style that hasn't inspired poetry, but as they say in Rome, *Quod facis bene fac.* What you do, do well."[53]

The concept of "try harder" is very difficult to define because most people assume all players and teams try hard. "Try hard" isn't really a style. It's an identity. When we asked players and coaches from opposing national teams what "try hard" meant to them as it relates to the USMNT, generally paraphrasing, their answers were: "There are certain teams that are just tough to beat even if you have superior skill;" "They [USMNT] made us work and run more than other teams;" "They made the game physical;" "They just didn't quit;" "They were like Atlético Madrid— you just didn't want to play them because you knew it was going to be a battle." Typically, the opposing national team players and coaches also pointed out that the USMNT had more skill than they were often given credit for. Generally paraphrasing, they said, "The USMNT would chase and compress space all night. They had grit. They were complicated and dangerous. If we made one mistake, they [USMNT] had some fast players with skills who could counter-attack and capitalize."

---

53. Beyond not being a "style," to simply describe the USMNT style as "try hard, run fast" and not thinking about tactics isn't completely fair for a number of reasons. The USMNT and selected players had more skill and tactical awareness than is often portrayed in the press.

Similarly, anyone who has played sports at a competitive level knows there are certain teams and players that, for lack of a more elegant way to say it, are just hard to play against. It is difficult to articulate exactly why these teams or players make things so difficult, but grit and determined effort are usually at the top of the list, and for better or worse, the USMNT had this spirit and reputation. Again, this isn't to say that others are not trying their hardest, but to an opponent, the effort seems even more extreme when taken into context with the probability of losing.

Starting with the World Cup in 1990, the USMNT have sought legitimacy. The USMNT weren't the first in America to seek legitimacy; America itself wanted to create legitimacy. In 1776, the main purpose of the writers of the Declaration of Independence was to spell out American ideals and principles; their other purpose was to start to create legitimacy. In 1776, the newly declared United States of America were fighting for global recognition as a sovereign nation.[54] While the former colonies wanted to be recognized as independent from British authority, there remained the real chance that no other country would look at them as anything more than unruly British subjects. Similarly, in the 1990s and 2000s, the USSF, USMNT, and fans were fighting for U.S. Soccer to be globally recognized and taken seriously. Most Continental army soldiers were farmers and merchants, not professional soldiers. Most had no formal military training, and what munitions they owned were personal firearms and possessions. They were underdogs against the British soldiers. Similarly, in the 1990s most USMNT players were essentially college players or played semiprofessionally, competing against players in the top European Leagues. Even today, most USMNT players don't play soccer in the Top Five Leagues in Europe. The USMNT are perennial underdogs. The grit, determination, and team cohesion that come with the underdog mentality are what made them and the American colonists so admirable and inspirational. Please note that there is a difference or subtle nuance between having an underdog mentality and believing you will win (or having that quiet confidence). Those two beliefs are not mutually exclusive.

---

54. It's always flawed to use an analogy between sports and war. We do here because it's often used and most would understand the real differences.

If we look at this idea within the broader historical context, it is easy to see the parallels and why this is important in understanding American soccer culture and style.

Because the odds were stacked against the American colonists, and the USMNT, strategy would be paramount. The American commander, George Washington, was aggressive by nature, but he understood what he had to work with and what he was up against. Overmatched, Washington decided to utilize irregular warfare such as ambushes and quick hit-and-run tactics against the British forces. He took advantage of his soldiers' passion (instead of professional occupation), will to win, and knowledge of the terrain. He knew if his army fought like the British, the Continental army would lose. Even though the British press—and even some founding fathers—thought the Continental army's tactics were unheroic, Washington decided to do what he had to with who he had to fight for legitimacy. The USMNT did the same. They did what they could in an American style of play that fit the players' skill level. Like their Continental army ancestors, the USMNT used quick hit-and-run tactics—quick counter-attacks. The USMNT's tactics, just like the Continental army's tactics, were labeled "unheroic" and "lacking style." The USMNT took advantage of their players' passion, will to win, and athleticism. Over time they developed a culture, identity, and authentic American style of playing soccer.

We tried to come up with a common language to capture the essence of American culture and American soccer style. At the time of the American Revolution, there was an intangible something that is known as the Spirit of '76. This spirit was personified by the beliefs and actions of the first citizens of the United States of America. Most Americans understand and identify with the Spirit of '76. The spirit captures the idea that, while Americans are aggressive by nature, they understand what they have to work with and what they are up against. Americans appreciate the courageous underdogs who break traditional rules, sacrifice, and turn perceived weaknesses into strengths. Americans root for underdogs who never quit. Therefore, within the context of the USMNT, they should embrace being authentic to who they are and what they have in terms of talent, culture, and history with the sport. Various foreign news articles during the 1994 World Cup used the words and phrases "fighters," "valiant," "inspired," "teamwork," "absorbing pressure," "threat on the break," and "fortuitous" to describe the players and play of the USMNT. Similar words and phrases could have been used to describe the Continental army during the Revolutionary War.

The *Why*, *How*, and *Who* of the USWNT

Comparisons between the USMNT and the USWNT have many flaws and require context.[55] However, we use the U.S. women's national soccer team (USWNT) as an example because the two teams, rightly or wrongly, are associated and linked. On the field, the USWNT have won four World Cups. Off the field, the USWNT have had tremendous success. For example, Nike sold more of their home jerseys on its website in the 2018–19 season than it had of any other men's or women's soccer team's jersey in a single season in its history—more USWNT jerseys were sold than the country of Brazil or the club Barcelona![56] In September 2020, Tobin Heath and Christen Press signed with Manchester United of the FA Women's Super League. The jerseys for the two USWNT soccer stars outsold all of the players on the men's side—surpassing Paul Pogba's jersey sales for the three days following his historic signing. Jersey sales indicate people wanting to identify with a player—the USWNT players have figured out their *why*, *how*, and *who*.

The USWNT and even their fans desperately want legitimacy, but it's in a different way than the USMNT. They aren't trying to prove the legitimacy of women's soccer in the U.S. anymore. They did that. Rather, their *why* evolved. They are trying to convince the world that women's sports belong—period. This impacts their approach and attitude.

---

55. Someone asked us if we wrote a book about the NBA's LA Lakers, would we mention the WNBA's LA Sparks? It's a good question. Probably not. But if we wrote a book about the LA Lakers, we would mention other teams that are associated with them—each of which would have flaws in comparison and need context. In this case, the USWNT and USMNT are associated. Just because one is a women's team and the other a men's team doesn't mean they can't be associated or compared at some level—recognizing the many flaws and context necessary in doing so.

56. Keep in mind that Nike.com isn't the largest seller of Nike sponsored jerseys.

When Mia Hamm was asked a question about the USWNT's overwhelming advantage in CONCACAF play, she said that she hoped that the USWNT could become an example to other federations in the region. Hamm wanted to believe these other countries would come to realize how allotting more funds and resources for a women's team might lead to great things. Badly beating underfunded CONCACAF teams was showing what was possible. The USMNT don't have that same purpose. Compare the USMNT in Trinidad & Tobago in 1989 and 2017. In 1989, the USMNT were underdogs trying to prove the legitimacy of soccer in the U.S. In 2017, they didn't have the same purpose. Actually, TV commentators said they had "blinded arrogance."

The USWNT's *why* evolved, rather than drifted or changed, and now has extended from women's sports belong to equal pay. This concept has empowered women in all facets of life, not just sports. What started out as a movement to prove that women's soccer in the U.S. is legitimate came to include that the women's soccer players should get just as much respect (and compensation) as the men, which evolved to include many other women's sports, and then even women more broadly, especially in the workplace. The mission has continued to evolve to include social justice for everyone. As the USWNT's mission has gained a higher purpose and evolved in such a positive way, they have grown their fan base.

Even though the USWNT are World Champions, remarkably, they very much are underdogs. From the very beginning, even while the USWNT looked to be underdogs in the 1980s, the team believed they always had a chance to come out on top—and they cherished the opportunity to prove their mission. They still have the same grit and determination and all the characteristics that are so commonly associated with being an underdog. Similar to the 1994 USMNT players who went out of their way to promote soccer and the World Cup, the USWNT players go out of their way to promote soccer and so much more.

While they don't necessarily have a rival on the field to help define their values and mission, they have powerful "rivals" (institutional and personal) who have not completely supported them, which provides a platform to highlight and reinforce their mission and values. Rivals help solidify identity and brands—the question casual fans are being asked is, "Are you *for* the USWNT and *equal pay* or *against* the USWNT and *equal pay*?" You have to choose a side. Same with other rivalries such as Real Madrid versus Barcelona (*El Clásico*) or "derbies" such as AC Milan versus Inter Milan (*Derby della Madonnina*)—even casual fans have to choose a side, which is essentially a way of life or set of values. The USWNT's attitude on and off the field reflects that they are playing for something greater than themselves, and remarkably they represent all people who like to root for or identify with underdogs fighting united as a team to reach seemingly unattainable goals.

The USWNT's *how*—style of play—and *who*—the players— authentically embrace who America is and who they are. The USWNT's first sports icon was reluctant superstar Mia Hamm, who would become a two-time Olympic gold medalist and two-time World Cup champion. Although she was one of the greatest women soccer players of all time, she directed credit to her teammates and best friends. She was as admired for her skill as much as her humility. Girls across America, and the world, wanted to be Mia Hamm.

The members of the USWNT are also not afraid to show *who* they are— and perhaps even go one step further than that by being so unequivocally themselves and constantly willing to put themselves out there and fight for what they believe in. The USWNT players are a bunch of characters who love and support each other—and that endears them to America. After Mia Hamm's brother sadly died, she missed a friendly game. She turned on the TV to watch, and saw that the USWNT were wearing black armbands in her brother's memory. Some players also express themselves with distinctive hairstyles, like the much-loved USMNT characters at the 1994 World Cup. The USWNT actively connect and engage with their fans more than most professional athletes to promote soccer and issues important to them, and themselves.

Jill Ellis, who won two World Cups in five years as coach of the USWNT, understood the value of drawing *how* from U.S. culture. In a 2016 interview with Tim Nash of *FourFourTwo*, Ellis said, "With such a diverse history and culture, it's difficult to summarize or gain a consensus on a style of play for our country. What we should embrace is being authentic to who we are. If you ask around the world, the U.S. are described as mentally tough, hard workers, athletic. They're not descriptors we want to disown. We are all those things." Mia Hamm also explained, "...We also wanted to get into a street fight and stand toe-to-toe with the toughest to put the ball in the back of the net. All the things we really felt represent the American spirit, we wanted our team to represent."

Many assume that the USWNT are popular because they win. Is winning a part of the identity? Absolutely. However, contrary to popular belief, winning isn't the most important thing for most fans; most fans *and players* care as much about *why* their teams win (mission and common purpose), *how* their teams win (style of play and values), and *who* their teams win with (the players, their passion, and their values) than winning itself.

The USWNT are popular because even though they win, they are underdogs still fighting for legitimacy in so many ways. Many people in America identify with the USWNT's *why*—many feel like they are the best at what they do and aren't recognized for it—and it's not just women. Regularly advancing to World Cup Finals and the Olympics provides the USWNT the opportunity and platform to showcase their *why*, *how*, and *who*. On the field, the USWNT have provided iconic images of pure joy: Brandi Chastain tearing off her jersey after her historic 1999 World Cup game-winning penalty-kick goal to Golden Boot, Golden Ball, and World Cup champion Megan Rapinoe's goal scoring celebrations. USWNT celebrative moments screamed, *Yes, I/we can!* Their fans are screaming the same thing—it's the aspiration of the idea of equal opportunity.

While everything is not always perfect as portrayed by the media, the USWNT are an example of a team that has brought together and inspired a passionate community by creating a sense of belonging and shared values felt so deeply that they are synonymous with one's identity. The history, feelings, moments, and emotions are all intertwined. It is impossible to tell where the USWNT fan's identity and USWNT's identity and purpose start and stop.

Chapter 2

An Explanation of *Why*, *How*, and *Who* and Expectations and Comparisons

Generally, the remainder of this book will go through various World Cups and other tournaments to explain and illustrate how and why the USMNT's *why*, *how*, and *who* have changed (including the meanings and perceptions) since the early 1990s. However, in order to provide context for the remainder of the book, in this chapter we will stop and explain more about *why*, *how*, and *who* and why they are important. *If you care more about the action and events and don't feel like you need more background or a deeper understanding of* why, how, *and* who, *please feel free to skip to the next chapter on the 1998 World Cup at any time.*

As a reminder, we believe the *why*—prove the legitimacy of U.S. Soccer—led to a *how*, which led to a culture and style of play. The Spirit of '76 American style of play uniquely reflected America's values, talent, traditions, and history with soccer's development in the U.S. The *how* also led to the players—the *who*—who were willing to sacrifice themselves and work together to prove U.S. Soccer legitimately belonged. We believe the *why*, *how*, and *who* can best be explained and illustrated using the "Golden Circle" below.

As we describe the various World Cups and tournaments throughout the book, we also explain and illustrate how and why the expectations changed over time. In order to provide context for the remainder of the book, at the end of this chapter we also stop and explain more about why expectations are important and their relevance to the happiness and satisfaction of fans. Afterward, we get back to the action of World Cups and other tournaments.

Golden Circle

Leadership expert Simon Sinek delivered one of the most popular TED Talks of all time. He is the author of *Start with Why: How Great Leaders Inspire Everyone to Take Action*. His talk focuses on how leaders at the most successful organizations think, act, and communicate. He uses his Golden Circle model to help explain.

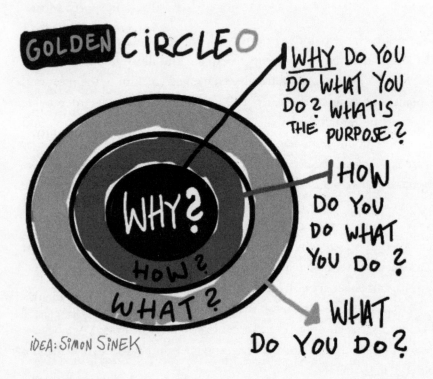

Humans respond most to messaging geared toward the parts of the brain that control emotions, behavior, and decision-making. According to Sinek, *why* is, above all, the message that an organization can leverage to spur others to action. *Why* is how you explain your purpose and behavior. Successfully conveying the *why* activates the limbic brain, the part that processes feelings such as trust and loyalty, as well as decision-making. If articulated successfully, the *why* can define value propositions, affect behavior, and move others to act as you might want them to.

So, what does *why* mean for the USMNT players or the players on any sports team? Players will be subconsciously thinking, *What's the mission? Why does the USMNT want to win? Why does anyone care? Why should I sacrifice for the team? Why should I do what is in the team's best interest versus my own? Why should I give extraordinary effort or risk injury or have extraordinary passion or have extraordinary loyalty?* The answers impact a player's and team's performance.

This holds true in every organization, but especially so in sports. Most athletes have relatively short careers. The average career duration of a professional soccer player in England is eight years (not all necessarily in the Premier League), and the average contract length is around 2.5 years. The average playing career for rookies in MLS, the NFL, and the NBA is 2.5, 3.3, and 4.5 years, respectively. Players have an economic incentive to try to maximize their earning potential during a very limited opportunity. Therefore, they have an incentive to prioritize themselves over the team. The *why* gives them the motivation for extraordinary effort and to care beyond themselves—this matters more and more because athletes are grinding to a physiological limit and performance is getting clustered.

Absolute skill has never been higher and relative skill has never been narrower. In the men's marathon at the 1932 Summer Olympics, the winner finished with a time of 2:31:36. The 20th-place athlete finished in 3:10:51, a difference of 39 minutes. In the 2016 Summer Olympics men's marathon, the winner finished with a time of 2:08:44. The 20th-place athlete finished in 2:14:37, a difference of six minutes.

In this vein, in 2008 running enthusiast and Stanford University biologist Mark Denny published a study attempting to determine if there

are absolute limits to the speeds animals can run. To do so, he analyzed
the records of three racing sports with long histories of documentation:
track and field and horse racing in the U.S., along with English greyhound
racing. By plotting winning race times back to the turn of the 20th century,
Denny was able to conclude that there is indeed a predictable limit to the
time it takes for a particular species to cover a certain distance. In fact, his
data show that horse and dog racing as well as some human track and field
events may already be there. We are definitely plateauing. Looking at the
horse racing data, which parallels what's happening in humans, winning
times in the Triple Crown haven't really improved since the 1970s—and
this is despite all of the millions of dollars being poured into breeding
faster horses. As Denny explains, horses can still be bred to improve on a
particular attribute; however, doing so comes with collateral physiological
drawbacks. "You can breed a horse to go faster than ever before or to
have stronger muscles but then its legs will break. It really looks like we've
maxed out the gene pool for thoroughbreds." The same is happening
with human athletes. With the gap between the best and the very good
getting smaller, those teams with players who are motivated to put forth
extraordinary effort and who care about the team more than themselves
will have a competitive advantage.

What does *why* mean for the fan? Fans will be subconsciously thinking:
*Why should I root for this team? Why should I spend my precious free time
(and money) going to see this team play or watching them on TV? Does the
team value what I value? Does the team play like I want it to play? Does this
team reflect me? Why* will differentiate one player or team from another.
The more aligned the *why* is among the sports team, players, and fans, the
more loyal, motivated, and passionate the collective group. Our brains are
capable of making deep, powerful, fast-acting, and emotional connections
when we can answer *why*. The more loyal, motivated, and passionate the
group is, then the more the players will give an extraordinary effort and
sacrifice for the team and fans on the field and the more fans and greater
fan intensity in the stands. It is a virtuous cycle. Off the field, the more
money fans spend on traveling with the team, stadium experiences, and

jerseys—the more money sponsors and broadcasters will pay to access the fan group.

Conventional wisdom is that the mission of a sports team is simple and obvious: win a championship. However, a mission is different from a goal in that the former is the cause and the latter is the effect; a mission is something to be accomplished, whereas a goal is something to be pursued for that accomplishment. Neel Doshi and Lindsay McGregor, former McKinsey & Company consultants and authors of *Primed to Perform*, proved through their research that "the highest performing cultures are built on the simple truth: *why* people work affects how *well* they work."

We ask a simple question: Why are the USMNT playing? It's not to win the World Cup. That is a goal. In 1990 and 1994, the USMNT and their fans had clear answers to *why?* The USSF, USMNT, and even the fans desperately wanted legitimacy—just like with the earliest Americans and the Spirit of '76. They wanted to show America belonged, and they had pride. They didn't care if they were underdogs; they embraced it. Their fans love the underdog. The USMNT transcend soccer in many ways. They appealed to the many dreamers. The dreamers need to believe that one day maybe they can achieve the impossible too. The compelling sports stories are the underdog stories—there is something romantic or heroic about winning as an underdog. Legends are made out of people and teams who overcome challenges to defeat the heavy favorites. The stories and journeys of the overlooked, counted out, or disregarded add a compelling layer to the games we love.

The organization's *how* is how you do what you do. According to Sinek, *how* messaging also affects behavior and emotion, again through the limbic brain. So, what does this mean for the USMNT or any sports team? Players will be subconsciously thinking: *What's our style of play? What values do we believe in?* (And, for coaches, *Which players do I put on the field?*). Fans will be subconsciously thinking: *Does this style reflect what I value and how I want to play? When I wear the team jersey, what does it say about me? What does it tell the world about me?*

In 1990 and 1994, the USMNT developed an answer to *how?* They would have the Spirit of '76. They played defense and counter-attacked.

They employed American grit, determination, and a "never-say-die" attitude. The iconic image of Brian McBride in the 2006 World Cup with blood pouring down his face after a star Italian player elbowed him in the left eye was a lasting visual representation of the grit and attitude. After being treated on the sideline, McBride went back and played the rest of the game. After the game, he received three stitches below his left eye. He wasn't a flashy player, he was a warrior.

We interviewed players and a coach from teams that faced the USMNT in the 1994 World Cup. One opposing player captured the sentiment of many when he said the USMNT were a "pain in the ass to play." They said the USMNT wouldn't quit. Grant Wahl wrote in his book *Masters of Modern Soccer*, "Claudio Reyna says that when he has spoken to soccer talent developers, especially in the Netherlands, they have noted that one area in which young American players excel globally is in their all-out push to win. The U.S. culture might not produce as many skilled players, but, man, they hate to lose. That's no small thing." The 1990 and 1994 national teams were responsible for setting this foundation in place, and it defined the values of the USMNT for almost two decades.

The USMNT were underdogs and utilized teamwork, unglamorous tactics, and hustle to compete. Americans can identify with that. Many fans marvel at the greats, but their skills and athleticism are not really relatable to most. And that is where the underdogs who aren't expected to reach the highest glories make sports more human. The attitude and values of underdogs attract fans. Players were willing to make sacrifices to be on the team and they didn't take anything for granted. After matches, the USMNT players genuinely seemed flattered people asked for their autographs.

Even as World Champions, the USWNT had an underdog mentality or values. John Powers of the *Boston Globe* wrote, "What makes Kristine Lilly and her US teammates special was not so much their gold-medal soccer skills as their gold-medal people skills. They understood what their fans wanted—a smile, a handshake, an autograph, an arm-around-the-shoulders photo. Just a moment's intimacy that would be remembered for a lifetime."

Included in the *how* is *who*. The fans will be subconsciously thinking: *Is that player like me? Do I want to be that player? Does that player have the same values as me? Is that player from where I am from? Did that player face some difficulties that I did? Do I want to play like that player? Would I buy a jersey with that player's name on the back?*

In 1990 and 1994, the USMNT developed an answer to *who?* The USMNT players were a cast of characters to whom most Americans could relate. They represented the eclectic melting pot of the U.S. with different backgrounds. Many of the USMNT players had unique stories and personalities, not to mention hairstyles, and weren't afraid to show it, which endeared them to Americans. Americans knew the players weren't the best in the world, but they also saw that they were willing to fight to win. Americans respected that and identified with their underdog status. They also had youth and potential, and those attributes attracted casual fans.

The most requested player for interviews during the 1994 World Cup was Alexi Lalas. He even was a guest on *The Tonight Show* before the tournament. He was born in Michigan to a Greek father, who was a professor, and an Anglo-American mother, who was a poet. The tall, 24-year-old defender had attended Cranbrook Kingswood School in Bloomfield Hills, Michigan. Even though he did not begin playing soccer until he was 11, he had developed his skills enough to be named the 1987 Michigan High School Player of the Year by his senior year. In addition to playing soccer, he was a member and captain of his high school hockey team, which won the state championship. Lalas was rated for the Ontario Hockey League midget draft in 1987, but was not selected. Lalas played soccer for Rutgers University from 1988 to 1991 and won college player of the year. As he did in high school, Lalas also played hockey in college, leading the team in scoring in 1989.

Lalas wasn't the best player on the USMNT, but he looked different from most. His red hair hung to his shoulders. His red-orange goatee was four inches long. He was a member of a rock band. As much as he was rock 'n' roll cool, he was Ronald McDonald dorky. He had an awkward, stiff playing and running style. However, he worked hard, covered a lot of space with his long strides, defended crosses into the box, and did the little things. He marked his man, tackled hard, and gave the ball to better players who could do something with it. He seemed like a hard-working knucklehead who, if he wasn't playing in the World Cup, would be drinking beer in the stands with his face painted rooting for the USMNT. Many Americans identified with him.

In the movie *Miracle* about the 1980 U.S. Men's Olympic Hockey Team, there is a scene where Herb Brooks is talking with his assistant coach Craig Patrick about the team he has chosen, and he says, "I'm not looking for the best players, Craig. I'm looking for the right ones." The question for the USMNT coach should be *who is the best fit* (can play the best within the U.S. style and has the American values fans identify with) for the team—and sometimes, the answer isn't *who is the best player*. Getting players with different socioeconomic backgrounds and languages to trust each other and work together and buy into a culture is a challenge for a coach, but it's part of the skill set a coach needs and a key reason why he or she needs a defined culture. Therefore, the coach should absolutely select the best fit with U.S. style and culture of the team.

As a side note, as it relates to familiarity, the breakdown of the 1980 U.S. Men's Olympic Hockey Team is a great case study. Nine players (45 percent) played for the University of Minnesota, where Herb Brooks coached. More than 60 percent of the players came from the state of Minnesota. The entire 20-man roster was made up of players from six colleges in total and came from only four states!

Table: Breakdown of the 1980 U.S. Men's Olympic Hockey Team

1980 U.S. Olympic Team					
College	# Players	% Team	Home State	# Players	% Team
Minnesota	9	45%	Minnesota	12	60%
Boston University	4	20%	Massachusetts	4	20%
Bowling Green	2	10%	Michigan	2	10%
Minnesota-Duluth	2	10%	Wisconsin	2	10%
Wisconsin	2	10%			
North Dakota	1	5%			

Getting back to players who are the best fit, Sweden, with one of the greatest players in history, Zlatan Ibrahimović, didn't qualify for the 2010 and 2014 World Cups. In 2018, without Ibrahimović, who didn't play in qualification matches, Sweden defied expectations and qualified for the World Cup. At the time, Sweden's leading scorer in qualifying was not even playing soccer in a European league. There was a debate over whether Sweden should include Ibrahimović on the roster for the World Cup. In one media survey in Sweden, two-thirds responded "no" because Ibrahimović didn't play a single minute in Sweden's improbable run to qualify. The word Sweden's fans emphasized most when describing the Sweden national team was *collective*. They said that the team represented them, no flash and no stars, working collectively. One fan said "they are stronger because they are, in theory, weaker." The coach didn't select Ibrahimović for the squad, and Sweden reached the quarterfinals of the 2018 World Cup, having helped eliminate Germany from the competition in the group stage.

It's not difficult for an organization to define *what* they do. For example, the USMNT play soccer for America. However, what is important is the *why*, *how*, and *who*. *What* messaging only engages with the neocortex—the rational part of our brain. According to Sinek, the neocortex drives decision-making less than the limbic brain. People respond to leaders and organizations better when they have a clear sense of *why* and *how* they do what they do, and when those leaders and organizations convey those beliefs passionately and authentically. The USMNT were authentic and passionate. They were not pretending to be anyone and embraced who they were. Win or lose, America loved them for it and watched their World Cup games in record numbers.

While writing this book, we learned another lesson: *when* you win also matters. National teams are ultimately judged on—and perceptions are made by—World Cup performances when the entire world is watching.

McKinsey, the management consulting firm, performed a study that demonstrated companies with defined (codified) and distinguishable cultures provided significantly higher returns. Each one of their cultures was authentic to their organization, not copied. The USMNT would probably benefit from writing down, or codifying, their mission and having the entire coaching staff and team buy into it. The evaluations of the coach and players should include living up to the mission and style of play. This is important because the coaches and players change so often for each cycle. It also will help reinforce that the focus should be on the mission, not the goal.[57]

Since I, Steven, wrote a book about Real Madrid and don't want to appear biased, I will use Barcelona, another club, as an example. Barcelona state they are "more than a club because when we play we want to win, but without neglecting our OWN STYLE.... More than a club because we feel that such VALUES as humility, ambition, effort, teamwork and respect are just as important a part of the way we play as winning…that's why we are more than a club, because we spend every day working hard to be the best and to make the world into a better place, by not only imagining a more prosperous future, but by really making it happen." (The emphasis is their own.) Barcelona's focus is on *why* and *how*.

Ronaldo and Messi and 60 Seconds

The *why*, *how*, and *who* matter because soccer is a highly improvised and team-oriented sport, even more so than basketball. Eleven soccer players interact in a fluid, rapidly unfolding manner. We examined Cristiano Ronaldo and Lionel Messi's scoring and learned how important teamwork is. On average, Ronaldo and Messi possess the ball 20 times a game, three seconds each time, for a total of merely one minute per 90-minute game. You read that right! Ronaldo and Messi touch the ball for around *sixty seconds per game*, around 1 percent of the game time.

Both Ronaldo and Messi are often fouled three to four times per game, reducing their 20 possessions to 16 or 17. Goals mean a lot more in soccer than points do in most sports. Quality shot opportunities in soccer are very scarce, so making the most of them is critical. Within those 16 to 17 non-fouled possessions, Ronaldo and Messi typically attempt four to six shots per game. Of Ronaldo's and Messi's four to six shots, 40 to 50 percent will be on goal and 40 to 50 percent of shots on goal (about 25

57. U.S. Soccer has an overall mission statement. The USMNT does not have a (public) team mission statement, which leaves the mission more open to interpretation and susceptible to change with every new cycle or coach.

percent of all shots) will actually result in a goal, which is ridiculously high compared to other star soccer players.[58]

The *why*, *how*, and *who* matter because, while star players like Cristiano Ronaldo and Lionel Messi can significantly impact a game, the stars need the ball passed to them at the right time and the right place from a teammate willing to pass them the ball. Their teammates all need to understand and buy into what their roles are for the team and be willing to do what is best for the team, not themselves. They need the *why* and *how*.

Too-Much-Talent Effect
Conventional wisdom is that bringing together the most talented individuals guarantees the best possible team performance. Adam Galinsky of Columbia Business School and Roderick Swaab of INSEAD conducted an analysis of data from basketball, soccer, and baseball that revealed that superstars are good for a team—up to a point. When there are too many star players on a single team, the data suggest players compete for status instead of cooperating as team members. The researchers dubbed their finding the "too-much-talent effect." A group of All-Stars can easily tip the balance away from coordination and cooperation to competition and petty rivalry. The too-much-talent effect is not as prevalent in baseball because a baseball player can hit a home run and score without help from a teammate.

Why, *how*, and *who*—a culture—not only improve effort, coordination, and cooperation, but also reduce the impact of the too-much-talent effect.

Changing Expectations and Comparisons: The Connection to Happiness and Satisfaction
The most loyal and passionate fans' identities are intertwined with the *why*, *how*, and *who* of their team. Of course, fans are "happy" or "satisfied" when their teams win. However, they are "happiest" and "most satisfied" when their teams win with the *why*, *how*, and *who* because, as

---

58. This includes 20 to 25 percent of their goals, which are from penalty or direct kicks.

previously mentioned, those things connect to the limbic brain, the part of our anatomy that processes feelings such as trust and loyalty, as well as decision-making and behavior.

Rakesh Sarin and Manel Baucells, in their book *Engineering Happiness*, explain happiness is influenced by things we don't have, were never going to have, and wouldn't have missed if the thought hadn't occurred. They conclude happiness equals reality minus expectations. Raise expectations beyond reality's capacity to meet them, and misery follows. Humans' thoughts and expectations are impacted by their environment and their culture. We will demonstrate that after the 1994 World Cup, the USSF, USMNT, media, and fans raised their expectations—thoughts started to creep into the collective view that if the USMNT could make the Round of 16 in the 1994 World Cup with some recent college graduates and a few players in Europe, then in four years the USMNT could make the quarterfinals. Were expectations beyond reality's capacity to meet them in 1998? The luck and background surrounding the win against Colombia and the laser beam free kick from more than 30 yards out that that Eric Wynalda would later admit "was the greatest goal of my life" against Austria provide some context. However, fans could only focus on the USMNT getting to the Round of 16 and "only" losing to Brazil 0–1. These feelings would become multiplied after the 2002 World Cup.

While happiness may be connected to expectations, cognitive psychologist Daniel Kahneman, winner of the 2002 Nobel Prize in economics, argues that satisfaction is based mostly on comparisons. He believes life satisfaction is connected to a large degree to social yardsticks—achieving goals. If we have faulty comparisons, we will never be satisfied. Putting aside the 2002 quarterfinal, even the 1994 Round of 16 without context (e.g., three teams qualifying from a group) can be used as a faulty comparison, setting up unrealistic expectations. When unrealistic expectations are not met, there is pressure to do something or be something different.

* * *

Generally, the remainder of the book will go through various World Cups and other tournaments to explain and illustrate how and why the *why*, *how*, and *who* of the USMNT have changed (including the meanings and perceptions) from the early 1990s as well as how and why the expectations and comparisons changed over time. The next chapter focuses on the 1998 World Cup.

Chapter 3

1998 World Cup: Team Chemistry

Rap Music Videos and Togetherness

Many people remember that the 1985 Chicago Bears had their own theme song and rap music video, "The Super Bowl Shuffle," which was released two months prior to their Super Bowl win. The song was actually nominated for a Grammy Award in 1985 for Best R&B Performance by a Duo or Group, eventually losing to "Kiss" by Prince.

Not many people recall "Victory," the 1990 USMNT's World Cup theme song and rap music video. The video, profiled by Adam Elder in 2014 in *The New Yorker*, was made shortly after the USMNT qualified for the World Cup for the first time in 40 years. Shelli Azoff, the wife of longtime music-industry mogul Irving Azoff, tried to help the USMNT players with their contracts and promotions. The song was written and produced by West Coast Rap All-Stars member Def Jef and DJ Eric Vaughn and came with a music video featuring shirtless members of the USMNT playfully kicking a soccer ball on a beach and cameos in the recording studio with sports celebrities O.J. Simpson and Marcus Allen. The chorus of the song is: "Togetherness and unity means victory in Italy / With dedication, heart, and soul, you have the tools to achieve your goal." Selected lyrics include: "Reaching higher / striving harder / always doing better because it's a part of / the winning spirit / you gotta keep your chin up…. Togetherness and unity / means victory for you and me / with intellect and self-respect / attain whatever you want to get /…. With dedication, heart, and soul / you have the tools to achieve your goals / when I was young my folks would demand / work hard for what you want be the best you can / stay out of trouble get an education / if you do you gain admiration / respect yourself as well as others / love your sisters and love your brothers…"

Coach Bob Gansler approved the players taking time off for the endeavor. He said, "Projects like that just bring the team closer together, and I think we had a pretty close bunch as it was. [Although] it wasn't my kind of music!" In hindsight, the project may seem silly; however, whether or not they knew it, the USMNT were tapping into a few important things. First, the endeavor was an opportunity for the players to do something fun and creative together outside of playing soccer. Today, national teams usually see each other for very limited and focused time. The coach recognized that bringing the team together was important. Second, the music video was a way for the USMNT to connect to fans. Today, players have social media. At the time, music videos were an innovative way for players to connect and share something about themselves with fans. The lyrics "togetherness and unity" were very much a part of the USMNT culture and identity. Connecting with fans beyond the soccer field was a part of the team culture. Lastly, the music video highlights the USMNT's search for legitimacy. There was a feeling that if music people were willing to write a song and produce a music video about them, and star athletes were willing to make cameos, then soccer in the U.S. was gaining legitimacy.

In April 1995, Bora Milutinović, the USMNT's 1994 World Cup coach, was told his contract would not be renewed, and he resigned.[59]

---

59. Milutinović would lead Nigeria to the knockout round of the 1998 World Cup. He set a coaching record for having taken four different teams to the knockout rounds of the World Cup. In 2002, he was the coach who led China to qualify for the 2002 World Cup, ending their 44-year drought. In a 2002 interview with Grant Wahl of *Sports Illustrated*, Milutinović said, "Four times my team goes through [to the knockout round]. I don't know how we go through, but we go through. I don't know anything, but I do everything."

The USSF wanted to widen the role of the USMNT coach to include developing other coaches and more administrative duties. Milutinović just wanted to coach. As the USSF searched for a replacement, Steve Sampson, one of Milutinović's assistants, took over coaching responsibilities as interim coach.

Sampson played soccer in college in California and then coached a public high school soccer team while he attended Stanford University's Graduate School of Education. After graduating from Stanford, Sampson was hired by UCLA as an assistant men's soccer coach. After UCLA won the NCAA men's soccer championship in 1985, Sampson became the head coach of Santa Clara University.[60]

Copa América 1995, Uruguay

Sampson's first test as USMNT interim coach was at the Copa América 1995 in Uruguay. An important part of USMNT history stems from this tournament. On the way to the tournament, the USMNT players wanted a better collective agreement with the USSF. Reportedly, the USSF offered a contract that would pay the players bonuses incrementally on how many times they had played for the USMNT. The players felt this was unfair and would divide the team. So, John Harkes called a captain's meeting in the back of the airplane and when they landed, the players informed their coach that they wouldn't practice or play until the matter was resolved.

It proved to be a game of chicken, and the USSF blinked.[61] It brought the players closer together. The USMNT felt empowered and understood that, together, they could accomplish goals. It would become a core value of the team. After successfully standing up to the USSF, Sampson told

---

60. On December 3, 1989, in Rutgers Stadium in New Jersey, Santa Clara played the University of Virginia, coached by Bruce Arena, for the NCAA Men's Soccer Championship. Santa Clara and Virginia were tied through regular time and four overtimes before NCAA officials stopped the game, much to the frustration of the players and two coaches, and named Santa Clara and Virginia as co-champions. The Final was played in frigid conditions as the wind chill was 10 degrees below zero at kickoff and dropped throughout the game. A perpetual stiff breeze took control of any ball kicked in the air.

61. A final agreement wasn't finalized until after the tournament because it required a vote that included more players. FIFA/CONCACAF were considering suspending the players from future competition if they didn't play.

the players that they needed to go out there and prove they deserved and earned what they fought for. The players were highly motivated.

The USMNT and Mexico were invited as guest participants in the Copa América 1995. The USMNT, which consisted primarily of 1994 World Cup players who were familiar with each other, their roles, and their style of play, unexpectedly defeated Chile 2–1. Eric Wynalda scored both goals. Sampson reflected, "I remember a team that wanted to attack, and did. They wanted to put opponents on their heels, and did. It was a team that wanted to prove their success in the 1994 World Cup was not a fluke. Beating Chile set the tone." They wanted to prove the legitimacy of soccer in the U.S.

The USMNT then played Argentina in Paysandú, Uruguay.[62] Argentina, still coping with the end of the Diego Maradona era, did not need to beat the USMNT to advance to the knockout round of the tournament. Therefore, the Argentina coach decided to rest nine members of their first team, including Diego Simeone (now head coach of Atlético Madrid). Predictably, with the USMNT mentality, the players viewed the Argentina coach's decision as a lack of respect. Eric Wynalda explained the team's approach: "I think collectively we said just don't give these guys time. One thing you learn as a footballer over time is that when you're hesitant, or scared to go in hard on someone, it's because you're afraid to get beat. There was an 'I've got your back' attitude on that team. If you miss the tackle, I'll be right behind you. No one let anybody down. Our mind-set was do not let them look up." In addition, the USMNT needed to beat Argentina, or at the very least tie them, in order to advance to the knockout round.

Sampson had also decided to be more attack-minded than his predecessor, Milutinović. Alexi Lalas explained, "To a certain extent, Steve took the shackles off. He followed that path that a lot of coaches take, in that he came in after a coach and was able to see what worked and what didn't. We were a very risk-averse team in the '94 World Cup, which I think was the right decision at the time, but I think Steve realized

---

62. Paysandú is located on the banks of the Uruguay River, which forms the border with Argentina.

if we were going to improve he had to give us more opportunities to go forward."

There was a sense on the team that players would do whatever they could to play and help the team win. For example, Milutinović had decided not to start Frank Klopas in any of the 1994 World Cup games.[63] When Milutinović was questioned about the decision, he said, "He can score, but what else?" When Klopas heard what his coach said to the media, he responded, "He said that? I don't know why he would feel that way. I can play wherever he needs me to play. This is the only time I've actually played striker. My five years in Greece, I played midfield and attacker. I'll play any position the team needs me to play." Sampson gave Klopas an opportunity.

During the game, Argentina struggled with the speed of wing-backs Cobi Jones and Earnie Stewart, who, while having the ability to get behind defenders, also put in tremendous efforts defensively. When hard-nosed midfielder Diego Simeone came on at halftime with Argentina losing 0–2, he tried to intimidate the USMNT players by telling them he was going to go through them.[64] The Americans responded. When Simeone touched the ball, Thomas Dooley hit him hard. When Simeone got up, Eric Wynalda ran past him and bumped him with a shoulder, and a few seconds later another player bumped him. When Simeone retaliated with a hard hit of his own, Wynalda tried to pretend like it didn't hurt. A few minutes later, Wynalda scored. Frank Klopas, Alexi Lalas, and Eric Wynalda each scored goals in the game.

The USMNT players were now much more experienced than in 1994, and they were sending a message that they wouldn't back down. They outworked, outplayed, and outsmarted the Argentinians. The USMNT had the Spirit of '76. Alexi Lalas reflected, "We were strangers in a strange land and had nothing to lose. There was next to no interest back home and we were underdogs. It was another example of a U.S. team being very comfortable in the underdog role and using it to our advantage.

---

63. Klopas had emigrated to the U.S. from Greece when he was eight years old and settled in Chicago.

64. Diego Simeone at the time played for Atlético Madrid—the club he now coaches.

Teams underestimated us and by the time they came to their senses the damage was done." Lalas brings up the underdog status, which was a very important element of the team identity and their *why*. He also raised another noteworthy point. Much of the interest in the USMNT back home from the 1994 World Cup had faded, because *when* matters too.

After the 3–0 win, Diego Maradona greeted some of the USMNT players near their locker room. He had tears in his eyes. He reportedly told the players who could understand Spanish, "I'm not crying because Argentina lost, I'm crying because it was so beautiful to see the Americans play so well." Later, Eric Wynalda revealed, "We went out that night and we drank quite a bit."

The USMNT then beat Mexico on penalties in the quarterfinals. Klopas scored the game-winning penalty kick. Sampson reflected, "Beating Argentina so convincingly marked the USA's arrival as a team worthy of respect on the world stage. Beating Mexico in the quarterfinals for the second time in a month raised the ire of a country not accustomed to competition in the CONCACAF region. What Milutinović began in his tenure was echoed in 1995 and beyond—that the United States was no longer the stepchild to Mexico in our region." Sampson's comments highlight the *why*—the legitimacy of soccer in the U.S.

In the semifinals, the USMNT lost 1–0 to Brazil, who played without their 1994 World Cup duo, Romário and Bebeto. Although the score in the loss was the same as the 1994 World Cup, the USMNT played much better. Alexi Lalas said, "We played 50 times better. For example, we actually touched the ball this time." In a sign of good sportsmanship, after the match Tab Ramos and Leonardo exchanged jerseys—indicating they had moved past Leonardo's elbow to Ramos' head in the 1994 World Cup. With a different mind-set and something to prove after the 1994 World Cup, the Colombians got their revenge when they beat the USMNT 4–1 in the third-place game. Asprilla and Valderrama each scored a goal. Uncharacteristically, the Americans seemed content. Sampson didn't play Harkes, Dooley, Balboa, or Wynalda because he wanted to give some of the younger players a chance. Sampson later admitted, "To be honest, we were all ready to go home after the semifinal." Lalas added, "Looking back, I think the third-place game against Colombia was a wasted opportunity.... Although we had matured as a team, we were still naive with regard to certain aspects of the game."

Unmistakably for the USMNT, in Uruguay there was a subtle change in mentality and understanding of the game. Before the Copa América, the USMNT had more of an emphasis on playing not to lose. During the tournament, the USMNT gained confidence in when and how to play to win without risking losing. It was a critical moment in the development of the USMNT and the Spirit of '76.

The players came away from the tournament believing that even though the USMNT didn't have any Ballon d'Or candidates, they had good players who had an extraordinary desire to prove it game in and game out—and they had the confidence that motivation and teamwork could close any gap in skill. They wanted to show that their advance to the Round of 16 at the 1994 World Cup wasn't a fluke. They backed it up with the Copa América in 1995. They wanted legitimacy, and the future looked bright for the USMNT.

Steve Sampson had never coached or played soccer for a professional club. There were reservations about him being appointed head coach. The USSF considered Timo Liekoski, a native of Finland who was an assistant to Milutinović at the World Cup and was coaching the U.S. Men's Olympic team as they prepared for the 1996 Olympics. The USSF had reportedly approached former Portugal coach Carlos Queiroz about being the coach, but he decided to coach Sporting Lisbon. In addition, the USSF reportedly spoke to Rinus Michels, who played for Ajax his entire career and had coached the Netherlands (and Johan Cruyff), to be a consultant and mentor to Sampson. In August 1995, after the Copa América success, Sampson became the USMNT's first native-born, full-time coach.

Sam's Army

There was another important change in soccer culture in the U.S. following the 1994 World Cup—the rise of a supporters' group. In 1995 Mark Spacone and John Wright co-founded "Sam's Army," utilizing a World

Cup website by Mark Wheeler. Sam's Army was an unofficial supporters' group for the USMNT. Although the use of the word *army* fits with the label Spirit of '76, it was inspired by the "Tartan Army," a name given to fans of the Scotland national team. The word *Sam* derives from Uncle Sam, a personification of the United States.

Previously, there wasn't an organized USMNT supporters' club, which are relatively common at European soccer clubs. The formation of Sam's Army indicates the beginnings of trying to be more European to add legitimacy. In addition, there isn't a comparable supporters' club for any other major sport's U.S. national team, which implies that there is something unique about soccer.

Sam's Army's first organized debut was at a USMNT versus Nigeria U.S. Cup match on June 11, 1995, at Foxboro Stadium. They wore all red, had leaders who led songs and chants that were accompanied by drummers, and stood the duration of the game. Their enthusiasm created a fun environment and a home-field advantage for the USMNT.[65] Alexi Lalas threw his jersey to the group in celebration of the USMNT's U.S. Cup victory to show his thanks for their support. Lalas knew how to connect to fans and show appreciation—*who* matters.

Qualifying for the 1998 World Cup and 1998 Gold Cup

The USMNT had finished its 16-game qualification campaign for the 1998 World Cup with eight wins, two losses, and six ties. The only USMNT defeats came on the road to Costa Rica at Estadio Ricardo Saprissa, where the hostile crowd threw coins, batteries, and other objects at the USMNT players. Mexico finished first in qualification, with the USMNT and Jamaica finishing second and third, respectively.

The 1998 CONCACAF Gold Cup was the fourth edition of the tournament. Brazil was invited again and brought their senior team. Jamaica shocked Brazil with a draw in the first round. In the semifinals on February 10, the USMNT played Brazil on a rain-impacted field at the Memorial Coliseum in Los Angeles. At halftime, the score was 0–0. Early

---

65. They also produced a bi-monthly fan magazine titled *Bookable Offense* that was mailed to group members.

in the second half, Coach Steve Sampson told 34-year-old, Belgrade-born Predrag (Preki) Radosavljevic to begin warming up. At that point the USMNT seemed more concerned with holding on defensively than getting forward. But Sampson had other ideas. On the hour mark, Preki replaced Roy Wegerle. If it had been a league or group game, Sampson might have opted for inserting an extra defender. Against Brazil in a knockout situation, he chose to go for an attacking midfielder who could deliver something special. USMNT goalkeeper Kasey Keller claimed, "Preki always had the ability to create something out of nothing." In the 65th minute, Preki struck a magical left-footed shot from over 30 yards into the top left corner. The moving, dipping, and swerving ball caught the Brazilian goalkeeper by surprise. The USMNT would hold on to upset Brazil 1–0.

The other hero of the evening was goalkeeper Kasey Keller, who had 10 saves, none of them routine. Shot after shot was saved by the American goalkeeper. His teammates were tirelessly hustling and supporting one another, getting enough pressure on shooters to make those saves possible. Brazil had underestimated the skill, determination, and grit of the American team. After a point-blank save from a Romário header, the Brazilian even reached out to shake Keller's hand. Following the match, Romário said, "That is the best performance by a goalkeeper I have ever seen."[66]

Keller described the USMNT's style of play: "As a team, you have to fight for everything and hope for the odd counter-attack or set piece to get yourselves into the game, and if your goalkeeper can make five to six saves and you take those chances, maybe you get a result. Most games, if a goalkeeper has to make 10 saves, he's probably going to lose 3–nil." Sadly, only 13,000 spectators were in the stadium to witness such an outstanding performance. The USMNT would go on to lose 0–1 to Mexico in the Final in front of a pro-Mexican crowd at Los Angeles Memorial Coliseum. Many Mexican fans booed during the playing of "The Star-Spangled Banner," pelted the USMNT players with debris, and threw fruit and

---

66. Kasey was the starting goalkeeper for Leicester City, and had flown all night after posting back-to-back Premier League shutouts of Manchester United and Leeds to arrive the day before the match.

cups of beer at fans trying to raise an American flag. The actions added to the rivalry.

Unfortunately, left back Jeff Agoos was injured in the match against Mexico. The USMNT were scheduled to play the Netherlands in a friendly across the country in Miami six days later. Steve Sampson told team captain John Harkes after a pregame practice that Harkes would start in Agoos' place at the left back position, rather than Harkes' usual central midfield spot. Harkes questioned the change. Sampson didn't appreciate his questioning, and it appeared to damage their relationship. Sampson was also trying to get the creative midfielder Claudio Reyna into the lineup. The USMNT would lose against the Netherlands.

On February 25, four days after that match, the USMNT were set to play Belgium in Brussels. Two days before the match, John Harkes, Eric Wynalda, and Joe-Max Moore returned to the team's hotel in Brussels early in the morning after a late night with other team members to celebrate Moore turning 27 on February 23. After hearing about the event, Sampson felt Harkes, the captain, could have set a better example. Still, Sampson started Harkes and Wynalda in the Belgium game, which the USMNT lost. Around the same time period, Harkes had missed a flight with Wynalda and another flight with Roy Wegerle. Harkes and Wegerle also missed a team bus trip. None of the missed transportation caused Harkes or his teammates to be late for a game or training session. However, the six-month buildup of issues caused Sampson's trust in his captain to deteriorate. Lastly, Sampson heard from another player that Harkes had "an inappropriate relationship" with Wynalda's wife.[67]

Around the time of and after the win against Brazil, many of the veteran players felt that Sampson increasingly started to micromanage. They believed he had gained enough confidence in his ability to change players and tactics that he made significant changes in an April 22, 1998, friendly match against Austria. He adopted a more offensive-minded formation and kept Balboa, Lalas, and Wynalda out of the starting lineup.

---

67. While Sampson tried to keep this last bit of private information confidential from the media, it was rumored. Twelve years later, Wynalda made the revelation to Grant Wahl of *Sports Illustrated*. Reportedly, Harkes has always denied or declined to comment on the accusations.

The USMNT won 3–0—two of the goals were scored in the 89th and 90th minutes. It was the USMNT's first victory in Europe in seven years. Sampson felt with the win, he had proved his new player selections, tactics, and formations worked. Unfortunately, the players didn't have the same conviction. In his book *Soccer in a Football World*, David Wangerin explains: "By now, the coach who had trusted his players and nourished their team spirit considered his apprenticeship over. Sampson had spent much of the previous year fighting for his job, and in the process settled into the more autocratic demeanor of the typical American coach, tinkering with line-ups and formations, placing a premium on video analysis and tactics, and identifying players who could 'do a job.'"

What many people didn't realize was that Sampson was making changes because of reservations he started to have about various players' sharpness. Several USMNT players returned from Europe to play in MLS, which started matches in 1996. Generally, the level of competitiveness and skill in MLS at the time was lower than most European Leagues. He believed the players lost a little edge by coming back to the United States, but at the same time believed that their return was important to the growth of the sport. In addition, he had concerns about several players who had injuries and were not at 100 percent and/or that age was having an effect. Lastly, with MLS starting for the first time, two distinct cliques developed between players playing professionally in Europe versus those in the U.S. Some players felt there was a lack of respect toward the players who played in MLS. Sampson seemingly favoring players by selecting players playing in Europe didn't help. These MLS players believed the lack of respect was not overt, but covert and could be felt.[68] Dynamics and perceptions are such important aspects of team chemistry.

Two months before the 1998 World Cup, Sampson removed Harkes, the captain, from the final list of 22 USMNT players.[69] The dismissal of Harkes from the squad, one of the most celebrated USMNT players at the time and a player Sampson had lauded two years previously as "captain for life," shocked the team and media. Sampson felt he had to leave Harkes

---

68. This becomes a continuing theme on the USMNT—especially later under Jürgen Klinsmann.
69. The squads were increased to 23 players in the 2014 World Cup.

off the team, but didn't fully disclose the main reasons to maintain privacy. Perhaps his decision could have been better explained and handled. With incomplete information, the move didn't make sense to the media, and Sampson was pummeled in the press.[70]

The oldest player on the USMNT, 37-year-old defender/defensive midfielder Thomas Dooley, was given the captain's armband. Dooley was born to a German mother and U.S. Army father and was playing in the Bundesliga. He was recruited to play for the USMNT for the 1994 World Cup. He had grown up dreaming of playing for the German national team. In contrast, the 31-year-old John Harkes grew up in Kearny, New Jersey, played soccer at the University of Virginia, and played professionally both in the U.S. and Europe. Like Tony Meola, the captain of the USMNT in the 1994 World Cup, Harkes had good connections and relationships with players who played in the U.S. and in Europe. Harkes also had a good enough relationship with Sampson that Harkes felt comfortable making suggestions as captain to his coach.

Then, surprisingly, three starters in the USMNT's win over Brazil—Balboa, Lalas, and Wynalda—were not starting final warm-up games.[71] In addition, Sampson recruited David Regis, who played defender in the Bundesliga, to start for the USMNT ahead of the popular Jeff Agoos, who was invaluable in qualification. Regis was a native of Martinique who spoke very little English but had an American wife and therefore was eligible for U.S. citizenship. Remarkably, Sampson assigned Jeff Agoos to be Regis' roommate and asked Agoos to help the person being recruited to replace him to pass his U.S. citizenship exam. While everyone was shocked, Agoos did what he was asked and tried to set an example of being an unselfish teammate. Regis received his U.S. passport on May 20, 1998, and made his USMNT debut on May 23, 1998, just weeks before the start

---

70. Not until 2010 did Wynalda talk about the situation, finally allowing Sampson to better explain. Sampson also later admitted he wishes he had never known about it. If he had been more transparent at the time, then that may have helped the team move, but he risked significant impact to two families. This additional context about the event makes Sampson's decision a little easier to understand.

71. Wynalda had recently had arthroscopic knee surgery.

of the World Cup.[72] Sampson reflected later, "I made a mistake allowing Regis to join so late in the game. It affected our chemistry. I probably should've left him off the squad and let Jeff Agoos play left back. But he was a good player, playing in the Bundesliga. It was very attractive. But hindsight is 20/20 vision. The stability and chemistry should've been more important than one player.... You can't underestimate the importance of chemistry." The players recognized Regis' talent, but they felt that, since he didn't help the team qualify for the World Cup and didn't make the same commitment and sacrifices, he should not have played—let alone started. Most players felt leaving the veteran players on the bench after everything they did for the USMNT was too much, especially with the formation changes and leaving Harkes off the team. In the end, soccer is as much about relationships and trust as skills and tactics. The relationships and trust had been broken.

Jeff Agoos, Alexi Lalas, and John Harkes (who wasn't on the team), all starters in the USMNT win over Brazil just four months earlier, wouldn't play a minute in the 1998 World Cup. Balboa would be used once as a sub in the 81st minute, after the USMNT was eliminated. Defenders Alexi Lalas, 27, and Marcelo Balboa, 30, played every minute of the United States' four matches in the 1994 World Cup and while playing side-by-side were considered anchors in defense.

The 1998 World Cup, France

The USMNT were not widely viewed as a soccer threat entering the 1998 World Cup, but clear strides had been made. In a 1998 article for the *New York Times*, Jere Longman wrote, "The United States is undeniably a better soccer team now than it was four years ago..." They were more accomplished. The USMNT beat Argentina 3–0 in the 1995 Copa América and Brazil 1–0 in the 1998 Gold Cup—both matches needed context. They were also more experienced. All 22 squad members were playing professional soccer in the tournament buildup. In 1994, that

---

72. At the time, a player needed a physical passport from the country he would represent. In addition, the materials for the passport had actually been lost during the process, causing further delays.

number was six. While soccer in the U.S. had made a lot of progress, it still was not a major sport. A pre-1998 World Cup Harris poll indicated that only 52 percent of Americans knew the World Cup was a soccer tournament and only 19 percent knew it was happening in France.

Before the World Cup draw, the aim of the Americans was to at least match their achievement in the 1994 World Cup by advancing to the knockout Round of 16. But the 1998 tournament rules were different; only two teams would advance from each group, whereas three had a chance in 1994. The USMNT were in Group F, with Germany, Yugoslavia, and Iran, who were ranked third, 36th, and 49th, respectively, at the time of the draw.[73] The USMNT were ranked 35th. Yugoslavia and Germany were the heavy favorites to go through to the knockout round. The Germans were fresh off winning the Euro 1996. Yugoslavia were full of European club stars and were considered a dark horse to win the tournament. Their star player, Predrag Mijatovic, had just scored the Champions League–winning goal for Real Madrid.

Besides dealing with internal personnel issues, Steve Sampson made several other big decisions just before the 1998 World Cup. Just a few months before the start, in Austria, he debuted a 3-6-1 formation, which features three defenders, six midfielders, and one forward, in contrast to the 4-4-2 formation typically used by the USMNT, which employs four defenders. The idea behind the 3-6-1 is to overload and clog up opponents in midfield and to pounce with counter-attacks. Theoretically, defenses were supposed to be confused about which and how many players would come forward in attack. He felt the strategy was necessary because of the USMNT's skill disparity compared to Germany and Yugoslavia.

This 3-6-1 is rarely used in international soccer. It relies heavily on energy, endurance, and speed. The system also requires players to be well-drilled in their roles and understand each other's positions. When the 3-6-1 works, the formation can be fast and lethal. But when it doesn't— the one forward isn't linking up well and efficiently scoring or the three

---

73. FIFA World Rankings as of October 1997. Seeding was different for the 1998 World Cup and the draw took place in December 1997, but we used those rankings to be consistent with how things worked in 2010 and 2014.

defenders are overwhelmed—a team can be exposed. Most importantly, a complex strategy change requires buy-in from players, but some of the players thought that the last-minute change in tactics after years of progress with the American style showed a lack of faith in the team.[74] In addition, Sampson kept several of the team's veterans on the bench while playing players with little or no national team experience, albeit with European credentials.

Sampson also chose to base the team at a secluded chateau in France. He didn't consult with the senior players before selecting the isolated Chateau de Pizay in the countryside north of Lyon. The Chateau offered a beautiful setting and magnificent food. However, some of the players were going stir-crazy because they found it too isolated, as if they were not even in the World Cup. They spent their days watching one TV with only French-language channels or playing cards. Some of the players lost significant money to others playing cards to pass the time, which impacted personal dynamics. This was in contrast to 1994, where Milutinović wanted the players to be close to the action and revel in the excitement.

1998 FIFA World Cup: Group Stage, Game 1
June 15, 1998, at Parc des Princes, Paris
USA 0–2 Germany
On June 15, 1998, the USMNT faced Germany at the Parc des Princes in Paris. Seven USMNT players were making their World Cup debuts, though 12 of the 22 players on the roster had played on previous World Cup squads.[75] Before the game, Germany players were literally laughing at the USMNT's new on-field formation. They told Eric Wynalda, "Got no chance. It's one against three," because Wynalda would be the one forward

---

74. Some players mentioned that assistant coach Clive Charles played a key role in keeping the team together. Charles was born in England to Grenadian immigrants, grew up playing street soccer, and began his career with West Ham United, where his brother John played. Later in his life he would coach at Reynolds High School in Portland, Oregon, and the University of Portland. He helped develop many outstanding future USMNT and USWNT players.

75. Kasey Keller had been on the 1990 team, and Joe-Max Moore on the 1994 team, but neither had played. Two of the three substitutions that were made in the game would also be World Cup debuts.

covered by three German defenders. Wynalda thought to himself, *I know. You're right.* It was a bad mind-set.

Germany dominated possession in the first half. Sampson believed that midfielder Claudio Reyna would be the key to the team's attack, but Germany smothered him and took him out of the game. In the ninth minute, some sloppy defense for the USMNT on a corner kick led to Germany's first goal. Jürgen Klinsmann, who would later become the USMNT coach, outleapt two defenders at the far post and headed the ball toward his teammate Andreas Moller in front of the center of the goal, who snuck past USMNT defender Mike Burns and then headed the ball in. Alexi Lalas and Marcelo Balboa (who were both out of the lineup) are 6'3" and 6'1", respectively. Klinsmann is 5'11".

At halftime, Sampson changed the tactical formation back to a 4-4-2 and began to attack. Frankie Hejduk, who replaced Mike Burns at right wing in midfield, had a diving header in the 52nd minute that came close, but otherwise the USMNT had nothing to show for their attack. In the 65th minute, Klinsmann beat USMNT defender Thomas Dooley, who missed trying to head the ball away. In the penalty area, Klinsmann controlled the ball with his chest, let the ball bounce once, shot, and scored to make it 2–0 for Germany. His great technical skill made it look easy. Since both German goals involved crosses and missed headers, the USMNT also seemed to really miss Lalas and Balboa's height and Jeff Agoos' experience. Germany would later lose to Croatia in the quarterfinals.

1998 FIFA World Cup: Group Stage, Game 2
June 21, 1998, at Stade de Gerland, Lyon
USA 1–2 Iran

The USMNT played Iran on June 21 at Stade de Gerland in Lyon. The Iran hostage crisis (1979 to 1981) was a more recent memory in 1998. It was supposed to be the most politically charged match in World Cup history.[76] But it wasn't. FIFA asked the teams to depoliticize the game as much as possible. The Iranian players shook hands with the Americans

---

76. An Iraq-based terrorist organization funded by Saddam Hussein had bought 7,000 tickets for the game and were planning to stage a protest during the match.

before the game, handed them white flowers symbolizing peace, and even posed with the USMNT for a picture.

On the field, the USMNT were heavy favorites. After the loss to Germany, they needed a win. As previously mentioned, a loss in the first game in a World Cup brings negative media and an urgency to win, which causes teams to press to score—leaving them vulnerable to counter-attacks. Sampson replaced five USMNT starters from the Germany match and scrapped the 3-6-1 formation for a 3-5-2 formation. Burns, Stewart, and Wynalda started on the bench. Sampson wanted assertive play in attack. In the third minute, McBride hit the crossbar. In the 15th minute, McBride hit the post. Reyna hit the post in the 33rd minute. In fact, the Americans came forward so aggressively and took so many risks that they were often left completely exposed on defense. And Iran took advantage. In the 41st minute, 5'9" midfielder Hamid Estili, who was left alone in the box, headed a ball (yes, another header with Lalas and Balboa on the bench) past American goalkeeper Kasey Keller to give Iran a 1–0 lead going into halftime.

The USMNT locker room at halftime was lacking positive energy. McBride reflected, "I don't remember anybody getting fired up and screaming at each other or yelling something positive."

In the second half, the USMNT continued to dominate play, but they just couldn't finish. In the 57th minute, Reyna missed on a bicycle kick in front of the net. In the 63rd minute, Preki missed wide on an open header. David Regis hit the goal post in the 68th minute. In the 79th minute, Hejduk sent a header right at Iran's goalkeeper.

Meanwhile, Sampson's all-out attack strategy had left the American side of the field vulnerable. In the 84th minute, an Iran forward started a counter-attack run and received the ball 10 yards into the American half with only Keller to beat. Iran doubled their lead. In the 88th minute, Brian McBride would score on a diving header—the only goal the USMNT would score the entire tournament. With the 2–1 loss, the USMNT would fail to advance to the next round of the tournament. Sampson later recalled, "We wanted three points so badly, we played naively. We opened up our lines too early. We wanted to score so badly, and opened ourselves up to the counter-attack, which is how they scored both goals. I learned later [from one of Iran's assistant coaches] that they used politics to motivate the team. At halftime, someone from their government came to the locker room. They took the players' passports and told them they wouldn't be allowed to return to Iran if they lost."

The USMNT were arguably the better team. The USMNT hit the goal post three times and the crossbar once and outshot Iran 27–15. However, the USMNT had serious defensive lapses. The loss was devastating. Losing to a soccer power was understandable. But Iran had never won a World Cup match, and 19 of their 22 players played in Iran.

Conflict within the USMNT began to leak to the press. Some players were vocal about their frustrations. On June 23, Amy Shipley of the *Washington Post* reported that Sampson had threatened to send home four players—Lalas, Wynalda, Balboa, and Stewart—before the Iran match for attitude problems. None of those players started in the loss to Iran. Stewart came into the game as a late substitute.

Amy Shipley also reported dissatisfaction with the strategy and decision-making employed by Steve Sampson had surfaced in the USMNT soccer camp. Alexi Lalas explained, "It's rather naive to think that a team that has gone through so much together can basically be rearranged and be expected to play with any consistency and cohesiveness. It just doesn't happen, especially in soccer.... The reality is, consistency comes from playing under a system for an extended period of time and understanding the role you play in that system. The basic core of guys have been involved for many years; their spirit and personality have been on the field for many years. If you look at it from a soccer standpoint, that's been a team that's won and gotten quality and historic results. I don't know where that team was.... I gave up trying to figure [Sampson] out a long time ago."

Another player, who requested anonymity at the time, added, "The reasons why we didn't play well were not because of this team. It has nothing to do with the ability of the players here. This team lost its chemistry months ago." Changing the *how* and *who* affected the players and destroyed the team chemistry. In many ways, this is the most interesting lesson about the 1998 World Cup for the USMNT.

1998 FIFA World Cup: Group Stage, Game 3
June 15, 1998, at Stade de la Beaujoire, Nantes
USA 0–1 Yugoslavia

Against Yugoslavia, Steve Sampson once again changed the lineup, and once again the USMNT lost. Sampson inserted substitutes Preki Radosavljevic and Marcelo Balboa—who hadn't played in the tournament—in the 58th and 81st minutes, respectively. Preki, who scored the winning goal against Brazil in the semifinals of the 1998 CONCACAF Gold Cup, was incensed at not being named to the starting lineup against his former country. The only players who didn't see any playing time were Alexi Lalas, Jeff Agoos, and backup goalkeeper Juergen Sommer. After reflection, Sampson regrets he did not utilize Agoos in the Yugoslavia match because Agoos deserved better for his dedication and sacrifices.[77]

Yugoslavia would later lose 2–1 in the Round of 16 to the Netherlands. By the time they exited in the group stage, the USMNT had all three of their matches and scored only one goal. Of the 32 teams in the tournament, the USMNT finished last.[78]

The Americans couldn't match their accomplishment in 1994 of having advanced to the Round of 16. The USMNT's 1998 World Cup performance was regarded as both a missed opportunity, after having beaten Brazil a few months prior to the start of the tournament, and complete failure. Afterward, Tab Ramos said, "From the beginning, this whole World Cup has been a mess...I blame the coaches for the losses. They didn't get the most out of what we had." Steve Sampson resigned four days after the loss to Yugoslavia. Sampson later reflected, "I think there was a raised expectation on the part of the media and the fans given our results in the Copa América, given our good run during the qualification

---

77. Agoos was among the last cuts, if not the last cut, for the 1994 World Cup USMNT. Many players were highly disappointed that Sampson did not play Agoos even one minute in the 1998 World Cup after being a key contributor to the USMNT qualifying, being so dedicated to the team, and being a team player. Agoos would have to wait until the 2002 World Cup to play, when he was 34 years old.

78. David Regis wasn't the reason the USMNT finished 32nd out of the 32 teams at the 1998 World Cup. In fact, he accounted well for himself despite the USMNT losing all three of their games. But his late inclusion on the roster was certainly a factor in a previously high-flying team crashing out in the USMNT's worst-ever showing at a World Cup.

phase. And then maybe the kiss of death from a perspective standpoint
was when we beat Brazil in the Gold Cup in '98. And so I think there was
a sense of unrealistic expectations…"

The unrealistic expectations were in part because of a faulty
comparison. When the USMNT beat Brazil in February, Brazil did not
have their captain Dunga or Ronaldo, Rivaldo, or Roberto Carlos in the
lineup. When Brazil lost to France in the 1998 World Cup Final, all four
of those players were starters. In fact, only two players, the goalkeeper
and defender Júnior Baiano, played in both the Gold Cup match against
the USMNT and the 1998 World Cup Final. Ronaldo (finished third in
voting), Rivaldo (fifth), and Roberto Carlos (13th) were candidates for the
1998 Ballon d'Or.

Germany and Yugoslavia had 23 and 16 players in the Top Five
Leagues—compared to five on the USMNT.

Table: 1998 World Cup—USA and Opponents (Group Stage)

1998 World Cup—USA & Opponents (Group Stage)					
Team	World Rank (Pre-WC)	Average Age (Team)	Average Age (Starters)	# Players Top 5 League	# Minutes Top 5 League
USA	35	28.3	26.7	5	11,025
Germany	3	29.8	30.4	23	71,933
Iran	49	26.8	27.5	3	4,058
Yugoslavia	36	27.5	27.4	16	38,336
Group Total (ex. US)	88			42	114,327

With only two teams advancing from the group stage, even if the
USMNT was firing on all cylinders, it was going to be a tough battle
to advance. The team chemistry issues and formation changes added to
the challenges. The difficult and unlucky draw with facing Germany first
didn't help. If the USMNT had faced Iran first, perhaps things would
have gone differently, as they would not have felt they had to press.

The USMNT fans and media may have started to have unrealistic
expectations of progress in an upward-trending straight line with a faulty
comparison, but the real challenge was the culture of the team.

Alexi Lalas added, "This was a team that was heading in the right
direction and improving on what they had seen in '94. In '98, that six
months before [the tournament], ultimately when Sampson did start
changing—formation, personnel, approach, and even his personality—

for me at least, he betrayed what I felt was the best part of Steve and what I felt was going to come to fruition and take us through '98."

We believe Lalas was right in that it is rather naive to think that a team that has gone through so much together can basically be rearranged, given a new formation, and expected to play with any consistency and cohesiveness. Familiarity comes from playing under a system for an extended period of time and players understanding the roles they play in that system. The USMNT had a basic core of guys with spirit and personality who had been involved for many years. The team had won and gotten good results. In hindsight, so many changes so close to the start of a tournament disrupted the familiarity, culture, and identity. It also caused the team to lose its chemistry. The players were no longer training together in Mission Viejo like before the 1994 World Cup. Players were spread out playing for various professional teams. Steve Sampson didn't have as much time with players. The USMNT needed to stick with a formation, style, and identity that they had developed and were familiar with.

Maybe the USMNT got unlucky with Iran and could have scored goals instead of hitting goal posts. Maybe the USMNT could have gotten a result, a draw, against Yugoslavia. Maybe, if Lalas and Balboa had played against Germany, the corner kick and cross would have been better defended. What was certain is the team had lost its unity. The margins between maybes and actual results are so small in international soccer that familiarity, culture, identity, and team chemistry matter even more.

Wynalda reflected, "This was a guy who was fighting for his job and wanted to say and do the right things. If you take the Sampson of the 1995 Copa América and have him coaching the 1998 team, I think it's a very different outcome. I don't think we lose to Iran. We probably lose to Germany, but then we have it all to play for against a very good Yugoslavia side and we might have gotten the tie to get through. At least we would have had a chance. I would say the same thing going into the '95 competition, where we've got a chance. That's all you really want to be able to say."

Remember "Victory," the 1990 USMNT's World Cup theme song and music video? The chorus of the song is: "Togetherness and unity means victory in Italy / With dedication, heart, and soul, you have the tools to achieve your goal." It's what the USMNT had relied on in the past but what was missing at the 1998 World Cup. The sad thing was that the USMNT's performance in the 1998 World Cup overshadowed their progress since the 1994 World Cup performance—*when* matters. They missed an opportunity to show the world they were legitimate, and that is what hurt the players the most. Eric Wynalda explained, "We had really lost a lot of respect from the world and internationally." They also missed an opportunity to show the quality of Major League Soccer. The USMNT's squad had 16 players from Major League Soccer, which didn't exist in 1994.

By 1998, the USSF, the players, and fans had very quickly forgotten about the enormous strides soccer in the U.S. had made in less than 10 years. The beginnings of a subtle (but devastating) shift in mind-set had started to occur. Short of progress in an upward-trending straight line, it was highly unlikely anyone would be happy or satisfied. This put an immense amount of pressure on the entire program and helps explain why changes happened.

Unfortunately, the enthusiasm from the 1994 World Cup did not carry over four years later. The 1998 World Cup was shown live on TV in the U.S. and treated as a major sporting event. However, ESPN ratings dipped about 50 percent overall from 1994. Encouraged by the TV audience in 1994, ABC rescheduled its popular daytime soap opera *General Hospital* to televise the USMNT match live against Germany. The game had lower ratings than a typical episode of *General Hospital*, and they were considerably worse than any USMNT match in 1994.

There was a positive. In 1998, the USSF signed a 10-year, $120 million sponsorship deal with Nike. In comparison, in 1990 Adidas sponsored the U.S. national teams for $100,000.

1999 Women's World Cup: USWNT Team Chemistry
The USWNT's team chemistry in the 1999 Women's World Cup was a stark contrast to the USMNT's 1998 World Cup. Astute observers noticed the importance of the team chemistry of the "'99ers"—the nickname of

the 1999 Women's World Cup USWNT—even as the media singled out star Mia Hamm. Author David Wangerin wrote, "The irony of the media's Mia-obsession was that American success had far more to do with team dynamics than individual brilliance. Some of the names might have seemed more appropriate for romance novels than shin-guards—Milbrett, Brandi Chastain, Lorrie Fair—but they were anything but a collection of lovelorn damsels, and their desire to play as hard for each other as they did for themselves had instilled an impressive chemistry and an egalitarian spirit."

By the start of the 1999 Women's World Cup, strong bonds had been formed. Kristine Lilly described why the team was special: "Not just because we won, but because of who our teammates were. That team was so special because we all knew our role." Julie Foudy, the team's energetic co-captain and self-designated videographer, was the embodiment of a selfless leader and echoed Lilly's sentiments. Foudy, now an analyst and reporter for ESPN and author of *Choose to Matter: Being Courageously and Fabulously You*, stated, "We were so lucky with our group. When Mia Hamm is your superstar and she is the most selfless, humble, and grounded person that never wants to take credit for anything, it's easy to have an awesome group of women come together." Often during matches, whoever scored a goal for the UWSNT would sprint to the sidelines to celebrate with the entire team. Both on and off the field, the USWNT showed the team chemistry and love they had for each other.

Tony DiCicco was the 1999 USWNT coach. Similar to Sampson, DiCicco changed formations. DiCicco broke away from the 3-4-3 that had been imprinted on the USWNT since the days of Anson Dorrance as coach and morphed into a 4-3-3. DiCicco kept the high pressure of the three-front, which was the USWNT's identity. He also implemented the change years in advance to give the team time to adapt.

Similar to Sampson's challenge of getting Harkes and Renya, who played the same position, on the field together, DiCicco had the issue of getting goal scorers Michelle Akers and Hamm on the field together. DiCicco moved star forward Akers from the front line into the midfield as an anchor on defense. Akers had joined the women's national team upon its founding in 1985, when she was 19 years old. She scored 10 goals in six games in the 1991 Women's World Cup, including two in the 2–1 victory over Norway in the Final, and was the team's leading scorer with 92 goals in 109 games. But a new generation of players was taking over. Forwards Hamm and Milbrett were world-class scorers. The team also had talented attacking midfielders in Foudy and Lilly. So DiCicco told Akers she would move positions and be the defensive anchor in the midfield. Instead of creating issues that could have impacted team chemistry, she embraced her new role and cleared the way for the 25-year-old Hamm to become the star scorer.

DiCicco coached with a calm demeanor and was popular with his players because he welcomed their suggestions. He listened when his players told him they had felt overtrained and fatigued during the 1995 World Cup in Sweden, when they finished a disappointing third. "Tony never felt like he knew everything," Hamm said in a telephone interview with Jeré Longman of the *New York Times* in 2017. "It was incredibly empowering. His security breathed so much confidence into all of us. What it told me was that I didn't have to be perfect 100 percent of the time. There were incredibly talented people around me, and they were going to help pick me up." Foudy said, "What made him such a special and successful coach was his ability to make the team into a cohesive unit that functioned not just as a team, but as a family."

In their quarterfinal game against Germany, the USWNT came from behind to win 3–2. They beat Brazil, who had eliminated them in the semifinals of the previous World Cup 2–0. The Final against China was in front of 90,125 fans at the Rose Bowl, the largest official crowd ever to watch women's soccer. In comparing the 1999 Women's World Cup Final to the Men's World Cup in 1994 at the Rose Bowl, David Wangerin wrote, "It, too, was decided on penalties, and suffered from a similar lack of open play and scoring opportunities."

For some reason, not only did American fans not seem to mind that there were no goals, they actually seemed completely absorbed by the tension of the game. In extra time, Lilly needed to head a ball off the line. With the match scoreless after extra time, both teams had to endure a nervy penalty shootout. Briana Scurry saved the third penalty kick to give the USWNT the lead. Chastain scored the decisive penalty kick to defeat China 5–4 in the Final.[79]

The broadcast of the match on ABC averaged close to 18 million viewers, a record at the time. In that pivotal moment of arrival for women's team sports in the U.S. and around the world, viewers saw Chastain, whose nickname was "Hollywood," remove and twirl her jersey and fall to her knees, pumping her arms in exultant triumph. What resulted was perhaps the most iconic photograph ever taken of a female athlete, a depiction of pure joy.

Caitlin Murray for Yahoo Sports explained, "When the USWNT first arrived to the mainstream American public in 1999 for the World Cup, it was unusual to see a group of strong female athletes sharing the spotlight. The media didn't quite know how to discuss them, calling the players "babes" and comparing their games to beauty pageants. Early in the tournament, a reporter asked Chastain point blank if the team would have attracted so many new fans if they weren't so attractive. But somewhere between Hamm's sensational opening goal against Denmark and Chastain's iconic penalty kick, people realized the USWNT was a collection of impressive athletes but, even better than that, together they brought out the best in one another." These very strong women worked as a team, challenging conventional wisdom that women can't be team players. History books are filled with outstanding individual female athletes who have taken over the sports world, from Billie Jean King to Serena Williams, Babe Didrikson Zaharias to Jackie Joyner-Kersee, Sonja Henie to Peggy Fleming, Shannon Miller to Simone Biles. But for the first time, the biggest star in the sports world was a group of women fighting together, led by captains Julie Foudy and Carla Overbeck. That in and of itself started to change perceptions and the way people think about women and girls think about themselves.

---

79. A little-known fact: Foudy was originally supposed to take Chastain's spot, fifth, in the penalty kick lineup until DiCicco made the switch. The USWNT had the easiest travel schedule in the tournament, while China had one of the most difficult. A forgotten fact: Chastain scored an own goal against Germany in the quarterfinals that almost helped eliminate the USWNT. The team picked her up and she delivered in the end.

Project 2010

The USMNT's disappointing results in the 1998 World Cup sparked a larger debate about player identification and development. The USSF had already commissioned Carlos Queiroz, the former coach of Portugal, and Dan Gaspar, Queiroz's longtime assistant, to research soccer in the U.S. and make recommendations to help the USSF. The cover of the 113-page report had the title WE CAN FLY: PROJECT 2010 with a photograph of Neil Armstrong with one hand planting the American flag on the moon—a photoshopped World Cup trophy was in the other hand and a photoshopped soccer ball was at his feet. The first page stated, "Winning the World Cup by 2010: Soccer's Equivalent to the Apollo XI Moon Landing.... Project 2010, as stated by U.S. Soccer, has set a goal of playing host to, and to be in a position to win the World Cup in the year 2010." According to interviews, the goal was more aspirational than literal. However, the document is evidence that expectations had changed, and the *why* or mission had started to shift to the *goal* of win the World Cup. The word *culture* is only mentioned 11 times in the report and never in the context of the USMNT. The word "style" is mentioned three times, including, "It's impossible to have a national style of play. The country is too big."

Carlos Queiroz coached Portugal U-20 to 1989 and 1991 FIFA World Youth Championship wins. After his junior-level success, he was hired to coach the senior team of Portugal (1991–93). After Portugal failed to qualify for the 1994 World Cup (placing third in their group behind Italy and Switzerland), he coached top Portuguese club Sporting CP (1994–96) and then the NY/NJ MetroStars (1996). He was selected to perform the project for a variety of reasons, including that he could bring an outsider/independent view, he had experience at all levels (youth national teams, senior national team, and professional clubs), and he was multilingual. It is informative that the USSF would hire a European coach for such a study—suggesting that the USSF, if not consciously, possibly subconsciously, may have felt a former European national team and European professional club coach could add legitimacy.

One of the results of Project 2010 was the U.S. Soccer's U-17 Residency Program at IMG Academy in Bradenton, Florida. With a lack of professional academies across the country, starting the Residency Program in 1999 gave young players the opportunity to experience an elite training environment, preparing them for a future in professional soccer. It was similar to the USMNT's Mission Viejo training camp. The residency camp closed in 2017, in part because of the growth of the U.S. Soccer Development and MLS Youth Academies.

Chapter 4

2002 World Cup: Luck and Other Factors in a World Cup

Backdrop to, and USMNT Players in, the 2002 World Cup

A unifying event (e.g., a tragedy, crisis, doubters) can crystallize a team's purpose and bring a team closer, which can help inspire extraordinary performance. In the 1998 World Cup, the USMNT finished dead last in the standings, having scored only one goal in three losses. The 2002 World Cup USMNT were determined to come back stronger and prove 1998 was a fluke and soccer in the U.S. was legitimate. Their mission, or *why*, took on additional emotional significance after the tragedy of 9/11 in the United States. The USMNT weren't just coming back stronger—a united nation was.[80]

In 1998, Bob Contiguglia, a Colorado kidney doctor, had become president of the USSF, and after a five-hour interview in Denver, he chose Bruce Arena to be the coach of the 2002 World Cup team. Arena was a successful coach at the University of Virginia, winning five national championships (four between 1991–94). At the club level, Arena took D.C. United to wins in two MLS Cups and one U.S. Open Cup. D.C.

---

80. A little-known fact: the USWNT were scheduled to play Japan in the Nike Women's Cup on 9/11.

United, under Arena, reached the CONCACAF Champions Cup semifinals in 1997, won the Champions Cup in August of 1998, and then won the Inter-American Cup in November. He coached the USMNT to qualification for the 2002 World Cup by finishing in third place in the final round behind Costa Rica and Mexico (ahead of Honduras, Jamaica, and T&T) with five wins, two draws, and three losses. Arena's final 23-man World Cup roster featured 11 players from MLS (Tony Meola was the only one who would not appear in the tournament), five from the English Premier League, and seven from other European leagues.

The USMNT were led by their captain, "Captain America," Claudio Reyna. The Springfield Township, New Jersey, native learned the game from his father Miguel, who moved to the U.S. in 1968 from Argentina, where he had played professionally. Reyna was eight years old when the NASL folded, which he recalls as "devastating." He had childhood memories of going to New York Cosmos games. At the time there were very few opportunities to watch soccer on TV in America. Reyna was 13 in 1986 when Argentina won their second World Cup and he remembers his dad and uncles crying and wrapped in Argentina flags.

Growing up, Reyna played youth soccer, along with Gregg Berhalter, for Union County SC, a team coached by his dad. Reyna played at Newark's Saint Benedict's Preparatory School, also with Berhalter.[81] During Reyna's three years with the team, Saint Benedict's went undefeated (65–0), while Reyna was named as the only two-time *Parade* magazine national high school Player of the Year and the Gatorade National Player of the Year, which is for the best student-athlete among the 12 primary interscholastic sports. Each of his three seasons at the University of Virginia, coached by Bruce Arena, the Cavaliers would win the NCAA championship. He also won the Hermann Trophy as the best college soccer player. As a then-20-year-old, creative midfielder, Reyna was on the USMNT 1994 World Cup squad, but did not play due to a pulled hamstring. After the 1994 World Cup, Reyna played in the Bundesliga, where he became the first American to captain a European club. In 2002, he was playing for Sunderland in

---

81. It's also the same school that Tab Ramos attended.

the English Premier League. Reyna gave the team something extra in the middle because he was an all-around player who could alter the tempo of a game. Both groups of players, those who played in America in MLS and those who played in Europe, knew and respected him.

MLS midfielder Cobi Jones, 31, was the most experienced player with 153 caps. Jones, at 5'7", grew up in Southern California and would often play soccer in the streets. His high school teammate at Westlake High School was Eric Wynalda. Jones, who had been cut from a few district teams, made the UCLA soccer team (1988–91) as a non-scholarship player and would help lead them to the 1990 NCAA Championship. Before he made the U-23 Olympic team, he was cut twice. At the 1992 Olympics in Barcelona, he would find himself as a 21-year-old who overcame so many obstacles representing his country along with USA Basketball's Dream Team. After the Olympics, he was part of U.S. Soccer's 18-month World Cup residency program in Mission Viejo before the 1994 World Cup. After playing in the 1994 World Cup, Jones signed with Coventry City of the English Premier League and played one season. After playing in the 1995 Copa América, he became a popular player in Latin America because an Argentine commentator gave him the nickname "Escobillón" ("swab"), due to his bleached dreadlocks and the similar pronunciation of his name and the word. He played a few games in Brazil after the 1995 Copa America before joining the LA Galaxy in 1996, which is where he was playing leading up to the 2002 World Cup. Oddly enough, his first coach with the LA Galaxy, Lothar Osiander, was the same coach cut him from the Olympic team.

Forward Landon Donovan and midfielder DaMarcus Beasley were the youngest players on the 2002 team. Donovan and Beasley were members of the inaugural class of U.S. Soccer's youth Residency Program at IMG in Bradenton, Florida. Donovan was named Player of the Tournament for his role in the U.S. U-17 squad that finished fourth in the 1999 FIFA U-17 World Championships before signing with German club Bayer Leverkusen later that year. Beasley also starred in the 1999 U-17 World Championships, winning the Silver Ball as the tournament's second-best player behind Donovan. Donovan and Beasley were both 20 years old when group play in the World Cup began; even so, the average age of the squad was 28.3.

The team had an incredible sense of familiarity. More than half the players on the 2002 World Cup team had been coached by two "godfathers" of American college soccer, Bruce Arena (University of Virginia, D.C. United) and Sigi Schmid (UCLA, 1999 FIFA World Youth Championship, LA Galaxy) or were graduates of the U-17 national team Residency Program at IMG Academy (Donovan and Beasley). In addition to the "Kearny Kids" and Cobi Jones and Eric Wynalda growing up together in Southern California, Clint Mathis and Josh Wolf had known each other since they were nine years old in the youth leagues of Georgia and both had attended the University of South Carolina. There were two other pairs of college teammates from the University of North Carolina and the University of Portland. These groups added familiarity, and formed a core foundation. In addition, the squad included six and 11 veterans of the 1994 and 1998 World Cup teams, respectively. David Regis was also on the 2002 USMNT roster but did not play any minutes in the 2002 World Cup.[82]

After the team chemistry issues in the 1998 World Cup, Bruce Arena felt that the most important characteristic in selecting a player was his commitment, passion, and desire to play for the USMNT above skill level. He also wanted a combination of veteran leadership, experienced players, young talented players, confident goalkeepers, and dynamic and explosive players. Landon Donovan said, "2002 was the perfect blend of experience and youth." The young players added some energy and brought an edge to the group. Frankie Hejduk, a Bob Marley fan and surfing enthusiast from Southern California who had played in college at UCLA, added positive energy.[83]

---

82. Reportedly, not one former teammate nor a single coach or U.S. Soccer official had been in contact with David Regis at least until 2014.

83. While he was only drafted in the seventh round (67th overall) of the 1996 MLS Inaugural Player Draft, his performance in the 1998 World Cup inspired Bayer Leverkusen to purchase his contract from MLS. In 2003, he returned back to MLS to play for the Columbus Crew. While he had an easygoing personality, on the field he had an incredible work ethic. He was the only USMNT player to have played the 1996 Olympics, 1998 World Cup, 2000 Olympics, and 2002 World Cup.

The 2002 World Cup: Expectations, Importance of First Match, and Luck of the Draw

Portugal, Poland, and South Korea were grouped with the USMNT and were ranked fifth, 43rd, and 28th respectively, while the USMNT were ranked 19th.[84] The bookmakers had given the USMNT 90–1 odds to win the tournament.

The gap in talent may not be as great as one might expect. When comparing players and minutes in the Top Five Leagues, the USMNT had just as many players as Portugal and Poland, but Poland and Portugal had almost double the number of minutes.

Table: 2002 World Cup—USA and Opponents (Group Stage)

2002 World Cup—USA & Opponents (Group Stage)					
Team	World Rank (Pre-WC)	Average Age (Team)	Average Age (Starters)	# Players Top 5 League	# Minutes Top 5 League
USA	19	28.3	27.4	8	12,652
Portugal	5	27.8	29.0	8	20,924
South Korea	43	26.7	27.7	1	577
Poland	28	28.4	27.8	8	19,580
Group Total (ex. US)	76			17	41,081

Most experts didn't think the USMNT could defeat their group stage opponent Portugal in the opener. Portugal had talent—at the time they had several world-class players and were dubbed as Portugal's *Geração de Ouro* (Golden Generation). Portugal's squad had three players on the ballot for the 2001 Ballon d'Or, including 29-year-old Luís Figo, who played for Real Madrid and finished sixth. Portugal's golden generation helped the team reach the semifinals of Euro 2000, losing 2–1 after extra time to eventual winners France, and secure second place at Euro 2004, losing to Greece on home soil. Most experts were not sure who would finish second in the group to Portugal. With South Korea and Poland in the group, the USMNT had a chance. South Korea had never won a game in the World Cup before 2002, and qualified automatically as co-hosts. It was Poland's first appearance at the World Cup since 1986. Poland's biggest win in the qualifying phase was a 4–0 victory over Armenia, while their biggest defeat was a 1–4 loss to Belarus.

---

84. FIFA World Rankings as of October 2001. The rankings at the time of seeding were different, but these figures were used to be consistent with the methodology in 2010 and 2014.

For the USMNT, Bruce Arena was upfront about his team's chances going into the tournament: "We're not going to win [the World Cup] because we're not a good enough team. I don't think anyone is going to be damaged by us saying that. I mean, how many countries have won it? If we can get a point in the first game, it will put the whole group in chaos."

Arena was setting realistic expectations about the USMNT's chances of winning the World Cup. In addition, he was right that the USMNT most likely needed at least a draw, resulting in a point, in the first game to have a chance to advance to the Round of 16. Since 1998 (when the draw was increased to 32 teams), less than 10 percent of the teams that lost their first match made it out of the group stage of the World Cup. The chances of a team getting past the group stage whose opening game ended in a draw increase to around 50 percent.

It wasn't just Arena who understood the importance of having realistic expectations. Figo said, "We'll go one step at a time. We'll try to pass through the first round, then see what happens. Argentina, France, Brazil, Italy, and even Germany have more of a chance of taking the title because of their previous experience in the Finals. They are teams that have already won the World Cup, so they know what it's like."

Unlike in 1998, when the USMNT stayed in a remote French village away from their families, in 2002 the team stayed at the JW Marriot in downtown Seoul, right in the center of the action. Arena placed few restrictions on the players, and they could spend any free time they wanted with their friends and family. The coach making the players accountable to each other to be responsible was a part of the team culture.

2002 FIFA World Cup: Group Stage, Game 1
June 5, 2002, at Suwon World Cup Stadium, South Korea
USA 3–2 Portugal
Before the game against Portugal, the coaches told the players that they felt the Portugal goalkeeper was shaky, and their central backs were a little slow. They talked about putting them under pressure. Arena said he wanted the team to play to win, and they had something to prove after the 1998 World Cup. The USMNT were without their injured captain,

Claudio Reyna, who had a strained thigh muscle, and without one of their most reliable scorers, Clint Mathis, who was not 100 percent. Six starters had never participated in a World Cup match. When Chris Armas went out with an injury just weeks prior to the 2002 World Cup, Pablo Mastroeni found himself a starter in the opening game.[85]

Due to the time difference, the USMNT played Portugal on ESPN2 at 4:55 AM ET. Those who got up early that morning were in for a treat. Four minutes into the game, a Brian McBride header from a corner kick by Earnie Stewart was redirected by Portugal's goalkeeper to John O'Brien, who immediately used his left foot to send the ball into the net.

A goal via a set piece.

In the 29th minute, a Landon Donovan cross into the box was deflected by defender Jorge Costa's back shoulder toward goal. The goalkeeper was unable to adjust and make the save at the near post. No one could believe the USMNT's luck, not even Donovan, who raised both arms in disbelief. USA 2–Portugal 0.

A goal via an own goal.

In the 36th minute, Tony Sanneh made a run down the wing and crossed the ball into the box to an unmarked, diving Brian McBride for a wonderful header to make it USA 3–0. McBride celebrated with multiple fist pumps with both arms.

A goal via crossing the ball in the box.

Three minutes later, Portugal would respond with a goal that resulted from a corner kick. A header on goal was blocked by a USMNT defender right to the feet of a Portugal player, who kicked the ball into the back of the net.

A goal via a set piece.

USA 3–Portugal 1 at halftime.

---

85. Mastroeni was the only man on the roster who didn't play in any of the 16 World Cup qualifying matches. He played in seven games for the USMNT in 2002—all resulting in shutouts. He wasn't even on Arena's original 30-man roster for the Gold Cup in January 2002, but injuries created an opening, and Mastroeni took advantage of his opportunity. He was a fan favorite for his fearless slide tackles and energy.

In the 71st minute, Portugal scored on a USMNT own goal. USA 3–Portugal 2.

A goal via an own goal.

Almost the entire second half was played in the USMNT's half of the field with the USMNT under intense pressure, but they held on valiantly. Portugal had two shots on target compared to seven for the USMNT.

Five goals were scored in the match: one own goal each and one set-piece goal each offset each other. The difference was the USMNT's goal from a ball crossed into the box.

When the final whistle blew, the players on the field and on the bench had disbelief on their faces. The win was the USMNT's first World Cup victory since the 2–1 defeat of Colombia in 1994. Dr. Robert Contiguglia, the president of the United States Soccer Federation, said, "We're there. We've shown we can play with anyone in the world."[86]

It is also worth noting that the match was played on June 5, 2002. On May 15, 2002, Portugal's Luís Figo helped Real Madrid win the Champions League in Glasgow, Scotland. He had been dealing with an ankle injury that had not healed, and had to be substituted off in the 61st minute of the Champions League Final. After celebrating the trophy in Madrid, he had little rest before flying to Asia. Portugal had last qualified for the World Cup 16 years prior, and Figo was determined not to miss his chance. Before the World Cup he had come close to being ruled out and said, "In normal conditions, I should be operated on and kept out for three months."

2002 FIFA World Cup: Group Stage, Game 2
June 10, 2002, at Daegu World Cup Stadium, South Korea
USA 1–1 South Korea

Like the USMNT, South Korea were responsible for an upset, winning their first match against Poland 2–0. When the USMNT players stepped onto the field, they were harangued by home supporters dressed in red.

---

86. When Contiguglia attended his first USSF annual meeting in 1980, he introduced a resolution stipulating the national team coach be American. He said, "If we're going to compete and show what we can do as a country, we needed to show that an American can do the job. I was shot down."

Tactically, with three points in hand and playing the host country, the strategy was to play smart and conservative and get at least one point with a draw to put the team in a position to qualify with at least a draw, and another point, against Poland—assuming Portugal would beat South Korea and Poland. Arena put Claudio Reyna, who didn't play against Portugal, into the midfield along with John O'Brian. Arena also decided to start Clint Mathis instead of Earnie Stewart. Mathis was an incredible talent but often alienated his coaches with his unique perspective on life, topped off by shaving his hair into a mohawk for the World Cup. In the previous year, the USMNT had zero wins, six losses, and two ties when playing in other teams' home countries.

South Korea outshot the USMNT 18–6, with seven corner kicks versus none for the USMNT. In the 24th minute, John O'Brien played a looping pass (a quasi-cross) that Clint Mathis brought down and controlled with his right foot and blasted into the net with his left. Arena's decision to start Mathis paid off.

A goal via crossing the ball in the box.

As Mathis scored, a South Korean player, Hwang Sun Hong, was off the field having his head wrapped after a collision, leaving his team short-handed. In the 39th minute, South Korea failed to convert a penalty kick. Friedel faked left, dove right, and got both hands on the ball. A South Korea player got the rebound but missed a shot wide. By chance, South Korea's most reliable taker of penalty kicks, Park Ji Sung, had hobbled off the field a minute earlier with an injured ankle.

In the 78th minute, an Ahn Jung-hwan header from an Eul-yong free kick gave South Korea the equalizer.

A goal via a set piece.

He celebrated by mimicking the movements of a short-track speed skater. The choreographed celebration seemed to imply that South Korea was finally getting revenge for the disputed gold medal won in the

Olympics four months earlier by American Apolo Anton Ohno against South Korea's Kim Dong-sung in Salt Lake City, Utah.[87]

In the 87th minute, South Korea had a chance when Choi Yong-soo sent a shot over the bar from 10 yards out. The USMNT held on for a draw.

Ray Hudson, working for ESPN's 2002 World Cup coverage, came up with a memorable quote after the game when he was expounding upon whether the USMNT goalkeeper should be thanking his defenders for their work. In his Northern English accent, Hudson said, "I'd be kissing their bums in the showers."

After 15 shots on goal to six for the USMNT, the South Koreans were displeased with the result. South Korea's coach said, "We deserved to win 3–1 or 4–1 because we created so many beautiful chances…. We were unlucky."

As the USMNT improved and expectations increased, a dual narrative appeared that would start to plague the team. On one hand, some felt lucky not to lose and proud of the performance. Bruce Arena said, "I'm going to take it and get out of town quick. We didn't only play against the Korean team, we played against a nation today. Give us a lot of credit." On the other hand, some were disappointed not to win. Defender/midfielder Tony Sanneh said, "It's disappointing, when you're up 1–0 at 80 minutes, you should win." The dual narrative reflects a change from gratitude or appreciation to regret or disappointment that can accompany a change in expectations. The win against Portugal was a comparison that needed context and set unrealistic expectations. In reality, the USMNT had four points after a game against Portugal and a game against a host country with home-field advantage. If the USMNT wanted to prove the legitimacy of U.S. Soccer, they could do it against winless Poland, who were up next. South Korea still had to face Portugal.

---

87. Kim Dong-sung finished first in the 1,500-meter short-track speed skating final. He took a victory lap with the South Korea flag. But suddenly, his celebration came crashing down—it was announced that the gold would go to his American rival, Apolo Ohno, and that Kim was disqualified for blocking Ohno on the last lap. The South Koreans implied that Ohno received a favorable ruling because the Games were in the U.S.

2002 FIFA World Cup: Group Stage, Game 3
June 14, 2002, at Taejon World Cup Stadium, South Korea
USA 1–3 Poland

Since Poland had lost their first two matches, there was no chance they could advance. They were playing for national pride. With nothing to lose, Poland changed a number of players who had not started in their previous two matches. The USMNT coaches had thought they thoroughly scouted Poland, but when they got Poland's starting lineup, they were unfamiliar with many of the players. Arena called the Polish American assistant who led the effort to scout Poland at his home in Connecticut, and he too wasn't familiar with many of the Poland starters. Any athlete will explain that when one team has everything to lose and the other team has nothing to lose and is using un-scouted and unknown players who are desperate to show what they can do, the game can be very complicated. The USMNT needed only a draw to advance to the knockout round.

Three minutes into the match, Emmanuel Olisadebe, who was born in Nigeria and after playing in Poland became eligible for Polish citizenship, made it 1–0 when he smashed home a deflection from a corner kick just under the crossbar. He just seemed to be one step quicker than USMNT defenders Jeff Agoos and Tony Sanneh, who were 34 and 31 years old, respectively.

A goal via a set piece.

In the fourth minute, a goal by Donovan was called back for him bumping a defender in the buildup while heading the ball into an open net. The call could have gone either way.

Referee judgment.

The disputed call seemed to cause the USMNT to lose focus. In the fifth minute, Poland was up 2–0 due to a left-footed redirection from a low cross into the box.

A goal via crossing the ball in the box.

The USMNT defender had been beaten in a sprint and muscled aside. The USMNT, despite their greater pressure and possession, were limited to speculative long-range shots. Friedel made a number of good saves to keep the USMNT in the game. While the USMNT pushed to score, they were exposed to swift counter-attacks. Substitute Marcin Zewlakow made it 3–0 in the 66th minute with a header from a cross into the box.

A goal via crossing the ball in the box.

Brad Friedel responded by denying his second penalty kick of the tournament. Then the USMNT's Clint Mathis would hit the post. In the 83rd minute, Donovan scored what amounted to be a consolation goal.

A goal via open play.

From only needing a draw to advance against winless Poland, it now seemed that the USMNT were finished, because everyone assumed Portugal, who had crushed Poland 4–0 a few days earlier, would beat South Korea—and Portugal and South Korea would advance.

The USMNT Advances to the Knockout Round of 16

Both group stage games (USMNT versus Poland and South Korea versus Portugal), only 115 miles apart, began simultaneously so that no team could conspire to produce a result unfairly eliminating one of the contending teams. The USMNT monitored the South Korea versus Portugal match on a TV in the press box and radioed reports to the bench.

Once South Korea and Portugal knew that the USMNT were losing 2–0 within five minutes of play, the two teams essentially quit competing, knowing that a 0–0 draw, paired with an USMNT defeat, would get them both to the Round of 16 and send the USMNT home. South Korean fans cheered wildly each time Poland scored a goal. But then, in the 27th minute, João Pinto of Portugal received a red card for a reckless and unnecessary tackle on Park Ji-sung. Portugal had to be more cautious the rest of the game, but the South Koreans didn't seem interested in attacking and making themselves vulnerable to a counter-attack. In the 66th minute the game changed. Portugal's Bento received his second yellow card and was sent off. Portugal were down to nine men. A few minutes later, South Korea scored. The American bench erupted, even though they were losing 0–3. The final minutes of South Korea vs. Portugal were tense. Portugal's Luis Figo sent a free kick wide by a foot. South Korea would hold on to win 1–0. Claudio Reyna would later say, "We definitely owe them [South Korea] a big thanks."

South Korea had seven points and finished first in the group. What is amazing is that they did this (and then advanced all the way to the semifinals) with only one player in a Top Five League.[88] Of the 23-man squad, there were 16 players who played in the domestic Korean league, five in Japan, and only two in Europe (Italy and Belgium). South Korea's performance should serve to dispel any lingering doubts about the importance of playing together as a team and the drastic impact that home-field advantage can have on results. The USMNT finished the group in second place with four points, and therefore advanced to the Round of 16. Portugal and Poland, each with three points, were out.

2002 FIFA World Cup: Round of 16
June 17, 2002, at Jeonju Stadium, South Korea
USA 2–0 Mexico
The USMNT, which finished second in their group, would face Mexico, which finished first in their group, in the Round of 16. The challenge for the USMNT was that they played Poland on a Friday and had to play Mexico on Monday—not a lot of time to recover. Mexico had one more day of rest. Mexico had surprised many experts by winning their group. Croatia pulled off an upset over Italy in the group stage, and then Mexico and Italy drew. Therefore, the USMNT could have been playing Italy instead of Mexico had the USMNT won their group. The USMNT versus Mexico match was the first, and so far only, match between the rivals in a World Cup. In terms of luck of the draw, the USMNT could have also faced other group winners, such as Brazil, Germany, and Spain.

The USMNT would now face their most bitter rival to prove to the world that the soccer in the U.S. was legitimate. It helped that the USMNT were familiar with Mexico and not intimidated. The team had won four out of five of their previous meetings with Mexico. The USMNT got a call from President George W. Bush, who told them he had a bet with the Mexican president Vicente Fox on the game. This put things in perspective for the team.

---

88. Ahn Jung-hwan, who played for Perugia in Serie A.

This time, Arena would make a change by debuting defenders Gregg Berhalter and Eddie Lewis. Donovan was also played in a different position from the previous match. Arena explained, "We played a 3-5-2, and the reason we did that was we didn't have enough guys that could play, because Frankie Hedjuk was suspended, David Regis couldn't really play—he had a bad knee. So, we had to kind of play with a back three and lean on the experience of Claudio and Eddie Lewis to hold down the flanks when needed. And they could certainly do that. I mean, if there was ever a time that Claudio gave for the team, that was it."

Arena had moved Reyna to the right, which seemed to surprise Mexico. Playing out wide gave him the space to play and get the ball. USMNT defender Tony Sanneh reflected on the strategy and said, "We were going to try to physically break them [Mexico] down, outrun them, and attack the goal. We knew we had some little advantages on set plays as well, and just tried to stay disciplined. We knew it was going to be chippy, so that was another big part of it, physically destroying them but mentally beating them as well." Sounds like the Spirit of '76.

Prior to the match, the USMNT players walked past the Mexico players, who were joking and laughing with one another. The Mexican media had been reporting that the USMNT couldn't beat Mexico when the match really counted. The attitude of Mexico's players and media gave the USMNT the impression that Mexico didn't take them seriously. Feeling slighted, the USMNT came out for the game highly motivated. To the USMNT, the game turned into a fight for legitimacy—right there and then.

Early in the match, the USMNT handled Mexico's pressure. Then, McBride took a free kick to Reyna on the right, who made a spectacular run and passed back to Josh Wolff at the near post. Off a Wolff pass, McBride then scored in the eighth minute from 12 yards out past two defenders.

A goal via a set piece.

The goal set the tone and Mexico looked rattled. After that, the USMNT seemed quite happy to sit back and let Mexico pass it around the midfield. After falling behind 1–0, Mexico's coach Javier Aguirre made a substitution just 28 minutes in, replacing talented winger Ramón Morales with 33-year-old striker Luis Hernández in an effort to add more power to the attack. Taking Morales out so soon seemed like desperation. As Mexico came after the USMNT, it opened more space for counter-attacks, which started to play into the USMNT's hands. Mexican players appeared to be arguing with or frustrated with each other. At halftime it was USA 1–0 Mexico.

In the 54th minute, Mexico was denied a sure penalty and possible red card when USMNT defensive midfielder John O'Brien, defending against a corner kick, jumped to head the ball and appeared to punch the ball away with his right hand in his own box. Mexico's players and coaches were calling for a penalty. The referee appeared to be looking into the congested area of players and did not see it.

Referee judgment.

Ten minutes after that, just when it felt like all the attacking pressure was on the USMNT's side, Eddie Lewis broke down the left-hand side of the field and made a cross to Donovan, who headed the ball into the back of the net in the 65th minute to make it 2–0. Donovan ripped off his shirt and fell to his knees in celebration. Lewis, who had a reputation of being even keeled and unemotional, joined in the big celebration.

A goal via crossing the ball in the box.

Of all players, Mexico didn't want Donovan to score. In Mexico, Donovan was the hated, menacing villain on the rival team primarily because he spoke enough Spanish to alienate them. Growing up, Donovan played with many Latin players and learned "soccer Spanish" by necessity, including trash-talking. His Spanish quotes were rarely picked up by the American media, but in Mexico his quotes were often distorted and would make national headlines.

Increasingly frustrated, Mexico started getting more aggressive. Later, an ugly challenge on Cobi Jones in the air heading the ball ended with Rafael Marquez being sent off in the 88th minute. The USMNT seemed to have a mentality or will to withstand the pressure that came and ultimately held strong to win the game.

For many years, the U.S.-Mexico matches were anything but a rivalry. From 1937 until 1980, Mexico was 21–0–3 against the USMNT. By the 1980s, the results were more respectable. Then in the 1990s, the USMNT would win most home matches. This World Cup win surpassed all others because it was on the biggest stage—and added another variable to the *why*, *how*, and *who*—the *when*.

In the locker room afterward, the group of players who didn't play seemed as excited and happy that they were as much a part of the victory as any starter. They all took their time showering and getting dressed before getting on the bus. When the team left the stadium, they passed Mexico's players boarding their bus. Almost all the USMNT players moved to the side facing Mexico's players so they could get a good look at them. The match was an inflection point. Mexico's coach at the time recalled, "To me, the rivalry between Mexico and the USA started from that moment. That's when it really intensified to what we see today."

Examining the official match statistics, Mexico had 67 percent of possession, more shots on goal (12–10), and the same shots on target (6–6). While the Americans struggled to maintain possession, it was the team's counter-attack that helped win the game.

Asked if the USMNT's performance meant they had entered the upper echelon of soccer, Arena responded, "Not even close. We're not pretending to be at the same level as the established teams, but the gap has closed considerably." U.S. Soccer was becoming more legitimate. He added, "It's a great day for U.S. Soccer."

2002 FIFA World Cup: Quarterfinals
June 21, 2002, at Ulsan Stadium, South Korea
USA 0–1 Germany
Having reached the quarterfinals or better in 13 consecutive World Cups, Germany were what the USMNT wanted to be—consistent contenders and World Cup champions.

Nearly four million American households woke up early to watch the 7:30 AM ET game on ESPN, the most who had ever watched a soccer match on the station before. The number also eclipsed all of ESPN's MLB telecasts that summer.[89]

The USMNT had enough confidence that they went on the attack from the start. The USMNT dominated time of possession in the first half and German goalkeeper Oliver Kahn pulled off two world-class saves against Donovan to keep Germany on level terms.

In the 39th minute, Michael Ballack, who is almost 6'3", headed a free kick from Christian Ziege to give Germany a 1–0 lead.

A goal via a set piece.

Tactically, Arena knew that this German team had one key strategy to beat his team, and that would be via set pieces given the German's physical characteristics (tall and strong). The USMNT tried to limit free kicks but eventually, Germany would get a critical one.

Later, with halftime looming, Germany's Miroslav Klose, 6'0", hit the post on a header; it should have been his sixth goal (all headers) of the World Cup. After the USMNT's possession and opportunities, it would have been extremely harsh for the USMNT to trail 2–0 at the break.

Germany spent the second half defending their lead. In the 50th minute, there was a decisive "what if" moment. Claudio Reyna's corner kick was flicked into the path of Gregg Berhalter, who had moved away from his defender toward the center back-post area. Berhalter lunged at it with his left foot, made good contact, and put the ball past the German goalkeeper. However, central midfielder Torsten Frings put his left arm out and blocked the ball right on the line and it fell to the goalkeeper. To many, this was clearly a handball; however, the referee either didn't see it or felt the handball was involuntary.

Referee judgment.

Sanneh seemed to be everywhere and looked like USMNT's man of the match. He had a great chance in the 80th minute on a free header about 10 yards out from a perfect cross from Mathis, but the ball went just on the wrong side of the upright. In the end, the USMNT could only find a few opportunities through Germany's superbly organized defense,

---

89. Remember close to 18 million viewers watched the USWNT beat China in the World Cup final in 1999 on a Sunday afternoon.

and when they could, they simply couldn't finish their chances. In the 83rd minute, the crowd started chanting "USA! USA!" The Germans seemed to be tiring at the end, but they held on and the match ended 0–1 for Germany. John O'Brien, 24 years old, was one of only three players, along with goalkeeper Brad Friedel and Tony Sanneh, to play every minute of all five games.

For the match, the USMNT had 58 percent of possession and outshot Germany 11–6, 6–2 on target. German goalkeeper Oliver Kahn would go on to win the tournament's Golden Ball, the only goalkeeper in history to have won the award for the best player in the World Cup.

Germany would eventually lose 2–0 to Brazil in the Final. The 2002 World Cup would be remembered as the tournament of Brazil's iconic trio of Ronaldinho, Rivaldo, and Ronaldo and the surprise semifinal appearances of South Korea and Turkey.

The general feeling was that the USMNT had outplayed Germany. Variables including the no-call on Frings' handball or Sanneh's missed header could have gone differently. Having said that, Germany's Miroslav Klose's header that hit the post in the first half could have gone in too. If the handball had been called, Frings would have received a red card, the ensuing penalty kick could have been scored, and the USMNT could have won in extra time or penalty kicks (a lot of *ifs*...). Even so, Bruce Arena would have had only 14 eligible field players for the semifinals due to yellow card suspensions (Berhalter, Pablo Mastroeni, Eddie Pope) and injuries (Jeff Agoos, Steve Cherundolo, Joe-Max Moore).

Two USMNT players receiving World Cup awards added to the legitimacy of U.S. Soccer. Landon Donovan was awarded the tournament's Best Young Player Award. Claudio Reyna was named to the tournament's All-Star team along with Germany's Michael Ballack (2002 UEFA Club Midfielder of the Year), Brazil's Rivaldo (1999 Ballon d'Or), and Brazil's Ronaldinho (2005 Ballon d'Or).

Reflections on the 2002 World Cup

In 2016, Grant Wahl of *Sports Illustrated* asked several USMNT 2002 World Cup stars, "What's wrong with the USMNT?" Several factors that we have discussed are mentioned. We highlighted some key words.

Brian McBride said, "In 2002 one of the most important parts is that we had a foundation that Bruce [Arena] had put in place: a formation, **a style of play**, but also a belief. We had a **unity in the group**. That's a tough thing [to achieve], especially in a national team setting, because **you're not together a lot** usually."

Claudio Reyna: "You want to have a **core group of players** that have earned through their club play and national team play being **called in consistently**. And that could be 15 to 16 players that we have to have on the roster more or less every important game. That allows the team to **develop a consistency** from game to game, tournament to tournament, **getting to know each other, getting to learn the way the team should play**. I think the amount of constant changeover from game to game [these days] makes it difficult for our team to establish any rhythm and consistency that you need to get results."

Carlos Llamosa: "In that cycle there was a chemistry we had as a team off the field and on the field. We were **like a family**. We enjoyed every single practice, every single game. We faced every game seriously with the same enthusiasm. That was a special **team with the chemistry**."[90]

John O'Brien: "We dictated games through **pace and intensity and defending well, through counter-attacking**. There were games like Mexico, where they controlled the game more than we did; we scored early and didn't have much of the ball. With Portugal, we beat them early. First half they were sleeping and we came out kind of firing. Same type of thing, though, with pace and getting the ball wide. During qualification, **when you're playing teams that are supposed to be lesser opponents**

---

90. Carlos Llamosa was born in Colombia and in 1991, at 22 years old, immigrated to the U.S. to join the rest of his family, who were at the time living in Queens, New York City.

and sit back against us, that's something we've had a hard time breaking down."[91]

Frankie Hedjuk: "He [Bruce Arena] brought that 2002 team together really from nothing. **Half were MLS guys, half were grinders in European leagues. He brought togetherness that no one really had before.** You know what he does? He finds fighters and battlers and guys who are willing to go into the trenches. **Maybe they're not the most skilled players, like myself, but they have the heart, the soul, and attitude the U.S. team needs.** Was I the best pick for left back in 2002 when I never played left back before in my life? No, I wasn't. But Bruce was like, **'I have to get this guy on the field because he's a battler and a fighter.'**"

Wahl wrote, "But **beyond chemistry, continuity, and a larger core group**, what was so special about the 2002 U.S. World Cup team that's lacking in the current U.S. team? For Reyna, the players on the 2002 **team were mostly at the peaks of their careers** and able to maintain possession of the ball better, which allowed the U.S. to control games more often."

In 2017, Arielle Castillo of MLSsoccer.com wrote an article titled "Legend of Dos a Cero: An Oral History of the US-Mexico 2002 World Cup clash." In comparing the USMNT today versus 2002, Bruce Arena said, "The **pride** is something that I think is lost today—how we worked really hard to build that team to have **the right values** and the **right kind of people on the roster and represent our country**. Just **good old-fashioned American values**; that's no longer the case anymore.... It didn't mean it was perfect all the time—it certainly wasn't—but those guys who wore the US jersey were fabulous."

USMNT players we interviewed explained that they were built around the philosophy of "fight," "grit," and "don't let your teammates down." They believe these values gave them the ability to overcome technical and tactical shortcomings. They also believe their mentality that the USMNT would never give up made them that much more difficult to play against.

---

91. John O'Brien was one of the few Americans who ventured to Europe as a teenager at the time—and made it. In 1994, he left his Southern California home at age 17 for Ajax Amsterdam and went on to win two Dutch Eredivisie titles.

Our interviews with opposing players and coaches in the 2002 World Cup confirmed this.

Keep in mind, all of these things were said in hindsight many years later after an extraordinary performance. It is easy to play Monday-morning quarterback, especially with time to reflect. One could easily argue the only real surprise for the USMNT was the upset over Portugal. Other than that, they tied South Korea; got hammered by Poland; beat Mexico, whom they had beaten four of the previous five times; and lost to Germany. If anything, one could claim their run (even though it was magical) shows how circumstantial success can be at the World Cup. Four points (one win and a tie) got them out of the group. South Korea beat Portugal when Portugal were down to nine players. In the knockout round, they drew a team they knew well and were also confident they could beat. It was a perfect storm. However, any team can only beat and do what is put in front of them.

Change in Expectations and Comparisons

As with the USMNT draw with South Korea, a dual narrative emerged with their loss to Germany. In 2013, Michael Cummings of Bleacher Report wrote, "It is a two-sided theme that reappears over the next decade [after 2002] and into the current day as U.S. Soccer continues its maturation in the world's game." In the moment, despite their disappointment, the USSF, USMNT players, and fans should have been proud of their performance against Germany and in the 2002 World Cup. The USMNT won unprecedented respect and added to the legitimacy of U.S. Soccer. Jack Edwards, an ESPN reporter, said, "It was just a prideful moment for this sport [U.S. Soccer] to able to stand on its own feet for once and say 'Yeah, we actually matter on the world stage.'" Only four years had passed since a disastrous, last-place finish at the 1998 World Cup in France. Americans were now labeled "valiant" by the BBC.

Bruce Arena, typically conservative in his remarks to manage expectations, said, "I think we demonstrated to the world that the United States belonged here. We expected to be the best team tonight. We weren't surprised at our performance." His remarks reflected a subtle shift.

Remember, just a few days earlier after beating Mexico, when asked if the performance of the USMNT thus far meant that the team was now in the upper echelon of the world game, Arena had responded, "Not even close. We're not pretending to be at the same level as the established teams, but the gap has closed considerably."

Goalkeeper Brad Friedel expressed the feeling of many by saying that the players realized the team "could've gone a little further." Years later, and upon reflection in 2017, Friedel would say, "The run itself in 2002 put U.S. Soccer on the map globally, in the eyes of other players around the world, the other staff around the world, the other federations around the world, the other leagues around the world. Really, that was probably the first time that people really got serious about what the United States could become in the future in soccer." Expectations were changing. In addition, future comparisons would now be made to reaching the quarterfinals. With the luck and other factors that were involved to get there, it was a faulty comparison and set unrealistic expectations.

It wasn't just the coach and players. A shift happened in the media as well. George Vecsey of the *New York Times,* who attended the game, explained the transformative effect the game had: "Three German sportswriters packed up their laptops [after the game] and stopped by our little American cluster. 'You guys outplayed us,' one of them said. 'You should have won.' 'One-nothing,' I said. 'Germany won.' I know these guys—good colleagues, always willing to explain the sport to bumpkins from the New World, like me, but there is no code for effusive sportsmanship in a soccer press room, only pragmatic judgments of who played well and who did not. From Old Europe came the rather startling possibility that the United States is now a player." Many, then, busily plotted their progress in an upward-trending straight line from the quarterfinals in Korea toward the ultimate "goal" of winning the World Cup.

While expectations changed, one reality didn't. Even with his successes, Arena, being an American coach, received no material offers from European clubs. A U.S. soccer coach was not considered legitimate in Europe. He returned to coach the USMNT for another four years.

Chapter 5

2002 World Cup:
The Ugly Truth
Behind the Numbers

Chapter Four went through the 2002 World Cup and detailed how each goal was scored. The margins between winning and losing are so small that various factors can have an incredible impact on the narrative—yet their contribution fades from storytelling and context in setting expectations and comparisons.

In this chapter, we will stop and go into more depth and data analysis on various factors behind the USMNT's 2002 World Cup scoring and winning, including goals from crosses, goals from set pieces, superb goalkeeping, no red cards, and distinctive speed for counter-attack goals—all part of the Spirit of '76. As a proxy for luck in 2002, we compare the difference between actual goals scored and model-based expected goals. Lastly, we explain home-field advantage generally and World Cup host nation advantages. *If you care more about the action and events and don't feel like you need more background or a deeper understanding of the factors behind scoring and winning, please feel free to skip to the next chapter on the 2006 World Cup at any time.*

Goals from Crosses

Crosses into the box represented the highest percentage of the USMNT's goals, 42 percent, which was above the 26 percent tournament average. Crosses developed as a part of the Spirit of '76 for many reasons. Crosses were traditionally a part of English and Scottish tactics, which were the first influences on how Americans learned to play. Typically, Americans learn to play soccer on large fields. With so much space, dribbling skills are not emphasized as much as speed, running, and athleticism. American-style soccer developed players who were especially talented in the air on crosses or balls in from set pieces (e.g., Brian McBride, Eddie Pope, and Tony Sanneh). In other countries, many players learn to play in constrained spaces. With limited space, dribbling skills in tight areas are emphasized.

The USMNT's reliance on crosses impacted the perception of legitimacy of U.S. Soccer. In a 2017 article titled "Art of Crossing Can Still Count in an Age of Crowded Penalty Areas," Sean Ingle of *The Guardian* wrote that in the last 30 years, crossing was seen as "a caveman tactic in a world of Renaissance artists…and an outdated and particularly English style of play." However, there is perception and reality. Garry Gelade, a statistical consultant who works with Premier League sides, showed that Serie A had more crosses from open play per game than the Premier League in 2010, with Ligue 1 and La Liga showing similar numbers to England.

The effectiveness of crosses has been debated amongst coaches, the media, and data scientists alike. Jan Vecer argued that crossing is not only ineffective because only one cross in 92 directly leads to a goal, but is actually counterproductive. In a detailed statistical analysis, he showed that teams that cross less score more goals, and he concluded that if Premier League teams stopped crossing altogether, they would score an extra 15 goals per season.

Garry Gelade demonstrated at Opta Pro Forum that Vecer had inadvertently not considered the effect of the state of the game—and that it is the current score that drives the number of crosses. In simple terms, teams tend to cross more when they are losing (especially on a counter-attack) and less when they are winning (to maintain possession), and this nuance would not be measured in that statistic. Said differently, Vecer's study muddles cause and effect. Teams don't score more goals because they cross less—they cross less because they score more. And that is quite different. It makes sense; a team in the lead will usually want to maintain possession and play more defensively than when they are behind so they won't cross the ball. There is no evidence that reducing crosses will increase the number of goals scored. Therefore, when people point out that a soccer power crosses fewer times than the USMNT, one needs to consider the soccer power is most likely scoring more and winning most of the game.

If you really want to assess the effectiveness of a cross, Gelade argued, one really needs to examine what happens in the six seconds after the ball is crossed into the box. He analyzed 35,000 crosses in the Premier League, from 2013 to 2015. Crosses led to assists for 414 goals—a miserable 1.2 percent success rate. However, when Gelade tracked what happened in the following six seconds, that percentage jumped, with a further 5,094 attempts on goal leading to 252 goals. There were also another 4,727 corners and 18 penalties, leading to another 80 goals. That brought the conversion rate from crosses from open play up to 2.2 percent—or one goal for every 45 crosses. Not enormously more productive, granted. But still much better—and a similar success rate to set pieces near the box.

Gelade was able to dive deeper. He demonstrated the numbers could be nudged further in the crosser's favor—depending on where the cross was made, where it was aimed, the angle of delivery, and whether it was closer to the near or the far post. Therefore, a cross from inside the box had a success rate of 7.6 percent if aimed toward the back post—double that of a cross hit to the near post. Of course, context is important. The quality of the cross and the player on the end of it matters too—something the data was not able to consider. Even with these caveats, Gelade's research is important because not only does it offer teams a better understanding of when crossing works best, but it also demonstrates that in an era when central areas are increasingly packed with defenders, putting the ball into the box has its place.

Goals from Set Pieces

Set pieces (defined as penalties, free kicks, and corners) accounted for 29 percent of the USMNT's goals in the 2002 World Cup, second-most after crosses into the box, and consistent with the tournament average. The thing about set pieces is that they are not considered a part of the "beautiful game," and many deride them as an "illegitimate" way to score goals. The USMNT's reliance on set pieces impacted the perception of their legitimacy.

Once again, there is an issue of perception versus reality. Set pieces are an important element for all teams at the World Cup, not just for the USMNT, and increasingly so. The winner of the 2018 World Cup, France, scored 43 percent of their goals from set pieces, which was in line with the tournament average (73 of 169 total goals scored), and up from a historical average of around 30 percent. In the 2018 World Cup as a whole, more than two out of every five goals scored during the group stages came from set pieces, which was a considerably higher proportion than at any previous tournament at the same stage. Five of the 11 goals in the quarterfinals, and two of the four scored in the semifinals, came from set pieces. Seventy-five percent of England's goals (nine out of 12 goals scored) at the 2018 World Cup came from set-piece situations. Harry Kane, the Adidas Golden Boot winner as the leading goal scorer at the 2018 World Cup, scored three of his six goals from penalties and another two from corner kicks. Alexi Lalas proclaimed that soccer has turned into a "set-piece orgy." As a Fox Sports commentator, he explained, "In a game that is often so random, [a set piece] is the one time where obviously it stops, and the players and the team and the coach can do something that alleviates some of the randomness. It's probably the closest thing we have to American football in a soccer game, and you ignore set pieces at your own peril. A set piece is to soccer what water is to life. You need it to survive, but it can kill you."

Superb Goalkeeping

Another component of the Spirit of '76 on which the USMNT relies heavily is exceptional goalkeeping. In 2005, Ihsan Alp of Gazi University in Ankara wrote an academic paper titled "Performance Evaluation of

Goalkeepers of the World Cup." After a rigorous analysis weighing goals against per game, penalty kicks saved, free kicks saved, corner kicks saved, and fast breaks saved, he ranked the most efficient goalkeepers of the 2002 World Cup. The top five in order were Oliver Kahn (Germany), Rüstü Reçber (Turkey), Brad Friedel (USA), Iker Casillas (Spain), and Gigi Buffon (Italy). Friedel was ranked ahead of two highly regarded World Cup winners. He finished behind Oliver Kahn, who won the trophy for the best player in the tournament, and Turkey's goalkeeper, as Turkey won third place primarily on his outstanding performance. Friedel had saved two of two penalty kicks (0 percent converted). Typically, 75 percent of penalty kicks are converted and 81 percent in World Cups. Friedel's saves, including a penalty kick, against South Korea were a key factor in the USMNT getting a point from a draw and advancing.

No Red Cards

The 2002 World Cup was the "dirtiest" World Cup on record, with the highest average number of red and yellow cards per game. In the 2002 World Cup there were 12 games with red cards (16 total red cards) in 64 matches (19 percent). Statistically speaking, one was more likely to see a game with a red card in the 2002 World Cup than a game ending in a 1–1 draw. In contrast to the 1990 and 1994 World Cups, the USMNT didn't receive any red cards and didn't ever have to play a man down. Obviously, it's common sense that red cards can hurt a team. Under FIFA rules, a player receiving a red is suspended for the following game. Likewise, the accumulation of two yellow cards in separate matches earns a player a suspension for the following game.[92]

Jan Vecer, Frantisek Kopriva, and Tomoyuki Ichiba of Columbia University's Statistics Department showed in an academic paper that when one of the teams receives a red card, its scoring intensity (expected number of goals scored during a game) is reduced to about 66 percent of

---

92. In 2010, the rules were changed so players are given a clean slate in the quarterfinals, just like in the Champions League, to help ensure big-name players would not be suspended for the Final. In 2002, Germany's Michael Ballack missed the World Cup Final after picking up a second yellow card in the semifinals.

the original intensity, whereas the intensity of the opposing team increases by a factor of 125 percent. As one would expect, receiving a red card earlier in the match increases the odds of losing substantially. The expected number of goals will increase if the weaker team is penalized, which makes sense, and at the World Cup is often true for the USMNT.

In a tournament, a player who receives a red card is ineligible for the next match. The World Cup allows a 23-man squad, usually including three goalkeepers, and typically during the course of a tournament a few players are not at peak physical and mental condition for a game because of various factors, such as an injury or cumulative physical exertion or even personal issues. According to Chris Anderson and David Sally, authors of *The Numbers Game: Why Everything You Know about Soccer Is Wrong*, the strength of a team crucially depends on the weakest player. An ineligible player will have a greater effect on a team that lacks depth or relies on physical attributes such as speed and fitness in a World Cup tournament. If the USMNT had beaten Germany in the quarterfinals, Arena wouldn't have had that many options for a lineup because of injuries and yellow card accumulations.

Distinctive Speed for Counter-Attack Goals

Landon Donovan and DaMarcus Beasley were young and fast additions to the 2002 World Cup USMNT. Their speed caused all kinds of problems for opposing teams. Donovan would be named Best Young Player of the tournament. At the time of the 2002 World Cup, FIFA.com stated, "He is a very good athlete, quick, strong, and mobile."

To understand the relative pace and acceleration of Landon Donovan and DaMarcus Beasley, we looked up their EA Sports FIFA video game ratings. The earliest we could find were from FIFA 2005 (which came out in October 2004). Obviously, these ratings are not perfect, and are subjective and debated, but they give us some sense. At the time, Donovan was 22 years old. His overall rating was an 84 with a potential of 93. His acceleration rating was 95, pace 90, ball control 86, and dribbling 83. At the time, Beasley was also 22 years old. His overall rating was a 78 with a potential of 90. His acceleration rating was 92, pace 89, ball control

85, and dribbling 85. Both Donovan and Beasley had higher acceleration numbers than Cristiano Ronaldo and Wayne Rooney, who are a few years younger than them.

We also included the FIFA 2019 ratings for Christian Pulisic and Kylian Mbappé for comparison. It is difficult enough to compare players within the same year, so to compare ratings across years is even more difficult because they are relative within each year.

Table: EA Sports' FIFA 2005 and 2019 Ratings

	FIFA 2005 (October 2004)				FIFA 2019	
	L Donovan	C Ronaldo	W Rooney	D Beasley	C Pulisic	K Mbappé
Age	22	19	18	22	21	21
Overall Rating	84	88	87	78	79	87
Potential	93	98	99	90		
Acceleration	95	91	90	92	93	96
Pace	90	93	92	89	91	96
Ball Control	86	86	85	85	82	90
Dribbling	83	92	85	85	87	89

According to the Bundesliga website, in his last season in the league Pulisic's top speed was 21.4 mph (34.45 km/hr), as compared to Mbappé's 22.5 mph (36.2 km/hr). This should help put their pace and acceleration numbers into perspective for USMNT fans.

Soccer players run in short bursts, using the time when the ball is on the other side of the field to recover. During the game a player might have 35 to 50 "sprints," depending on the player's position. Most of these are of relatively short duration, on average about 22 yards in length. Taking the players' average of 45 "sprints," they "sprint" about every two minutes. So, it's like doing 45 short sprints with a 90- to 160-second recovery jog in between.

The sprint distances have a meaningful impact on the number of goals as well. Jan Vecer, a former teacher in the department of statistics at Columbia University who is working on a book titled *Soccermetrics: Science of Soccer Statistics*, believes "the sprint distances have a large positive effect on the goals." His hypothesis is that the critical statistic is the acceleration, which captures the change from the fast play to sprints. More importantly, it is not the absolute value of the acceleration, but rather the difference over the opposite team. He believes players can benefit enormously from being able to accelerate to a level that can overrun the defenders of the opposite team. His hypothesis is that the lower scoring rate in the Champions League (goals per game) is primarily due to the acceleration differential being smaller in comparison to the competition in the domestic leagues. Speed not only helps a player score goals for himself but also creates space and opportunities for his teammates, as defenders can't help their teammates and leave a speedster alone. In addition, a player is able to sprint back from offense to help with defense. Speed increases the pressure on the opposing team's players and attacks and reduces their space to maneuver.

Anyone who watched the French national team in the 2018 World Cup saw that 19-year-old Kylian Mbappé's speed combined with his superb finishing skills were key differentiators amongst elite players, whose skills are getting harder to distinguish over time. His two goals against Argentina in the Round of 16 made him the first teenager to score a brace (two goals) in a World Cup game since Pelé in 1958. Both came from quickness of thought and action, along with the skill and poise needed for the finish. His goal from 25 yards out in the Final against Croatia happened in a flash, as the defender had to play off him to respect his speed. The goal also made him the second teenager after Pelé to score in a World Cup Final.

When playing for their countries, Ronaldo and Messi are not surrounded by as many world-class players as they are in their clubs and don't have as much familiarity and practice time with their national teammates. Therefore, national team defenders can try to focus on working together to crowd and stop players like them. At their clubs, players like Ronaldo and Messi have more teammates who are also world-class and are more familiar with where and when they will go and want the ball, so defenders can't cheat and help as much. It impacts their efficiency. For example, Ronaldo's and Messi's average goals per game are 1.02 and 0.87 during their Real Madrid and Barcelona club careers, respectively. In the Champions League, where club competition is the greatest, their averages are 1.04 and 0.81, respectively. However, they have a drop-off to 0.70 and 0.40 in non-friendly competitive national team matches, respectively. Ronaldo's drop-off may be less than Messi's because Ronaldo has world-class speed.

It is much harder to defend world-class speed, especially if the team has other capable finishers. Kylian Mbappé averages 0.56 goals per game in the Champions League and 0.50 in non-friendly competitive national team matches. Landon Donovan averaged 0.39 goals per game playing in his professional club career as compared to 0.36 goals in national team competitions.

In explaining the advantage of speed combined with conditioning, Landon Donovan said, "The advantage doesn't come because you can run more than someone over 90 minutes. The advantage comes when, in the tenth minute, I'm sprinting back and making another guy chase me. By the end of the game, that guy's worn down, but I can still keep going at the same pace. That might mean the difference between a half-yard or a yard to make a play."

Proxy for Luck: Difference Between Actual Goals Scored and Expected Goals (xG)

Expected goals (xG) is the number of goals a team (or player) would be expected to score based on the quality and quantity of shots taken. Expected goals is a metric that assesses the chance of a shot becoming a goal. Every shot is compared to thousands of shots with similar characteristics to determine the probability that this shot will result in a goal. That probability is the expected goal total. An xG of zero is a certain miss, while an xG of one is a certain goal. A xG of 0.5 would indicate that if identical shots were attempted 10 times, five would be expected to result in a goal. Some of the characteristics/variables include location of shooter (How far was it from the goal and at what angle on the field?), body part used (Was it a header or off the shooter's foot?), type of pass (Was it from a through ball, cross, set piece, etc?), and type of attack (Was it from an established possession? Was it off a rebound? Did the defense have time to get in position? Did it follow a dribble?). A word of caution: some xG models do not consider defensive pressure and lack context. While xG is a valuable tool, it is only a tool and doesn't provide the entire picture.

As shown in the table below, in the 1998 World Cup the USMNT scored one goal, but the expected goals were 2.4 for a minus-1.4

differential. This implies that the USMNT had a little bad luck. In 2002, the USMNT scored seven goals, but the expected goals were 3.6 for a plus-3.4 (Goals For-xG). This implies that in 2002, the USMNT had a lot of good luck in scoring. The USMNT have never been so efficient at shooting—41.3 percent of their shots were on goal. Keep in mind that Brad Friedel also saved two penalty kicks. One of them, versus South Korea, changed the result of the game and led to one point and advancing. The plus-3.4 and plus-2 penalty kicks are a big swing. Obviously, with more data points over time luck starts to even out, and the USMNT is a plus-1.4 in xG from 1998 to 2014. We included other information, such as shots, shots on goal, and possession, from USMNT performances in World Cups in their respective chapters, but included them in the table below for context and comparisons.

Table: Summary of USMNT World Cup Goals and Expected Goals from 1998 to 2014

United States	Games	GF	GA	GD	GF/Game	xG	GF—xG	xG/Game	Shots	SOG	OnTarget%	Poss%
1998	3	1	5	-4	0.3	2.4	-1.4	0.8	50	12	24%	54%
2002	5	7	7	0	1.4	3.6	3.4	0.7	63	26	41.3%	48.6%
2006	3	2	6	-4	0.7	1.7	0.3	0.6	31	2	6.5%	50.2%
2010	4	5	5	0	1.3	5.1	-0.1	1.3	67	24	35.8%	48.9%
2014	4	5	6	-1	1.3	5.8	-0.8	1.4	44	14	31.8%	43.8%
Total							1.4					

Below is a summary of the top four finishers of each World Cup from 1998 to 2014. As expected, the teams in the top four had a lot of goals, but also a lot of luck. In the 2002 World Cup, champion Brazil scored 18 goals, while their expected goals (xG) was 9.5, an extraordinary plus-8.5 difference. In the comparison, the USMNT's expected goal difference was plus-3.4. The USMNT have not had as much relative luck as other countries—2002 is the only year in which the USMNT's goals scored minus goals expected was higher than the tournament average.

**Table: Summary of Top-Four Finishers in World Cup Goals
and Expected Goals from 1998 to 2014**

1998	Games	GF	GA	GD	GF/Game	xG	GF—xG	xG/Game	Shots	SOG	OnTarget%	Poss%
France (1)	7	15	2	13	2.1	10.0	5.0	1.4	166	54	32.5%	53.6%
Brazil (2)	7	14	10	4	2.0	6.6	7.4	0.9	99	37	37.4%	52.8%
Croatia (3)	7	11	5	6	1.6	6.6	4.4	0.9	102	35	34.3%	42.1%
Netherlands (4)	7	13	7	6	1.9	7.6	5.4	1.1	144	54	37.5%	60.8%
United States (32)	3	1	5	-4	0.3	2.4	-1.4	0.8	50	12	24.0%	54.0%
Tournament Average	4	5.3	5.3	0	1.2	3.7	1.7	0.9	60	20	32.3%	49.5%

2002	Games	GF	GA	GD	GF/Game	xG	GF—xG	xG/Game	Shots	SOG	OnTarget%	Poss%
Brazil (1)	7	18	4	14	2.6	9.4	8.5	1.4	116	48	41.4%	48.9%
Germany (2)	7	14	3	11	2.0	7.2	6.8	1.0	124	35	28.2%	49.9%
Turkey (3)	7	10	6	4	1.4	4.5	5.5	0.6	80	27	33.8%	52.6%
Korea Republic (4)	7	8	6	2	1.1	7.2	0.8	1.0	112	45	40.2%	55.6%
United States (8)	5	7	7	0	1.4	3.6	3.4	0.7	63	26	41.3%	48.6%
Tournament Average	4	5.0	5.0	0	1.1	3.5	1.5	0.9	56	18	31.3%	49.9%

2006	Games	GF	GA	GD	GF/Game	xG	GF—xG	xG/Game	Shots	SOG	OnTarget%	Poss%
Italy (1)	7	12	2	10	1.7	7.3	4.7	1.0	98	38	38.8%	48.7%
France (2)	7	9	3	6	1.3	6.7	2.3	1.0	92	33	35.9%	48.9%
Germany (3)	7	14	6	8	2.0	7.2	6.8	1.0	140	42	30.0%	52.6%
Portugal (4)	7	7	5	2	1.0	7.2	0.0	1.0	123	44	35.8%	55.0%
United States (25)	3	2	6	-4	0.7	1.7	0.3	0.6	31	2	6.5%	50.2%
Tournament Average	4	4.6	4.6	0	1.2	3.4	1.2	0.8	58	19	31.3%	49.2%

2010	Games	GF	GA	GD	GF/Game	xG	GF—xG	xG/Game	Shots	SOG	OnTarget%	Poss%
Spain (1)	7	8	2	6	1.1	8.9	-0.9	1.3	126	35	27.8%	64.5%
Netherlands (2)	7	12	6	6	1.7	6.5	5.6	0.9	97	43	44.3%	52.4%
Germany (3)	7	16	5	11	2.3	8.7	7.3	1.2	106	37	34.9%	51.7%
Uruguay (4)	7	11	8	3	1.6	6.5	4.4	0.9	99	40	40.4%	42.2%
United States (12)	4	5	5	0	1.3	5.1	-0.1	1.3	67	24	35.8%	48.9%
Tournament Average	4	4.5	4.5	0	1.2	3.8	0.8	0.9	57	18	29.4%	49.0%

2014	Games	GF	GA	GD	GF/Game	xG	GF—xG	xG/Game	Shots	SOG	OnTarget%	Poss%
Germany (1)	7	18	4	14	2.6	15.9	2.2	2.3	99	48	48.5%	60.0%
Argentina (2)	7	8	4	4	1.1	10.1	-2.1	1.4	108	33	30.6%	53.6%
Netherlands (3)	7	15	4	11	2.1	13.1	1.9	1.9	89	40	44.9%	49.6%
Brazil (4)	7	11	14	-3	1.6	11.8	-0.8	1.7	112	44	39.3%	52.8%
United States (15)	4	5	6	-1	1.3	5.8	-0.8	1.4	44	14	31.8%	43.8%
Tournament Average	4	5.3	5.3	0	1.2	5.6	-0.3	1.3	53	18	33.3%	49.4%

Home-Field Advantage

Of the 20 World Cups, the host nation has been the champion six times (30 percent). Additionally, the hosts have made at least the semifinals six additional times, indicating that there may be a home-field advantage. Part of this may be that in the past, host nations have been soccer powers, as every team that has won the World Cup has hosted the event at some point. Recently, however, countries with less historical success at soccer have played the role of host and have done pretty well. This advantage probably helped the USMNT in 1994 (this also helps put the USMNT 1994 performance into more context), South Korea in 2002 (Japan, co-hosts with South Korea, also won their group), and Russia in 2018 (Russia lost to Croatia in the quarterfinals in penalty kicks). Since the

World Cup began in 1930, only host South Africa in 2010 failed to make it past the initial group stage.

There are many theories behind the reason for home-field advantage at a World Cup. According to an academic paper titled "Home Advantage in European International Soccer: Which Dimension of Distance Matters?" Nils Van Damme and Stijn Baert of Ghent University wrote that among the most debated theories are (1) crowd effects, (2) referee bias, (3) territorial effects, (4) travel effects, and (5) familiarity effects. Theories (1), (2), and (3) each relate to the fact that the home team typically receives stronger support from the crowd, which motivates the players of the home team and which tends to influence the referee's decisions in favor of the home team. Therefore, not surprisingly, many studies have found the larger the crowd, the greater the home-field advantage.

In 2003, Thomas Dohmen published a paper titled, "In Support of the Supporters? Do Social Forces Shape Decisions of the Impartial?" in which he analyzed the neutrality of referees during nine German Bundesliga seasons. He found that home-field advantage was smaller in stadiums with a running track surrounding the field than those without a running track. Why? Apparently, when the crowd sits closer to the field, the officials are more susceptible to getting caught up in the home crowd emotion. He wrote: "The social atmosphere in the stadium leads referees into favoritism although being impartial is optimal for them to maximize their reappointment probability." Referees are humans, impacted by senses like sound and a desire to be liked. Referees tend to favor the home team, as they systematically award more injury time in close matches when the home team is behind. Further evidence for similar home bias comes from referees' mistaken, or at least disputable, decisions to award goals and penalties. The severity of social pressure, measured by the crowd's composition and proximity to the action, determines its effect.[93] In a low-scoring game where opportunities to score goals are very valuable, like soccer, the referee decisions matter.

---

93. All of this assumes the home crowd is larger than the visiting crowd. This is not always true for USMNT matches.

Even in a game like basketball, where there are numerous opportunities to score, the proximity of fans and their reactions seem to have an influence on referees. According to professors Michael Lopez and Gregory Matthews' academic paper "How Often Does the Best Team Win? A Unified Approach to Understanding Randomness in North American Sport," in the NBA, the home team has the highest percentage of beating a team of equal strength (62 percent, as compared to 54 percent in MLB). NBA fans can sit right on the floor and referees make many quick judgment calls throughout the game that can lead to high-probability scoring opportunities (free throws) or changes of possession. American football, in which crowd reactions to key plays (e.g., pass interference or unsportsmanlike conduct) can influence a referee's decision, has the next highest home-field advantage percentage (59 percent).

Theories (4) and (5) address the fact that the away team may experience fatigue due to travel-related factors and that the home team has the advantage of being familiar with the circumstances of the city and the stadium, both resulting in a higher relative productivity of the home team. Crucial with respect to (4) and (5) are the actual distance between home and away teams, difference in altitude, difference in climate, and cultural differences. The cultural differences, travel distances, and overcrowded calendar most likely impacted the 2002 World Cup results, helping co-hosts South Korea.

USMNT fans often ask about Mexico's home-field advantage playing in Estadio Azteca in Mexico City, which is 7,200 feet (2,195 meters or 1.4 miles) above sea level. In addition, the stadium is often drowning in air pollution from the city, and Mexico prefers to play important matches in midafternoon, under the hottest sun. The sightlines are also difficult, as it's 20 yards from the touchlines to the dugouts and the playing surface is separated from the crowd by unsightly fencing and moat work. The environment creates an enormous problem for opponents.

According to a 2017 academic paper by Richard Pollard of California Polytechnic State University and Vasilis Armatas of National and Kapodistrian University of Athens titled "Factors Affecting Home Advantage in Football World Cup Qualification," every 1,000 meters

(3,280 feet) in altitude difference is worth an average of 0.115 of a goal advantage for the home team. This implies that at 2,195 meters, 1,000 equals 2.195, multiplied by a 0.115 advantage, equals a 0.25 goal advantage, assuming most American players play at sea level. Los Angeles and New York are 285 and 33 feet above sea level, respectively.

While not all of Mexico's players play at high altitudes most of the season, many of them are more familiar with playing at high altitude (most big matches are played in the Estadio Azteca in Mexico City) and play in the Mexican league (so they would play a few matches in Mexico City). Home-field advantage helped Mexico win the 1999 Confederations Cup, beating Brazil 4–3 in the Final at home as the host nation. Mexico's best progression in World Cups has been reaching the quarterfinals in both the 1970 and 1986 World Cups, both of which were staged on Mexican soil.

World Cup Host Advantage

Since 1974, the host nation has been treated as a seeded team, which provides the host nation an easier group and better chance to advance to the knockout round. This helped host countries the U.S. (1994), South Korea and Japan (2002), and Russia (2018), all of whom advanced to the knockout rounds. South Korea and Russia advanced to the semifinals and quarterfinals, respectively. As previously mentioned, South Africa (2010) is the only host nation that has failed to advance to the knockout round.

Talent Effect of Hosting a World Cup

We believe hosts of the World Cup receive a positive talent effect. The 2002 World Cup in South Korea and Japan had a similar effect to the 1994 World Cup in the U.S. In the 2018 World Cup, South Korea defeated Germany 2–0 in what was nicknamed the "Miracle of Kazan." Kim Young-gwon and Tottenham Hotspur's forward Son Heung-min scored the two goals for South Korea; they were born in 1990 and 1992 and were therefore 12 and 10 years old during the tournament, respectively. In interviews, Son has said, "I watched the [2002] games on TV…everyone [was] wearing red shirts in 2002, including myself…every moment in 2002 was fantastic." In the English Premier League, South Korea had Ki

In 1989, Paul Caligiuri (white jersey) scored "the shot heard around the world" against Trinidad and Tobago for the USMNT to qualify for the 1990 World Cup. (AP Images)

Christian Pulisic reacts to the USMNT's 1–2 loss to Trinidad and Tobago in 2017 and being eliminated from the 2018 World Cup. (AP Images)

A USMNT player is carried over water on the playing field in Trinidad and Tobago in 2017. (AP Images)

In the 2010 World Cup, Landon Donovan scored the last-minute, game-winning goal against Algeria. The USMNT won their group and advanced to the Round of 16. (Getty Images)

Teammates pile on Landon Donovan (not visible) following his goal.
(Getty Images)

Sunil Gulati introduces Jürgen Klinsmann (right) as the new USMNT coach in 2011. (AP Images)

Alexi Lalas celebrates his goal against England in the 1993 U.S. Cup. The USMNT won 2–0. (Getty Images)

The USWNT "'99ers," coached by Tony DiCicco, won the 1999 Women's World Cup at the Rose Bowl in Pasadena, California. (Getty Images)

The USWNT, coached by Anson Dorrance, won the first Women's World Cup in China in 1991. (AP Images)

Sung-yueng (born 1989), Lee Chung-yong (1988), and Son Heung-min (1990). Before the 2002 World Cup, no South Korean had ever played in the English Premier League.

In the 1994, 1998, and 2002 World Cups, there was only one player on the entire South Korean roster who even played in one of the Top Five Leagues in Europe. After 2002, however, the trend started to change. The host nation has home-field advantage, and if the host nation takes advantage and does well, its players gain more exposure. In 2006, there were two players playing in one of the Top Five Leagues, four in 2010, six in 2014, and three in 2018.

Japan has seen a similar effect. In 2018, Japan had a noteworthy tournament as well, finishing 1–1–1 in group play and eventually losing to very talented and eventual third-place finisher Belgium in the Round of 16. The rise in the number of Japanese players in the Top Five Leagues in Europe was initially slower than that of South Korea, but has seen an even more dramatic uptick in the past two World Cup cycles. In 1998, Japan did not have a single player on the roster who played outside of the domestic league. In 2002, there were only two players playing in one of the Top Five Leagues in Europe, the same number in 2006, and only one player in 2010. It took until 2014 to finally see the impact, but it was impressive nonetheless. In the 2014 World Cup, Japan had 10 players in the Top Five Leagues in Europe (six in the Bundesliga, two in the Premier League, and two in Serie A), and by 2018, that number had increased to 11. Since 2002, Japan and South Korea have also been the only two Asian nations to qualify for each subsequent World Cup.

Similarly, the USMNT's peak in talent was in 2006 to 2010, defined by number of minutes in the Top Five Leagues. The peak resulted from the energy and excitement of the 1994 World Cup being held in the U.S. and the identity of the team inspiring a group of talented young boys. One of the conditions for the U.S. to host the World Cup was that a domestic top-tier league was created to promote and grow the sport. These boys would now have the opportunity to play in newly formed Major League Soccer (which started playing matches in 1996) and 12 to 16 years later would reach peak soccer age in 2006 to 2010. For players not ready or able to go to Europe, Major League Soccer provided an opportunity for them to continue to develop. In addition, we believe the excitement of Pelé and other stars playing in the U.S. in the mid to late 1970s may have had a similar effect, leading to a generational talent boom in the early to mid-1990s.

If one doubts the ability of sport to take off after hosting a major event or stars having the ability to raise the profile of and interest in a particular sport, think of what happened to Spanish Olympic sports and Spanish basketball following the 1992 Olympics and "Dream Team" in Barcelona. Prior to 1992, Spain had previously earned 26 medals in 16 summer games. Since 1992, Spain have won 124 medals in seven summer games. In the 1992 Olympics, Spain lost to the Dream Team 122–81 and didn't qualify for the knockout rounds. In the 2012 Olympics, Spain, led by Pau and Marc Gasol, received a silver medal after losing 100–107 to the USA, led by Kobe Bryant, Kevin Durant, and LeBron James.

Chapter 6

2006 World Cup: Is Soccer in the U.S. Really Legitimate?

In 2003, Tim Howard was sitting in a Los Angeles dorm room during the national team's January training camp when he answered a call from an unrecognized number. Howard revealed to Gabby Carrier of the Colorado Rapids what happened next: "Hi. This is Tony Coton, a goalkeeping coach of Manchester United. We're interested in you and we're going to keep tabs on you." Tim remembered, "Once Manchester United called, I could have taken that to my grave. I didn't have to play a minute in Europe. I was like 'I made it, Manchester United called me.' I was over the moon...I wanted to get over there and prove myself..." Just like U.S. Soccer, Tim wanted to prove he was legitimate.

Tim Howard was born in North Brunswick, New Jersey, the son of an African American truck driver and his Hungarian wife, who worked for a container packing distributor. His father moved out when Howard was young and his parents divorced when he was three. Afterward, Howard lived with his mother. In the sixth grade, Howard was diagnosed with Tourette syndrome and obsessive-compulsive disorder (OCD). He would habitually count things and try to achieve unattainable perfection, and he learned relaxation techniques to ease his symptoms.

When Howard was 12 years old, Tim Mulqueen, a onetime assistant coach for the U.S. U-17 soccer team, saw his potential at a camp. He offered Howard free soccer coaching. A few years later, Peter Mellor, a former professional goalkeeper who was coaching for the USSF, saw Howard at an Olympic Development Program camp and placed him into the program. While Howard attended North Brunswick Township High School, he was a soccer and basketball star. In 1997, Mulqueen became the coach of the North Jersey Imperials of the United Systems of Independent Soccer Leagues and the goalkeeping coach of Major League Soccer's MetroStars (now the New York Red Bulls). Howard turned professional before graduating from high school when he signed with the Imperials. In 1998, Mulqueen brought Howard to the MetroStars. When Howard joined the MetroStars, he moved to Kearny, New Jersey. Tony Meola suggested he should live in Kearny, because, as he puts it, "It is a soccer town and a great place to live." Howard won MLS Goalkeeper of the Year award in 2001 after recording four shutouts and 146 saves. Then, in the middle of the 2003 season, Howard received a call notifying him that Manchester United wanted to sign him.

When Howard, then 24 years old, arrived at Manchester United's training grounds, legendary manager Sir Alex Ferguson stopped the team's practice drills to introduce him, and within moments the soon-to-be Red Devil was shaking hands with some of the biggest names in the soccer world, including Roy Keane, Rio Ferdinand, Ryan Giggs, Paul Scholes, the Neville brothers, Nicky Butt, and Ruud van Nistelrooy. At the time, the USMNT had a few players, such as goalkeepers Brad Friedel (signed with Liverpool in 1997 at 26 years old) and Kasey Keller (signed with Leicester City in 1996 at 27 years old) play in the English Premier League, but not Manchester United. No native U.S. player had ever managed to crack the Manchester United lineup. By the time Howard joined, under the coaching of Sir Alex Ferguson, Manchester United had won the English Premier League eight times from 1992–93 to 2002–03. In 2003, Manchester United was such a global powerhouse that its $258 million in revenues ranked No. 1 in the Deloitte Football Money League Rankings, $58 million ahead of second-place Juventus and $86 million ahead of sixth-place Real Madrid. Howard was being brought in to challenge Fabien Barthez, the goalkeeper for the French team that won the 1998 World Cup, 2000 Euros, and 2003 Confederations Cup. A young American-born player regularly starting for Manchester United was uncharted territory. In the blink of an eye, U.S. Soccer was pretty legitimate in at least one position, goalkeeper, which was a start.

In 2002, to the surprise of many, the USMNT made it to the quarterfinals, and played so well there many agreed the USMNT had appeared to outplay eventual tournament finalist, Germany. After a dismal performance in 1998 where they finished 32nd out of 32 teams, the USMNT had shown they deserved to be on the world stage. The USMNT's performance raised the expectations of their fans and the country alike. Simply playing in the World Cup was no longer a measure of success. By the time of their fifth consecutive World Cup appearance in Germany in 2006, U.S. Soccer fans and casual observers now expected the team to advance to at least the quarterfinals. This shift wasn't just due to their 2002 World Cup performance, but also to their 2006 World Cup qualifying performance.

With four games remaining in qualifying, the USMNT needed one more victory to qualify for the 2006 World Cup. Up next: Mexico. After a scoreless first half at Columbus Crew Stadium on September 3, 2005, the USMNT took the lead with a goal from midfielder Steve Ralston in the 53rd minute. Ralston was not always in the starting XI at Oakville High School in St. Louis and didn't have any major college scholarships. He went from playing at a local community college to being an All-American at Florida International to being drafted by a team in MLS, where he became the all-time career leader in assists, appearances, starts, and minutes played.

Four minutes later, Claudio Reyna delivered the ball to DaMarcus Beasley, who finished to make it 2–0, the final score line of the match— the same score as the 2002 World Cup Round of 16. Besides the win, the game was famous for Oguchi Onyewu's intimidating stare toward Mexico's Jared Borgetti during the game, which became known as "The Staredown," and remains an iconic image of the USA-Mexico rivalry and the toughness and grit of the USMNT. The USMNT had qualified for the 2006 World Cup with three matches to go. A few years earlier, no one would have thought it possible.

Ths USMNT's performance at the 2002 World Cup and in the CONCACAF qualifications for the 2006 World Cup and being ranked seventh in the world going into the tournament meant the expectations of the fans and the team themselves had risen sky-high.

2006 World Cup, Germany

When the draw for the 2006 World Cup was held in December 2005, the USMNT were hoping to avoid some of the better teams in the tournament. However, even with the USMNT winning CONCACAF qualifying and having a higher ranking at the time, due to the seeding system, which includes past performances, FIFA gave Mexico the No. 1 seed from the CONCACAF region. The USMNT had been drawn into Group E with the Czech Republic (ranked third), Italy (ranked 12th), and Ghana, which, despite being ranked 51st, were the African champions and recognized as a formidable force.[94] Only two teams would advance to the knockout rounds. It was considered the "Group of Death" for the tournament.[95] If 2002 was about good luck for the USMNT, 2006 was arguably about trying to overcome some tough luck, starting with the draw, and dealing with higher expectations. Despite the team's world ranking, the bookmakers had given the USMNT 100-1 odds to win the tournament, worse than they did at the 2002 World Cup (90-1).

Head coach Bruce Arena had used 46 players in the qualifying matches for the 2006 World Cup. When the final 23-player roster was announced, it included 12 players from the 2002 World Cup squad. Some of the stars from 2002 were on their last legs with the national team, while its younger stars were beginning to form the core of the future of the squad. For core players Kasey Keller and Claudio Reyna, 2006 would be their

---

94. Using October 2005, the same as what is used for the USMNT. Also, to be clear, this is not what was used for seeding at the time, but stays consistent with the most recent World Cups so that we can compare apples to apples.

95. The USMNT would be placed into a tougher group in 2014.

fourth World Cup, and it would be the third for Brian McBride and Eddie Pope. The young phenoms at the 2002 World Cup, Donovan and Beasley, were joined by rising talents such as Clint Dempsey, Oguchi Oneywu, and Eddie Johnson. Of the 23 players who made the trip to Germany, 18 would see minutes in the tournament.

Arena knew it was important during the World Cup that his players got to be with their families and enjoy themselves. So he had the team stay in a hotel in the center of Hamburg, Germany's second-largest city. He was trying to avoid the mistake made by his predecessor at the 1998 World Cup, when the players were stuck in a chateau outside Lyon, France. The atmosphere was more relaxed than the 2002 World Cup— some of the players brought golf clubs. Some players believe, in hindsight, it was maybe too relaxed. The Eagles invited the USMNT to their Farewell Tour concert in Hamburg on June 3, which the players couldn't attend for security reasons.

2006 FIFA World Cup: Group Stage, Game 1
June 12, 2006, at Gelsenkirchen
USA 0–3 Czech Republic
The Czech Republic were making their first appearance in the World Cup as a separate nation. Their last participation had come in 1990 when, as Czechoslovakia, they beat a young, inexperienced USMNT 5–1 en route to reaching the quarterfinals.[96]

In the 1990 tournament, it took 25 minutes for the Czechs to score. On June 12, 2006, the Czechs scored five minutes after the opening whistle. After the USMNT won the ball on a failed free kick by the Czechs, goalkeeper Keller quickly punted the ball upfield trying to free Bobby Convey on the left wing. However, Convey wasn't there, and the Czechs quickly took advantage and counter-attacked the Americans, whose defense was left disorganized and vulnerable. Czech defender Zdenek Grygera raced down the right flank, fielded a long pass from David Rozehnal, and launched an accurate cross to the sprinting Jan

---

96. Czechoslovakia split into a separate nation from Slovakia in 1993.

Koller. Koller nudged the 6'1" defender Eddie Pope aside, gaining some space. At 6'7½", Koller had a significant advantage. He headed the ball into the net from three yards out for a 1–0 lead.

At the time, the Czechs thought with a lead they would win the game. They had studied the USMNT closely and believed they could not easily break down disciplined and talented teams. The Czechs knew that when the USMNT tried, they would be vulnerable to counter-attacks. The Czechs added two more goals in the 36th and 76th minutes. Looking like what the Associated Press described as a "bewildered World Cup newcomer again," in reference to the 1990 match, the USMNT managed only one shot on goal during the entire game. The Czechs were all over Donovan and Beasley, the breakout stars of the year.

Arena wasn't often critical of his players in the media, but after the match, he said, "Landon showed no aggressiveness tonight…. We got nothing out of Beasley on the night." Convey was singled out as one of the few U.S. players who had "the courage" to attack. After the game Keller said, "We didn't play well. We didn't compete. We didn't make the plays…. It was just a shame. We definitely gave the game away, and that's what we're frustrated about."

The USMNT had Italy up in five days' time. Reyna said, "We all have to learn quick, especially the young guys…. We can't wait months or years to get better. We have to get better quickly, and I think we can do that."

Four years of planning and expectation, and two years of qualifying, unraveled disastrously in five minutes for the USMNT. As the World Cup entered its fourth day, the Americans suffered the ignominy of the tournament's most lopsided loss. "It was embarrassing," said Donovan. Coaches and players know losing the first game in a World Cup usually means the team is out of the tournament. They know that it impacts the mind-set of the team—negativity and doubt from all angles, especially the media, can start to consume a team's camp. They know their chances of advancing significantly decline. Turkey was the only team in the two previous World Cups to lose their first match and yet advance out of the group stage. Many highly ranked tournament favorites who lost their first game have quickly fallen apart in recent World Cups, including France, Germany, and Spain.

The USMNT hoped to possess an edge in speed, fitness, and health. But it was the supposedly aging and hobbled Czechs who proved to be the more lively, imaginative, and determined team, even with four starters over the age of 30. Pavel Nedved, the 2003 European Player of the Year, bounced around the field with his springy blond hair. The Juventus midfielder gave no hint that he would soon turn 34. He collected rebounds, deflections, and loose balls and carved through the midfield and defense. Juventus had been knocked out of the Champions League tournament in the quarterfinals in early April and had comfortably won Serie A by 15 points.[97] So, Nedved was rested.

Arena's lineup was four defenders, five midfielders, and one striker: a 4-5-1. Donovan was being utilized as a striker. Beasley was played out of position by being slotted on the right wing. Clint Dempsey was on the bench with Eddie Johnson, another young striker and the team's leading goal scorer (along with Donovan) during the qualifying campaign. Beasley criticized Arena's positioning of him in the second half, essentially at right back, after defender Steve Cherundolo was removed. "I was back there defending the whole time," Beasley said of Arena's tactical switch. "I don't know what he wants me to do." Beasley added that he did not expect to start in the Americans' next match, against Italy. Upon reflection years later, Arena acknowledged the confusion that had inadvertently been created, and how detrimental it was for the team: "A lesson I'll always take away from that game is that you never want to hear your players talking about not knowing their roles. Team chemistry and team communication were always my focus, going back to my first days as a coach, and I'd always taken the view that you wanted your players as comfortable as possible with what you expected of them. [What] DaMarcus said after the Czech Republic game…was ultimately on me…other players talked about having the sense that not everyone knew their role."

---

97. Before the title was awarded to Inter after the Calciopoli scandal.

Some of the key USMNT players said the team thought they were better than they were and thought they were good enough to compete with the best in the world because of the 2002 result. They believed the hype. They said in doing so, they lost their underdog mentality and grit.

The defeat for the USMNT was much more disheartening than the 1990 loss. Expectations were much higher. The 1990 American team was composed mostly of amateurs. This was a squad of professionals, ranked seventh in the world. Half of the USMNT team had played in a previous World Cup.

The Czechs were highly motivated to beat the USMNT. They didn't want to lose and be negatively compared to the 1990 Czech team. They also knew they couldn't take the Americans lightly and would need a win to have a chance to advance because they knew Italy were particularly strong. While the Czechs beat the USMNT, they paid a heavy price. They may have been rested for the first game, but they were still "too tired and old." During and after the game, key players were injured and exhausted. With a depleted team, the Czechs lost their next two matches against Ghana and eventual winner Italy. It was the luck of the draw that the USMNT faced the Czechs first, who were ready for them and willing to sacrifice everything for a chance to advance. Italy and Ghana benefited.

2006 FIFA World Cup: Group Stage, Game 2
June 17, 2006, at Fritz-Walter-Stadion, Kaiserslautern
USA 1–1 Italy
The USMNT dug themselves into a deep hole in their first match, losing 3–0 to the Czech Republic. That created a situation where the team needed to respond with an improved performance, and hopefully a victory, against Italy. The USMNT players were highly determined to prove they had the skills and grit to compete with a soccer power. The teams would meet on June 17, 2006, in Kaiserslautern, Germany, where lots of Americans resided due to a military base located there. This was the moment the USMNT desired, but they were going against one of the favorites to win the tournament.

Arena used the 4-5-1 formation again and also chose this opportunity to give up-and-coming 23-year-old striker Clint Dempsey his first chance in the World Cup. Dempsey, who would later go on to become one of the most celebrated USMNT players of all time, grew up in East Texas and always played with intensity—as if he had a chip on his shoulder.[98]

The USMNT came out on the attack, hoping to keep Italy on their toes and grab an early goal. However, it was Italy who struck first. In the 22nd minute, USMNT midfielder Pablo Mastroeni brought down Francesco Totti, giving Italy a free kick from 26 yards. Midfielder Andrea Pirlo put the ball low and Alberto Gilardino got behind the USMNT's defense, and his diving header off a set piece went into the back of the net to make it 1–0 Italy. It was uncharacteristic of the team to give up a set-piece goal. Several players made mental mistakes. Once again, the USMNT gave up an early goal, and the team struggled to score against disciplined defensive teams. There is a reason Italy's style of play is known as *catenaccio*, or "door bolt." Once they take a 1–0 lead, Italy rarely give it up.

However, something strange happened soon thereafter in the match. In the 27th minute, the USMNT took a free kick from the right flank and Italy defender Cristian Zaccardo tried to clear it with a volley. However, he badly mishit the ball with his left ankle and shanked it into his own net to tie the game at 1–1.

In the 28th minute, as Italy midfielder Daniele De Rossi went for a high bounce in the USMNT half of the field, he inexplicably threw an elbow into the left side of Brian McBride's face. It was a bizarre action. Blood poured down McBride's face as the Uruguayan referee Jorge Larrionda pulled out a red card. Referees keep an eye out for elbowing in particular. De Rossi was ejected, and Italy would have only 10 men for the rest of the match. The image of McBride walking off with his bloody face (he would later require three stitches) is one of the lasting images in U.S. Soccer history, representing the grit that defined U.S. Soccer.

---

98. Dempsey would be the first USMNT player to score a goal in three different World Cups.

Given the man advantage, the USMNT dialed up the aggression. Then, in the final minute of the half, Mastroeni harshly slid into Pirlo's left ankle with both feet, cleats up, and drew a red card.

In the 47th minute, USMNT defender Eddie Pope tackled Gilardino from behind, drawing his second yellow card of the match and thus a red card and mandatory ejection. Tens of thousands of USMNT supporters booed. The USMNT were now down to only nine men—a goalkeeper and eight field players. Three players were sent off in one match for just the fourth time in the history of the World Cup. The USMNT had gone from being about to go into halftime tied with Italy and having a man advantage to being down a man and fighting for their lives. The USMNT had a suspicion that the referees might give out more red cards and had practiced playing with 10 men versus 11. However, they never practiced nine versus 10, which is very different because of the spacing.

In June 2003, during a Confederations Cup match in France, Larrionda also generated controversy when he awarded Turkey a disputable penalty kick, and Turkey scored again later on a play that appeared to be offside. Larrionda was banned for six months in 2002 by Uruguay's soccer federation for unspecified "irregularities."

In the 52nd minute, the USMNT almost gave an own goal to Italy when Bocanegra's defending header from a set piece deflected off the USMNT's crossbar. The USMNT bravely continued to attack, and in the 66th minute DaMarcus Beasley, who had been substituted in for Dempsey a few minutes prior, appeared to score the go-ahead goal. Beasley sprinted into the penalty area and drilled a low shot into the net. The USMNT seemingly had a 2–1 lead, but McBride appeared to be clearly offside on the pass. The goal was called back. The USMNT was kept in the game largely because of an incredible performance from Keller that included a terrific save on a close-range toe-poke by Del Piero.

For the game, Italy had four shots on target compared to three for the USMNT. The USMNT defense played very well. While the game ended in a 1–1 draw, the clear winner in the hearts and minds of soccer fans were the Americans. After the game, Arena said, "When it was finally over, the players collapsed to the field in exhaustion. I really don't think they had any more to give. Not many teams could hold their poise like that. That's the kind of team the U.S. should be putting out there." Despite the red cards, they employed the grit, determination, and "never say die" attitude that would come to define the USMNT's identity.

The draw gave the USMNT their first point in any World Cup match in Europe. With Ghana having upset the Czech Republic, the point earned meant that the USMNT could advance if they defeated Ghana and Italy also beat the Czechs. Going into the tournament, the USMNT felt like if they could get a point in their first two matches, they would have a chance to advance. The USMNT may have been drained from playing so many minutes with only nine men, but they held on to their goal of advancing. For Italy, they stretched their unbeaten streak to 20 matches, the longest streak by the country since 1939. Italy would go on to win the 2006 World Cup by defeating France in penalty kicks, with Zinedine Zidane receiving a red card in the 110th minute of extra time. To provide context to the USMNT's performance, Italy didn't lose a game the entire tournament, beating Germany 2–0 in the semifinals. Italy tied two teams—the USMNT and France in the Final.

2006 FIFA World Cup: Group Stage, Game 3
June 22, 2006, at Frankenstadion, Nuremberg
USA 1–2 Ghana

The USMNT needed to beat Ghana to advance on June 22 in Nuremberg. It was an overcast afternoon and the weather was a lot cooler than it had been for the previous two games. The odd chants of "USA, USA" didn't seem to bother the small contingent of Ghana supporters, who were already singing and dancing and seemed confident they could at least get a draw and advance to the next round.

Ghana and the USMNT had to make changes to their lineups after the previous matches' red-card ejections. The USMNT put Jimmy Conrad in central defense to replace Eddie Pope, while Eddie Lewis moved into midfield at left wing in the absence of Pablo Mastroeni. DaMarcus Beasley also returned to the lineup in midfield, on the left side, where he generally felt more comfortable. Some observers were surprised that

Bruce Arena came out again with a 4-5-1 formation, instead of a 4-4-2. Also, he decided not to start Eddie Johnson, one of the team's fastest, most dangerous strikers. Most observers thought Johnson would likely start alongside Brian McBride. As a sub against the Czechs, Johnson did what few other USMNT players did that day—shoot.

From the start, the USMNT were on the attack, with Clint Dempsey and Lewis pushing up to join McBride. But, for the third straight match, the USMNT fell behind. In the 22nd minute, as Dempsey played a pass back to Claudio Reyna on the right flank, 27 yards from the USMNT goal, Ghana midfielder Haminu Draman dispossessed Reyna of the ball in the American defensive third. Reyna's left ankle bent awkwardly from the contact, and he dropped to the ground. Draman slotted the ball inside the far post, giving Ghana a 1–0 lead.

Reyna was carried off on a stretcher. He returned briefly before he was replaced by Ben Olsen in the 40th minute. Reyna had played solidly in the World Cup, and many wondered if the USMNT might fall apart without their captain. Instead, the USMNT fought back and in the 43rd minute, Dempsey blasted in an equalizer off a quick counter-attack with a right-footed volley from a mind-boggling curving cross by Beasley, who had stolen the ball in the midfield. Dempsey celebrated his first goal ever at a World Cup with a little heel-to-toe dance.

The excitement didn't last long. Only four minutes later, German referee Markus Merk made a call that altered the course of the game for the USMNT. Defender Carlos Bocanegra failed to clear a ball in the American end, popping it up instead. The ball was then headed into the penalty area, where the 6'4" Onyewu, jostling for a header, made contact with the 5'8" Razak Pimpong. Onyewu flicked the ball away with his head, but Merk ruled that he had fouled Pimpong from behind, taking him down. Merk awarded Ghana a penalty kick, and midfielder Stephen Appiah coolly drove it into the upper left corner while Kasey Keller dove the other way to put Ghana up 2–1. The penalty kick seemed to take an emotional toll on the USMNT. Inexplicably, the USMNT gave up early goals in all three matches and against the Czechs and Ghana they conceded second goals just before halftime. Now they would need to score two goals in the second half to advance.

Almost immediately in the second half, it was apparent that Ghana's strategy was to waste time, put all of their men behind the ball, and force the USMNT to try to break them down. The attack in the second half was far more effective when Johnson came off the bench in the 60th minute for Steve Cherundolo. The USMNT rallied and produced a couple chances—including a McBride header off the post from four yards out in the 67th minute after great wing play from Lewis—but could not put the ball into the net, a chronic problem at the 2006 World Cup. A minute later, Onyewu headed a free kick from Landon Donovan, but the ball sailed just over the crossbar.

The USMNT seemed to find it difficult to come up with fresh ideas of how to break down the stubborn Ghana team and in the end, it just wasn't meant to be. The USMNT were eliminated from the World Cup with the 2–1 defeat to Ghana.

The USMNT had 55 percent of possession and four shots on target to Ghana's three. The USMNT took 31 shots during the tournament with only four on goal and only scored twice, and one of those was an own goal.[99] It should be no surprise that in 1998 and 2006 the USMNT had 54 and 50 percent of possession, respectively—their opponents were willing to dare the Americans to come at them, especially after conceding early goals and leads, and counter-attack.

With another referee's judgments on Reyna being dispossessed and Onyewu's penalty, the narrative could have been different. Ghana would go on to lose 3–0 to Brazil in the Round of 16. Italy beat Australia 1–0 after a controversial penalty during stoppage time in the Round of 16, and would go on to win the tournament.

Argentina and Brazil were eliminated in the quarterfinals, leaving an all-European Final Four for only the fourth time (after the 1934, 1966, and 1982 tournaments). The tournament had a record number of yellow (345) and red (28) cards.

---

99. ESPN reports were used for game-by-game statistics. Data from OPTA was used for full tournament statistics.

Only four years after reaching the quarterfinals in 2002, the USMNT exited without a victory and with only one goal of their own in three matches. As in 1998, the USMNT finished last in the tournament. The team managed only two shots on goal during group play, the lowest of any team at the 2006 World Cup.

The USMNT played a 4-5-1 formation every match, which is considered a more defensive approach. However, the USMNT fell behind 1–0 with early goals in every match with this more conservative system. After the group stage of the 2006 World Cup, FIFAworldcup.com carried out a survey among their readers to find out which teams had failed to live up to expectations—the USMNT finished first. After 2002, few observers questioned players' decisions to play in MLS. After 2006, many observers questioned if more American players should have more ambition to play against a higher level of competition in Europe to improve. The perception was that the USMNT players were not skilled enough to score if teams played disciplined defense.

When examining the number of players and minutes in the Top Five Leagues, the USMNT were at a significant disadvantage compared to Italy and the Czech Republic.

Table: 2006 World Cup—USA & Opponents (Group Stage)

2006 World Cup—USA & Opponents (Group Stage)					
Team	World Rank (Pre-WC)	Average Age (Team)	Average Age (Starters)	# Players Top 5 League	# Minutes Top 5 League
USA	7	28.3	28.7	6	12,312
Czech Republic	3	28.5	28.5	12	34,419
Italy	12	28.2	27.4	23	76,704
Ghana	51	24.6	23.5	7	13,733
Group Total (ex. US)	66			42	124,856

The best chance for the USMNT would have been to play Ghana in the first group match or at least not play the fresh Czech Republic in the first match. The order of the draw could have impacted the narrative.

The tournament was a sign of the growth of the sport in the U.S., as almost 10 million people watched the U.S.-Italy game, and 120 million watched at least a minute on television. This compares to 2002, where in the U.S., a gross audience of more than 85 million TV viewers, or an average of 1.3 million per match, watched the World Cup. The largest U.S. audience for a single match was the nearly seven million viewers (four million live) who watched Germany defeat the USA 1–0 in the quarterfinals. That game was broadcast live on ESPN, and replayed later that day on ABC. The Final of the 2006 World Cup between France and Italy had a 7.0 television rating on ABC, which was higher than the NBA Finals. Tens of thousands of Americans traveled to Germany to watch the World Cup. The USSF was allocated 19,000 tickets and received over 60,000 requests. As recently as the 1998 World Cup in France, only a few hundred supporters and Sam's Army were spotted in the stadiums.

The American Outlaws

By the 2006 World Cup, Sam's Army had grown to over 10,000 unofficial members. However, sometime after the 2006 World Cup, the membership started to decline. The original young trailblazers of Sam's Army from the 1990s had gotten older and their lives and responsibilities had changed.

In 2007, Korey Donahoo, Justin Bruken, and Ben Cahoon in Lincoln, Nebraska, founded the American Outlaws, another unofficial supporters' group for the USMNT, as well as the USWNT. In 2010, the American Outlaws provided a travel package for members to attend the World Cup in South Africa. The American Outlaws can be readily identified by their red membership shirts and American flag bandanas, and most often sit behind one the goals during the games waving scarves, banners, and flags. They are frequently accompanied by a drum corps made up of members dressed like popular American icons such as George Washington (Spirit of '76) and Rocky Balboa (the "underdog"). While they take inspiration from European club supporters' groups (including painting tifos and holding up supporter scarves), their traditions and rituals also take inspiration from the engagement of college football, complete with night-before parties to meet fellow fans, tailgating hours before games, marching into the stadium, and a supporter section. Over time, the American Outlaws have become the primary supporters' group. As of 2020, they have 30,000 members and 200 chapters, and have become the public face of U.S. Soccer fandom.

Chapter 7

Coaches' Second World Cup Cycles: Can They Work?

2006 Second World Cup Cycle

After the 2006 World Cup, the time was most likely right for a definite change of leadership—a fresh start. It was the second time that the USMNT didn't win a game and finished last in a World Cup hosted in Europe. In 2006, Bruce Arena had momentum from a highly successful qualifying tournament. He was criticized for experimenting with personnel placement—most notably putting DaMarcus Beasley on the right side, where he was uncomfortable. However, putting aside the reversion to the mean, we believe Arena was dealing with what we label the "too-tired-and-old effect" and "blinded-by-loyalty-and-experience effect," which are common for coaches who coach a second World Cup cycle. In addition, while probabilities indicate a coach will have a poor second cycle, Germany's Joachim Löw and France's Deschamps showed it can be done, and we explain the similarities as to why. However, in 2018, on his third cycle, Löw and Germany eventually succumbed to the "too-tired-and-old effect" and the "blinded-by-loyalty-and-experience effect."

In order to better understand and provide context for what happened to the USMNT in 2006, in this chapter we more closely investigate and explain these effects. *If you don't feel like you need more background or a*

179

deeper understanding of these topics, please feel free to skip to the next chapter on the 2010 World Cup.

Too-Tired-and-Old Effect

In 2006, the average age of the USMNT team was 28.3 years old, which was exactly the same as in 2002. However, the average age of the starters (defined by the starting lineup for the first match of each World Cup) in 2006 was older, at 28.7 (29 median), versus the 2002 average of 27.4 (28 median). In addition, the average age of the 12 players who were on both teams was 29.8, past what is considered peak age in soccer. Compared to World Cup champions in the modern era (1994–2018 World Cups), where the average age of both the team and the starting XI was 26.5, even the 2002 USMNT starters were older on average. And 2002 was interesting in that there was a good balance between the young up-and-comers and older veterans, whereas in 2006, that wasn't as much the case—the team simply aged.

The too-tired-and-old effect matters because speed, endurance, and peak age are more important than ever in soccer today. With the high pressing tactics, this is even more pronounced because once a player loses the ball, the player immediately attempts to win it back.

Too Tired

Age matters because veterans get tired—too tired. In the 1970s, an average soccer player ran approximately 2.5 miles per 90-minute game. Today, an analysis of the maximum running distances of players in Champions League games shows that the average soccer player runs approximately 7.1 miles in a game (the minimum is 3.5 miles; maximum is 8.5 miles). The largest distances are covered by central midfielders (approx. 7.5 miles), followed by outside midfielders (approx. 7.45 miles), outside defenders (approx. 7.1 miles), forwards (approx. 7.0 miles), and central defenders (approx. 6.6 miles). Studies have shown that with the increased distances covered today, players slow in the second half of play. The rules of soccer, unlike basketball, limit the ability to rest players. In basketball, coaches can rest older players to keep them fresh for key moments. The San

Antonio Spurs, for example, won the NBA Championship in 2014 by resting their three biggest stars on the bench 43 percent of the time. In contrast, soccer's limit of just three substitutions per game puts a premium on endurance above all else. The only way for a player to compensate for fatigue is with craftiness and technique—a tremendously difficult feat for even small losses in speed and stamina.

While this is probably intuitive, it raises the obvious question—so what? The answer lies in the timing of when the most goals are scored. Using the 2014 World Cup as an example, if each match is broken down into 15-minute increments and then the number of goals that were scored in each part of the game are added up, an interesting pattern emerges: 41 of the 171 goals scored during the entire tournament (24 percent, compared to the 16.6 percent that 15 minutes represents) came between the 76th and 90th minute of the match.

In basketball, during the regular season there is one primary team goal: win the NBA Championship. In soccer, however, for the big clubs with the best players, they are often vying for several trophies in a single season. Players also have obligations to their national teams, which rely upon them to perform at the highest level in international competitions. Many of the club tournaments and international qualifiers and friendlies go on during the regular season while the clubs are competing for their domestic championships. All of these competing priorities especially impact the club teams with the best players on national teams. They also impact the countries with many players on teams that advance to the semifinals or finals of European or domestic tournaments or are fighting to the end of the season for a league trophy or standing. The domestic league standings matter in European soccer because it is the top two to four clubs that qualify for the Champions League the following year (and for teams at the opposite end of the league table, relegation is at stake).

The multiple priorities profoundly complicate the leadership challenge for soccer team coaches and decision-makers. The best players who play on the best teams get too tired (and if they are older, the effect is more pronounced), and that often leads to suboptimal performance, or even worse, injury. It is noteworthy that the risk of injury increases dramatically for players whenever they exceed 3,000 to 3,5000 minutes played in a season (which roughly equates to 33 to 39 full 90-minute matches). To put this into context, this amount of playing time is not uncommon for a world-class superstar whose team competes not only in its respective domestic league, but also in the Champions League and domestic cups over the course of a single season. For example, in the 2018–19 season, Cristiano Ronaldo played in 43 matches totaling close to 3,650 minutes representing Juventus in Italy's Serie A and Messi played in 50 matches totaling just over 4,000 minutes representing Barcelona in Spain's La Liga. In the context of the World Cup and the impact this can have, Portugal's Luís Figo showed up for the 2002 World Cup with an injured ankle and only a few weeks' rest after winning the Champions League with Real Madrid. Given the above statistic, it is not entirely surprising Figo was injured—he had just come off a 47-game season, having played close to 4,000 minutes total.

Too Old

In an interview with the media, Arena admitted that some of the veteran players who were instrumental in getting the team to the 2006 World Cup were a little too old by the time the tournament actually started—they were "simply not good enough to make us better in 2006." The World Cup is a unique challenge in and of itself because not only does a coach have to put together the best team to qualify for the tournament (otherwise there is no World Cup), but the team also has to achieve peak performance at a discrete moment in time that occurs once every four years. This creates a frustrating dichotomy where the benefit of the qualifying campaign is to have players play together and become familiar with each other in an international setting, but by the time the World Cup actually happens, those same players might not actually be the best for the team.

The first two years after a World Cup are somewhat of a wash—it is a time for a coach (new or old) to test new players and give younger guys a shot and to experiment with lineups and different combinations of players to test chemistry. The next one to two years, however, get much more serious and the focus shifts to identifying the 23 players who give a country the highest chance of success, and qualification is at stake. The reality is that a lot can still happen in those two years as players age—for better or worse. Younger players can get the necessary experience needed to be ready to compete. Older players are susceptible to a decline in performance as they pass peak age, and each position may be different depending on many factors. Everyone is at risk of injury, regardless of age, although, as we go into in more detail shortly, older players are at much greater risk. And so picking the team and then making decisions about who to start, playing time, etc., is extremely difficult.

Many key veterans in 2006 were past peak age—or "too old." For the USMNT, a player like Jeff Agoos is the perfect example of where this effect was particularly pronounced, even in 2002. Agoos is arguably one of the most talented USMNT defenders in history, having been named MLS defender of the year in 2001 and one of the MLS All-Time Best XI in 2005, and having won five MLS championships over the course of his career. During his prime in MLS, he was playing about 30 games per season, averaging more than 2,500 minutes. However, at the time of the 2002 World Cup, Agoos was 34 years old and unfortunately, he was slightly slower than he was at peak age, especially for international competition. (Father Time is undefeated.) In 1994, Agoos was one of the last players cut from the final squad; in the 1998 World Cup, in spite of coming off a stellar domestic and qualifying season, he did not play a single minute during the tournament, as Sampson made late changes. The 2002 World Cup was his last chance. Arena chose to go with his veteran defender for the first three group stage games, where he scored an own goal versus Portugal and then suffered a calf injury versus Poland that caused him to miss the rest of the tournament. Agoos seemed to be just a half step behind those he was charged with defending, and like Figo, with his age and wear and tear on his body over the seasons, his injury was not at all surprising.

Earnie Stewart, the second oldest on the team in 2002 at 33 years old, fits this pattern as well. Similar to Agoos, Stewart was a fixture on the USMNT and was instrumental in the qualifying campaign.[100] He also had

---

100. Stewart was named Honda Player of the Year, having led the team with five goals and played every minute of every match.

plenty of time on the field, starting twice and appearing in four games, but he too was unable to stay healthy. In the opening match against Portugal, Stewart's corner kick led to the first USMNT goal. Unfortunately, he limped off at halftime with a strained left groin, an injury that forced him to miss the game against South Korea and limited his effectiveness against Poland and Mexico.

In hindsight, Arena maybe could have selected or utilized younger players in 2006 as preparation for 2010, similar to Bob Gansler's controversial decision to favor youth over experience for the 1990 World Cup, which would help set up the USMNT for the 1994 World Cup. However, the expectations were to win now, as the team had reached the quarterfinals in the 2002 World Cup. The expectations from an unfair comparison pressured the coach to take fewer risks and favor experience.

The Economist's Study

In a July 2014 article titled, "Player Age in Football: The Clock Is Ticking," *The Economist* tried to analyze the impact of age in a World Cup. Admittedly, this is difficult because so many other variables also influence performance. In order to isolate the age factor, *The Economist* compared teams of otherwise roughly similar skill. One simple way they controlled for overall quality was to limit the study to defending World Cup champions, all of whom were good enough to win a title four years before the tournament in question. *The Economist* found that within this group, age seems to have a remarkably strong impact. The single strongest factor that influenced performance was probably the (close to) home-field advantage: teams that played on their own continent performed nearly six places better in the final standings than those that had to travel farther afield. But after adjusting for the effect of geography, a one-year increase in average age was associated with a four-place drop in performance. In other words, if a reigning champion simply brought back its roster from four years before, its mean age would increase by four years, and it would be expected to finish a dismal 17th. Although the sample of defending champions is small, the examples seem compelling.

When Italy repeated as the champion in 1938—they are still one of only two teams to win back-to-back World Cups—they had the second-youngest team of any returning champion in tournament history.

Brazil won the tournament and their first World Cup title in 1958 by defeating host country Sweden 5–2 in the Finals. This was also the debut of 17-year-old Pelé, who would go on to lead Brazil to two more World Cup titles in the next three cycles (1962 and 1970). The average age for this team was 25.3 and there were only two players on the team who were aged 30 or above.[101]

One-third of World Cup winners won with an average age below 26, including Spain in 2010. On the other hand, France in 2002 and Italy in 2010 had two of the oldest squads after winning their respective World Cups, and neither won a single match.[102] As of today, Italy is the only team to have won a World Cup with an average player age older than 28, which happened when they defeated France in the final in 2006.

**Table: Average Age of Team and Final Standing
for Defending FIFA World Cup Champions**

Team	Defending Team	Average Age of Team	Final Standing*
2018	Germany	26.5–27.0	20–25
2014	Spain	27.5–28.0	20–25
2010	Italy	28.0–28.5	20–25
2006	Brazil	28.0–28.5	2–5
2002	France	28.0–28.5	25–30
1994	Germany	28.5–29.0	2–5

*Adjusted for continental advantage

---

101. When Brazil repeated as champions in 1962 by defeating Czechoslovakia 3–1, the average age of the team was 27.3 and there were eight players aged 30 or above. Amazingly, Brazil used only 12 players during the entire tournament, which is a record that has never been broken. This feat would essentially be impossible in modern times, given player fatigue and the increased physical demands of today's game. The number of games played by a typical player in a club season at that time (for the Brazilian team, it was in Campeonato Brasileiro Série A by the time the 1962 World Cup came around) was a fraction of what it would be today, and is likely the reason why some of Brazil's aging stars, in addition to their immense talent, could continue to be effective in each successive game of the tournament. In 1966, the average age of the Brazilian team dropped back below 27, but they didn't make it out of the group stage. In 1970, when Brazil became champions for the third time in history, the average age of the team dropped again to an astounding 24.4 years old, with only two players over the age of 30.

102. France seemed to have learned its lesson, as the average age of the 2018 World Cup winning team was 25.6 and the average age of the starting lineup for the first match was 24.2!

The Economist discovered that if the oddsmakers placed a greater weight on this variable, they would have been far more bearish on Spain's chances in 2014—when they didn't advance out of the group stage. Spain's players in the 2014 World Cup had an average age of 28, two years older than those who won in South Africa in 2010. Based on that factor alone, they would not even have been expected to reach the quarterfinals. Why does age seem to be a key factor in World Cup performance? While there is clearly some value to experience and mastering the intricacies of the game, as we previously mentioned, the raw physical demands of soccer at the highest level have grown significantly.

Peak Age

Many factors (such as genetics, diet, conditioning, and previous injuries) determine a player's peak age, and it can vary significantly from athlete to athlete. The timing may vary but unfortunately the results are unavoidable: athletic performance declines for a player after a peak age. Also, the older a player is, the longer it takes to recover to be able to compete at peak performance. When analyzing data, it is important to understand context. Age is often neglected when reviewing statistics. Sian Allen and Will Hopkins, at the Sports Performance Research Institute in New Zealand, examined scientific literature to determine the age at which athletes competing in various sports hit peak competitive performance. They found male sprinters hit their peak around 25 years of age; male Olympic distance triathletes peak at 27 years old; male marathoners are their best at the age of 30; and male triathletes in the Ironman, which consists of a 2.4-mile swim, a 112-mile bicycle ride, and a 26.2-mile run, are at their best at the age of 32. Generally, the authors noticed that athletes competing in "sprint" events requiring explosive power peak much sooner than athletes competing in endurance or game-oriented events, perhaps because older athletes are able to use experience and savvy to their advantage. Glaringly missing from the review was soccer because there are so many variables that impact performance. However, they believe soccer peak age is probably closer to sprinting (25) than endurance (32). As a result, many estimate modern soccer players tend to peak under age 28, but will vary by position as well as style of play and tactics used.

Ideally for any national team, the best players would play in two World Cups at the peak of their career. When other countries have had successful second cycles, many players on the final roster made their World Cup debut in their early twenties, and were therefore right in the middle of their "peak age" on the second cycle. In the U.S. however, this happens less frequently, with many players making their debut at much older ages (i.e., over the age of 28), which is a problem. For the USMNT, in 1998 those players who had not previously played in a World Cup were on average 27 years old, with three players over the age of 28. In 2002, the average age of that cohort dropped to 25.5 years old, with four players 28 or older. In 2006, that number jumped to 26.5 (on Bruce Arena's second cycle as coach), and there were again four players aged 28 or older. In 2010 under Bradley, the average age dropped back down to 25.1, with four players 28 or older. And in 2014, the average age of players making their World Cup debut jumped back up again to 26.5, with six players aged 28 or older, and five of those six were *over the age of 30*. Based on this data, it is no surprise that the USMNT struggled leading up to the 2018 World Cup—the core of the team was just too old.

On the 2010 Germany World Cup team, the average age of the players making their World Cup debut was 24.1, and three of those 16 players (19 percent) were 28 or older. It is also notable that nine of those players making their debut were 23 or younger, including future stars such as Thomas Muller, Mesut Özil, Toni Kroos, and Jérôme Boateng. For France, Raphaël Varane and Paul Pogba are two great examples of players who got an opportunity (and did incredibly well) in 2014 at the age of 21, and then went on to be even more effective in 2018.

Blinded-by-Loyalty-and-Experience Effect

Coaches are understandably reluctant to leave stars who helped them exceed expectations in the previous World Cup cycle and/or who helped them qualify for the current World Cup on the bench or off the team altogether. The coaches have personal relationships with these players who have delivered for them in key situations. Let alone how much it can aggrieve fans, promoting a newcomer over a veteran is an asymmetric risk. However, the preference toward veterans could easily sow friction among players, which impacts team culture and chemistry.

Kasey Keller was another big name to see more playing time in 2006, having been a member of the 1990 (backup to Tony Meola), 1998 (starter), and 2002 (backup to Brad Friedel) World Cup teams. He and Claudio Reyna were also the first two members of the USMNT to be named to four World Cup rosters. There were two players on the team, Brian McBride and Eddie Pope, who had played in the two previous World Cups, and then another eight players (including Landon Donovan and DaMarcus Beasley) who had played in the one prior. Overall for the 2006 team, 12 players had previous World Cup experience with 18 tournaments between them. That compares to 2002, where 11 players had previous experience (six had played in the two previous World Cups and five had played in one) with 17 tournaments between them.

There is only one other USMNT World Cup team (loosely speaking) that has had as much experience as the 2006 team, and that was the 23-man roster put together by Bruce Arena that made up the USMNT for the ill-fated qualifying game in 2017 against Trinidad & Tobago. There were 14 players (60 percent) who had previous World Cup experience, with a combined total of 25 tournaments between them. One player, Beasley (35 years old), had played in the four prior World Cups. Two players, Clint Dempsey (34 years old) and Tim Howard (38 years old), had played in the three prior. Four players had played in the two prior, and then the remaining seven players had played only in 2014. Unsurprisingly, the average age of the team at the time was 29.6 and the average age of the starting XI for that game was 27.2. Like in 2006, Arena fell into the trap of being overly reliant on veterans and players he was more familiar with.

The evidence suggests that coaches would be well advised to seriously reconsider relying on too many players over 30 years old at a World Cup because of the precipitous decline after peak performance or ability to maintain their level for the calendar during a World Cup or risk of injury. The older Czech team that the USMNT played in 2006 had several players who were injured or could not play a full 90 minutes the next match after beating the USMNT in the first match. They may have been rested for their first game against the USMNT, but they were still "too tired and old." With a depleted team, the Czechs lost their next two matches against Ghana and eventual winner Italy.

Germany's Second and Third Cycle

In the 2010 World Cup, Joachim Löw coached Germany to a third-place finish, the same as Jürgen Klinsmann in 2006. The average age of the team in 2010 was 25.0, and for the starters the average was 24.8. In the 2014 World Cup, on his second cycle, in which Germany won, the team aged slightly to 25.7, and the average age of the starters was 25.9. Löw selected 11 players from the previous squad, six of which were starters both times and whose average age was 27.2. Given how young the team was in 2010, this is where gaining experience was actually helpful.

After winning the 2014 World Cup, Löw was given an opportunity to repeat. In the 2018 World Cup, Germany lost to Mexico and South Korea and had a nervy, last-gasp win over Sweden. Germany finished 22nd, the worst any German team had done in the history of the tournament. In the 20 World Cups that have taken place since 1930, which Germany did not enter, the team has participated in 19 of them (the only one they missed was in 1950, when they were banned), never finishing worse than 10th place (and seventh in modern times, which equates to reaching at least the quarterfinals every single time). To say that 2018 was a disappointment would be an understatement. The average age of that team was 26.7, which is still fairly young. The average age of the starting XI, however, was 27.4, which is older than that of any team that has won the World Cup since 1998 (and in 1998, France won in France). Löw selected nine players who were also on the 2014 team, six of whom had played in 2010 as well. Even more importantly, seven of the nine were starters in both 2014 and 2018, whose average age in 2018 was 29.4, and four of the six were starters in all three World Cups (2010, 2014, 2018), whose average age was 30.0.

Germany qualified for Russia with a perfect record of 10 wins but, as Mats Hummels admitted after their defeat to South Korea, the last time the team had played well together was late 2017. One year made a big difference and revealed Löw's misguided loyalty. Of the six players on the German squad who were playing their third World Cup, *all six of them started*. Their average age was 29.5. It was the too-old effect and being blinded by loyalty and experience. Despite only recently returning from a fractured foot that kept him out of play since September 2017, Bayern Munich's goalkeeper Manuel Neuer (32) was selected over Barcelona's Marc-André ter Stegen (25) to start. Neuer made his first appearance since his injury on June 2, 2018, in a 2–1 friendly defeat to Austria. Toni Kroos (28) is the midfielder who controls Germany's tempo. Nevertheless, he was mentally and physically tired from a long season campaign culminating with winning the Champions League with Real Madrid on May 26, 2018. Germany's first match against Mexico in the 2018 World Cup was June 17. He was a shadow of his usual self in Russia, only redeeming himself with the winning goal against Sweden—the too-tired effect. For the 2017–18 season, Kroos had played a total of 43 matches and 3,570 minutes. In 2018, Löw clearly went with experience, and the results showed the consequences of what happens if players are past their peak age. Experience is only valuable up to a point.

Coach Löw could have gone with more youth. Germany won the previous year's 2017 Confederations Cup without their older stars, but Timo Werner (22) was the only emerging star to be given a regular starting berth in the senior team. Leon Goretzka (23), who led Germany's midfield brilliantly at the Confederations Cup; Niklas Süle (22); and Julian Brandt (21) were only given their chance when Löw's first-choice stars were suspended or injured. Seven of the starting XI against South Korea did not feature in the Confederations Cup. Germany's U-21 team had won the European Championship the previous summer, and Germany's U-23 team finished second in the 2016 Olympics. Yet none of them were present in Russia, and that is telling. Löw also decided to omit Manchester City's Leroy Sane, the Premier League's Best Young Player the previous season, from the World Cup squad. According to Opta, Sane recorded the highest top speed in the Premier League.

Any coach or player will tell you that the margins between success and failure can be incredibly fine. German defender Mats Hummels had a relatively easy header six yards out against South Korea in the 86th minute. If he had scored, Germany probably would have made it through to the Round of 16. Instead, the ball hit his shoulder, bouncing out—just as Germany was.[103]

France's Second Cycle

France won the 2018 World Cup with Didier Deschamps on his second cycle after finishing seventh in 2014. But similar to Germany, the average age of the team and the starters both declined from the 2014 World Cup to 2018 World Cup, and of the four players who started both years, the average age was 27.0. Keep in mind, the 2018 World Cup was French speedster and goal scorer Kylian Mbappé's first—similar to Landon Donovan's first in 2002. They both won the Best Young Player Award at their respective World Cup debuts. Second cycles can work if there is a perfect blend of experience, youth, and clearly defined expectations and roles for players.

Similar to the USMNT team in 2002, France had a great mix of youth (and speed) and experience, and a formidable leader in captain and goalkeeper Hugo Lloris, 31 at the time. To put France's mix in perspective, there were 15 players on the team who were 25 or younger, which was complemented by five players in their thirties. This meant that the team was made up of a core group of young players who saw a lot of time on the field and then had a solid handful of veterans, including their captain.[104]

In addition to Mbappé, Paul Pogba and Raphaël Varane, both 25 in 2018, were two notable young players who started in both 2014 and 2018. Pogba, a mainstay on Manchester United, played almost every minute of every game in 2018, scored a crucial goal in the Final, and saw significant minutes in 2014 as well, when he won the Best Young Player Award for his performance. Varane, who plays for Real Madrid and had

---

103. South Korea scored the winning goal in the 90th minute +3 off a set piece—a corner kick.

104. Of the players in their thirties, only Lloris started and of the players who were 25 and under, eight of them started.

already won four Champions League titles by 2018, also saw significant playing time in both World Cups. He played all 90 minutes of every game in 2014 except for the last group stage game versus Ecuador, was nominated for the Best Young Player Award (but lost out to Pogba), and then in 2018 played every minute of every game. With France's victory, Varane became only the fourth player to be a World Cup champion and Champions League winner in the same year, after Christian Karembeu (1998), Roberto Carlos (2002), and Sami Khedira (2014). All the players, like Varane, were playing for Real Madrid at the time they won the World Cup.

Chapter 8

2009 Confederations Cup: Second Place at a FIFA Tournament

Bob Bradley

After the 2006 World Cup, in mid-July 2006, Dan Flynn, the USSF's general secretary, and Bruce Arena flew into New York's La Guardia Airport and met with Sunil Gulati for five hours at the United Red Carpet Club to debrief about the tournament. In March 2006, Gulati, a 46-year-old economics professor at Columbia University who had also served six years as vice president of the USSF, had been elected president of the USSF by the membership of U.S. Soccer, the sport's governing body.

After the meeting at the airport, Gulati announced the USSF would not be renewing Arena's contract. Gulati said, "For him to be there eight years is unrivaled. He has given the U.S. credibility worldwide and achieved in the summer of 2002 what has caused so much consternation because the expectations were so much higher." With the statement, it appears Gulati was acknowledging the fight for the legitimacy of U.S. Soccer, and that 2002 had reset expectations. Those rising expectations, a result of the USMNT having advanced to the quarterfinals in the 2002 World Cup, were clearly not met at the 2006 World Cup. Arena was the longest tenured among the 32 coaches at the 2006 World Cup. With a 71–30–29 record, at the time, Arena was also the most successful national team coach in U.S. Soccer history, surpassing Bora Milutinović, who went 30–35–31 from 1991 to 1995, and Sampson, with a record of 26–22–14 from 1995 to 1998.

In a 2006 article, Jack Bell of the *New York Times* wrote, "Arena, who often was bluntly outspoken about his team and the state of the game in the United States, was able to forge a special bond with his players as he assumed the mantle as the de facto spokesman for American soccer. As an accomplished American coach, he seemed to have been the right man at the right time. *That equation appears to have changed amid rising expectations and an American sporting mentality that assumed there would be a natural progression from quarterfinalist four years ago.*" (Our italics for emphasis.) We believe Bell was right: the USSF, USMNT, media, and fans had developed unrealistic "rising expectations" from a flawed comparison and then added an unrealistic "natural progression."

Gulati said the search for Arena's successor would not be restricted to someone who "holds a U.S. passport or resides in the U.S." but added that the next coach would need "some knowledge of American soccer, experience, leadership, a track record of success." It seemed like an obvious reference to Jürgen Klinsmann. Klinsmann, who lived in Southern California with his family near the USMNT training base at the Home Depot Center in Carson, California, had won the World Cup as a player and coached his native Germany to a third-place finish at the 2006 World Cup. Many considered Klinsmann the best replacement because he had serious World Cup and European soccer credentials, which added "legitimacy," and was familiar with America and soccer in the U.S. However, he reportedly withdrew his candidacy at the time because he wanted more say in how the USMNT was operated than the USSF was willing to give him.[105]

Gulati named Bob Bradley the interim coach of the USMNT. Bradley had been coaching MLS' Los Angeles–based Chivas USA, and had been

---

105. Reportedly, Klinsmann wanted control over almost all areas, including marketing—which is not typical for a national team coach.

MLS coach of the year in 2006 for reviving the club. Unfortunately, the flirtation with Klinsmann seemed to linger over Bradley's tenure as interim couch. In a December 8, 2006, article in the *New York Times* titled "After Klinsmann Says No, a Temporary Solution Is Found," Jeré Longman wrote, "Gulati was believed to have favored a coach like Klinsmann who had the international recognition and the standing to assertively influence the direction of soccer in the United States."

Bob Bradley played at Princeton and landed his first job as a coach, at Ohio University in 1981, when he was 22. He was Arena's assistant at Virginia in 1983 before taking over as the coach at Princeton in 1984. He rejoined Arena as an assistant with D.C. United when Major League Soccer began operations in 1996 and then became the first coach of the Chicago Fire when that team joined MLS in 1998. Bradley won the MLS Cup title with Chicago in 1998 and led the league in career victories with 124.

Bradley was given the opportunity to win the job as the full-time national team coach while other candidates were being considered. He was widely considered to be a future USMNT coach, perhaps for the 2014 World Cup cycle. By the end of the year, as the USSF continued their search for a permanent successor to Bruce Arena, the USMNT dropped to 31st in the FIFA rankings.

Bradley seized his opportunity and quickly went about building a strong foundation for the team, introducing younger players to the squad and approaching the job as though he already was, or would soon become, the permanent coach. His tenure began successfully, and after a series of promising friendlies that included a 3–1 victory over Denmark in January 2007 and a 2–0 win over Mexico in February 2007, the USSF removed Bradley's interim title and officially named him manager on May 15, 2007. Although happy with the wins, an American competitive sporting attitude, unrealistic expectations, and flawed comparisons still led many media members and fans to be somewhat disappointed that a "high-profile European or international coach" wasn't hired. The disappointment resonated from their feeling that such a coach would add legitimacy to U.S. Soccer. Undeterred, Bradley continued his success that summer, leading the USMNT to the 2007 Gold Cup Final on June 24, where they beat rival Mexico 2–1 for the second time in four months.

Bradley's approach is simple. He is a coach who leaves no detail to chance. His players all know their roles and responsibilities, and he is meticulous for ensuring that the "fit" of the team is always good. Bradley's teams are organized and tough to play against. He doesn't win with flair. More important than tactics, Bradley had a philosophy on the team overall. He said, "In 1980, the U.S. hockey team was together for months…. We must become a real team like that. We have to value our time together, play collectively with belief. We must develop that kind of attitude. The Italian team [who won the World Cup in 2006], they were blood brothers. We must build on that first…"

Bradley was smart enough to realize the team needed to embrace its underdog status. While some wondered if the USMNT had a style, Bradley embraced the Spirit of '76. Bradley utilized players who would complement Donovan, Dempsey, and Beasley. He tried to have the USMNT take advantage of transitions and counter-attacks. His goal was to force teams into turnovers at the top of the box, then get the ball to one of the fullbacks, who would take it as high as possible until passing it off to Donovan or Dempsey. Up top, he believed Charlie Davies and Jozy Altidore complemented each other. Davies ran the channels, while Altidore could hold the ball in tight spaces. They created more time and space for Donovan, Dempsey, and Beasley out of the midfield.

2009 Confederations Cup, South Africa

The Confederations Cup is sometimes called the mini World Cup or a pre–World Cup.

The FIFA Confederations Cup is held every four years with winners of the six regional championships from CAF, CONMEBOL, CONCACAF, UEFA, AFC, and OFC being eligible to play in the prestigious tournament. The host country and the reigning World Cup winner are included in order to bring the number of participants to eight. The USMNT qualified for the 2009 Confederations Cup in South Africa by winning the 2007 CONCACAF Gold Cup.

In June 2009, the USMNT settled into their three-star hotel in Pretoria, South Africa, a one-hour drive north of Johannesburg.[106] They felt removed from the rest of the world as they lived, trained, and played matches together for almost three weeks. The tournament served as a way for the team to get to know each other better, as they normally just flew into towns to play a friendly or qualification match and then immediately had to head back to other obligations. The tournament also allowed the team to preview a few South African soccer stadiums and experience the winter climate of South Africa in June before the 2010 World Cup.

The Americans were in a group with five-time World Cup champion Brazil; 2006 reigning World Cup champion, Italy; and reigning African Cup of Nations winner, Egypt. Only two teams would advance to the semifinals, and Brazil and Italy were the massive favorites.

In the USMNT's opening match against Italy in Pretoria, midfielder Ricardo Clark received a red card in the 33rd minute for a late, clumsy tackle on Gennaro Gattuso. After the match, Gattuso said that a yellow seemed more appropriate. The game was scoreless at the time. The Americans even took a 1–0 lead in the 41st minute after Jozy Altidore was taken down by Giorgio Chiellini in the penalty area, and Landon Donovan scored on the penalty kick. However, it was too much to ask the Americans to play a man down for nearly two-thirds of the match at an altitude of 4,000 feet.

Forward Giuseppe Rossi, 22, entered for Gattuso in the 57th minute and the game changed. Rossi grew up in Teaneck, New Jersey, but just short of his 13th birthday he moved to Italy to play for the Parma youth academy in Italy's Serie A.[107] His parents were born in Italy. His father coached soccer and taught Italian and Spanish at Clifton High School. Rossi's father believed his son needed to go to Italy to live and breathe soccer to reach his potential. In 2006, he was invited to a pre–World Cup training camp with the USMNT by Bruce Arena but declined, stating his

---

106. At the time, FIFA was monitoring a global outbreak of swine flu that started weeks before the tournament.

107. Teaneck, New Jersey, is a 20-minute drive from either Kearny, New Jersey, or Yankee Stadium.

dream was to play for Italy.[108] One minute after entering the game, Rossi stripped a USMNT midfielder and blasted a left-footed slicing shot from 30 yards out past a diving goalkeeper Tim Howard to just inside the post, tying the score 1–1.

In the 72nd minute, midfielder Daniele De Rossi, who had received a red card for his vicious elbow to Brian McBride in the 2006 World Cup, blasted a 35-yard shot into the back of the net. It seemed as if two USMNT defenders may have impeded Howard's sight and maybe even deflected the ball. Rossi scored another goal around four minutes into added time, leading Italy to a 3–1 victory. The score seemed to be a setback from the 1–1 result in the 2006 World Cup. However, the USMNT were leading 1–0 and then—with a red card and playing at 4,000-foot altitude with a man down—events need to be taken in context.

Three days later the USMNT would have to play Brazil, whose stars included Real Madrid attacking midfielder Kaká (Ballon d'Or 2007 winner), Sevilla striker Luís Fabiano, Manchester City forward Robinho, Bayern Munich defender Lúcio, Barcelona defender Daniel Alves, Inter Milan goalkeeper Júlio César, Benfica midfielder Ramires, and Inter Milan defender Maicon. Kaká and Lúcio were members of the 2002 World Cup–winning team as well, in addition to Gilberto Silva and José Kléberson. While there were plenty of household names on the Brazil squad, all eyes were on Kaká because he was considered one of the best, if not the best, in the world. Brazil won the trophy in 2005 and had 13-8 odds to win the tournament, after favorites Spain.

The USMNT had scored in every game they had played since a 0–0 friendly draw with Argentina in June 2008. Many wanted to see how 19-year-old Altidore, who had scored six goals in his last 11 appearances, would do. However, many expected the USMNT's undoing to be on defense—which had recently been conceding an average of more than a goal a game.

---

108. Rossi would later fail to make a World Cup team for Italy. It was understandable, but unlucky for the USMNT, that he chose to pursue playing for Italy. One can only imagine if the USMNT had one more talented forward. Rossi was Altidore's teammate at Villarreal in Spain's La Liga. In 2004, when he was 17 years old, Manchester United bought his contract from Parma. In 2007, Manchester United sold Rossi for a reported €10 million transfer fee.

The USMNT were losing 2–0 to Brazil by halftime. The Americans didn't shoot once at goal in the entire first half. Then, in the 57th minute, USMNT midfielder Sacha Kljestan made an ugly tackle on Ramires after losing the ball and received a red card. Another red card for the Americans! Brazil would score in the 62nd minute to make it a lopsided 3–0 defeat. A large American audience watched live on ESPN, and there were plenty who took to websites, blogs, and email to express their frustration. Gulati said, "I think it's great that Americans have this kind of passion. I don't think it's great that they have my Columbia University email address." Gulati received more than 200 emails, most of them demanding Bob Bradley be fired as coach and criticizing the USMNT for a lack of drive, effort, and organization.

Bradley had a different take. Even playing with 10 men against Brazil, he saw a squad that never gave up. Although they were down a man, the USMNT almost scored, hitting the crossbar, and gave up only one goal. He decided against using his third available substitution in the game to send a message to his team that he would support players on the field who would fight until the end.

The USMNT moved from a hotel in urban Pretoria to a lodge on the game preserve in the North-West Province of South Africa for their last match in the group stage. Being closer to nature seemed to help them reset and escape the criticism. Although the USMNT lost their first two matches, they were still eligible to advance following an upset victory for Egypt over Italy that kept the USMNT from being mathematically eliminated. Egypt had scored the game's only goal on a header from a corner kick set piece. Still, the reality was that in order to finish second in the group and avoid being eliminated, the USMNT had to defeat Egypt by three goals while Italy would have to lose to Brazil by three to advance on a goals-scored tiebreaker. Rossi's late goal in added time had put the USMNT into a deeper hole against Italy. In two games, the only goal the USMNT had scored was on a penalty kick.

Unlike the USMNT, Egypt was having a very respectable tournament. After beating Ivory Coast and Cameroon on their way to their African Nations trophy, Egypt's good form had continued in their 2010 World

Cup qualifiers. They had 25-1 odds to win the tournament, better than the USMNT. They lost to Brazil 4–3, with Brazil scoring on a late penalty kick in added time. Then, they shocked the world by beating Italy 1–0. It was highly likely the team would at least be tired (not only from the match but from reportedly staying up late celebrating) and Bradley felt they could be susceptible to a letdown after such an emotional high from beating Italy.

Coach Bradley met with the team as well as many individual players separately. He met with Clint Dempsey to talk and strategize about the upcoming game. Dempsey is renowned for his ultracompetitiveness. He told his coach that he believed the team still had a chance and needed to go for it. Other players expressed the same feelings. It was the self-driven, fighting spirit that Bradley was hoping and waiting for. Bradley used a classic 4-4-2 formation (which would shift to 4-2-2-2 at times) and kept most of his starting lineup, hoping for an early goal. He did start Charlie Davies at forward, thinking that his speed would expose the exhaustion that Egypt might feel after their two grueling matches. Bradley's hunch would prove prescient.

The Americans started the game aggressively. In the 21st minute, after a throw-in from the left flank, forward Jozy Altidore sent a low cross toward the near post. The ball popped free after an Egyptian midfielder slid into the head of his diving goalkeeper. Davies kept hustling in the confusion, and ricocheted the ball into the net. It was Davies' second goal ever for the USMNT.[109]

Leading Egypt 1–0 at halftime, the American players were told that Brazil were beating Italy 3–0 at halftime. Brazil's Luís Fabiano scored in the 37th and 43rd minutes, and then, luckily for the Americans, Italy let in an own goal just before halftime. If the USMNT could score two more goals, and if the margin in the Italians' game did not change, they would advance.

---

109. Sadly, Davies was left off the U.S. roster for the 2010 FIFA World Cup when he was not cleared medically by his French club team after a devastating car accident in the fall of 2009.

In the 52nd minute, a shot by Altidore was stopped by a handball at the goal line, a clear violation that apparently went unseen by the referee. In the 63rd minute, the USMNT took a 2–0 lead on a give-and-go between Michael Bradley and Landon Donovan. The third goal the USMNT needed to take them into the semifinals came in the 71st minute, on an inch-perfect 40-yard cross from Jonathan Spector to Dempsey, who headed the ball into the net from seven yards out. The usually even-keeled Bob Bradley pumped his arms in celebration.

After the match, Donovan said, "Soccer is a funny game. Anything can happen. This is one of the things Americans are capable of. We have a spirit a lot of people don't. We showed it tonight." How right he was—a Spirit of '76. The USMNT, improbably, would be in the semifinal against Spain. The day after the USMNT's win over Egypt they went out on a safari and enjoyed a little bit of South Africa.

When describing the Egypt match for *Howler* magazine in 2012, Matt Doyle wrote, "It took more than two years to come together, and throughout critics dismissed it as linear and uninspiring. But talk of that nature vanished after the 2009 Confederations Cup in South Africa. The final group stage game for the U.S., against Egypt, isn't remembered as well as it should be…it was the Egypt match, which wasn't just a "must-win" but a "must-pummel-into-submission," that showed how well Bradley's group could perform when firing on all cylinders. Davies and Altidore were relentless in finding space, and when the U.S. pushed forward with numbers it was like an avalanche: 'try hard, run fast' at its finest. The notion of controlling the tempo was never at issue: instead, they simply tried to push it as high and hard as it could possibly go. Two of the three goals (Dempsey and Michael Bradley) were scored at pace, and Egypt's 3–0 humiliation reinforced scouting reports on the U.S. around the world: when they're running, they're dangerous."

Spain entered the semifinal match at the 2009 Confederations Cup ranked No. 1 in the world, with a world-record 15 straight wins and 35-match unbeaten streak. Having not tasted defeat since being beaten in 2006, Spain were the heavy favorites to win the tournament with 11-8 odds to win (the USMNT's were 33-1). Spain hadn't conceded a goal in

424 minutes and had only conceded two goals in 16 games. They qualified for the tournament by winning Euro 2008. In the group stage, Spain easily won their three matches by a combined eight goals to none. Spain's starting lineup included Real Madrid goalkeeper Iker Casillas, defender Sergio Ramos, and midfielder Xabi Alonso (who joined Real Madrid in 2009); Barcelona defender Puyol, defender Gerard Piqué, midfielder Xavi, and striker David Villa (who joined Barcelona in 2010); Arsenal midfielder Cesc Fàbregas (who came through Barcelona's La Masia); and Liverpool striker Fernando Torres and winger Albert Riera. They were coached by Vincente del Bosque, who had played for and coached Real Madrid (winning two Champions League titles as coach). Needless to say, Spain were overwhelming favorites.

Often overlooked is that the USMNT had lost to Spain 0–1 after a goal from Xavi in the 78th minute in Spain on June 4, 2008. Therefore, the USMNT knew what to expect and believed they could compete, even though most observers gave them no chance on June 24, 2009.

Bradley's plan was to clog the middle and make Spain's short passes more difficult. When forced out to the wings, he believed Spain were less dangerous. Spain were magicians on the ball, but not strong executing crosses and heading the ball. At 6'4", defender Oguchi Onyewu was much taller than all of the Spanish players. The USMNT backline that night featured Carlos Bocanegra (who played for Stade Rennais), making his first start at left back since March 2007, playing alongside Jay DeMerit (Watford), Oguchi Onyewu (A.C. Milan), and Jonathan Spector (West Ham United)—all of whom played in Europe.

With the American defense on lockdown, the USMNT nearly scored in the seventh minute as Davies' bicycle kick off a Dempsey cross went just wide of the goal. A minute later, another Davies shot went wide. Spain, playing with the attacking trio of Fernando Torres, David Villa, and Cesc Fabregas, were unable to penetrate the USMNT defense.

The game, played at a frenetic pace, included a series of attempts on both sides, but the USMNT were the ones to score first. In the 27th minute, Altidore, 19, ended Spain's shutout streak at 451 minutes. Dempsey played a one-two with Davies and looked for Altidore, who was being marked by his Villareal teammate Joan Capdevila. Dempsey's pass was deflected by Xabi Alonso, but Altidore was able to shoot the ball, which hit Casillas' hand but still went into the net for a 1–0 lead.

With the USMNT hanging on to preserve the lead, Spain upped the pressure in the second half. Shots rained on Howard's goal, but he denied them all. Spain could not find the breakthrough, and their hopes of reaching the Final were crushed when Dempsey made it 2–0. Donovan's low cross should really have been cleared by Ramos at the far post, but Dempsey showed quick reactions six yards out to prod the ball away from the Real Madrid defender and past Real Madrid goalkeeper Casillas. With four minutes left to play, Michael Bradley was ejected following a late tackle on Xabi Alonso. Despite being reduced to 10 men, Spain could not break through the organized USMNT defense, and when they did they were misfiring. Meanwhile, Howard seemed unbeatable in goal. No matter how slick, accurate, and quick the Spanish *tiki-taka* passing was, the USMNT seemed a half-step ahead.

The USMNT won the game 2–0. The USMNT were exhausted from playing and defending Spain's attack over and over. Spain had 11 shots, six on target, compared to the USMNT's four shots, two on target. Spain's goalkeeper had no saves (the USMNT had two shots on target and two goals), compared to Howard's six saves. While outshot, the USMNT still played as equals against Spain. The USMNT powerfully reminded soccer fans, and themselves, that grit and teamwork can transcend skill level. The Spirit of '76 can work.

Former French international Marcel Desailly, working as a BBC commentator that evening, said, "I was certainly impressed by USA. Each of their players have a very good level of discipline and they did not make a single mistake to allow Spain to score. The Spanish played in too tight a space." After the match, Spain's Torres said, "When you play against Spain, everybody's watching the game. So maybe all the people can see they [the USMNT] have fantastic players and a fantastic team."

For many American fans, the USMNT's stunning 2–0 victory over Spain in the 2009 Confederations Cup in South Africa was probably the second-biggest upset by an American team, behind only the 1980

Olympic "Miracle on Ice" by the hockey team over the Soviet Union. In an article titled "U.S. Victory Was a Miracle on Grass," George Vecsey of the *New York Times* captured the sentiment when he wrote, "The inequity is what made this match such a spectacle. The Spanish players are regulars for Barcelona and Liverpool in the richest leagues of Europe.... The Americans play in the earnest Major League Soccer or are mostly role players and reserves in Europe.... But for these 90 minutes...the Americans were better than the Spaniards, brave and smart and lucky, too.... Nobody in the American soccer federation will dare to claim that this was the day the country came of age in the world's most important sport.... But this was a step.... For loyal American fans, it feels so good precisely because it was an upset."

The bad news for the USMNT was Michael Bradley received a red card—and in the 87th minute—which meant he was ineligible for the next match. It was totally unnecessary because the result was assured. Bradley would now miss the Final against Brazil. The USMNT had gotten a red card in three matches at the tournament and in the 2006 World Cup—challenging the execution of the tactic of playing smart.

The USMNT would face Brazil in the Final. Benny Feilhaber, who had been a valuable reserve, replaced the suspended Michael Bradley. Bob Bradley's tactics for the match would be similar to what he used against Spain—4-4-2, pressure the ball, clog the middle, and look for the counter. There was one difference in that Benny Feilhaber would allow Dempsey to play more forward, closer to the opponent's goal. However, Brazil were better headers of the ball than Spain, and able to come from deeper positions with devastating speed. In an interview before the match, Coach Bradley said, "We need to step on the field and play our game, an aggressive, smart game with energy and speed."

The USMNT tactics worked well in the first half on a cold night in the South African capital because of the overwhelming presence of Onyewu on defense and Howard in goal. Kaká and Robinho were neutralized. Then, on a counter-attack in the 10th minute, right back Jonathan Spector curved a Beckham-like cross from a very deep position on the right side of the box that was neatly redirected by Dempsey with a side-footed volley

10 yards out, past the Brazilian goalkeeper for a 1–0 lead. Dempsey's goal broke Brazil's 315-minute shutout streak. After the goal, Dempsey gave his best impersonation of Michael Jackson, who had died just days before, by setting up in the middle of the field and showing off his own version of Jackson's famous leg kick. Afterward, Dempsey said, "I was actually surprised that it went in, to be honest, just got a good bounce and it got past the keeper. It was something we talked about before the game and it was just good to show love to Michael Jackson for the good times he's given us through his music."

In the 27th minute, the Americans scored again on a brilliant counter-attack, one of the most magnificent goals in USMNT history. Davies and Donovan broke out in a two-man sprint downfield against two Brazil defenders. Donovan found Davies on the left with a one-touch pass, and Davies returned the ball to Donovan, now on the edge of the box. Donovan brought it down with one touch on his left side, twisted the last defender Ramires, and with his second composed touch, belted a shot across his body and to the left of the Brazilian goalkeeper into the corner for a 2–0 lead. Donovan's goal gave the USMNT their first and only two-goal lead ever against Brazil. After Donovan scored, he pointed to Davies, who ran over to Donovan and lifted him into the air. The goal showcased the very best of the Spirit of '76. Donovan's goal was a quick counter-attack that utilized speed. The USMNT showed they could score world-class, clinical goals.

The Brazilians naively kept trying to come infield and the USMNT defense was stifling them. Also, the Brazilians seemed to have difficulty with the USMNT's physical strength. The USMNT went into halftime up 2–0.

The Guardian live match bloggers stated, "I couldn't care less who wins, and am rather enjoying the U.S.'s industrious, streetwise performance…. Easily the best 45 minutes this team has played in a decade. It's often said that a person in trouble needs to hit rock bottom before being able to recover and grow. Perhaps that's what happened to this team following the earlier 0–3 loss to Brazil. It does not even remotely look like the same U.S.

team. Unbelievably disciplined on defense and shockingly comfortable with possession—by American standards, at least. Hope it lasts."

In the locker room, the coaches and players talked about how Brazil would throw everyone forward, especially at the beginning of the half, desperately looking for a goal. They talked about keeping a good defensive structure.

It took just 39 seconds into the second half for Brazil to get back into the match. Fabiano received a pass from Maicon with his back to the goal at the top of the box. He took a touch before swiveling, then instantly blasted a shot through the legs of DeMerit and past Howard into the corner. And it was downhill from there. In spite of having an early 2–0 lead against Brazil in the Confederations Cup Final, the USMNT would eventually lose 3–2, with Brazil's last goal coming from a corner kick set piece.

The USMNT failed to hold their nerve tactically and keep two men up for counter-attacks. Instead, they chose to sit back and desperately tried to hold on. *The Guardian* bloggers typed, "It seems to me that this tournament has shown how effective tactics can be, highlighting the importance of a good coach with plans. How else to explain the USA's success against Spain and the game so far.... The U.S. have been heroic, but they look spent." The USMNT had failed to hold on to arguably the most dangerous lead in sports (2–0). Brazil had 31 shots with 13 on target compared to nine and four for the USMNT.

The match was considered one of the greatest ever in the tournament's history. Nearly four million viewers tuned in to watch, making it the most-watched non–World Cup game in USMNT history. In addition, it was at the time the third-most watched of any competition—following the 2002 World Cup quarterfinal against Germany and 1994 group stage match against Colombia. Americans watched a close-up of Dempsey's face as he accepted his medal for second place. It captured all the emotions the entire team was undoubtedly feeling. He seemed sad, pissed off, and proud at the same time, knowing he had a chance to win and yet honored to be in the position. In his book *When America Wins the World Cup*, Matthew Kolesky wrote, "It was that hunger to prove to America and the world that we [USMNT] are so close to the next level, ready to take the next step up." Legitimacy was the mission.

Regardless of the final outcome, the Americans had made their point. The USMNT beat Spain and came within 45 minutes of their first FIFA trophy. For the first time in U.S. Soccer history, the USMNT were not only a serious contender on the international scene, but also showed they could get results against soccer powers. Dempsey won the Bronze Ball, and Howard won the Golden Glove.

Just when the USMNT seemed outplayed and were on the verge of getting sent home, they came back to show grit, determination, and spirit in demonstrating the legitimacy of U.S. Soccer. In many ways, USMNT fans identified with the team because they never quit until the final whistle, and this would become a more prominent core value of the USMNT in the 2010 World Cup. They benefited from some luck, such as Brazil scoring three goals and conceding none to Italy; incredible efficiency in the game against Spain and the first half of the game against Brazil; and an astonishing goalkeeping performance by Howard. They also made things harder on themselves with red cards. In the second half of the game against Brazil, the team could have used Michael Bradley. The danger of these positive results was rising expectations against the flawed 2002 comparison.

Qualifying for the 2010 World Cup, South Africa
The USMNT finished first in CONCACAF qualifying for the 2010 World Cup. The top three teams to qualify were the United States, Mexico, and Honduras (in order). The USMNT had six wins, two draws, and two losses (away to Mexico and Costa Rica) for 20 points. Mexico had six wins, one draw, and three losses (away to the USMNT, Honduras, and El Salvador) for 19 points.

Core Value of the Team: Never Quit
On October 14, 2009, the USMNT played Costa Rica at home during World Cup qualifying. Two days before the match, forward Charlie Davies was seriously injured in a car accident and remained in a coma. Fans were holding signs bearing No. 9, Davies' jersey number.

The USMNT had already mathematically qualified for the World Cup and were down 0–2 after 23 minutes. The USMNT kept creating chances, but Costa Rica goalkeeper Keylor Navas, who would go on to win three straight Champions League trophies with Real Madrid, made several incredible saves. It seemed like it was just not going to be the USMNT's night. With nothing to play for, some teams may have reduced the intensity. But finally, in the 71st minute, Landon Donovan managed to get a shot off that was saved, but Michael Bradley was there for the rebound to make it 1–2. In the 83rd minute, Oguchi Onyewu suffered an injury. Coach Bradley had already used his three allotted substitutes, so the USMNT were forced to play a man down.

At 90+5' and with the final seconds ticking away, second-half sub Robbie Rogers, who wore the No. 9 jersey that night, sent in a left-footed corner kick. An unmarked Jonathan Bornstein headed it past the goalkeeper and a defender on the line from six yards to tie the game 2–2, and RFK Stadium erupted. Jozy Altidore lifted his jersey to reveal his undershirt imprinted with "Davies 9" and started pounding his chest. The memorable header pushed the USMNT to a first-place finish in the World Cup Qualifying Hexagonal, and also made Bornstein an instant hero in Honduras, who leapfrogged over Costa Rica and into the 2010 FIFA World Cup.

Davies, who remained in a coma for two weeks and didn't see the game live, later reflected, "I wasn't there, and I've only seen it on replay, but I have goosebumps...any time someone brings up that match and that goal and seeing how you guys celebrated after. I was unconscious in the hospital, but at the time, to see how you guys could come together—you could see the love, the belief—everything was there."

Dedicated Home Stadium Debate

During the qualifying tournament, Mexico, Honduras, and the USMNT's average attendance per match were around 98,000, 34,000, and 31,000, respectively. The USMNT do not have a dedicated national stadium like some of the other CONCACAF teams, including Mexico and Honduras. On August 12, 2009, attendance reached 104,499 for Mexico's 2–1 home win against the USMNT. In comparison, the USMNT beat Mexico 2–0 at Columbus Crew Stadium in front of 23,776 fans, the stadium's maximum capacity.

This information raises three obvious questions: First, should the team have a dedicated stadium the way Mexico, for example, do with Azteca? While the USSF has had conversations about a dedicated stadium, it has never been seriously considered. Second, if the USMNT ever wanted to have a home stadium, where should it be? And third, how big should it be?

Playing games in the same place would allow the U.S. teams to develop routines for training and game days and to learn the intricacies of a particular field. Fans would have a place they identified the U.S. teams with and it also would be an identity for players. A designated stadium would help solve the complex scheduling process of matching CONCACAF schedules with local stadium obligations as well as coordinating travel.

There has been sporadic talk over the years about finding the national team a permanent home, but then basic obstacles arise such as erratic and seasonal weather patterns, differing needs in terms of the size of the stadium, different time zones, and ensuring the crowd is pro–United States. In addition, the USSF has to cater to the wishes of the TV networks and their preferred days and start times. Finding places where the crowds would be favorable is a unique challenge that very few other countries face because the U.S. is a country of immigrants, and the home team is not necessarily always the favorite or most supported team in many U.S. cities where the immigrant population is large or particularly concentrated.

For any game against Mexico, this is all the more challenging. In spite of what would be a forgivable assumption, the most popular soccer team in the United States is not actually the USMNT; rather, it is the *Mexican* men's national team. The team regularly fills NFL stadiums, even for meaningless friendlies. TV ratings for the Mexico team are higher than the USMNT. The Mexican league (Liga MX) draws bigger audiences on U.S. television than any other soccer league in any language—more than the EPL, UEFA Champions League, and certainly more than MLS. When Telemundo won the U.S. Spanish-language World Cup television rights for the eight-year period from 2015 to 2022, it paid FIFA $600 million, which was $175 million more than Fox Sports paid for the U.S. English-language TV rights. Because of the Mexican national team and large Hispanic community in the U.S. who are passionate about soccer and their—or their relatives'—original countries, no country in the world pays FIFA more money for World Cup TV rights than the U.S. Also, Mexico plays more games in the U.S. than it does in Mexico! You'd be hard-pressed to come up with another example where this is the case.

The other major challenge, and one that certainly cannot be overlooked, is that many within the USSF are still very focused on growing the game in the United States and support the notion that playing in a variety of venues helps promote the game and teams in a geographically large and diverse country. The USMNT have a history of touring, and every stop along the way is seen as an opportunity to increase the fan base, raise the popularity of the team, and get more young boys and girls interested in the game. In comparison to the U.S., other larger geographic countries (e.g., Australia, Canada, and Russia) play a majority of their important international matches at a select few stadiums, which has the benefit of familiarity and appropriate infrastructure, but is still somewhat limiting in terms of trying to maximize the amount of people who have exposure to and relatively easy access to the games. Additionally, even some geographically smaller nations like Spain and Italy do not have national stadiums, but instead allow their national teams to play big games at a variety of venues. Given the number of cities in both countries that can consistently fill a club team's stadium, this is not surprising.

For the U.S., the arguments in favor of having one national stadium are just as strong as those against, and there are examples to draw from other countries where either solution, or some balance of something in between, is successful. Regardless, what goes without saying is that stadium selection is an incredibly complicated and important business and can have a larger-than-expected impact on the team's performance. As a result, whatever solution the USSF decides to implement should be carefully analyzed, with all factors considered.

Stadium selection is controllable, and while there are obvious commercial benefits to hosting a USMNT game in a city like New York, which has the largest population in the U.S., there are some downsides as well—first and foremost being the number of immigrants that live in and around New York City. "Home games" often feel like "away games." The margins are so small and the differences between qualifying or not for the World Cup are tiny, so any home-field advantage helps. The USSF can better control the supporters to be pro-American in smaller stadiums because they can more closely monitor the allocation and sale of tickets. However, a smaller stadium means smaller ticket receipts and therefore smaller revenues.

Typically, the USMNT and USWNT coaches have input in where and when matches will be played. Unfortunately, things don't always go as planned. For example, a qualifying match between Costa Rica and the USMNT on September 1, 2017, had been scheduled before Bruce Arena took over the team from Klinsmann. Costa Rica's team arrived at Red Bull Arena in New Jersey, where the USMNT should have had an advantage. But it didn't work out that way. Bruce Arena said, "We stepped on the field. About half the stadium was supporting the U.S. and the other half Costa Rica. We don't know how those people get tickets—fans of the opposing team. But they manage to get them all the time.... We also made a real big mistake as a federation in putting that game in New York. Every game in qualifying is a battle. And every advantage you have, you gotta take advantage of that, and we did not do a very smart job in picking that venue."

Chapter 9

2010 World Cup:
U.S. Soccer Is Legitimate

The Greatest Moments in U.S. Soccer History

In July 2019, *Sports Illustrated* published an article that listed the greatest moments in U.S. Soccer history. Two of the eight mentioned have to do with the 2010 World Cup, which indicates how special it was. Interestingly, the 2002 World Cup was not mentioned! The list is below.

No. 1. In 2019, the USWNT reaching their third consecutive FIFA World Cup Final and winning their fourth World Cup title overall. *Sports Illustrated* wrote, "The men have received plenty of mentions for their achievements over the past century, but they aren't a patch on the women, whose efforts far surpass anything their counterparts have done."

No. 2. In 1950, the USMNT beating England 1–0 in the World Cup in Brazil. At the time, England were often referred to as the "Kings of Europe," with a postwar record of 23 wins, four losses, and three ties. England had beaten Italy 4–0 and Portugal 10–0 in the weeks leading up to the tournament. Conversely, the USMNT consisted of semiprofessional players, most of whom had other jobs to support their families. Their professions included high school teacher, hearse driver for an uncle's funeral home, letter carrier, and dishwasher. One player had to cancel attending because he couldn't get time off from work.

The USMNT had lost their last seven international matches by the combined score of 45–2. The coach told the press that his players were "sheep ready to be slaughtered" and the English *Daily Express* wrote, "It would be fair to give the U.S. three goals to start." The result of England 0–1 USA was considered so unimaginable that one London newspaper presumed the postmatch telegram they received from their representative was a typo and published a score line of England 10–1 USA.[110]

No. 3. In 1991, the USMNT and USWNT winning their first major silverware. The USMNT won the Gold Cup and the USWNT won the World Cup.

No. 4. In 1994, the U.S. hosting the 1994 World Cup.

No. 5. In 2007, David Beckham signing with the LA Galaxy.

No. 6. In 2007, Kristine Lilly becoming the first player to achieve 300 caps (appearances in a game at an international level), the "Triple-Century." Lilly retired with 345 caps over 23 years. She made her debut for the USWNT while she was still attending high school. She participated in the 1991, 1995, 1999, 2003, and 2007 Women's World Cups, winning in 1991 and 1999. She also competed in the 1996, 2000, and 2004 Olympics, winning gold in 1996 and 2004 and silver in 2000. The most caps for any male player from any country is 184 over 16 years. Christine Rampone Pearce is the only other player to have more than 300 caps; she has 311.

---

110. To add to the discussion of dual nationals' contributions to the USMNT, Joe Gaetjens, who scored the lone goal, was originally from Haiti. While studying at Columbia University, he declared his intent to become a U.S. citizen to be eligible to play for the USMNT, but after the World Cup he never completed the process. He played for Haiti before and after playing for the USMNT, and also could have played for Germany. Geoffrey Douglas, a professor at the University of Massachusetts Amherst, wrote a book about the match titled *The Game of Their Lives*. Joe Gaetjen's son Lesly Gaetjens wrote a biography about his father: *The Shot Heard Around the World: The Joe Gaetjens Story.*

No. 7. A goal from the 2010 World Cup to be remembered. To be discussed later.

No. 8. A first since 1930 from the 2010 World Cup. To be discussed later.

2010 World Cup, South Africa

In the 1994 World Cup, many of the USMNT's players played together growing up, in college, or in Mission Viejo. They had formed tight bonds. By 2010, fewer players had long relationships and familiarity. Landon Donovan and DaMarcus Beasley played together at the IMG Academy Residency Program in Bradenton. Tim Howard and Jonathan Spector played in the Premier League together. Clint Dempsey and Ricardo Clark were both ex-Furman players. A younger group of players had been teammates on various U.S. youth teams. In addition, the players would get together for short periods of time. Bob Bradley added dual nationals Edson Buddle (Jamaica), Robbie Findley (Trinidad & Tobago), and Hérculez Gómez (Mexico) to the team even though they had not participated in qualification. However, they were known to most of the players because they had played in and won trophies in MLS. Gómez had been a sensation in the Mexican League and Buddle had been tearing up MLS for LA Galaxy. They were brought on to help fill the void left at forward by the absence of Charlie Davies, who had not recovered from a serious car accident. A few other players were dealing with injuries or were not at their best form. The coaches wanted players who were in their best form, had good personalities, and fit into the group. The players viewed them as necessary to fill holes, not take spots away, which was different when David Regis, who didn't participate in qualification, was added to the 1998 World Cup squad.

However, the players seemed to unite around being underdogs and with common grudges against the media who slighted them, especially ex-USMNT commentators. The best quote exemplifying the team's attitude came from Michael Bradley. After beating Egypt in the 2009 Confederations Cup 3–0 and qualifying for the semifinals against Spain,

Bradley said, "When everything is against you, everyone wants to say how bad you are, everybody wants to write you off, all the f--king experts in America, everybody who thinks they know about soccer, can all look at that score tonight and let's see what they have to say now."

On October 11, 2009, Jeré Longman of the *New York Times* wrote, "This appears to be the most talented American squad over the past six World Cup cycles, certainly the one that can most dependably score goals. What can be expected in South Africa.... Will this American team match the second-round advance of 1994 or the quarterfinal appearance of 2002? Or will it exit meekly in the first round as in 1990, 1998, and 2006?" The 2002 World Cup result was and is an ever-present comparison. Longman was right; it was the most talented USMNT by total number of players and minutes in the Top Five Leagues. The USMNT also had three players in European competitions—Dempsey (Fulham, Europa), Howard (Everton, Europa) and Onyewu (Milan, Champions League)—their most ever. Dempsey appeared in the 2010 Europa League Final for Fulham.

The USMNT were placed in Group C for the 2010 World Cup with England, Algeria, and Slovenia. By FIFA rankings, the USMNT were favored to finish second in the group, behind England—whom the bookmakers had at 6-1 odds to win the whole tournament. Still, the bookmakers had given the USMNT 90-1 odds to win the tournament, the same as 2002.

Eric Wynalda said, "The best draw we've ever had in any World Cup." England were the heavy favorites to win the group. All 23 of England's players played in the Top Five Leagues, playing a total of more than 75,000 minutes. In comparison, the USMNT had 12 players playing a total of over 23,000 minutes. However, the USMNT had more minutes in the Top Five Leagues than Algeria and Slovenia.

Table: 2010 World Cup—USA & Opponents (Group Stage)

2010 World Cup—USA & Opponents (Group Stage)					
Team	World Rank (Pre-WC)	Average Age (Team)	Average Age (Starters)	# Players Top 5 League	# Minutes Top 5 League
USA	11	26.9	27.2	12	23,265
England	7	28.4	27.8	23	75,016
Slovenia	49	26.7	26.7	8	16,187
Algeria	29	26.2	25.8	12	18,822
Group Total (ex. US)	85			43	110,025

Commenting on England's group, the British paper *The Sun* wrote, "The best group since the Beatles." Luckily for the USMNT, the three stadiums where they would play their group matches were all within easy driving distance of the team's headquarters—and they had played in all three stadiums during the 2009 Confederations Cup. Even more luckily, the team's headquarters were at high altitude, just like the stadiums, and the team would have weeks before the start to acclimate.

After spending two straight World Cups in urban hotels in Seoul, South Korea, and Hamburg, Germany, the USMNT were in the countryside. The team stayed at the Irene Country Lodge in Pretoria. Families and friends stayed at a hotel around 20 minutes away. The team was surrounded by police with holstered guns and bulletproof vests. For the 23-man roster and about an equal number of coaches and support staff, the general atmosphere was much more "tightened up" than 2006. However, it wasn't all serious. Stu Holden and Jay DeMerit came up with songs in their room, which they dubbed "Studio 214," about their teammates to sing on the bus rides.[111] The slogan on the side of the bus read, LIFE, LIBERTY, AND THE PURSUIT OF VICTORY! with the Stars and Stripes painted alongside.[112]

The USMNT's first match was against England on June 12 in Rustenberg, the place where the USMNT had defeated Egypt 3–0 in the Confederations Cup. Since the draw in December 2009, many Americans had been looking forward to the match because it was an opportunity to fight for the legitimacy of U.S. Soccer against the country that invented

---

111. Holden and DeMerit also would use their vuvuzelas to alert players of team meetings to "make sure their teammates were on time."

112. "Life, Liberty and the pursuit of Happiness" is a well-known phrase in the U.S. Declaration of Independence signed in 1776.

the modern game. The game's backdrop had a little bit of an American Revolutionary War undertone.

2010 FIFA World Cup: Group Stage, Game 1
June 12, 2010, at Royal Bafokeng Stadium, Rustenburg
USA 1–1 England
Heading into the World Cup, England were 6–2–1 in friendly play, losing only to Spain and Brazil. England beat the USMNT in a friendly 2–0 at Wembley Stadium in May 2008. England had such stars as Liverpool and England captain Steven Gerrard (2005 Ballon d'Or third-place finisher and 2009 English Footballer of the Year), Manchester United forward Wayne Rooney (2009–2010 Premier League Player of the Season), Chelsea midfielder Frank Lampard (2005 Ballon d'Or runner-up), and Chelsea defender John Terry (UEFA Club Defender of the Year 2005, 2008, and 2009). Before the game, Roy Hodgson, who coached several Americans in the English Premier League, said, "The U.S. are well-organized and well-drilled, athletically very good and with players with a lot of experience playing in England or Germany, but that could be a like-versus-like contest. That could actually be quite good for England. It'll be like a Premier League game, with two teams with a similar style. They'll know how England plays, but we won't be surprised with what they're going to come with. And I think that England have just got far too much quality for the U.S." Then–Vice President Biden was in attendance.

Four minutes into the game, taking advantage of the USMNT's nerves and susceptibility to giving up early goals, Steven Gerrard gave coach Fabio Capello the perfect start when he slid Emile Heskey's pass beyond goalkeeper Tim Howard with the outside of his right foot. Instead of building on the 1–0 lead, England seemed content, and the USMNT calmed down and got into the flow of the game. Then Landon Donovan created a great chance when he sent an inviting cross into the box, but the ball was headed wide by Jozy Altidore.

Five minutes before halftime, Clint Dempsey shot a ball toward goal from around 25 yards, and West Ham United's goalkeeper Robert

Green mishandled what should have been a routine save.[113] England fans collectively groaned as they watched the ball agonizingly roll slowly over the line as Green tried to recover.

A USA goal via lucky long-range shot.

Dempsey had even turned away after taking the shot, assuming that the goalkeeper would make a routine save. However, he turned back in time to see the ball cross the goal line. Instinctively, he started to celebrate—then stopped, not sure if he should believe what he had just seen. Dempsey certainly worked hard to get off the shot that produced the fortunate goal, bobbing and weaving through traffic and twice turning England's midfielder Steven Gerrard around. That created enough space for him to get off a strong shot with his weaker left foot. For Dempsey, the goal was his second in World Cup play, making him only the second American to score in two World Cups.

As one publication reported the day after the match, "Robert Green will not have wanted to wake up this morning—if he managed to sleep at all that is. Of all the scenarios he might have envisaged, the worst came to pass." England coach Fabio Capello opted not to name his first-choice goalkeeper until the day of England's opening match. Capello, unconvinced about usual starting goalkeeper David James' fitness (40 years old), chose Green (30 years old) to start ahead of the inexperienced Joe Hart (23 years old), who had been consistently the most impressive of the three goalkeepers in training before the tournament.

Capello was forced to deal with another personnel issue when James Milner, usually one of the most trusted players on the team, had to be replaced in the 31st minute after receiving a yellow card shortly before. Milner had come down with a stomach virus the week before the match and missed an entire week of training. He was looking particularly sluggish. The England coach feared a second yellow (red card) would follow, given he was repeatedly fouling the speedy Americans. Then, Ledley King, one

---

113. England coach Fabio Capello later suggested the new World Cup Adidas Jabulani ball was to blame for Green's error. The high-tech ball was heavily criticized by the players, particularly by goalkeepers, who claim its movement in the air is unpredictable. Green admirably blamed himself.

of England's staunchest defenders, had to be substituted out after 45 minutes with a groin injury.

The score at halftime was 1–1. In the 52nd minute, it looked like England would take the lead when Heskey had a breakaway with only the goalkeeper to beat. Fortunately for the USMNT, Heskey unconvincingly shot the ball straight at Howard for an easy save. In the 64th minute, it was the USMNT's turn and England fans' hearts were in their throats when Altidore exploited his speed as he raced past Jamie Carragher toward goal, but Green partially made amends for his earlier gaffe when he deflected Altidore's shot wide. Rooney was relatively quiet all match, but soon thereafter almost surprised Howard with a shot from long range that flew just wide. At the end, England seemed to have been worn out by the Americans.

Even though England had 58 percent of possession and nine attempts on target as compared to the USMNT's five, the USMNT matched them. The USMNT definitely proved the legitimacy of U.S. Soccer with a subtlety that almost served to undermine what they had accomplished— after the game, the USMNT were celebrating as if they had won. It was understandable. They had embraced being an underdog and matched the soccer power, whereas the English players were distraught.

The next day an article in *The Guardian* titled "England v USA: Draw Brings World Cup Feel-Good Factor to America: USA's Result Against England is Front-Page News in the US" stated, "In one of the greatest sporting upsets since the day before yesterday, when Robert Green decided goalkeeping was the new charity, the USA woke up yesterday and decided it was the new Norway, the plucky footballing underdog come good." The *New York Post*'s front-page headline captured the mood of the United States: USA WINS 1–1. Gawker wrote, "America does not suck at soccer—it's safe to care about the World Cup," while ESPN recognized the paradox of a superpower being an underdog in soccer: "Cue a litany of condescending adjectives not normally associated with the world's last superpower: spirited, feisty, gutsy, brave."

2010 FIFA World Cup: Group Stage, Game 2
June 18, 2010, at Ellis Park Stadium, Johannesburg
USA 2–2 Slovenia

It was the first-ever meeting between Slovenia and the USMNT. Slovenia had won seven of their last eight matches and beaten Algeria 1–0 in their first group match, so it was important for the USMNT to get a result.

The USMNT started the match tentatively, and before they knew it, they were down 0–2 by halftime. It felt like another game, another early letdown. To the outside world, the USMNT were effectively out of the 2010 FIFA World Cup. The players were surprised at how calm and pragmatic Coach Bradley was given how high the stakes were at the time. During halftime, the team spoke about believing they could come back and win.

Coach Bradley then made two switches—bringing Maurice Edu and Benny Feilhaber in for Robbie Findley and Jose Torres, then shifting Dempsey up to forward. Findley had a yellow card for a handball that actually hit him in the face (the yellow would cause him to miss the Algeria game, where his pace would have helped), and the one thing the USMNT couldn't afford was to go a man down if Findley drew another card.

In the article "What Is American Soccer?" for *Howler* magazine in 2012, Matt Doyle explained the sentiment around Bradley: "...At the World Cup in South Africa, doubts about Bradley's coaching remained. Was he an astute tactician whose ability to make in-game adjustments won his team results, or was he myopic and stubborn to the point that he was forced into those adjustments out of desperation?" Bradley changed tactics at halftime, shifting from an "empty bucket" (two holding midfielders play deep with to other midfielders much farther up the field on the wing along the touchlines so there isn't a playmaker in the middle—hence the "empty bucket") 4-4-2 to a 4-1-3-1-1. Then the USMNT would start a spirited fight to dig out of the hole they had created for themselves.

Doyle described the change, "Whatever the case, by shifting from an 'empty bucket' 4-4-2 to a 4-1-3-1-1 after going down 2–0 to Slovenia in the second group game, Bradley unleashed Donovan to become a U.S.

legend. Unshackled on the right flank, Donovan took control of the game."

Not long after the formation switch, a Slovenia player missed a simple clearance, and Donovan took full advantage. Donovan tracked the ball down the right-hand side, took a few touches as he raced into the box, and fired the ball from close range directly over goalkeeper Samir Handanovic's head into the roof of the net from a tough angle.

A goal via counter-attack based on a long, direct pass.

Doyle wrote, "It was a blast that seemed filled with all the angst and agitation of the previous four years, and it woke the U.S. up. Benny Feilhaber, a halftime sub, raised hell up and down the left flank, Altidore created space, and Michael Bradley ran himself into the ground. They didn't quite reach the anarchic energy of the 2002 team against Germany but—finally—this was a U.S. team that could use the ball to both generate chances and snuff out opposition momentum."

Michael Bradley's equalizing goal, with eight minutes left, was proof of his father's in-game tactical prowess. In the 80th minute, Coach Bradley pulled Onyewu and sent in forward Hérculez Gómez in a brilliant tactical gamble. The USMNT went to a 3-4-3 formation, something Feilhaber later said they'd never done before, even in practice. This formation put Dempsey in more of a free role, which meant he could at any given moment drop deep into midfield or appear in the box, and when he did, the Slovenians had difficulty tracking him. So, Dempsey had more than enough time to find Donovan at midfield, and Donovan to find Altidore at the top of the box. With the Slovenian defense keying on Gómez, no one was left to watch Bradley bursting out of midfield. Altidore headed Donovan's cross into empty space, and Bradley finished.

A goal via counter-attack based on a long, direct pass.

With Bradley's goal in the 82nd minute to tie the game at 2–2, the USMNT were back in the World Cup. The goal revitalized the large U.S. support base and the chants of "USA! USA!" were heard above the wailing noise of the vuvuzelas. No team had ever come back from a 2–0 halftime deficit to win a World Cup match, but the USMNT sought to do just that.

The USMNT almost pulled ahead in the 85th minute when Malian referee Koman Coulibaly, taking charge of his first World Cup game, ruled out what looked like a perfectly good Maurice Edu goal. Donovan's free kick was swung into the Slovenia area and Edu volleyed the ball into the net.

A goal via set piece that should have stood.

Edu ran off in celebration, but the referee blew his whistle for an apparent infringement as the players jostled for position in the penalty area. To the frustration of the USMNT, he didn't fully explain what his call was. The play-by-play on FIFA's website listed the result of the play as a holding foul by Edu, but upon replay a Slovenia player used his left arm to impede Edu's movement while a few other Slovenia players wrapped their arms around some USMNT players.[114]

The USMNT's chances to reach the knockout rounds would have been far higher if they had won, but they were still in contention. Coach Bradley described a key value of the team: "This team has shown it keeps fighting to the end. It's a credit to the mentality of the players that they are willing to fight for 90 minutes. This is something we've seen time and time again." He also described the overwhelming sentiment: "There was one moment in the second half it seemed like one point gained, and another when it felt like two points lost." The USMNT, who now had two points from two games, were set to play Algeria in Pretoria in their final Group C match with a chance to advance. Thankfully, the England versus Algeria scoreless draw meant a USMNT win against Algeria would put them into the Round of 16.

2010 FIFA World Cup: Group Stage, Game 3
June 23, 2010, at Loftus Versfeld Stadium, Pretoria
USA 1–0 Algeria
Algeria had scored only one goal in their previous seven matches, a penalty against the United Arab Emirates. However, no team should be taken lightly in the World Cup. In the 1982 World Cup, Algeria defeated West

---

114. The reason for the call is a mystery to this day. The only consolation for American supporters is the fact that the referee never officiated another World Cup game.

Germany, a two-time World Cup champion, 2–1. West Germany would later lose to Italy in the 1982 Final.

When the USMNT's bus drove up to the stadium, they were greeted with the American Outlaws and other USMNT fans enthusiastically screaming, chanting, and singing. It meant so much to the USMNT to have their support so far from home, Bob Bradley and some of the players teared up.

The match with Algeria got off to an explosive start and there were chances at both ends. Algeria attacking midfielder Karim Matmour sent a shot narrowly over Tim Howard's bar in the first minute, and five minutes later Algeria striker Rafik Djebbour rattled the crossbar with a volley. DeMerit was literally tasting blood—he split his tongue open in a collision shortly after the match started.[115] Shaken into action, the USMNT went straight to the other end. Hérculez Gómez forced the first save of the game from Algeria. Gómez, in for the suspended Robbie Findley, then sent a volley of his own too high from Steve Cherundolo's cross. A run from Donovan set up the clearest chance of the first half, but when his first effort was blocked, Jozy Altidore took control of the ball and blasted it just over the crossbar in what seemed to be a certain goal. Though Djebbour was causing problems for the USMNT defense and proving difficult to knock off the ball, most of Algeria's goal threats were coming from distance. A Matmour strike from 25 yards out was pushed aside by Howard just before halftime. The USMNT should have scored in the 60th minute, when a combination of a good run and cross from Altidore and a defensive slip left Clint Dempsey with a perfect shooting chance. He essentially had an empty net at a position near the penalty spot, but hit the post. In yet another good chance, Altidore headed a ball straight at the goalkeeper off of a cross from Dempsey.

A draw looked inevitable as the assistant referee held up the LED board indicating four minutes of stoppage time. The USMNT were taking big risks to try to score, and the defenders did an unbelievable job of stopping counter-attack after counter-attack.

---

115. DeMerit would get it stitched up after the game.

In the 2014 World Cup, John Brooks, a second-half substitute, scores the game-winning goal against Ghana in the 86th minute. (Getty Images)

In the 2002 World Cup, the USMNT celebrate beating Mexico 2–0 ("Dos a Cero") to advance to the quarterfinals. (Getty Images)

In the 2006 World Cup, Brian McBride played all 90 minutes in a 1–1 draw against Italy. After the game, he received three stitches below his left eye. (AP Images)

The American Outlaws cheer and wave scarves during the Copa América Centenario semifinal against Argentina in 2016. The USMNT lost 0–4.
(Getty Images)

Borussia Dortmund midfielder Giovanni Reyna (upper left), Juventus midfielder Weston McKennie (lower left), FC Barcelona defender Sergiño Dest (upper right), and Chelsea winger Christian Pulisic (lower right) lead the USMNT's youth movement ahead of the 2022 World Cup. (Getty Images)

The USWNT are much more than a national women's soccer team.
(Getty Images)

Weston McKennie wore an armband reading JUSTICE FOR GEORGE *in May 2020 following the killing of George Floyd by police.* (Getty Images)

The USMNT wore warm-up jackets with BE THE CHANGE *on the front and personal messages on the back prior to a Wales friendly in November 2020. Although U.S. Soccer repealed its policy requiring players to stand for the anthem in June 2020, they stood with arms linked.* (AP Images)

Tim Howard making one of his 16 incredible saves against Belgium in the 2014 World Cup Round of 16. The USMNT lost 1–2. (Getty Images)

After Howard made a save from what could have been a more dangerous header, he threw the ball forward to Donovan up in the midfield. In the stands, Ian Darke was calling the game alongside ESPN colleague and former USMNT captain John Harkes. Darke came to life with his English accent: "Landon Donovan! There are things on here for the USA! Can they do it here?"

Donovan, going at full speed, found Altidore in the penalty area. Darke: "Cross!" Altidore then passed the ball over to Dempsey, who attempted a shot in the box and in front of goal. Darke: "And Dempsey is denied again!" The Algeria goalkeeper made a save, but the ball bounced off of him and into the path of Donovan, who had kept running, following play. The kid from San Bernardino County—who trained at the IMG Bradenton residence academy, turned pro at 17, and made his first World Cup team at 20—ran at the ball in full speed and slotted it into the net.

A goal via counter-attack.

Darke: "And Donovan has scored! Oh, can you believe this? Go, go USA! Certainly through! Oh, it's incredible. You could not write a script like this!" Donovan raced toward the corner flag, slid on his belly, and collided with teammate Stu Holden, with frosted hair tips, at the corner flag. They were met almost immediately by the entire USMNT bench in a massive pileup. After the final few minutes of play, the referee blew the whistle. The USMNT won 1–0. Greatest moment No. 7: a goal from the 2010 World Cup to be remembered.

In a 2013 article "Remembering the USMNT in the 2010 World Cup" for ussoccerplayers.com, Clemente Lisi wrote:

> Nearly four years later, the goal remains an Internet phenomenon. For the first time in American soccer history, one goal meant so much to a nation continuing to grow its love for the game. It seemed, for a moment anyway, that the United States was no different than Brazil, Argentina, Italy, or countless other countries where soccer is a religion. It was a collective moment where a nation could celebrate the success of its soccer team. Donovan's strike may have surpassed Paul Caligiuri's epic goal in 1989 against Trinidad & Tobago that qualified the Americans for a World Cup for the first time in 40 years. At the time,

soccer was not what it is today in this country. There was no pro soccer
league. The National Team was seldom on TV. Caligiuri's goal created
no collective sigh of relief. There was no mass celebration in homes
or bars across the United States. It was before the digital age where
iPhones and YouTube became repositories for every human emotion
and experience—no matter how big or small. This is the moment
no one on that will forget. Whether you were one of the 36,000 in
attendance that night on June 23 at Loftus Versfeld Stadium in Pretoria
or watching on television at home or in a bar in this country, it is a
moment—a goal—that will live on in your memory forever... The
goal set off celebrations on the field, in the stands and in millions of
American homes and bars.

In an article titled "And Donovan Has Scored!," Brian Straus of *Sports
Illustrated* quoted Ian Dark in an interview: "It became clear to me, over
time, that it was the breakthrough moment in the rise of popularity of the
game in the U.S.…. I think a lot of people in past years would ask, 'Why
aren't there more goals? Why is it so dull? Nothing happens.' And I think
the way that happened, the incredible high at the end of a goalless game, I
think a few people said, 'Okay, I get it now. That was amazing.'"

Straus continued his article and wrote, "Gradually, videos of American
fans 'getting it' were uploaded to YouTube. They showed bars and
restaurants and a group of people watching through a window on a New
York City street and a guy throwing himself down a flight of stairs, all
exploding in joy." On YouTube, a USMNT fan uploaded a compilation
of celebrations, complete with the theme from *Rudy*, that quickly had
millions of views. One of the players said, "To see all of their reactions, I
think that re-energized us. Look at all the people behind us. Look at all the
people now that are going to support us for the next one. It made us feel
like we were doing it for more than ourselves. We're on the cusp of having
a country that doesn't really care about soccer, really care about soccer."

It was a collective moment where a nation could celebrate the success of
its national team and the legitimacy of soccer in the U.S. It didn't matter
that the USMNT had just beaten Algeria, who were not considered a
traditional soccer power. It was as much the *how* and *who* as the *what*.

President Bill Clinton, who was in the stands, captured the reason why Americans were so passionate: "I like people who don't quit.... We are not keen on quitters in my family."

Greatest moment No. 8: a first since 1930 from the 2010 World Cup. The USMNT won the match and Group C in the most dramatic circumstances possible. Donovan's goal advanced the USMNT to the Round of 16 as the group winner and relegated England to second place just when they thought they had secured the top spot. It was the first time since 1930 that the Americans had won their group.

The USMNT left it to the end, but there can be no arguing with the justice of the final group table. England scored twice in three matches. The USMNT scored four and had a perfectly good winner disallowed against Slovenia. The goal was also Donovan's fourth World Cup goal of his career, tying him with Bert Patenaude from the 1930 World Cup on the USMNT's all-time list. The game also marked Donovan's 11th World Cup appearance, tying him for the USMNT record alongside Cobi Jones and Earnie Stewart. That day, Donovan also became the only USMNT player to score multiple goals in two different World Cups.

One goal on essentially the last play of a match completely changed the narrative. Brian Straus quoted Donovan in an interview: "The crazy thing is you're on the verge of being completely sad after the game, going home, packing your bags and leaving the next morning and within a few minutes you're in this euphoric state and in the back of your mind you're still in the tournament. Where do we go next? Who are we playing?"

Carlos Bocanegra noticed President Clinton outside the locker room and invited him in to celebrate. President Clinton took off his jacket, rolled up his sleeves, and grabbed a beer. The players were shocked President Clinton knew all their names. Donovan described what happened in the locker room: "My recollection of it is just being so hectic and finally getting back to the locker room, seeing guys with beers open, seeing President Clinton, seeing a bunch of our U.S. Soccer staff in there, half the room is sort of a look of relief from the suits in the room and the rest of the coaching staff and the players are just elated." The room was so chaotic that they couldn't locate a phone to receive a phone call from

President Barack Obama, who would eventually speak to the team after dinner the following day.

The USMNT's three group stage games in South Africa averaged more than 11 million viewers in the U.S. That was up 68 percent from the 2006 World Cup. If there was going to be a goal that defined both the Spirit of '76 and when American soccer soared into the mainstream, what better than Donovan and his teammates not giving up, working together, and scoring a goal on the counter-attack in the last minute. In that one play, all fans witnessed, in all of its glory, the Spirit of '76. The USMNT's last-minute goal also changed the 2010 World Cup narrative for England. Instead of winning the group and playing Ghana, as runners-up England had to play Germany in the Round of 16, which they lost 1–4.

The win had also reignited expectations of the USMNT. Ryan Pine of *The Philly Soccer Page* was at the game and reflected on July 2010: "Landon Donovan had just given us—no, check that—a whole nation a lifeline. We didn't have to go home short of the knockout stages again. We were through! The dancing and singing carried on long into the night. It was well over an hour from when the whistle blew before we even considered leaving the stadium. The whole car ride back, we listened to the radio and reports of Lando's wonder strike. It was, undoubtedly, the single greatest sporting moment I had ever witnessed and one of the most important goals to ever be scored by the United States national team. As we split a pizza that night back at Terra Casa, we dreamed aloud of a U.S. *semifinal* berth for the first time since 1930 and the first time in the current 32-team format." (Our italics for emphasis.) The issue was that the 2002 World Cup quarterfinal result had set the bar. The progress in an upward-trending straight line was back on. No one was dreaming of merely a quarterfinal anymore.

After the team beat Algeria, in the midst of all the excitement, Bradley and Tom King of U.S. Soccer secretly arranged to get family and friends to the USMNT hotel. When the team arrived, they were so surprised and happy. Conveniently, it also solved the problem of the players wanting to go to the family and friends' hotel with the Round of 16 match only days away. After everyone left that night, it was back to business—the team had a meeting.

2010 FIFA World Cup: Round of 16
June 26, 2010, at Royal Bafokeng Stadium, Rustenburg
USA 1–2 Ghana

The Round of 16 match against Ghana was called the Black Stars versus the Stars and Stripes because of each team's nickname. *The Guardian* bloggers wrote: "It's a tough one to call. I've missed two of Ghana's matches, but am reliably informed they play 'lovely football' but tend to lose their heads in the final third—a fact apparently borne out by the fact that their only two scores in the tournament to date have come from the penalty spot. The US, on the other hand, have been fairly impressive on fairly limited resources and in Landon Donovan have one of the players of the tournament thus far. I expect…Ghana content to sit back, absorb whatever is thrown at them, and attack on the break." The bookmakers had the USMNT as 4-5 favorites (55.6 percent), while Ghana were 6-5 (45.5 percent). The USMNT won their group without having had the lead in any of the total 270 minutes of normal playing time.

Ghana beat the USMNT 2–1 in the final group game in the 2006 World Cup before losing to Brazil in the Round of 16, so the USMNT wanted payback. Ghana qualified second from Group D behind Germany following a tense final round of matches that saw three teams level on four points. The last African nation to win a World Cup knockout round match was Senegal, when they beat Sweden 2–1 in the Round of 16 in 2002.

After the Algeria match, Bradley was being touted as a tactical genius, but when he released his lineup for the game, the USMNT fan base and media collectively scratched their heads. After solid play from midfielder Benny Feilhaber and midfielder Maurice Edu in both the Slovenia and Algeria games, Bradley reverted to midfielder Ricardo Clark and forward Robbie Findley. It seemed Bradley was concerned Feilhaber didn't have the fitness level to play 90 minutes, and he thought that bringing him into the game later and moving Clint Dempsey forward would be a good way for the USMNT to change the game. The decision to use Findlay may have had to do with losing Charlie Davies, because having a fast player up front with Jozy Altidore could make the USMNT more dangerous.

As they walked onto the field in their all-white jerseys, some of the USMNT players noticed President Bill Clinton in attendance sitting alongside Mick Jagger. When the game started, the USMNT went on the attack and enjoyed the majority of possession. Ghana came out defensive, literally, starting five defenders to absorb pressure. It seemed Ghana's strategy was to soak up pressure and try and break with pace with their speedy outlets.

Then, in the fifth minute, Ghana's Kwadwo Asamoah stripped the ball from Clark near the center circle and quickly passed it to midfielder and speedster Kevin Prince Boateng. Boateng, who had switched nationalities before the tournament after representing Germany at the U-21 level, took six steady touches toward a tentative USMNT back line and from about 25 yards out drove a low shot past the diving Tim Howard's near post for the opening score. Unfortunately, the USMNT conceded yet another early goal.

In the seventh minute, Ricardo Clark crashed into Boateng and picked up the first yellow card of the game. Ghana's plan seemed to be crowding the midfield as much as possible, pressing the USMNT high up the field, knocking them off the ball at every opportunity, forcing mistakes, and generally playing the opposite of the way many predicted with Ghana starting five defenders. Steve Cherundolo was dispossessed by a Ghana player midway through the first half, then fouled him and picked up a yellow card. Ayew took the free kick that Howard had to punch away. Michael Bradley managed to force a save from Richard Kingson at the other end, but found himself back on the defensive shortly afterward, heading a clearance over his own bar.

In the 23rd minute, Dempsey found Michael Bradley inside the Ghana area on the left, but his cross was blocked by Richard Kingson before Robbie Findlay could make contact from close range.

After 30 minutes, Coach Bradley sent on Maurice Edu for Clark. Clark had a yellow card and seemed at risk of getting another. The decisive move was also an attempt to stiffen the American midfield and cut down the space available to Boateng. It was a necessary early substitution, but one that could cost a tired USMNT team later. Edu's substitution brought some positivity to the USMNT side, and immediately the Americans responded. In the 35th minute, young Ghana defender Jonathan Mensah gave the ball away to Dempsey, who placed a perfect pass to the feet of Findley. Findley failed to compose himself and drove an off-balance shot right into the hands of the Ghana goalkeeper Kingson. Kingson, who had struggled against Australia, looked a lot more confident, not only stopping shots but safely claiming crosses. Dempsey was very good. His energy and effort were incredible. He took knock after knock. He kept fighting for every ball and was a real offensive spark.

The USMNT went into halftime down 0–1. Ghana looked to be the better team and deserved their lead. Their lone goal was fantastic, but again it was because the USMNT cheaply gave the ball away. The USMNT looked tired and, after what they had been through in previous games, it was unclear whether they would have enough energy left to turn the game around.

The players believed they could come back and win. They were the first back out on the field. Coach Bradley made some second-half adjustments. The struggling Findley came off for the more dangerous Feilhaber. The USMNT changed from Bradley's favored empty bucket to a more flexible, free-flowing 4-4-1-1 that shifted shapes depending on whether they possessed the ball and where the ball was—the USMNT found itself in 4-3-3, 4-4-2, and 4-3-2-1 shapes—thanks to the intelligent movement of the players, who were finally playing to the best of their strengths. For example, when the USMNT possessed the ball, two of the team's best creative playmakers, Donovan and Dempsey, technically acting as midfielders, had the freedom to come inside into good pockets of space to receive the ball and create opportunities.

Feilhaber was born in Rio de Janeiro and his family moved to the U.S. when he was six years old. In 2006, he turned down an offer to play for Austria (his paternal grandfather is Austrian) and said that he would instead focus on earning a place on the USMNT. Feilhaber allowed the

USMNT to match Ghana's midfield, drifting more and more centrally or where he could find pockets of space where Dempsey wasn't, allowing Dempsey to move higher up the field with more space and options to create.

Right away, in the 47th minute, the USMNT could have leveled the match. The USMNT found open space down the right and the ball was played by Altidore to Feilhaber on the edge of the six-yard box. He tried to poke a right-foot shot over the onrushing goalkeeper and into the right-hand side of the goal, but Kingson stuck out his left hand and managed an excellent save.

As Michael Bradley pushed forward from the midfield and the Dempsey-Donovan duo played just off Altidore, the USMNT began to dictate possession and create chances. There were several reasons this formation worked so well. First, it put all of the players in positions where they generally excel. Michael Bradley is best in a box-to-box role. His deep-penetrating runs into Ghana's box were a constant threat. Donovan and Dempsey could play off each other—when one went forward, the other dropped deep into the midfield to get the ball. When one crossed the field, so did the other. They were able to link up frequently and get in central space. Both were difficult for Ghana to deal with.

In the 62nd minute, Dempsey cheekily nutmegged 19-year-old defender John Mensah and made his way into the penalty area, forcing Mensah to bring him down as he tried to get past. Donovan then coolly hit the ensuing penalty kick in off the left-hand post.

Goal via set piece.

It was Donovan's 45th international goal, making him the all-time leading scorer in World Cups from the CONCACAF region, with five goals.

With around 15 minutes left, Kingson had to come racing a long way off his line and made a brilliant sliding save on Altidore, which was another excellent piece of goalkeeping but also an indication of how the match had swung in favor of the USMNT. For most of the second half, the USMNT employed the patient, probing style that had served them so well. They were enjoying their best chances of the match as normal time ran out, but they could not repeat their heroic late efforts from the previous two matches that would result in a goal. It seemed the fear of losing by both sides slightly overcame the desire to win in the last 10 minutes.

In extra time, in almost a direct repeat of the opening goal, the USMNT were caught early in the first period by a Ghana goal. When a high ball came down the middle, Gyan absorbed the impact of Bocanegra's shoulder, stayed on his feet, accelerated away from the USMNT captain, and from 15 yards out beat Howard in the same unstoppable manner as Boateng did. Just as they had done at the start of the game, the Black Stars hit the Stars and Stripes with a devastating quick counter-attack in the opening minutes. It was third time in four matches the USMNT had conceded an early goal. Although some nervous defending by Ghana late in the extra period gave the USMNT chances, the USMNT could not come back again.

Typically the losing team just wants to get back to the privacy of their dressing room, but there were a lot of USMNT players just sitting on the bench with towels draped around them, looking utterly despondent. BBC Radio 5's Danny Mills said, "It was a hard-fought game which could have gone either way but it was settled by a moment of pace, power, and opportunism when Asamoah Gyan burst through onto a long ball. Credit to both teams, great game, great entertainment." A blogger for the BBC wrote, "However much it may not be the most popular sport in the US, I've got more respect for the American team after this World Cup. They've played some good stuff and their football is improving very quickly now. The rest of the world better watch out in a couple of years."

During the match, Altidore made a few noteworthy runs and almost scored, but ultimately failed to register a single goal in the entire World Cup. While his play was good at times, for whatever reason, the finish was not there. In fact, none of the USMNT goals came from forwards. Charlie Davies, one of the USMNT's best forwards, was still not cleared to play after his car accident, which was particularly disappointing because Altidore and Davies had displayed beautiful chemistry in the 2009 Confederations Cup.

When reviewing the statistics from the game, it could have gone either way. Ghana had 51 percent possession. The USMNT took 20 shots and six were on goal, compared to Ghana's 16 and six. Howard had four saves compared to Ghana's five.

At that point, Donovan was tied for most goals in the tournament with three goals over four games. Thomas Müller of Germany would eventually win the Golden Boot with five goals in six appearances.[116] Only 145 goals were scored at South Africa 2010, the lowest of any World Cup since the tournament switched to a 64-game format. This continued a downward trend since the first 64-game World Cups were held 12 years earlier, with 171 goals at France 1998, 161 at South Korea/Japan 2002, and 147 at Germany 2006.

Ghana moved on to face Uruguay, who had defeated South Korea 2–1, in the quarterfinals in Johannesburg. Uruguay, the only South American team to reach the semifinals, beat Ghana in a penalty shootout after a 1–1 draw in which Ghana missed a penalty at the end of extra time after Luis Suárez controversially handled the ball on the line.

The USMNT finished the tournament in 12th place, ahead of England (13th) and Mexico (14th). The pretournament world rankings had the USMNT at 14th, England eighth, and Mexico 17th. The USMNT scored five goals—three counter-attacks, one set piece (one set piece that should have stood), and one lucky long-range shot. The USMNT averaged 1.3 goals per game, higher than eventual champion Spain. The USMNT didn't receive a red card in the 2010 World Cup. In the 2002 World Cup, the USMNT had plus-3.4 goals higher than expected (higher than the tournament average of plus-1.5), while in the 2010 World Cup the number was minus-0.1 (below the tournament average of plus-0.8). The 2010 USMNT didn't have the same luck as 2002. Ultimately, the dismaying USMNT habit of conceding early in the 2010 World Cup, which also was an issue in the 2006 World Cup, caught up to them.

In a June 2010 article in the *New York Times* titled "Mixed Results for the U.S.; Uncertain Future for Coach," George Vecsey wrote, "This can

---

116. Germany won the third-place playoff.

only be considered a sign of progress for soccer in America: the head of the United States Soccer Federation is not bubbling with glee after the team got as far as the World Cup Round of 16. Facing something between a ticker-tape reception and a tomato barrage, the bulk of the United States team headed to Washington." In characterizing the USMNT's performance, he quoted Gulati as saying the team had "mixed results." In describing the result of the last match, he quoted Gulati as saying "an opportunity missed."

The USMNT wanted to prove the legitimacy of soccer in the U.S., especially after the 2006 performance. If nothing else, they proved they had spectacular heart, will, and teamwork—and fight to the finish.

Perceptions, Language, and Stereotypes

Prior to the 2010 World Cup, the play-by-play announcers for the English-language television in the U.S. were primarily American. USMNT fans seemed content with Americans calling soccer matches and didn't seem to mind that the American commentators had, for the most part, never announced European soccer matches. The lead announcers for the 1990–2010 World Cups were, in order, Americans Bob O'Neal (1990), Roger Twibell (1994), Bob Ley (1998), Jack Edwards (2002), and Dave O'Brien (2006).

Starting in 2010, things changed. Martin Tyler, an English football commentator, led ESPN's coverage of the 2010 FIFA World Cup. A few months prior, Fox used Tyler's Sky commentary for the 2010 UEFA Champions League Final. This was the first time the Champions League Final was broadcast on a major American television network. Ian Darke was hired to be the ESPN commentator for its coverage of the 2014 World Cup for the American market. He became known to the American public as the English commentator for Landon Donovan's last-second goal. The magic was in the moment itself, but Darke's giddy description of the USMNT's goal against Algeria cemented a special place for him in the hearts of American soccer fans. We believe it also meant more because he was English—there was some sort of implied higher authority, legitimacy, or expertise. We believe Martin Tyler and Ian Darke are talented and deserving commentators. However, we also believe that the selection of English commentators reflected the drift or change in what was needed to add legitimacy. Intentionally or not, their English accents reflected some higher authority on the sport, now that Americans' expectations had risen.

Language and stereotypes in the media also would diminish the USMNT's legitimacy. When the USMNT beat or tied a European soccer power, the media headlines, such as BLUNDER HANDS U.S. DRAW WITH ENGLAND or U.S. TIES ENGLAND ON GOALIE GAFFE, implied the only way the USMNT could tie England was through luck or an English mistake. These perceptions and stereotypes also restricted the opportunities in Europe for some USMNT players and coaches.

Meanwhile, language and stereotypes in the media were contributing to the USMNT's drift from embracing being an underdog fighting for legitimacy. During our research, when reading and listening to the commentary of the 2010 USMNT versus Ghana match, it was hard not to notice what seemed to be stereotyping by Western media and soccer commentators. James Wells wrote, "ESPN's coverage of this game has been rife with stereotypes of African football. Ghana are 'powerful, physical, and explosive' but the U.S. is 'tactically stronger.' Just now, viewers were informed that the U.S. can't compete physically with Ghana and will have to outsmart them. It's true that Ghana have some great athletes, but all teams at this level are full of athletes. And tactically naive? I haven't seen it. They're certainly not tactically weaker than the USA based on what I've seen..."

While writing this book, research done by RunRepeat in 2020 found that broadcast commentators were not only far more likely to praise white players for their intelligence, leadership qualities, and versatility, they were also substantially more likely to criticize Black players for what they regarded as the absence of those attributes. Black players were four times more likely than their white counterparts to be discussed in terms of their strength and seven times more likely to be praised for their speed. Commentators help shape the perception we hold of each player, deepening any racial bias already held by the viewer. It's important to consider how far-reaching those perceptions can be.

The USSF and USMNT should actually have been more proud of their progress. Unfortunately, while the USMNT were actually progressing with their mission to prove the legitimacy of soccer in the U.S., many had shifted their primary focus to a goal, which was to progress to the semifinals of the World Cup (or at least match the 2002 quarterfinal). If Bob Bradley had lost the Round of 16 game versus a perceived soccer power, he probably would have received more credit for winning the group in the 2010 World Cup. The fact that the loss wasn't to a European or South American soccer power and the USMNT were slightly favored was "an opportunity missed." The United States, with all of its resources, losing—to an African nation, no less—in two straight World Cups was hard to accept by U.S. media and fans. The narrative changed because, in part, expectations changed, but also perceptions, language, and stereotypes had an impact.

Chapter 10

Summer 2011 to 2014: Klinsmann Arrives

A European Coach with Credentials like Klinsmann Adds Legitimacy to U.S. Soccer

After the 2010 World Cup, many observers wondered if hiring a European coach was what was needed to show more progress and advance further than the 2002 World Cup quarterfinals. In 2010 George Vecsey of the *New York Times* wrote, "Gulati did not seem to agree with American fans who insist *it is time to hire a major European coach.*" (Our italics for emphasis.) He quoted Gulati as saying, "An American coach understands the mentality of the American player." Vecsey wrote, "He added that he would be interested in an American coach who had played in a World Cup final and had coached in a World Cup final, 'but we don't have one of those.'"

On June 25, 2011, the USMNT lost 2–4 to Mexico in the Gold Cup Final. According to an article in the *New York Times* by Jeré Longman, "There seemed to be a growing feeling that the Americans had stagnated in their progression while the fast, young, creative Mexican team had surpassed the United States as the region's top team." The USMNT had beaten Mexico in the 2002 World Cup Round of 16; therefore many fans saw losing to them as a step backward. On July 28, 2011, the USSF

239

fired Bob Bradley and hired Jürgen Klinsmann. Sam Boden of the *New York Times* later wrote, "To Gulati, Klinsmann was what U.S. Soccer needed: a coach *European enough* to command the players' respect, but *American enough*." (Our italics for emphasis.) The word "European" often accompanied any introduction or description of Klinsmann in the U.S. media. The drift to wanting to be and play "more European" resulted in Klinsmann being hired as coach, but the drift was already occurring before that. His hiring just accelerated the belief that the USMNT needed to act and play more like Europeans in order to be more successful.

Klinsmann was as close to being an American as a foreign-born coach of the USMNT could be. He lives in Southern California, is married to an American model, had spent time working with the LA Galaxy, and was familiar with many of the players in the U.S. Unlike his immediate predecessors, Klinsmann was a top player at the highest levels of international soccer. He played a key role in West Germany's victory in the 1990 World Cup and was captain of the team when they won the 1996 European championship. He coached Germany to a third-place finish in the 2006 World Cup. His pedigree was very legitimate.

However, there was something that the fans and media often overlooked—no foreign coach has ever won the World Cup, and only two have reached the Final (in 1958 and 1978). Understanding a country's soccer culture, identity, and style matters.

Europeanization of American Soccer Accelerates

When Klinsmann took over the USMNT, his mandate was to take American soccer to the next level, and to accomplish this many believed he had to "Europeanize American soccer," a phrase used in a June 2014 article Cameron Abadi wrote for the *New Yorker* titled "Jürgen Klinsmann's Soccer Mandate."

In the article, Abadi wrote, "Klinsmann thinks that the U.S. team can help to shake the country out of its apathy. But he says that winning won't be enough; the team will have to win in a recognizably American style. 'It has to be our goal to develop a style in which Americans will recognize themselves,' he says. 'They have to be in front of the television and say,

"Yes, that's my team.'" Klinsmann admits that this is a bit of a challenge in such a diverse country where 'no one is completely American.' But Klinsmann believes that the team's playing style will eventually resemble something like the country's assertive entrepreneurial culture. 'Americans are proactive,' he tells me. 'You want to be world leaders in everything you do. So, on the field, you shouldn't just sit back and wait.' Although American teams have traditionally depended on counter-attacking—a type of strategy that involves exploiting an opponent's aggression— Klinsmann hopes that his players will soon be more assertive and creative on offense." Above all else, he wanted to rid the U.S. team of its underdog status and mentality.

Klinsmann promised to no longer rely on an American style of superb goalkeeping and counter-attacks. He wanted to instill a proactive, possession-based game that was modeled on the 4-3-3 of Europe. In a November 2016 article titled "Jürgen Klinsmann's Biggest Mistake Was Showing American Soccer What It Really Is," Aaron Gordon of Vice wrote, "Klinsmann got the job and provoked so much enthusiasm among American soccer fans early on precisely *because* of his promises to take the game to opponents, to compete with the best…. From the beginning, Klinsmann keyed on American ambition: *America will play like a top country, against top countries, and aggressively compete with them.* He understood our culture well enough to know this promise would get a lot of people on his side, including USSF executives and board members. Many fans, of course, also loved the idea." (Italics Gordon's, not ours.)

In a June 2014 article in the *New York Times* titled "How Jürgen Klinsmann Plans to Make U.S. Soccer Better (and Less American)," Sam Borden wrote, "Klinsmann believes that if the United States is ever going to really succeed at a World Cup, a specific and significant change must occur within the team. That change does not necessarily have to do with how the Americans play; rather, it has to do with the American players being too American. Put simply, Klinsmann would like to see his players carry themselves like their European counterparts—the way he used to."

Klinsmann's comments were forward-thinking and progressive, which matched the belief that the USMNT needed to act and play more like Europeans in order to advance and be more legitimate. The problem was the USMNT's *how*—the Spirit of '76—already existed because of America's soccer culture, history with the sport, and skill level.

While it is in theory possible to copy a certain style of play with enough talent and time, it is impossible (not to mention counterproductive) to try to copy a culture or appropriate an identity. Sam Borden explained, "Bruce Arena, who coaches the Los Angeles Galaxy, told me recently that instead of trying to get American soccer to mimic European culture, U.S. Soccer officials should simply look inward.... The people that run our governing body think we need to copy what everyone else does, when in reality, our solutions will ultimately come from our culture. Come on, we can't copy what Brazil does or Germany does or England does. When we get it right, it's going to be because the solutions are right here." We believe Arena was right that solutions will have to come out of American soccer culture. Klinsmann looked to American culture, but did not fully appreciate or understand the context of why and how the USMNT's style and identity developed and why and how soccer is perceived in the U.S.— and he wasn't alone.

Another problem of trying to Europeanize American Soccer was, according to Borden, "...While other countries tweak their traditional blueprints, the Americans are still working on the plans for a foundation. Should they kick the ball long and chase it? Use big bodies to defend with physical aggression? Rely on what Pia Sundhage, another European brought in to coach Americans (the women's national team, in her case), described to me as 'the incredible energy that only Americans have'?" Indeed, this was a problem because the USMNT already had an identity or "foundation." Observers may not have liked it or thought it was good enough to consistently beat soccer powers and progress to a World Cup semifinal or final. But the *how* was there.

Did Skill Level Meet What Was Required to Play Europeanized American Soccer?

The USMNT had developed an identity and style of play that was progressing. However, while their skill level was often underappreciated, the USMNT didn't have an entire squad of players competing in the Top Five Leagues in Europe on a regular basis or players receiving votes for the Ballon d'Or, let alone six of them on the team like most World Cup champions. Since the trophy's inception in 1956, players from 20 different countries have won the Ballon d'Or, with even more players from even more different countries finishing in the top three.[117] Still, the U.S. hasn't even come close. And that is something many observers don't take completely into context when developing expectations.

In fairness, Klinsmann did briefly allude in his introductory press conference to the fact that the USMNT didn't have the talent necessary to play such a style. This is obvious—so obvious that when he said it no one paused—and yet everyone largely ignored it in pursuit of what was an unrealistic goal of progress in an upward-trending straight line to win the World Cup. The idea that everyone thought Klinsmann could immediately progress to win was preposterous. In his same November 2016 *Vice* article, Aaron Gordon wrote, "Luckily for Klinsmann, Americans were sick of hearing about our talent shortfall, and were thus ready to accept a manager not just telling us otherwise, but promising to play like it, too. Klinsmann, in his dual role as technical director and head coach, claimed he would find and develop the talent to play proactively and then integrate it into the national team. He promised to overhaul the American youth system, no matter how impractical that was, a necessary step toward playing the way he said Americans crave."

As previously mentioned, the peak in talent in soccer in the U.S. resulted from the energy and excitement of the 1994 World Cup being held in the U.S. and the identity of the team inspiring a group of talented young boys. These seven- to 12-year-old boys, 12 to 16 years later, would reach peak soccer age in 2006 to 2010. The minutes in the Top Five

---

117. Germany tops the list with five players winning seven Ballons d'Or.

Leagues support this. The challenge was the USMNT skill level, defined by players and minutes in Top Five Leagues, was actually declining. While Klinsmann alluded the USMNT didn't have the talent to play the style he would like, he did not fully appreciate that there would be a drop-off in skill level that would further challenge his future plans.

The Challenges Klinsmann Faced Compared to Being Coach of Germany
Evaluating and Monitoring Players Across Different Countries and Continents

When Klinsmann began coaching the USMNT, he had to evaluate the skill level of each player. This was a lot more complicated than his experience in Germany, where most players played in the Bundesliga or other Top Five European leagues. There were an established career path and pecking order in Germany and Europe. Most German players tried to work their way up from bottom-half Bundesliga table teams to play for one of the top Bundesliga clubs like Bayern Munich or Borussia Dortmund, who could pay the most and were consistently playing for trophies. A few elite German players may move from Bayern Munich to top clubs in Europe that have even more financial resources or a willingness to spend more than Bayern, such as Real Madrid or an English Premier League club.

In 2006, while Klinsmann was head coach, 21 of the 23 players on the German team played in Germany. The other two players, Jens Lehmann and Robert Huth, played in the Premier League at Arsenal and Chelsea, respectively, and while Huth spent his entire career in England, Lehmann had played at Dortmund for a number of years before being transferred to Arsenal in July 2003. Of those who played in Germany, four played for Bayern Munich; three each for Borussia Dortmund and Werder Bremen; two each for Borussia Mönchengladbach, Bayer Leverkusen, and VfB Stuttgart; and then one each for Hertha BSC, VfL Wolfsburg, Schalke 04, Hannover 96, and FC Koln. With an established system and level of competition, and players playing against each other more consistently, it was relatively easy to evaluate and compare players. In many ways, the German clubs already did this for the German coach. For example, generally a German starter for Bayern Munich was better than his German backup on the bench. Typically, the backup on the bench was better than most German players in the Bundesliga at his position—if not, Bayern Munich had the resources to get the German player they wanted. A competitive German ordering system existed in the Bundesliga.

In contrast, the USMNT players played in a wide range of European leagues, MLS, and Liga MX, and for different reasons. On the USMNT 2014 World Cup team, there were five players who were playing in the Bundesliga at the time, on five different teams. Elsewhere in Europe, there were four players in England, one in France, one in the Netherlands, and one in Norway. The rest of the team, with the exception of DaMarcus Beasley, who was playing in Mexico at the time, played in MLS.

The USMNT coaches have to try more players as a result of players being spread across so many different leagues and countries. In winning the 2014 World Cup, Germany used 38 players in qualification. The USMNT used 60 players, over 50 percent more. We provided Spain for 2014 as context, who used 39. We also included the USMNT for the 2010 World Cup, who used 59.

2014 WC Qualification—All USA Players

2014 WC Qualification	USA 2014	Germany	Spain	USA 2010
# Games Played	16	10	8	16
# Players (Pool)	60	38	39	59
# Players (Appearance)	38	24	28	43
Average Age (Pool)	25.1	24.0	25.7	25.3
Average Age (Appearance)	25.5	24.1	26.0	24.7

This delays the establishment of a core group of players who are familiar with each other.

Players with Different Competitive Experiences Causing Different Levels of Conditioning

German (and European) players who play in the upper echelon of European professional clubs often play in the Champions League or Europa League tournament—the highest levels of club competition. Players playing in these tournaments also become mentally accustomed to high-pressure matches against elite competition in a knockout format, which helps them prepare for the knockout rounds of the World Cup. Putting aside the experience of the tournament, the German coaches can see how the players are competing with top players from other countries.

German (and European) players who play in the upper echelon of European professional clubs are also used to playing matches with a few days' rest as they compete in their domestic league, Champions League (or Europa League), and domestic knockout tournaments. This busy calendar causes players to build physical and mental fitness and understand how to recover. Players in MLS and players on European clubs not competing in European tournaments or going far in tournaments don't get used to the same demands. In a World Cup, players are expected to play every few days. A USMNT player may not be used to playing all three group stage games coming within a few days, typically at the same level. So, a USMNT coach and player have to adapt.

Players who played in both Top Five Leagues and MLS explained that in MLS, the pressure and wear and tear on the body isn't quite the same. It isn't just physical, either; obviously, a player's body needs time to recover and it's helpful to have experience playing back-to-back, hard games, but mental toughness needs to be developed as well. It is physically, mentally, and emotionally challenging for a player to play at his peak performance level in successive games in fairly short order.

Another difference is national European teams often play other national European teams, which tend to be highly ranked in their regional tournaments (Euros) and World Cup qualifying matches. Playing against the best players and teams sharpens skills and exposes areas for improvement. If we compare the teams in CONCACAF versus UEFA, the contrast is pretty striking. The total rankings for the 2017 Gold Cup, which the USMNT won, was 653 (if we add up each team's FIFA World Ranking at the time). Twelve teams total competed in the tournament, with an average rank of 65.3.[118] This compares to the 2016 European Championship, which had 24 teams competing with a total rank of 496 and an average rank of 20.7. While we would certainly expect the average

---

118. Note that the average would have been higher, as French Guiana and Martinique were not FIFA members and therefore did not have a FIFA World Rank.

rank for the Euro teams to be much lower, it is shocking to see that even with twice the number of teams, the *total rank* is lower as well, by a sizeable margin![119]

We discovered in our interviews that internationally, the perception of Mexico is that they are a very good team, but many of their players lack the competitive match experiences of the Top Five Leagues or Champions League or the experience of playing matches with very little rest while juggling European tournaments, domestic tournaments, and the domestic league. In addition, the international perception is that Mexico playing relatively weak competition in CONCACAF as compared to UEFA (Europe) and CONMEBOL (South America) hinders their development and "match toughness." Some international players and coaches attributed these factors to Mexico's not advancing past the Round of 16 in the World Cup, except when they reached the quarterfinals in the 1970 and 1986 World Cups—both times Mexico were the hosts and had home-field advantage.

Team Chemistry Impacted by Cliques

After Klinsmann arrived, various cliques emerged or became more distinct based primarily on where the players played and/or grew up (language)—including those who played in Europe, those who grew up in Germany and primarily spoke German, those who grew up in the U.S. and played in MLS, and those who played in Mexico and/or spoke Spanish. While cliques existed in the past, there was a feeling among many of the players that the effect was greater under Klinsmann for a variety of reasons, ranging from MLS becoming more prominent to Klinsmann's own decisions. This was in contrast to the 2010 World Cup USMNT group who felt there was an incredibly special and close bond.[120]

---

119. The USSF invited CONMEBOL to play a tournament with CONCACAF in 2020, which CONMEBOL turned down.

120. In fairness, it is not unusual for organizations to have cliques and it highlights another issue: the team seemed to lack a player who could consistently unite the team. For example, the 1980 Olympic Hockey team had Mike Eruzione to unite the players from Minnesota and Boston; in 1994, the USMNT had Tony Meola to unite players in Europe and those at Mission Viejo; and in 1999, the USWNT had Carla Overbeck to unite the players from UNC and other colleges.

Klinsmann didn't have to deal with as many cliques as coach of Germany because most of the players played in the Bundesliga, were familiar with each other, and primarily spoke German. In addition, players knew and respected the informal hierarchy of which clubs in the Bundesliga or Europe consistently were generally considered better than the others. It was as if there were a competition ladder. Such an informal hierarchy didn't exist in the USMNT because the players were so dispersed and MLS doesn't have a consistently dominant team like Bayern Munich. Without a respected informal hierarchy, it opened the door to more misperceptions and stereotypes, which contributed to the cliques as well as criticisms of player selection.

Challenging the Status Quo

Klinsmann and his staff brought a sense of competitiveness and ambition to the national team. Under Klinsmann, a player's spot was never guaranteed. He created a mind-set of a player never letting himself get too comfortable. If a player was in his prime and playing in MLS, Klinsmann saw that as a wasted opportunity—for the player and country. In the early 1990s, before MLS, there was a sense of pride that an American could go to Europe and make it—the underdog. By the time Klinsmann took over, MLS was becoming more powerful and the perception had changed within some circles that the U.S. had "lost" a player to European soccer. The change impacted the team culture and chemistry. Klinsmann was trying to introduce competitiveness at every level.

On the other hand, many players felt like they were constantly being held to German standards and practices. For example, Klinsmann would have most of their days fully scheduled, many times for meetings that were not directly related to soccer, and would even list what the players were required to wear off the field—which often was an uncomfortable team track suit. There isn't anything inherently wrong with this. We are giving this background to explain how the USMNT went from a relatively loose environment of even bringing golf clubs to the 2006 World Cup to a stricter one under Bradley leading to the 2010 World Cup, which many players believed was a tightening adjustment that took time to get used to but a necessary one, to an even more regimented environment under Klinsmann leading up to the 2014 World Cup, which many players felt had gone too far. Many felt Klinsmann was imposing German culture on them. Some players didn't mind and some felt Klinsmann's changes were necessary.

How Winning Can Hide Ugly Truths: Firsts in Italy and Mexico...

On a chilly February 12, 2012, night in Genoa, Italy, the USMNT, ranked 31st in the world, beat Italy, ranked eighth, in a friendly match. It was the first time the USMNT had beaten Italy, and the USMNT were missing a few of their players due to injuries or illness, including Landon Donovan, the team's leading scorer. In 10 games under Klinsmann, the USMNT were 5–4–1, but their four other victories were over Slovenia, Panama, Venezuela, and Honduras.

Italy controlled possession though most of the game, but the USMNT defenders (captain Carlos Bocanegra, Clarence Goodson, Steve Cherundolo, and German American Fabian Johnson) were well-organized and kept a good shape and line. Tim Howard also had some key saves. Then, in the 55th minute, Fabian Johnson ran forward with the ball and crossed it to Jozy Altidore, who, with his back to goal near the penalty spot, softly touched it off to the top of the area to set up a shot for Dempsey, who hit a well-placed right-footed hard drive across his body into the low corner of the net. With 16 goals in the season for Fulham, Dempsey became the American career scoring leader in the English Premier League with 43 goals. Desperate to score, Italy made multiple substitutions over the next 15 minutes to bring on fresh-legged attacking players. However, the Americans held on to win, with defenders blocking or deflecting several threatening shots at goal. Italy dominated stretches of the game and outshot the USMNT 19–4, and were called offside nine times as compared to none for the USMNT. After the match, USMNT midfielder Michael Bradley said, "We fight for respect every time we step on the field." Bradley understood the USMNT's *why*.

In August 2012, the USMNT beat Mexico, in Mexico, for the first time in 75 years of matches, bringing the American record to 1–23–1 at Estadio Azteca. We previously discussed home-field advantage. Both clubs didn't have their "full" squads. Dempsey and Bradley couldn't make the friendly due to club commitments. Donovan was substituted because of an injury scare. Mexico controlled the ball most of the game, and most of the game was played in the Americans' third. The USMNT defense, led by Geoff Cameron, was tremendous, but the USMNT couldn't effectively hold on to the ball when they got it back. Fortunately for the USMNT, Mexico were unable to create chances or finish. Then, in the 80th minute, three USMNT substitutes got involved in one of the Americans' rare ventures forward. A great run by Brek Shea unlocked the Mexican defense before he crossed into the box, cutting behind a defender. Terrence Boyd got to the ball and, facing away from goal, blindly backheeled it toward goal. It found defender Michael Orozco, who just poked it over the line. He had just been substituted in. The USMNT would barely hold on. Tim Howard made two highlight diving saves on shots from Javier "Chicharito" Hernandez, and, as announcer Ian Darke called the game in his English accent, "covered himself in glory." It was just Mexico's fourth loss in Azteca's 46-year history.

It was Orozco's fifth cap. Orozco was born in California to Mexican-born parents. While Orozco may have been born and raised in the U.S., he was noticed at the age of 17 by Mexican club Necaxa and invited for a tryout. He eventually signed with the club, but never saw any first-team action. In 2006, he signed with San Luis, another Mexican first-division team. He started all three games for the U.S. in the 2008 Olympic Games in Beijing.[121]

---

121. In 2010, Orozco was loaned to the expansion Philadelphia Union from San Luis. He was interviewed in March 2010 by ussoccerplayers.com and Clemente Lisi asked, "You've made the move from Mexico's Primera Division to Major League Soccer. What do you think are the biggest differences between both leagues?" Orozco's response, "The speed of play is just different. In Mexico it was slower and more technical. Here in the U.S. it is more fast-paced, physical, and more like the European style."

The Ugly Truth When Looking More Closely

But…Chance Cook for Bleacher Report wrote, "Sometime around the 70th minute I started mulling over ideas for a postgame analysis article for the USA versus Mexico friendly. Even if it were to end in a tie, which at that point it looked as though that was the best the U.S. could hope for, I was still going to write of the United States' failure in Azteca stadium. If you look at the game stats, the United States was destroyed. They were out-possessed 66–34, lost total shots by 19–7, and were awarded ZERO corners to Mexico's 11. That said, all too often stat sheets don't show the entire story of the game. Despite seemingly never having the ball in a scoring position, and having their closest scoring opportunity come on an awesome defensive deflection by Kyle Beckerman to prevent a counter-attack opportunity, the U.S. was able to net a late winner."

In his September 2012 *Howler Magazine* article "What Is American Soccer?," Matthew Doyle, who watched more than 50 hours of USMNT game tape to study the American style of soccer, wrote,

> What makes Klinsmann's set-up different is that he throttled back from the openness of the Bob Bradley years, and shied away from the balance of the Arena years. Defensive-minded players crowd the midfield, sending a simple message: "We dare you to beat us from the flanks." Mexico took that dare, attempting 39 crosses in their 1–0 loss; a year previous in the Gold Cup final against Bradley's U.S., they'd attempted only 10. Yes, El Tri dominated possession both times, but against Klinsmann's scheme they didn't really trouble Tim Howard until the altitude took its toll in the final 10 minutes. Routinely dropping more creative players for a three-man defensive midfield trio—he's even made it four, on occasion—runs counter to the attacking, expressive soccer Klinsmann has talked about in interviews. It could be that Klinsmann sees the development of the team as a staged process—and he wants to shore up the defense first. Or, it could be that he's simply committed to choosing players who play in Europe and that doing so creates a defensive-minded roster. Either way, given those personnel choices, and Michael Bradley being played so deep, even more of the creative onus has been placed on Donovan—now working narrower and with less space—and Dempsey, the one player who's blossomed

under Klinsmann. The offense has subsequently sputtered, producing nearly a goal less per game than it had under Arena or Bradley.

As of September 2012, when the article was written, Klinsmann's teams were averaging about 1.2 goals per game (so about 0.5 goal less than under Arena and Bradley), although at this point it was a very limited dataset, the team having played only 18 games with the bulk of them being friendlies. This compares to Klinsmann's total average over the course of his tenure as coach of the USMNT of 1.84 GPG including friendlies and 2.02 excluding friendlies, which is a higher average than Arena and Bradley. (See appendix.)

Table: Comparing Goals For and Goals Against for Arena, Bradley, and Klinsmann

Match Data	Bruce Arena (1998–2006)	Bruce Arena (Total)	Bob Bradley	Jürgen Klinsmann
Total Matches (Incl. Friendlies)	130	148	80	98
Total Matches (Excl. Friendlies)	70	84	48	47
Avg. GFPG (Incl. Friendlies)	1.67	1.69	1.68	1.84
Avg. GAPG (Incl. Friendlies)	0.80	0.79	1.21	1.14
Avg. GFPG (Excl. Friendlies)	1.77	1.82	1.90	2.02
Avg. GAPG (Excl. Friendlies)	0.84	0.83	0.83	1.15
Avg. GFPG v. Mexico	1.14	1.13	1.40	1.25
Avg. GFPG v. Top 20	1.12	1.11	1.33	0.73

Klinsmann actually used much of the aggressive tactics and style that he described in public against weaker opponents. However, in high-profile matches against stronger competition he was much more pragmatic, which caused confusion and started to cause players and observers to question his tactical acumen and hype. Klinsmann's average goals per game against national teams ranked in the top 20 (proxies against stronger competition) was 0.73 (a minus-1.29 difference versus his average 2.02) as compared to 1.33 (minus-0.57) and 1.12 (minus-0.65) for Bradley and Arena, respectively.

Qualifying for the 2014 World Cup: Friendly Fire

One doesn't need to be a sociologist to predict that the mismatch of expectations and realities would start to cause issues with the group. In March 2013, a Sporting News article by Brian Straus titled "Friendly Fire: U.S. Coach Jürgen Klinsmann Methods, Leadership, Acumen in Question" stated that among the 22 individuals they spoke to with ties to the USMNT, including 11 current players based in MLS or abroad, there was near-unanimity regarding the players' flagging faith in Klinsmann, his staff, and his methods, along with the squad's absence of harmony. The article revealed players felt that constant lineup changes and building resentment over the perceived importance and attitude of the German-born players were harming team chemistry. The article reported that for several U.S.-born players, the increasing stature of Jermaine Jones, Danny Williams, Fabian Johnson, and Tim Chandler (and to a far lesser extent, Terrence Boyd), all Americans who had spent most of their lives in Germany, was harming team chemistry. The cliques and lack of respected informal hierarchy were causing challenges.

Klinsmann responded that he could only get the players to another level by bringing in new players and challenging the older players in every training session and making them uneasy. Unfortunately, those tactics only work to the extent that the players actually trust the coach and therefore the process, which was not necessarily the case at that moment in time. Klinsmann's actions had the opposite effect from what was intended—instead of motivating the players and pushing them to be better, all it did was breed more distrust and team chemistry issues.

The article revealed the players didn't agree with the style of play Klinsmann promised the public. The *Sporting News* article quoted an anonymous player saying, "They want us to play the beautiful game, but we're not a technical team like the Germans. We're not Spain or Brazil. What we're good at is we work hard, we fight, and we compete. We have great athletes and we're a good counter-attacking team. Maybe we need to go back to what we're good at." Klinsmann responded that he could only get the players to improve and play an aggressive style by playing the style during matches, even if that meant losing games.

Soon after the article, the USMNT went on a winning streak. And as the cliché prophesies: winning cures everything. Winning also conceals drift. However, when the winning stops, often, the consequences of the drift that was left unabated can be worse.

In September 2013, the USMNT qualified for the 2014 World Cup after beating Mexico in Columbus, Ohio, (and Honduras tied Panama

1–1). The final score was 2–0 ("Dos a Cero," in Spanish), which was becoming a storied score line in the USMNT's rivalry with Mexico. The USMNT had defeated Mexico in Columbus 2–0 in four straight World Cup qualifying cycles (2002, 2006, 2010, and 2014) and the Round of 16 in the 2002 World Cup—the most important game the two teams have ever played. For context, Mexico was in disarray—having just fired their head coach and being wracked with suspensions and injuries. However, the USMNT were not quite at full strength, either. The USMNT were missing three players—Jozy Altidore, Matt Besler, and Geoff Cameron—who were suspended because of yellow card accumulation, and, far more importantly, were without midfielder Michael Bradley, who had a sprained ankle.

Never-Quit Attitude Still Intact

On October 15, 2013, the USMNT were playing Panama away with little to play for and many of their top stars not playing. A win for Panama would qualify them for the World Cup. After 90 minutes, and going into injury time, the USMNT were losing 1–2. At the same time, Mexico was losing to Costa Rica. A loss to Costa Rica and a Panama win against the USMNT would eliminate Mexico from the World Cup for the first time since 1982. Mexico's fans were desperate for the USMNT to score. If the USMNT lost, Mexico would finish fifth in qualifying.

The USMNT could have intentionally not pressed and let their rival not qualify. However, one of the main values of the USMNT is to never quit. At 90+3', Graham Zusi scored to tie the game 2–2. Aron Johannsson scored at 90+4', to win the game 3–2. The result knocked Panama out and gave Mexico a chance to face New Zealand in a two-game playoff for a place in the World Cup, which Mexico would win.

Andrew Keh of the *New York Times* wrote, "The United States has now qualified for seven straight World Cups. This time, they experienced some early hiccups and tentative performances before coalescing as a team over the summer. Players now are touting this group as the deepest-ever American squad, and competition for jobs will remain heated entering the final two qualification games." A few days later, the USMNT vaulted six spots in the FIFA World Rankings to become the No. 1–ranked team in the CONCACAF region and No. 13 in the world. It was the best showing for the USMNT in the rankings since July 2010.

Luck of the Draw: Group of Death

The USMNT (ranked 13th in the world) were drawn in the same group with Germany (second), Portugal (14th), and Ghana (23th). Only the top two teams of the group would advance to the Round of 16. All four teams made the Round of 16 in the 2010 World Cup. The combined World Ranking of 52nd for the entire group was the lowest in the tournament— making it the "Group of Death."

Germany was one of the strongest teams in the tournament and would ultimately win. Portugal had a talented group of players led by Cristiano Ronaldo, one of the world's best and most dominant players. Ghana, who were supposedly the weakest opponent in the group, had eliminated the USMNT at the Round of 16 in 2010. In addition, the USMNT would have to battle the most grueling travel schedule among the 32 teams in the tournament—almost 9,000 miles for their three group stage matches, more than double the average for all teams in the tournament—including a visit to the Amazonian jungle city of Manaus, with its extreme humidity and hostile weather.[122]

A Contract Extension

Gulati, with approval from U.S. Soccer's board, gave Klinsmann a contract extension for another four years even before a single game was played in Brazil. It was a surprising show of confidence, and in the new deal Klinsmann also was made technical director of the federation, further strengthening both his power and his connection to U.S. Soccer.[123] The

---

122. To highlight the luck of the draw, Mexico (No. 24) was in Group A with Brazil (No. 11), Croatia (No. 18), and Cameroon (No. 59) (a total of 112). In the 2014 World Cup, Mexico, with both Javier "Chicharito" Hernandez and goalkeeper Guillermo Ochoa in top form, would advance to, and eventually lose in, the Round of 16 for their sixth-straight World Cup. Just a few months prior, Mexico needed help from the USMNT to even qualify.

123. This was a controversial decision as, reportedly, Klinsmann didn't actively scout players in their domestic leagues—he would most often scout players when they played MLS games in Los Angeles, near his home. Many U.S. players in European leagues felt they were not being properly scouted.

USMNT won a team-record 16 games in 2013, including 12 in a row, another team record, from June through August. However, a disappointing showing in Brazil could leave Klinsmann and U.S. Soccer in an awkward position, especially if the team were to play poorly. In many ways, Klinsmann was becoming the face of U.S. Soccer. His background and credentials added legitimacy and attracted attention.

Final 23 Players; Landon Donovan Cut

On May 14, 2014, 30 players were invited to the final training camp before the 2014 World Cup at Stanford University. Training was intense. On May 22, Klinsmann cut his squad to the final 23 players, one week earlier than expected and without notifying the USSF in advance. His decision to utilize 25 days, instead of 14, to try to build team chemistry and prepare with the players actually going to the World Cup made sense. Not telling his bosses and colleagues at USSF in advance, especially knowing the potential controversies, indicated issues.

Forward Terrence Boyd; midfielders Joe Corona and Maurice Edu; and defenders Brad Evans, Clarence Goodson, and Michael Parkhust, all of whom had contributed to the USMNT in qualifying, were cut. Evans had been a regular choice by Klinsmann at right back during qualifying and scored perhaps the most important goal during the campaign (for a late win at Jamaica). Evans and Goodson were seen as leaders in the locker room. Michael Parkhust provided a spark against Mexico.

However, it was Landon Donovan being cut that captured the headlines. Klinsmann said, "As a coach, you have to make a decision based on what you want to execute in Brazil, what you want to see, how do you want to build those components into the entire group. And then I felt—we coaches felt—the guys that we chose, they're a little step ahead of Landon in certain areas." Donovan was scoreless in seven games with the LA Galaxy during the season, and Klinsmann dropped him from the USMNT for the first half of 2013 after Donovan took a four-month sabbatical. Asked for specifics, Klinsmann said Donovan "maybe is not the one now anymore to go one against one all the time or going into the box or finishing off." But the coach praised "his outstanding passing game, his experience, which is a big factor always." However, for various reasons, many (including players and media members) felt that Klinsmann's decision was primarily driven by personal reasons and not soccer-related ones—which Klinsmann has denied.

Donovan was widely considered the best USMNT player in history and had helped the USMNT qualify for the 2014 World Cup. He was the career leader for the USMNT with 57 goals and 58 assists. With 156 international appearances, he was seeking to play in the World Cup for the fourth time. Jeré Longman of the *New York Times* wrote, "Still, to anyone following the national team closely, Donovan's exclusion did not come as a great surprise, whether one agreed or disagreed with the decision. Klinsmann had openly questioned whether Donovan's desire, commitment, and skill had ebbed to the point that less-experienced forwards like Chris Wondolowski and Aron Jóhannson deserved instead to be named to the World Cup team along with Jozy Altidore and Clint Dempsey…. He had also come to view Donovan as a forward, no longer an attacking midfielder…" Bruce Arena told the *San Jose Mercury News*, "If there are 23 better players than Landon, then we have a chance to win the World Cup." Grant Wahl of *Sports Illustrated* flatly stated, "Cutting Landon Donovan will prove to be a mistake." Donovan handled the situation with dignity and class.

In soccer, there is the emotional and the rational. Donovan was 32 years old and past peak age. An honest Donovan admitted to ESPN, for their first episode of *Inside: U.S. Soccer's March to Brazil*, "I can't train 12 straight days in a row and have 12 great days in a row. Physically it is not possible. My body breaks down, I'm getting older." As previously discussed, coaches in their second cycle often do not make such difficult decisions to cut proven, older players, and their teams suffer. We also learned something interesting when researching our book about Serie A, which has the oldest average squads among the Top Five Leagues. Players revealed that the entire team typically can only practice to the intensity and fitness of the weakest player, which impacts team fitness and chemistry. This was an issue in Italy because there was a tendency to keep fan-favorite older players.

We are not agreeing or disagreeing with Klinsmann's decision to cut Donovan, but based on data analysis, it was an understandable decision. The research supports not playing players past peak age. However, Donovan was an American sports icon and helped grow soccer in the U.S. We believe the key issues were the timing, communication, and expectations—and the biggest issue was that Klinsmann selected players who didn't meaningfully contribute to qualifying. Donovan played in five matches for a total of 405 minutes in qualification, higher than 10 players on the final squad.

For all the hoopla about Klinsmann bringing in "a bunch of German Americans," Klinsmann's final 23-man roster for the 2014 World Cup was "more American," "more MLS," and "more diverse" than perception. The squad had five players born outside the United States, the same as the 2002 team. The team had nine Black Americans, the highest ever, and four players with Hispanic origins, which was above average. The team also included Chris Wondolowski, who is of half–Native American descent through his mother, who was born into the Kiowa tribe from Oklahoma, of which Chris is also a member, and DeAndre Yedlin, who is a quarter Native American, a quarter Black American, and half Latvian. There were 15 dual national players compared to 16 in 2010. While only 11 players had college careers (the lowest since the 1990s, with the typical number being somewhere between 15 and 18), there were six players who had never left the U.S. to play overseas at any point in their career, which was higher than 2006 and 2010. In 2010, for example, that number was zero, meaning every single player on that team had played abroad at some point. Klinsmann did wish he had more time to evaluate Jordan Morris, who was 19 and at Stanford at the time.[124] Klinsmann's 23-man squad had 10 MLS players, and four were starters. In comparison, there were four MLS players and two starters on the 2010 World Cup USMNT. While

---

124. Before the World Cup, the USMNT trained at Stanford and played them in a closed-door scrimmage. Morris impressed Klinsmann with his ability to read the game, speed, and one-on-one skill. Morris, who made the All-Pac-12 first team his freshman year, received an invitation to the first USMNT camp after the 2014 World Cup—before a friendly with the Czech Republic. He was the first active college player to be on the USMNT in a long time.

most USMNT coaches encouraged their players to test themselves and improve in Europe, Klinsmann was the most publicly vocal about it.

Five German Americans making the final cut for the 2014 World Cup team was more than expected. Two of the German American picks were anticipated to have meaningful minutes, if not start—Jermaine Jones, 32, who had first played under Bob Bradley, and Fabian Johnson, 26, who first played for Klinsmann. Both were the sons of Black American servicemen who married Germans. Both FC Nürnberg's Tim Chandler (24 years old) and Hertha BSC's John Brooks (21), sons of Black American servicemen playing in the Bundesliga, made the final 23, which wouldn't have been foreseen a few months prior by observers. Chandler was given his first cap by Bob Bradley in 2011, but he only played in one game for 2014 World Cup qualifying. Brooks had not participated at all in 2014 World Cup qualifying. Brooks would later score the winning goal in a crucial game for the USMNT in the 2014 World Cup.

One German American player selected received the most attention— Julian Green, 18, who played for Bayern Munich II (the reserve team). At the beginning of the year, he wasn't considered a realistic possibility. He didn't participate in 2014 World Cup qualifying. He trained with the USMNT ahead of their friendly match on March 5, 2014, and filed for a one-time switch to play for the USMNT on March 18. Prior to his senior international appearance, Green played internationally for the German and American youth teams due to having dual citizenship. He was born in Tampa Bay to a Black American serviceman and German mother, but grew up in Germany with his mother. On March 24, FIFA approved Green's change to play for the USMNT.

Green essentially played the same position as Donovan, and therefore was often portrayed as being the player who kept Donovan off the team. His late addition reminded some observers of Steve Sampson's decision to add David Regis. Unlike Sampson, Klinsmann didn't have Green replace a starter or change the tactical scheme just months before the World Cup.

The German American players were unfairly portrayed by some as mercenaries. They were the sons of current or former American servicemen who were protecting or had protected America—saying they were not "real" Americans or didn't care as much was ridiculous. Over the years, there have been many players on the USMNT who were not born and/or raised in the U.S. Many of them made significant contributions—people didn't complain then. What was different?

Many argue the difference with Klinsmann was that he was German, selected several German Americans, and was vocal that players should play in Europe—and he cut an American icon and the face of American soccer. This argument implies he was being criticized for doing what he was hired to do—Europeanize American soccer to win a World Cup. It doesn't completely make sense. The real underlying issue was that he selected players who didn't participate in qualifying.[125] Soccer is viewed as the equal-opportunity sport in the U.S., and if players didn't put in the hard work and make the sacrifices in qualifying, then the feeling is they shouldn't have the reward of going to the World Cup to represent their country and fans—similar to how the majority of Sweden fans didn't want Zlatan Ibrahimović to be selected for the 2018 World Cup after he didn't help with qualification. Klinsmann underestimated or didn't fully appreciate the impact of adding players who were not a meaningful part of the qualifying campaign—this holds true when looking at caps and

---

125. Players did mention one exception for broad team acceptance if a player was added and didn't help in qualification—recognized need. For example, Bob Bradley selected Hérculez Gómez for the 2010 World Cup even though he didn't participate in qualifying. He played forward, a position the USMNT unexpectedly needed to add—forward Charlie Davies was not granted medical clearance to play by his club team. The perception was Bradley was astutely filling an unexpected opening. It helped that Gómez was known to most players. He had played for the USMNT in the past and played in MLS. He was a budding young star in MLS before a severe knee injury derailed his progress and he was released by Kansas City. He had to revive his career with Mexican club Puebla. After a remarkable season in Liga MX, where he became the first American to lead another country's domestic league in goals, Gómez was a comeback story. Gómez also played in Puebla's high altitude, comparable to the heights of the cities in South Africa where the World Cup games were to be played. Lastly, there wasn't an obvious reason to accuse Bradley of favoritism.

minutes played. Who you win with is just as important as winning.[126] The fact that Klinsmann was German, combined with the number of German American players he selected who did not meaningfully contribute to qualifying, as well as their being selected after a shortened tryout camp, unintentionally created a perception of favoritism, which goes against the idea of equal opportunity.

Some believe Klinsmann made good choices in his selection of German American players for the 2014 USMNT World Cup roster. During the 2014 World Cup, the USMNT scored five goals. Three of them were scored by the German American players with two key goals coming from players who had not participated in World Cup qualifying matches: Brooks scored the winning goal against Ghana and Green became the youngest USMNT player to score in a World Cup.

---

126. Those who watched the movie *Miracle* may remember that Herb Brooks tests his team by giving a new player an opportunity to make the team right before the Olympics, after the other players endured so much work and sacrifice. He justifies the move by arguing that the new player could potentially help the team win. The team eventually objects to the new player taking a spot from an existing player "because we're a family." Not only did Herb Brooks send the new player home, but when Jack O'Callahan got injured in an exhibition match against the Soviet Union on the eve of the Olympics, which would force him to miss games and leave the team shorthanded in the opening rounds at the Olympics, Herb Brooks decided to keep him— sending a message to his team that who he wins with is more important to him than winning. In a *Sports Illustrated* article, Brooks revealed that when the final seconds were ticking down before he would win the 1980 Olympic men's hockey gold medal, his thoughts were on Ralph Cox, the last player Brooks had to cut from the team.

Chapter 11

2014 World Cup: What Happened to the *Why* and *How*?

2014 World Cup Expectations

In 2002, Bruce Arena was upfront about the USMNT's chances going into the tournament: "We're not going to win [the World Cup] because we're not a good enough team. I don't think anyone is going to be damaged by us saying that. I mean, how many countries have won it? If we can get a point in the first game, it will put the whole group in chaos."

In 2010, Bob Bradley took a similar approach to Arena, but the difference this time was that the team and fans both had much higher expectations, especially after the 2009 Confederations Cup 2–0 defeat of Spain. Headlines such as EXPECTATIONS HIGH FOR TEAM USA AHEAD OF WORLD CUP dominated mainstream media.

Ahead of the 2014 World Cup, Jürgen Klinsmann was in something of a bind. He was supposed to be the coach who would advance further than 2002 and take to the USMNT to at least the semifinals. In a March 2013 article on Forbes.com titled "It's Time to Raise Our Expectations of Jürgen Klinsmann and the U.S. Men's Soccer Team," Monte Buke wrote, "We—the burgeoning U.S. soccer public—can be patient.... We have been patient ever since that glorious run to the quarterfinals in the 2002 World Cup."

Conventional wisdom was that if an American coach who spent 20 years coaching college and two years coaching in MLS could take the USMNT to the quarterfinals of a World Cup, then a World Cup champion with World Cup and Bundesliga playing and coaching credentials should be able to take the USMNT to at least the semifinals. Reportedly, the USMNT was paying Klinsmann $2.5 million per year, three times more than his predecessor. In a February 2014 interview, Klinsmann said, "The American mentality is really very impressive. They always want to be first.... The ambition has to be to reach a World Cup semifinal, and what we have to do is work to create the right kind of atmosphere for that to happen…you still have to set goals for yourself and ask yourself: 'How far can I go?' If you're Brazil, Argentina, or Germany you have to reach the Final, and if you don't, then you've failed. That's the way it's always been. USA have to try to go further than they've ever been before." In his quote, Klinsmann specifically mentions "reach a World Cup semifinal." It is further evidence of the expectations of a straight-line progression.

Just before the World Cup, however, Klinsmann started to try to manage expectations: "You have to be realistic. Every year we are getting stronger. We don't look at ourselves as underdogs. We are not. We are going to take the game to Ghana and they will take it to us and it will be an exciting game and then we go from there. For us now talking about winning a World Cup, it is just not realistic. If it is American or not, you can correct me." As anticipated by Klinsmann himself, these comments were not received well in the court of American public opinion because unrealistic expectations and false comparisons were already set. We admire Klinsmann's attitude that the USMNT would go into a tournament thinking they were going to win, and it was an attitude the USSF wanted when they hired Klinsmann. However, the comment that the USMNT were no longer "underdogs" also signaled the drift occurring. Being the underdog or having an underdog mentality and values and fighting for legitimacy was part of the identity of the team.

2014 World Cup, Brazil

The 2014 FIFA World Cup was the tournament's 20th. It took place in Brazil from June 12 to July 13, 2014. It was the second time that Brazil staged the competition, the first being in 1950, when Brazil lost to Uruguay in the Final. For the first time in awhile, every World Cup–winning team—Argentina, Brazil, England, France, Germany, Italy, Spain, and Uruguay—qualified for the 2014 tournament. In addition, for the first time at a World Cup, match officials used goal-line technology, as well as vanishing white spray to mark free kicks.

The USMNT were grouped with Germany, Ghana, and Portugal in the Group of Death. According to rankings and number of minutes in the Top Five Leagues in Europe, the group was one of the hardest in the modern era. As for the USMNT, the combined ranking of their group stage opponents was 39 as compared to 85 in 2010 and the next hardest, 47, in 1994. With their tough group, the bookmakers had given the USMNT 150-1 odds to win the tournament, worse than 2002 (90-1).

Portugal and the USMNT's starters were much older than those of the other teams.

Table: 2014 World Cup—USA & Opponents (Group Stage)

2014 World Cup—USA & Opponents (Group Stage)						
Team	World Rank (Pre-WC)	Average Age (Team)	Average Age (Starters)	# Players Top 5 League	# Minutes Top 5 League	TMV ($ MM)
USA	13	27.3	29.1	10	23,042	$86
Ghana	23	24.9	24.8	11	23,153	$142
Portugal	14	28.2	29.4	10	25,377	$440
Germany	2	25.7	26.7	23	72,515	$778
Group Total (ex. US)	39			44	121,045	$1,359

Germany held a distinct advantage in terms of players in the Top Five Leagues and number of minutes played. Ghana and Portugal had a similar number of players and number of minutes played in the Top Five Leagues to the USMNT.

2014 FIFA World Cup: Group Stage, Game 1
June 16, 2014, at Arena das Dunas, Natal
USA 2–1 Ghana

The American Outlaws supporters' group chartered two full planes carrying more than 500 people to the game and had demand for more. They all hoped to see their team gain revenge against Ghana, who had eliminated the USMNT from the last two World Cups. As they awaited their team, they forcefully blew into their vuvuzelas. And they danced to the official song of the 2010 World Cup—Shakira's "Waka Waka (This Time for Africa)."

For this matchup, the overall level of talent between the two teams was similar based on the number of players and the minutes played in the Top Five Leagues in Europe. The biggest difference was that the Ghana team were significantly younger than the USMNT team, with the average age of their starting lineup at 24.8 years old versus 29.1 for the USMNT. This was a recurring theme over the years: when the two teams faced off in 2010, the average age of the starting lineup for Ghana was 24.5 years old versus 26.9 for the USMNT, and in 2006, it was 23.5 for Ghana versus 28.3 for the USMNT.

Before the game, President Barack Obama sent a public video message to the USMNT saying, "Go Team USA. Show the world what we are made of." The inspiration must have worked—29 seconds into the game, Clint Dempsey scored. Off a throw-in, Jermaine Jones found Dempsey on the left wing making a run into the Ghana box, and the Seattle Sounders striker did the rest. Dempsey let the ball run and stylishly stepped over it before confidently tapping it forward with the inside of his right heel. The ball now perfectly placed in front of him, he cut behind Ghana's right back and beat the goalkeeper with a low left-footed shot, which hit the inside the far post and went in. It was the fifth-fastest goal in World Cup history. Dempsey had scored in three successive World Cups, with two of his three goals coming against Ghana. The American fans were dancing in the aisles, as many hadn't even gotten to their seats yet.

In the 21st minute, Jozy Altidore pulled up, then reached down and grabbed the back of his leg as he was sprinting for a ball down the sideline. Altidore, the son of Haitian immigrants and a graduate of the IMG Bradenton Residency program, was stretchered off with a hamstring injury. Aron Jóhannsson, born to Icelandic parents studying in Alabama and a graduate of the IMG Bradenton Residency Program as well, was thrown into his first World Cup game with no warm-up.

Dempsey also had an injury scare in the 34th minute when he took a shin to the nose on an aerial challenge. His nose was bleeding and broken, but he would finish the game. The injury scares continued in the 40th minute when defender Matt Besler, the Notre Dame All-American and Academic All-American from Kansas, momentarily grabbed his hamstring. After a couple moments, he seemed to be able to walk it off. Besler did not return to play in the second half and was replaced by John Brooks, a 21-year-old German American making his World Cup debut for the USMNT.

As for the play on the field, Ghana settled down after the goal and began to take control of possession, picking away at the USMNT defense. However, they failed to connect with their attackers and create good chances on goal.

The USMNT back line held off Ghana until the 82nd minute, when Ghana's Gyan found a streaking Ayew with a sublime back heel touch that allowed the striker to cut inside into a pocket of space. Ayew did the rest and fired a left-footed inside-out shot past Howard to his near post to even the game at 1–1.

Four minutes later the USMNT won a corner kick, which was taken by Graham Zusi, the two-time NCAA champion with the University of Maryland. Geoff Cameron drew the attention of two Ghana defenders, which allowed 6'4" Hertha Berlin defender John Brooks enough space in the box to rise and bury his header off the ground and into the back of the net past Ghana's goalkeeper. He became the first American to score as a substitute at a World Cup, in the 86th minute of a highly contentious game, no less. Brooks scoring this goal was so improbable that ESPN's commentator of the match, Ian Darke, promptly exclaimed: "He couldn't even have dreamt it." Amazingly, Brooks actually did dream it two days prior. "Yeah, it's unbelievable," Brooks said after the game. "I said I had a dream, I told some teammates that I dreamed that I had scored in the 80th

minute and we won the game. Now it [turned out to be] the 86th minute and we won the game, so that was good." The goal in the dream was also a header scored from a corner. Brooks' first international goal proved to be both highly prescient and decisive.[127] The USMNT would win 2–1. However, the team lost two key players to injury.

Ghana had 59 percent of possession and 21 shots compared to the USMNT's eight. However, Ghana only had eight shots on goal compared to seven for the USMNT. Any hope of advancement out of the Group of Death was predicated on a positive result against Ghana.

The USMNT scored more than once for only the third time in their past 12 World Cup games. Although Klinsmann wanted the USMNT to progress past relying on great goaltending, counter-attacks, and set pieces, it was a set piece that was the difference. For the weeks leading up to the World Cup, Klinsmann focused on set pieces, giving the players recordings of the different plays to help them study and memorize. During short sessions together during the season, the players often don't have the patience to work on set pieces. But during the weeks before a World Cup, there is a lot more focus and attention to detail given to set pieces. After the match, Klinsmann said, "We trained over and over on set pieces and it was well-deserved.... We have a great spirit and fight until the last minute." The American Spirit of '76 style of set pieces and fighting until the end was still intact.

Then–Vice President Joe Biden stopped by the U.S. team's locker room to congratulate them. A shirtless DaMarcus Beasley showed Biden a coin Biden had given him four years earlier.

2014 FIFA World Cup: Group Stage, Game 2
June 22, 2014, at Arena da Amazônia, Manaus
USA 2–2 Portugal

Portugal lost to Germany 4–0 and needed to beat the USMNT to control their own destiny. Cristiano Ronaldo's participation had been in some doubt following a stint of tendonitis in his left knee after winning the

---

127. Brooks wouldn't be used the rest of the World Cup.

Champions League with Real Madrid, reminding observers of the doubts about Figo's fitness against the USMNT in the 2002 World Cup after winning the Champions League, also with Real Madrid. Ronaldo had played an incredible 4,030 minutes over the course of the season. While Ronaldo did end up starting, Portugal had to make several other changes due to injury, whereas Klinsmann made only one, introducing Graham Zusi to replace the injured Jozy Altidore.

Zusi, from Longwood, Florida, was never a youth national team prospect and was the first-ever Orlando-area high school graduate to be called up to the USMNT. His paternal grandmother was born in the Dominican Republic. His play for Kansas City Sporting led to a call-up to the January 2012 national team camp under Klinsmann. Zusi was 25 years old when he received that first invitation, well behind the curve of many USMNT regulars.

The USMNT had the same number of players in the Top Five Leagues in Europe as Portugal and almost the same number of minutes played, but Portugal had more star power—three players from Champions League winners Real Madrid, Cristiano Ronaldo, defender Fábio Coentrão (who was injured in the match against Germany), and defender Pepe (who was suspended for the match due to a red card against Germany). The transfer market value of Portugal's players was more than five times greater than the USMNT, and Portugal would go on to win the 2016 European Championship two years later. However, the USMNT were lucky as Portugal's usual starters Fábio Coentrão and Pepe, both starters at Real Madrid, couldn't play in the match.

At kickoff, the temperature was near 90 degrees Fahrenheit and humidity nearly 70 percent. In the fifth minute, Geoff Cameron completely botched a clearance attempt on what seemed like an ordinary ball into the USMNT box. The ball went right to Portugal winger Nani, who was wide open at the far post. Manchester United's Nani's right-footed shot from the right side of the six-yard box to the high center of the goal gave Portugal the early lead. The early goal caused the Americans to chase the game to create decent chances.

As the half continued, the USMNT began to play with more confidence. Clint Dempsey just missed on a free kick in the 14th minute, pushing it just over the crossbar. Michael Bradley came close twice, first in the 23rd minute when his shot from far out went a bit wide, then in the 29th minute when a low shot from outside the box rolled just wide of the far post. The match featured the first water break of the tournament in the 39th minute because of extreme heat.

In the second half, the weather seemed to have more of an effect and the pace seemed to slow. Portugal controlled the opening 10 minutes of the second half and put the USMNT defense under steady pressure. But then, the USMNT should have equalized in the 55th minute when Fabian Johnson's cross back across the box found Michael Bradley standing in front of an open net. The USMNT midfielder's shot looked sure to go in, but Portugal's defender Ricardo Costamade made a magnificent goal-line clearance, covering for his goalkeeper, who was out of position after trying to block Johnson's cross. Bradley's hands covered his face in shock.

In the 62nd minute, Cristiano Ronaldo got loose on the counter and had a good chance to test Tim Howard. Instead, Ronaldo's shot was wildly off target, leaving spectators with no doubt that he wasn't 100 percent healthy.

The USMNT finally got the break they needed when in the 64th minute, following a cleared corner kick, the ball fell to German American Jermaine Jones 20 yards from goal. Jones took a touch to sidestep Nani before bending in a brilliant shot from his right foot from outside the box around a Portugal defender and to the bottom right far corner beyond the frozen Portuguese goalkeeper. Even Ronaldo admired the curve and placement from that distance as the ball nestled into the side netting. Jones celebrated his first World Cup goal by pounding the U.S. Soccer crest on his jersey. Jones later explained Beasley was yelling at him to shoot, and so he did.

In the 81st minute, Zusi spotted Dempsey alone in front of the Portuguese goalkeeper and put the ball over a sliding Portuguese defender and in front of the striker. The captain Dempsey guided the ball in off his midriff from close range for a shocking late lead. Dempsey, with a black eye, broken nose, and swollen cheek, let out a loud roar and ran to the bench to celebrate with his teammates. Klinsmann was running up and down the sideline and gave Zusi an embrace and kiss on the head.

Klinsmann then substituted Wondolowski for Dempsey to waste time and get fresh legs. In the 91st minute, Klinsmann did the same with ex-Maryland star defender Omar Gonzalez coming on for former Maryland teammate Zusi.

In the 94th minute, with less than 30 seconds left on the clock, Ronaldo got free on the right and launched a perfect cross to Silvestre Varela, who blasted the ball past Howard with a diving header to even the match at 2–2. When the final whistle blew, the win and guarantee for the USMNT to advance to the knockout round was gone. Now, a loss against Germany in their third group stage match would possibly leave the Americans needing to win a tiebreaker with Portugal or Ghana.

Portugal had 52 percent of possession, 17 shots, and seven on target, compared to 10 and five for the USMNT. This match would turn out to be the most-viewed soccer match ever in the United States, with reportedly more than 24.7 million viewers tuning in (split between ESPN and Univision). ESPN also said at the time that 18.2 million people watched on its network alone, which made it the most-watched non-American football event in the network's history.

2014 FIFA World Cup: Group Stage, Game 3
June 26, 2014, at Itaipava Arena Pernambuco, Recife
USA 0–1 Germany
Jürgen Klinsmann tweeted a note excusing the entire U.S. workforce from their offices to watch the Germany-USA match, scheduled for the middle of the workday in the United States. All employees had to do was print the attachment, fill in Klinsmann's presigned note, turn it into their boss, and stay home to watch the game.

The game would be played in monsoon-like conditions. Heavy rain in Recife left fans navigating flooded roads on the way to the stadium. Germany thrashed Portugal 4–0 in its opening game before being held 2–2 by Ghana. Germany had seven players from Bayern Munich, including six starters and one key substitute, defender Jérôme Boateng, midfielder Mario Götze (substitute), midfielder Toni Kroos, defender Philipp Lahm (captain), midfielder Thomas Müller, goalkeeper Manuel Neuer, and midfielder Bastian Schweinsteiger; three from Arsenal (all starters, defender Per Mertesackler, midfielder Mesut Özil, and midfielder Lukas Podolski, who had played at Bayern Munich); and four from Borussia Dortmund (including starting defender Mats Hummels). In the 2013–14 season, Bayern Munich was coached by Pep Guardiola, and they won the Bundesliga by 19 points over Borussia Dortmund, UEFA Super Cup (beat Chelsea), and FIFA Club World Cup (qualified by winning the 2013 UEFA Champions League when the beat Borussia Dortmund), and were semifinalists of the 2014 UEFA Champions League (lost to Champions Real Madrid).

To say this German squad was particularly talented would be an understatement. Not only did every single German player play in one of the Top Five Leagues in Europe, but the total number of minutes played eclipsed that of the USMNT by a factor of three. Germany was also much younger than the USMNT, with an average age of 25.7 (and 26.7 for the starters), and one inch taller on average.[128]

Before the match started, there had been some conspiracy-theory speculation that Klinsmann might conspire with Germany Coach Joachim Löw, one of his close friends and his assistant coach in the 2006 World Cup, to arrange a draw that would allow both teams to advance.

Conspiracy theories were put to rest early—Germany clearly came to attack. At one point, Germany had completed 76 passes to the USMNT's seven. For the tournament, Germany would come to dominate on this metric, averaging 630 passes per game, the highest in the tournament, with an 86 percent pass completion percentage. In comparison, the USMNT averaged 427 passes per game with an 82 percent pass completion percentage.

The seemingly inevitable goal from Germany came in the 55th minute, when Howard, who was excellent and finished with five saves, made a

---

128. Germany was the tallest team in the tournament; the USMNT ranked eighth.

diving stop on a header from a play initiated from a corner kick, but could not keep the rebound away from Müller, who from just inside the box buried his shot into the side netting.

The Bayern Munich forward Müller scored his ninth World Cup goal in as many games. Müller's rate at scoring goals in the World Cup matched Brazil legend Pelé's, who also found the net nine times in his first nine matches in the tournament. After the match, Müller said, "We were dominant. All the Americans did was sit back deep in their own half, and when that happens, it just becomes a patience game." Germany had 63 percent of possession and six shots on target compared to three shots total and none on target for the USMNT, and would go on to win the tournament.

Now, with the USMNT losing 0–1, they needed Portugal, playing simultaneously about 1,200 miles away, to tie or beat Ghana to advance. About 10 minutes before the end of the USMNT match, Cristiano Ronaldo scored to make it 2–1 against Ghana. Ronaldo's goal would prove decisive: Portugal would win; and the USMNT, predicted by many not to get out of the Group of Death, advanced to the Round of 16. The USMNT finished with a win, a tie, and a loss in the group stage, securing second place in Group G. The Americans, who had reached the knockout rounds in consecutive World Cups for the first time, were to face Belgium, the winners of Group H.

2014 FIFA World Cup: Round of 16
July 1, 2014, at Itaipava Arena Fonte Nova, Salvador
USA 1–2 Belgium

The USMNT had lost to Belgium 2–4 on May 29, 2013, at home and 0–1 in Belgium on September 6, 2011, in international friendlies. Belgium started the 2014 World Cup as group favorites but beat all their group stage opponents with the smallest margin, one goal. Belgium had a core group of star players such as Wolfsburg midfielder Kevin De Bruyne, Atlético Madrid goalkeeper Thibaut Courtois, Tottenham Hotspur midfielder Mousa Dembélé, Manchester United midfielder Marouane Fellaini, Chelsea midfielder Eden Hazard, Tottenham Hotspur defender

Vincent Kompany, Everton forward Romelu Lukaku, and Napoli forward Dries Mertens. Similar to Germany, Belgium was much younger and had more club-level experience in Europe. Seventeen players played in one of the Top Five Leagues, and another three played in the top league at home. While the difference with the USMNT in number of minutes played wasn't quite as extreme as the German team, the Belgians still nearly doubled the Americans. In addition, the value of their players was almost six times that of the USMNT.

Table: 2014 World Cup—USA and Belgium (Round of 16 Opponent)

Team	World Rank (Pre-WC)	Average Age (Team)	Average Age (Starters)	# Players Top 5 League	# Minutes Top 5 League	TMV ($ MM)
USA	13	27.3	29.1	10	23,042	$86
Belgium	5	25.5	25.5	17	44,043	$515

Jozy Altidore was supposed to have a great World Cup, but he was injured in the team's first game against Ghana and was sidelined for the USMNT's other two games against Portugal and Germany. However, Altidore practiced with the team ahead of the game. Altidore, 24, originally from Livingston, New Jersey, got his start in professional soccer with the New York/New Jersey MetroStars, now known as the New York Red Bulls, at age 16. In 2008, Spanish club Villarreal signed him for $10 million, pitting him against some of the world's best players. He played for Villarreal until 2011, followed by two years at Dutch club AZ Alkmaar, and in 2014 played for the English Premier League club Sunderland. Altidore is often linked to Haiti, where many of his relatives live—he wears a wristband bearing both the Haitian and American flags during every game and in 2006, went on a service trip to Haiti with rapper Wyclef Jean. After the catastrophic earthquake of 2010, he was active in helping to raise money for victims. Sadly, in spite of being cleared to practice, Altidore would not start or play against Belgium.

Geoff Cameron was given the start over Kyle Beckerman. Cameron was a defensive midfielder, which would allow Jermaine Jones to push higher up the field and take some of the offensive responsibility off Michael Bradley and mark Belgium's Marouane Fellaini, whom Cameron had experience playing against in the English Premier League.

Ben Smith of *BBC Sport* would characterize the match in the following way: "This was a battle of flair against function. Belgium, with their jet-heeled forwards and unquestioned technical superiority, against the organization and energy of the United States." Bars across America were full at 2:30 in the afternoon for the start. The bloggers at *The Guardian* wrote before the game, "I know there are some Americans out there who are relatively new to the game of 'soccer,' so lest there be any confusion after your magnificent, triumphant, and heroic defeat at the hands of Germany, be aware that if you lose tonight's match you are definitely out of the tournament."

Just 42 seconds into the start, Belgium's Divock Origi showed his searing speed and almost opened the scoring. He got in cleanly behind one of the USMNT defenders and fired a low, hard diagonal shot at Tim Howard, who managed to block the ball with his foot and put it out for a corner. In the 15th minute, as if there weren't enough action already during the course of play, there was a field invader wearing a Superman T-shirt. In the 17th minute, Cameron picked up a yellow card for a silly, unnecessary challenge on Dries Mertens and would be forced to play more conservatively for the rest of the match for fear of being ejected. In the 22nd minute, Graham Zusi lost the ball in midfield and Jan Vertonghen picked out Kevin De Bruyne, whose shot was a foot wide of the left upright about 10 yards out, with a mostly open net. In the 25th minute there was another bad miss for Belgium, who seemed to always be threatening. By the 27th minute, Belgium already had their sixth corner kick. In the 30th minute Fabian Johnson suffered a hamstring injury and was replaced by Seattle Sounder DeAndre Yedlin.[129]

When U.S. President Barack Obama started watching the game in the second half, all he could see was increasing one-way traffic facing his team. In the 47th minute, Dries Mertens attempted a looping header past Howard, who pulled off a highlight save by tipping it over the bar. In the 54th minute, Jan Vertonghen brilliantly squared the ball across the face of the USMNT six-yard box, where it could have easily been poked in for a

---

129. Yedlin was the first signee of the Seattle club to come through their development program.

tap-in goal. Luckily for the USMNT, not one, but two Belgium players missed. In the 56th minute, Origi leapt up to connect with a cross, heading the ball toward the top right-hand corner. Howard was beaten on the play, but the ball bounced off the top of the crossbar. In the 70th minute, Origi missed another great chance, firing a shot straight at Howard. In the 72nd minute, Chris Wondolowski came on for a tired Zusi. In the 76th minute, Origi played a short pass behind the USMNT defense for Kevin Mirallas, who attempted to roll it past Howard into the corner, but Howard spread himself out and managed to get a cleat on it, putting the ball out of bounds for another corner. In the 78th minute, Howard made another spectacular save, diving low to his left to keep out a shot by Eden Hazard. In the 84th minute, Origi had another great chance, and all Howard could do was tip it over the crossbar. In the 90th minute, Belgium took their 16th corner of the match, while the USMNT had four corners.

Then, almost miraculously, two minutes into stoppage time a looping backward header fell to Wondolowski six yards out, and he saw Belgium's Courtois charging toward him. Wondolowski connected with the ball after a short bounce. On the ESPN broadcast, Taylor Twellman brought USMNT fans out of their seats: "He's in!" Twellman's boothmate, Ian Darke, added: "Wondolowskiiiii!" Wondolowski tried to loft it over Courtois' arms, but the ball went high and wide of the goal. For a moment, American fans were despondent. "Flag was up anyway, wouldn't have counted," Darke said, explaining that Wondolowski had been offside. The linesman had put up his flag, but replays showed that a Belgium player had played him onside.[130] It was heartbreaking miss, and the best opportunity for the Americans. Cameras showed Klinsmann with his hands over his mouth in disbelief. Later, in unreserved accountability, Wondolowski would tweet an apology to everyone and his teammates.[131] He wanted to let fans know that he felt their pain and felt terrible.

---

130. There was lingering confusion about whether the flag was raised for an offside call, but apparently it was to signal for a goal kick after the miss.

131. He posted: "I'm gutted to have let down everyone but especially my teammates. It's been an incredible ride but I know this will make me stronger." Wondolowski would go on to be named MLS's 2012 Most Valuable Player and in 2019 break Landon Donovan's MLS goal-scoring record.

At full time, it was still 0–0. *The Guardian* bloggers wrote, "USA have been wonderful tonight. Almost to a man, their largely ordinary players have given everything tonight, wringing out every last drop of effort for the good of the collective. Belgium have had a touch more class, but so many of their big names have under-performed. Fellaini has done little or nothing, Hazard hasn't done much more and De Bruyne has gone very quiet after a good first half." Before extra time, Belgium substituted Romelu Lukaku for Divock Origi, and Lukaku would change the game.

Three minutes into extra time, Kevin De Bruyne slotted a ball into the bottom left-hand corner of the net past Howard after running onto a pull-back from Lukaku, who had previously won the ball down by the right touchline and worked into the penalty area before passing it off. Realizing he had finally been beaten, Howard fell back on the grass, arms and legs outstretched.

In the 104th minute, De Bruyne received a pass wide on the left flank and paused, waiting to pass it to Lukaku, who then rifled the ball past his Everton teammate Howard to the near post. Four of Belgium's six goals at the World Cup had been scored by substitutes. At halftime in extra time, the USMNT's Julian Green came on for Alejandro Bedoya. One minute after play was initiated, Green showed perfect technique on his first touch after receiving a pass from Bradley, then used his toe to volley a shot from seven yards out into the back of the net. Green, at 19 years old, became the youngest player in USMNT history to score in the World Cup, and was the youngest player from any country to score at the 2014 World Cup.

In the 23rd minute of extra time, Courtois denied Clint Dempsey with an incredible save as the USMNT almost pulled off a well-executed free kick outside the penalty area. Bradley played it diagonally along the ground to Yedlin, who flicked it to an open Dempsey, who made a run toward goal. Courtois charged forward and spread his giant body in front of the ball to smother the shot. It was the USMNT's best and last opportunity.

With chants of "USA, USA" in the 48,000-seat stadium, the USMNT kept searching for an equalizer until the final whistle. The goal never came. The match finished 1–2. Three draining group games for the USMNT in

far-flung locations—including a trip to the stifling heat of the Amazon—
left the team gasping for air at the finish, but the USMNT never gave up
and came close to tying a couple of times in the final minutes, but couldn't
quite connect.

A sensational performance by Howard (exceptional goalkeeping and
never giving up were still hallmarks of the USMNT) gave the USMNT a
chance, remarkably and opportunistically, to beat Belgium at the end of
regulation time in the Round of 16. In his 104th cap, 35-year-old Howard
single-handedly kept the USMNT in the match, recording 16 saves.[132]
The most recorded saves in World Cup history previous to Howard was
13 in 1978. Howard had to make 2.5 saves for every one for the opposing
goalkeeper. Lukaku and Howard swapped shirts after the exhilarating
game.

The onslaught by Belgium was also one for the record books: their 30
shots and 20 shots on target were in the top five in history. The USMNT
took 12 shots, five shots on target, many of them coming in extra time.
Belgium had 19 corner kicks to four for the USMNT. Remarkably, the
USMNT had 53 percent possession even though it felt like one-way traffic
for most of the game.

Klinsmann promised proactive, dynamic soccer, and less reliance on
outstanding defense and goalkeeper performances. It was an invigorating
idea, but it never materialized consistently. The team relied on old-
fashioned American hustle and grit in the 2014 World Cup, far more
than technical skill for long stretches—and that went against elevated
expectations. Over four games, the USMNT were outshot 94 to 44 and
41 to 17 on goal.

---

132. There were reports or rumors that Klinsmann did not want to start Howard against Belgium.
The people we interviewed with knowledge of the situation emphatically stated that those reports
or rumors were not true.

Table: USMNT Shots, Goals, and Possession in the 2014 World Cup

2014	Goals	Corners	Shots (Including Blocked)	SOG	Saves	Free Kicks	Possession
USA	5	15	44	17	28	59	44.8%
Opponents	6	33	94	41	11	53	55.3%

Among the seven USMNTs that have qualified for the World Cup in American soccer's modern era, Klinsmann's side took the fewest shots per 90 minutes, yielded the most, and eclipsed only the 1994 squad in possession. The bad luck of Jozy Altidore injuring his hamstring in the team's first game against Ghana and being sidelined for the USMNT's other games seemed to have had an impact. Clint Dempsey was often left high up the field alone to try to create opportunities to score.

The USMNT ran more than any other team in Brazil with an average of 77 miles (124 kilometers) per match, more than 2.5 miles (4 kilometers) more distance covered than the next-closest team, champions Germany. Michael Bradley ran more than any other player in the opening matches.

In the book *FIFA World Cup and Beyond*, Shakya Mitra wrote, "Praised for athleticism and effort, the USMNT didn't stand out for style or technique, content to cede possession and rely on the counter-attack. An enhanced quality or standard of play, however, was not evident." And this was the issue for Klinsmann—after everything he had promised, expectations and hype didn't meet reality.

For the first time in World Cup history, all eight teams to win their groups went through to the quarterfinals. While Germany defeated Argentina (with Lionel Messi) in the Final 1–0 for their fourth World Cup (and first title since Germany's reunification), the 2014 World Cup forever will be remembered as the tournament Germany beat host Brazil (without Neymar, who was injured) 7–1 in the semifinal. With regard to CONCACAF, while the U.S. and Mexico lost in the Round of 16, Costa Rica beat Greece on penalty kicks in the Round of 16 to advance to the quarterfinals and then lost to the Netherlands on penalty kicks in the quarterfinals. Costa Rica's performance was generally overlooked. They would become tougher to beat in the future—home or away.

Klinsmann and the raised expectations surrounding him had increased interest in the USMNT. In terms of audience at the 2014 World Cup,

1,363,179 tickets, or about 60 percent of the total sold, were purchased by Brazilians, and the U.S. had the second-largest number of tickets purchased with 196,838. Argentina and Germany followed with 61,021 and 58,778, respectively. Clint Dempsey said, "I remember a time playing games in the States, World Cup qualifying games or a friendly, when you felt like you weren't in your own country, you weren't at home. And then now we're at the point that we're going down to a World Cup, playing in Brazil, and you're feeling that home away from home. So, it's pretty special. It gives you that confidence, that belief, that people are there supporting you."

Almost 25 million viewers in the U.S. watched the USMNT versus Portugal and 26.5 million watched the Germany versus Argentina Final. The 2–2 draw with Portugal, with global superstar Cristiano Ronaldo being a key draw for casual fans, was the most-watched soccer game in American history, according to Nielsen figures. Keep in mind that baseball's 2013 World Series averaged 15 million viewers on Fox, while the NBA Finals delivered a similar figure for ABC. Average viewership for all 64 matches on ESPN in the U.S. increased 39 percent from the 2010 World Cup in South Africa. "This hasn't been an overnight sensation; it's been building and growing for 25 years. We're excited to see our fan base grow and more and more people involved in the World Cup," Neil Buethe, U.S. Soccer's senior manager of communication, told CNN.

Dempsey became the face of the USMNT with team mainstay Landon Donovan left off the final 23-man roster. After the tournament, he was a guest on popular TV shows. The starring role was lucrative for Dempsey off the field, as he racked up endorsement deals with Degree for Men, Electronic Arts, Modelo, Mondelez International, Oberto, PepsiCo, and Upper Deck. He reportedly earned an estimated $3.5 million annually from sponsors in addition to his $6.7 million salary from the Seattle Sounders of MLS. Times had certainly changed from the 1990s, when players had a tough time making ends meet.

Jürgen Klinsmann Fired

Any momentum from the 2014 World Cup stalled almost immediately afterward, starting with the Americans finishing fourth in the 2015 CONCACAF Gold Cup. Their semifinal loss to Jamaica was their first to a Caribbean team on home soil since 1969. In the game for third place against Panama, the USMNT were outshot 25 to five (12 to two on target) and thoroughly outplayed.

In March 2016, the USMNT lost to Guatemala in World Cup qualifying, their first loss to them since 1988. In November 2016, the USMNT lost to Mexico in Columbus, their first home World Cup qualifying loss to their rivals since 1972. And their 4–0 loss to Costa Rica four days later was their worst shutout loss in qualifying in more than three decades. Sam Borden of the *New York Times* wrote, "Klinsmann's team looked alternately disorganized, dispirited, and—perhaps most damningly—uninterested." Andrew Helms and Matt Pentz of the Ringer commented further on the significance of the loss and the state of the USMNT, "Historically, the USMNT had been known for its grit and fight—a team that exceeded the sum of its parts. But Klinsmann's tenure had cracked that collective spirit, and it was exposed in ruthless fashion in the match against Costa Rica. It wasn't just that the team lost 4–0; it was how the side capitulated under pressure. The humiliating defeat exposed the team's broken culture, and most importantly revealed that most of the group had given up on Klinsmann."

The USMNT had started the Hexagonal round of World Cup qualifying with consecutive defeats, the first time a USMNT team had ever done that. The USMNT hadn't beaten an opponent in the top 70 of FIFA's World Rankings in a competitive match in their previous eight attempts. Critics commented that Klinsmann played too many players out of position, which caused them and the team to struggle, not to mention made some players unhappy. Klinsmann would deny this. He had several rifts with players who felt that not only were they playing out of position, but also his tactics and their roles were not clear. Some players described routinely not knowing their roles on the way onto the field. Constant clashes in expectations and roles highlighted the team's problems. Klinsmann response to the losses and criticism was, "The fact is, we lost two games. There is a lot of talk from people who don't understand soccer or the team." What Kinsmann failed to understand or appreciate is that the *why*, *how*, and *who* were becoming less clear.

Klinsmann was fired in November 2016. Kevin Baxter of the *Los Angeles Times* wrote, "Klinsmann also was hurt by his high expectations. He promised nothing short of a revolution, predicting five months before his sacking that the U.S. would reach the semifinals of the 2018 World Cup. But when results failed to match his expectations, Klinsmann deflected the blame toward his players, their approach, and the U.S. soccer culture in general." Eric Betts of *Slate* wrote, "Jürgen Klinsmann is delusional. He took over the U.S. men's soccer team in 2011, promising a new, beautiful style of play. It was all empty bluster."

In the end, Klinsmann's winning percentage was 64.9 percent in tournament matches (excluding friendlies), as compared to 67.1 and 67.7 percent for Bruce Arena (1998–2006) and Bob Bradley, respectively. The average World Rankings of the USMNT opponents were 49.9, 57.1, and 58.0 for Arena, Bradley, and Klinsmann, respectively. The total number of minutes in the Top Five Leagues for the USMNT players in the 2002, 2006, 2010, and 2014 World Cups were 12,652, 12,312, 23,265, and 23,042. Klinsmann never had a marquee win against a top-10 FIFA-ranked team in a knockout round of a major tournament, while Arena (2002 World Cup Round of 16 win over No. 7–ranked Mexico) and Bradley (2009 Confederations Cup semifinal win over No. 1–ranked Spain) had one each. Klinsmann advanced out of the toughest group stage in the World Cup in USMNT history in 2014 with the group's seedings totaling 39 (excluding the USMNT); 1994 group's total of 47 was the second-toughest. (See appendix.)

Chapter 12

2018 World Cup: Did Not Qualify

Trying to Qualify for the 2018 World Cup, Russia

In November 2016, Bruce Arena was hired to replace Jürgen Klinsmann. He was a logical choice. He coached the USMNT from 1998 to 2006. He was familiar with the teams, travel, and environment involved with the CONCACAF qualification process. He was also very familiar with the growing core of MLS players on the USMNT, which would make the transition quicker and easier. A mind-set—just qualify for the World Cup—clouded the urgency of trying to identify and address the underlying fundamental problems of drift from a mission.

As with every World Cup qualification campaign since 1997, CONCACAF held a six-team, home-and-away round-robin group known as the "Hexagonal," or "Hex," as its final and decisive round. As a result of the abolition of the February and August fixtures from the FIFA calendar, the "Hex" for the first time was not contained within a single calendar year, but instead began in November 2016 and concluded in October 2017.

In 2016, the USMNT lost to Mexico at home, after Klinsmann implemented a new 3-5-2 formation with which the team only had limited practice before the match.[133] Things got so bad in the first half that Michael Bradley reportedly ran over to Klinsmann and told him that they needed a change. The team would later switch to a more familiar 4-4-2.

The last time the Americans lost a qualifier at home was on September 1, 2001. Since then, the USMNT had rattled off 30 games at home without defeat against a variety of opponents. Then they lost to Costa Rica away under Klinsmann. In 2017, under Bruce Arena, the team would beat Honduras 6–0 at home, tie Panama 1–1 away, beat Trinidad & Tobago 2–1 at home, tie Mexico 1–1 away, lose to Costa Rica 0–2 at home, tie Honduras 1–1 away, and beat Panama 4–0 at home. Arena's final record came out to two wins, one loss, and three draws. With the two defeats under Klinsmann, the USMNT were 2–3–3 overall. Occasional wins were false positives and concealed the truth—the team had lost its original grit, fight, and collective spirit.

Arena desperately tried to resurrect the culture he had nurtured in the early 2000s, but the drift had gone on for too long. There was no clear *why, how*, or *who*. For too many, the *why* was *just qualify and we will figure it out*—and that just wasn't compelling or inspirational enough.

In hindsight, maybe people could have made the difficult decision Bob Gansler did in 1989—favor youth and build for the future with a mission. While the skill and experience level may not have been as high, young players could have better accepted the role of underdogs fighting to prove the legitimacy of soccer in the U.S. However, there wasn't much time, big dollars were at stake, and expectations were high.

On October 10, 2017, the USMNT (ranked 35th) had to play away at Trinidad & Tobago (ranked 78th) for their final match. With at least a draw, the USMNT would qualify for the 2018 World Cup. Even if they lost, it would take an unlikely combination of results (Mexico, ranked 16th, losing to Honduras, ranked 72nd, and Panama, ranked 52nd, beating Costa Rica, ranked 26th) to eliminate the USMNT. However, Honduras and Panama had home-field advantage.

---

133. This was the last time the USMNT had used a true three-at-the-back formation since a friendly against Chile in 2015.

Table: Information about Teams in the 2017 Hex Qualification for 2018 World Cup

Team	Hex Finish	World Rank	# Players Home Country	# Players MLS	# Minutes MLS	# Players Top 5	# Minutes Top 5
Mexico	1	16	11	2	3,323	5	6,065
Costa Rica	2	26	9	7	14,899	2	6,264
Panama	3	52	4	7	11,560	0	0
Honduras	4	72	14	4	7,530	0	0
USA	5	35	16	16	37,171	4	9,156
T&T	6	78	11	3	7,146	0	0

Arena decided to field the same starting XI that played four days earlier in a 4–0 rout of Panama in Orlando. While the starting XI had an average age of 27.2 years old, they may have been too tired. Trinidad & Tobago's starting XI had an average age of 25.6.

On paper, the USMNT's starting XI were much better than Trinidad & Tobago. Eight of the starting XI USMNT players were playing or had played in one of the Top Five Leagues or played in the 2014 World Cup. In comparison, none of Trinidad & Tobago's starting XI had played in one of the Top Five Leagues in Europe (none had even played in Major League Soccer) or a World Cup. However, Arena may have fallen into the same trap as Germany Coach Joachim Löw in his third cycle at the World Cup—favoring experience and familiarity too much. Fourteen of the 23-man USMNT were 30 or older. It seems rational to go with more established players to reduce risks, but the data shows typically too many older players and players who are too tired have negatively impacted performance. Regardless of the "too-tired-and-old effect," conventional wisdom was that the USMNT could beat T&T on talent alone. As we discovered earlier, other factors such as mission, luck, and home-field advantage also have an impact.

As for team chemistry, in a 2020 *BSI: The Podcast* interview, Arena contrasted the 2017 USMNT with the 2002 World Cup team: "Everybody on that [2002] team wanted the team to succeed. And not to be critical of other groups, but the team I had in 2017, that I inherited, as a coaching staff we talked and said if we can get through this year and qualify for the World Cup, we have to make a dozen changes to this team because we just didn't have the right characters and a lot of guys weren't in it for the right reasons. And I think those things are important, especially for the U.S. team that you could argue is not as talented as most of the teams you are going to see in the World Cup. We [in 2002] had the right balance of talent and the right kind of mentality and team spirit...there are a lot of intangibles that people don't talk about, like team chemistry and being committed to the program, that are important to national teams."

The USMNT versus T&T match would be played at the smaller Ato Boldon Stadium instead of Hasely Crawford Stadium due to the larger stadium's issues with its floodlights. Heavy rain in the days preceding the match meant that the field at Ato Boldon Stadium was soaked, impeding practice the day before the match. ESPN FC had a video titled, "USMNT Encounters a Moat on the Trinidad & Tobago Training Pitch." The video captured images of players getting piggyback rides onto the pitch to avoid their feet getting soaked by the water surrounding the field—with a soundtrack used in old comedy films. ESPN FC wasn't alone—many U.S. media outlets and the USSF displayed similar images. The USMNT did not have the Spirit of '76, embracing an underdog status or mentality similar to the American Patriots in 1776. Their mentality came across as more of the superior British attitude against the Patriots.

The USMNT lost to Trinidad & Tobago 1–2 in front of 1,500 spectators (not some large hostile crowd), Honduras beat Mexico 3–2, and a late goal from Panama gave them the win over Costa Rica 2–1.[134] While some USMNT supporters blamed bad luck for an early own goal and near-misses by Clint Dempsey and Benny Feilhaber against Trinidad & Tobago, the USMNT also benefited from a last-gasp goal-line clearance by DeAndre Yedlin and a superb save by Tim Howard denying T&T from close range. Perhaps the USMNT didn't have enough talent to win on talent alone.

When asked what happened, T&T's coach explained, "There was a lot of fire in our eyes. I think they were a bit overconfident and a bit disrespectful because they came in yesterday and rain fell on the pitch and they were giving each other piggybacks over the water and all kind of stuff.... Rain fell, it's not our fault. They made a big scene out of it.... They learned their lesson." Those who watched the game could see the USMNT lacked intensity or urgency.

---

134. Replays would later show that Panama's first goal didn't appear to cross the line.

The USMNT finished CONCACAF's Hexagonal round of qualifying with 12 points, five fewer than they earned in any previous qualifying cycle since the format began in 1997. Panama's 13 points were the fewest ever earned by a third-place team in the format, one fewer than Jamaica earned in the 1998 qualifying cycle. The Americans did earn one point more than fourth-place Mexico in the 2014 cycle.[135] Had the USMNT qualified by finishing third in a six-team group with only three wins and 12 points from 10 games, it would have been more an indication of how forgiving the qualifying competition is. The USMNT had largely been kept in contention by the brilliance of Christian Pulisic and Clint Dempsey. Pulisic had five goals, the most in the Hex. Dempsey, who finished with four goals, was tied for second.

The failure for the USMNT to qualify made national and international news overnight. ESPN FC hosted a segment on the game and openly criticized the "blinded arrogance" that the USMNT team had. ESPN FC commentator Alejandro Moreno, who won three MLS cups and played for the Venezuela national team, criticized the players' commitment and passion for the game. ESPN FC commentator Hérculez Gómez, who played for the USMNT in the 2010 World Cup and won two MLS cups, criticized the USMNT's lack of focus on the match, claiming that during the T&T game USMNT players on the bench were asking for the scores from the other matches in qualifying.[136,137]

---

135. In 2014, Mexico got help from a USMNT win to have a playoff with New Zealand, which they won and qualified and then advanced to the Round of 16.

136. Remember, in comparison, when Mia Hamm was asked a question about the USWNT's overwhelming advantage in CONCACAF play, she said that she hoped that the USWNT could become an example to other federations in the region. Dominating CONCACAF teams was showing what was possible. It's a striking contrast to the USMNT.

137. When the USWNT beat Thailand 13–0 in the 2019 World Cup in the group stage, they were heavily criticized in the media, especially for celebrating after the later goals. Keep in mind goal differential matters in a group stage match. The values of the USWNT are that they should play hard no matter the score—that is the best way to respect your opponent and the game. The same applies to Germany. When Germany beat Saudi Arabia 8–0 in the 2002 World Cup, including scoring a goal off of a free kick in stoppage time, the media didn't criticize the score line or their celebrations, which included a backflip. The USWNT 13–0 victory was a World Cup record, men's or women's—and there have been plenty of mismatches in men's World Cups. We are not arguing what values are right or wrong. We are just pointing out possible stereotype differences.

ESPN FC commentator Shaka Hislop, a former goalkeeper who represented Trinidad & Tobago in the 2006 FIFA World Cup, said, "Speaking from personal experience, not only is this the worst U.S. team I have seen [in the last 20 years], this is the most arrogant U.S. national team that I have seen in the last 20 years. And that is not just down to the players, that is down to everybody from U.S. Soccer [federation] through the media that comes through the coach and onto the players." Hislop provided evidence of the drift normalized by the USSF. He explained, "You go down to Trinidad & Tobago in the tropics, rainy season, the pitch is wet. U.S. Soccer from their official Twitter account is taking photos of the pitch with the water in the foreground…it was nowhere as bad as they were trying to suggest…and the message that is sent…is, 'Here we are, U.S. Soccer, in this little backwater nation having to play to qualify.'" Hislop then provided evidence of the drift normalized by the U.S. media. He said, "…This is where the U.S. media gets involved. If the U.S. media sits there the day before a World Cup qualifier and asks a question about Europeans competing in CONCACAF that is the media also blinded by their own arrogance."[138]

Remember, in November 1989, the USMNT were the underdogs with something to prove against Trinidad & Tobago, whose government had declared the following day a national holiday because they were so confident they would at least get a draw and advance. By October 2017, a lot had changed—the USMNT had drifted from an underdog mentality with something to prove to "blinded arrogance."

---

138. This reminds some observers of Hope Solo of the USWNT annoying Brazilians at the 2016 Olympics in Rio when she posted a photo on social media of herself covered with mosquito netting and armed with insect repellent in response to her concerns about the Zika virus. Although not the intent, her actions were interpreted by Brazilians as her implying Brazil was a "backwater nation." Unfortunately, her actions diverted attention from all the positive things she has done advocating for equality, and her many outstanding contributions to U.S. Soccer. And then, in the same competition, after the USWNT lost to Sweden in the quarterfinals she criticized Sweden as "a bunch of cowards" because their defensive tactics were not, in her opinion, "very Olympic-spirited." Again, she unintentionally created a perception of arrogance. It's like the British criticizing the American Patriots in 1776 for guerrilla war tactics. Sweden smartly dropped back defensively and absorbed pressure against a better team—and beat the USWNT in penalty kicks. Sweden didn't break, or even bend, any written or unwritten rules. They are not the first team, and won't be the last, to "park the bus."

The Aftermath of Not Qualifying for the 2018 World Cup

After not qualifying, Bruce Arena resigned as coach. Sunil Gulati did not seek reelection for president of the USSF. In June 2018, the U.S., Mexico, and Canada secured the 2026 World Cup. In August 2018, Carlos Cordeiro was elected president of the USSF in a heated election. A lifelong soccer fan, Cordeiro had served in various roles with U.S. Soccer since being appointed as the federation's first Independent Director in 2007. Prior to USSF, Cordeiro worked at Goldman Sachs.

In December 2018, former USMNT player (2002 and 2006 World Cups) Gregg Berhalter, who was coaching the Columbus Crew, was hired as USMNT coach. It makes sense that the USSF would hire a former USMNT player who knew the history, traditions, and values of the national team as well as soccer in the U.S.[139] Berhalter grew up in New Jersey and played youth soccer for Union County SC and high school soccer with Claudio Reyna. He (and his wife) played college soccer at the University of North Carolina and was captain of the U.S. U-20 team at the 1993 U-20 World Cup. After his junior year at UNC, he signed with a Dutch club—at the time it was rare for an American to get a contract to play in Europe. He was a member of the U.S. U-23 team that went to the Netherlands to play four games. Legendary Dutch coach Rinus Michels, whom U.S. Soccer had hired as a technical advisor, was on the trip. Berhalter impressed a few Dutch clubs and Michels' endorsement helped. He played professionally in the Netherlands from 1994 to 2000. Almost every player or coach in the Netherlands has been influenced by legendary coach and player Johan Cryuff. After Cruyff's passing in 2016, Berhalter said: "Most teams that play the way we [Columbus Crew] play, a lot of the inspiration has started from ideas of his and ideas of teams he's been on, whether that's Holland in the mid-70s to his foundation that he laid with Barcelona. I mean Barcelona, what they're doing now is a direct

---

139. No foreign coach has ever won the World Cup, and only two have reached the final match: George Raynor of England, with Sweden in 1958, and Ernst Happel of Austria, with the Netherlands in 1978.

relation to him." Berhalter also played in the English Premier League and Bundesliga before playing in MLS.[140]

The 45-year-old Berhalter left the Columbus Crew to take over a national team that hadn't had a permanent head coach in 416 days because U.S. Soccer was distracted with the World Cup bid, which was the top priority. In August 2019, former USMNT player Earnie Stewart and former USWNT player Kate Markgraf were hired as general managers of the USMNT and USWNT, respectively.[141] Their responsibilities include shaping the soccer culture and playing styles of their respective teams. Former USMNT player Brian McBride was later hired to succeed Earnie Stewart, who was promoted to sporting director of the USSF.[142]

WARNING: Europeanizing American Soccer Continues

As coach of MLS' Columbus Crew, Gregg Berhalter was vocal about his admiration of Barcelona's style of play under coach Pep Guardiola, which was influenced by Johan Cruyff, who played and coached at Barcelona. Guardiola's tactical framework included building play from the back and maintaining possession, which required silky-skilled defenders (Barcelona's Dani Alves, Carles Puyol, Gerard Piqué) with impeccable spacing and decision-making. Guardiola's philosophy also featured two solid center midfielders (Barcelona's Iniesta and Xavi), and a floating playmaker (Barcelona's Lionel Messi) in lieu of a second striker. Berhalter consciously emulated Barcelona's style at Columbus with Argentine Federico Higuaín—a playmaking central attacking forward/midfielder, commonly referred to as a No. 10. Under Berhalter, Columbus qualified for the playoffs in 2014, 2015, 2017, and 2018. They reached the MLS

---

140. Berhalter took coaching certification classes in Germany.

141. Markgraf ended her career with a high school championship, state club championship, NCAA Division I championship, Olympic gold medals, and a FIFA World Cup Championship. We believe Markgraf was a great hire and will help the USWNT.

142. We do believe that many good USSF changes and decisions have been made, starting with Berhalter being hired as coach, as well as Earnie Stewart and Brian McBride being hired by the USSF. They are all highly respected and well liked and know the traditions and values of the USMNT. Current USMNT players feel team chemistry is improving, but a lot of work and time are necessary to improve familiarity and trust.

Cup Final in 2015, but lost at home 2–1 to the Portland Timbers. At the time, Columbus ranked 13th in MLS in total base salary.

Berhalter describes his style of offensive play as "an attacking-based team…using the ball to disorganize the opponent to create goal scoring opportunities."[143] The idea is that if teams believe the USMNT are confident enough to play out of the back they might bring pressure—leaving space in their defensive third to exploit. To "disorganize the opponent" is to create unpredictable options or difficult decisions for the opponent. He believes that the USMNT needs to be equipped with ways to break down CONCACAF opponents who don't attack like many soccer powers. Berhalter has conviction that the USMNT have players with the ability to play his style. Berhalter's mission (*why*) is to change how people view American soccer. In many ways, his style is an opportunity to highlight the skill level of American players. It's important to understand that Berhalter's desired style is influenced by his experiences in Europe. It helps explain why his style is different from the Spirit of '76.[144]

As of November 2020, under Berhalter's guidance, the Americans have lost two games to rival Mexico by a combined 4–0 score and three more to opponents ranked beneath them in the current FIFA World Rankings (No. 26 Venezuela, No. 47 Jamaica, and No. 75 Canada). Being a national team coach is not like being a club soccer coach—one can't just sign a player to fill in a gap somewhere on the field. One has to deal with the skill level and experience level of the national eligible players. In addition, the USMNT are not a club team that meets on a daily basis for seasons at a time and can build bonds, trust, and relationships—familiarity. The players come in for a short time and then head back to their respective teams with their differing playing styles and cultures. On top of this, in order to evaluate players, Berhalter has been experimenting with many different players and

---

143. In a 2018 interview with Alexi Lalas, Berhalter said, "First and foremost, people want to see exciting soccer." This may be true. To generate revenues, clubs need to be focused on the entertainment aspect of soccer. This is not necessarily true for national team soccer. It is an important difference between club and international soccer. People only have one national team to watch, while there are many clubs to choose from.

144. Just because Berhalter's style is inspired by styles predominantly from Europe, it doesn't mean it won't be successful.

lineups, having used 50 different players since taking over as coach. Bruce Arena, Bob Bradley, and Jürgen Klinsmann used 49 to 59 different players over various years. (See appendix.) The current USMNT players are a young group establishing themselves on the international stage. It makes sense to give many players an opportunity and see how they respond; however, it's just another challenge to implementing a different system and creating familiarity. As of this writing, time is precious as the global pandemic compresses the 2022 qualifying cycle. Berhalter is asking a lot of his players. It might be too much.

Under Berhalter, the USMNT have played just nine matches against teams in the top 50 of the FIFA rankings: two losses to Mexico (1–0, 3–0), draws against Uruguay and Chile, a 3–0 loss to Venezuela, two wins over Costa Rica (2–0, 1–0), and a win-loss split (0–1, 3–1) against Jamaica. In total, the USMNT scored eight goals and their opponents scored 11 goals. However, as Bill Connolly of ESPN pointed out, the USMNT's expected goals were 14.9 (6.9 goals fewer than the eight they scored) and their opponents' expected goals were 8.3 (2.7 goals fewer than the 11 goals they scored) in this nine-match sample. Therefore, in fairness, it could have been bad luck, and we previously mentioned how much luck matters in the narrative.

Loss to Canada

On October 15, 2019, the USMNT was stunned in CONCACAF Nations League play, suffering a 2–0 defeat to Canada. It was the first time the USMNT had lost to Canada in 34 years. It wasn't just the loss, either; the USMNT had just three shots on goal and were outplayed. While the loss is not at all comparable to the loss to Trinidad & Tobago in a qualification match for the World Cup, many in the media were critical of the performance.

Alexi Lalas' reaction to losing to Canada: "I'm not angry. I'm not sad. I guess I'm just apathetic…. The 2–0 loss to Canada was bad. Was it Trinidad & Tobago bad? No…. But this team looks…confused and most disappointing of all it looks soft…. Yes, there is a price to pay for progress, but if it means losing the essence of what has fueled this team for the last

25 years, then I don't think it's worth it.... This was yet another warning shot. The time has come to say goodbye to romance. Gregg Berhalter needs to change his tune, because right now no one wants to hear it."

Taylor Twellman of ESPN said, "Listen, you can lose games; that's part of sports.... What is alarming to me is what you are getting from the United States...you've got to roll your sleeves up, you've got to dig in, you've got to fight...at one point you look at it and you're saying well we've got the Christian Pulisics, Weston McKennies, and Josh Sargents of the world...I don't care, the team needs to show up on the same page and act as if they are committed to the program."

While Berhalter believes that the young group of players haven't had enough time and matches to form an identity, what Lalas and Twellman are getting at—putting aside style—is that the team didn't appear to them to have an underdog mentality or an identity of grit. The explanation from some that it is because the players make more money now and care less doesn't make complete sense. All the nations that win have players who make lots of money. Cristiano Ronaldo is one of the most highly paid players—he cares a lot about international performance. The explanation from others that this generation is "soft" doesn't make sense. The other teams have players from this same generation.

A month after the USMNT lost to Canada, they beat Canada 4–1 in Orlando with Jordan Morris (Seattle Sounders), Gyasi Zardes (Columbus Crew), and Aaron Long (New York Red Bulls) all scoring. The USMNT were without some players due to injury, including Michael Bradley and Pulisic. With the victory, Berhalter became the second-fastest manager to 10 wins (17 games) in USMNT history. The USMNT then cruised to a 4–0 win over Cuba. Josh Sargent (Werder Bremen) and Jordan Morris scored two goals each. The USMNT took the top spot in 2019 CONCACAF Nations League Group A, with a superior goal difference to Canada, and advanced to the semifinals of the Nations League.[145]

---

145. Berhalter, McBride, and Stewart are very focused on team chemistry and culture. An example of a change made under Berhalter to improve team chemistry and culture is that, when possible during camps, the players sit at one long table instead of a few round tables, which tend to separate into cliques.

In 2020, USMNT development was interrupted by the global COVID-19 pandemic. In November 2020, Berhalter named a 24-player roster for just its second camp of 2020. The roster's average age was almost 22 years old. Nine of the players were on clubs in the UEFA Champions League, the most in team history. With the MLS season still underway and playoffs on the horizon, the roster was exclusively made up of players playing professionally outside of the U.S. A total of 10 players were seeking their first cap with the senior USMNT. The USMNT played friendlies against Wales (0–0 draw) and Panama (6–2 USA win). While it is difficult to dig too deep into the performances considering the various circumstances, there were plenty of reasons to be excited about the USMNT's future. But to manage expectations, the U.S. ranks 25th and 28th as a nation in number of players and minutes, respectively, in the 2020–21 Champions League as of November 28, 2020, in the group stage.

Chapter 13

Revisiting Player Identification and Development

In an ESPN FC segment after the USMNT lost to Trinidad & Tobago in 2017, an exasperated ESPN FC studio host Dan Thomas turned to a panel of experts and said, "Let's just focus on the 90 minutes in Trinidad & Tobago. This was a Trinidad reserve side, with nothing to play for, who were the worst team in the Hex, who hadn't won in nine matches.... How can this possibly happen? Just because they [USMNT] weren't good enough." After a lively debate, ESPN FC commentator Steve Nicol, who won the Champions League with Liverpool and played for the Scottish national team, responded, "Nobody stood up. Nobody showed any real strength of character..."

The USMNT weren't good enough and didn't show any real strength of character because of the consequences of the drift of the team's *why*, *how*, and *who*. In their quest to play like and be like something they are not— European—the USMNT lost the essence of what fueled them—fighting for the legitimacy of soccer in the U.S. Not only were the scrappy defense and quick counter-attacking of the Spirit of '76 missing, key values of the Spirit of '76 had faded as well. The grit was missing. An attitude of blinded arrogance replaced underdog mentality and determination. They were *less* than the sum of their parts, which they could not afford to be because the margins between winning and losing are so small.

When we interviewed opposing coaches and players about the USMNT, many felt the team "have lost something"—"a little less physical" and "a little less determined." A player from a CONCACAF nation that qualified for the 2018 World Cup revealed, "We used to dread playing them, almost fear them…and now we don't." A European who won the World Cup rhetorically asked, "Why do they [USMNT] want to be like us? Play like us?" Then he added, "The U.S. don't have the same system, same culture, or same skill level. America is a great country. They should be proud to be and play like Americans. In trying to be like us, they lost the best of who they were."

This drift was not deliberate; rather, the drift happened so slowly that the modification in meaning of *why* (the mission) became normalized by the USSF, the USMNT, the fans, and the media. Since there wasn't an immediate catastrophe, there was a long incubation period with warning signs that were either misinterpreted, ignored, or missed completely. Selected wins or performances were misinterpreted as either issues being resolved or, worse, progress. Not qualifying for the last two Olympics (2012 and 2016) with U-23 players and, after reaching the quarterfinals in the 2002 and 2005 U-17 World Cups, the U.S. U-17 not reaching the quarterfinals again until 2017 (and not even qualifying in 2013) were ignored by many. Even more alarming than not qualifying for the Olympics, the U.S. reached the U-17 World Cup quarterfinals in 1991, 1993, 2003, 2005, and 2017 and the semifinals in 1999. (See appendix.) The U-17 and U-23 team performances can give a sense of the talent pipeline.

Those arguing the U.S. missing the Olympics or never being higher than 12th from the 2007 to 2015 U-17 World Cups doesn't matter are missing the *why*—prove the legitimacy of soccer in the U.S. Those arguing many soccer powers don't care about qualifying—the U.S. is not a soccer power—are dismissing the identity of being an underdog. In both arguments, there is an implicit attitude of arrogance.[146] For the U.S., the tournaments are very important building blocks, and missing meaningful games against the best competition are lost opportunities to improve.

The precipitous drop of players and minutes in the Top Five Leagues was completely missed. Those arguing that some players moved to MLS are missing that the identification and development of players had stagnated. A very public disaster eventually would happen—in this case the loss to Trinidad & Tobago and not qualifying for the World Cup—that the USMNT could not hide from. Not qualifying exposed the drift that had gone on too long and had gone too far.[147]

After the loss to Trinidad & Tobago, soccer experts identified many topics related to soccer in the U.S. that should be revisited. Re-examining why and how things are done shouldn't diminish how much extraordinary progress has been made and shouldn't suggest that a complete overhaul of U.S. Soccer is necessary. The USMNT had many successes—the 1994 Round of 16, 2002 World Cup quarterfinal, 2009 Confederations Cup Final, 2010 World Cup Group Winner and Round of 16, and 2014 World Cup Round of 16. For most of the 20th century, Mexico were superior to the USMNT—that changed. MLS is thriving. There are currently 26 clubs, and four expansion clubs. There has been growth in the number of U.S. players in Top Five Leagues. Each year more American soccer fans watch games from leagues all over the world, and they are getting more knowledgeable. The simple fact that people are so passionate about the USMNT that this book could get published is a tribute to the many unheralded people whose contributions to soccer in the U.S. don't get enough recognition.

---

146. The U.S. qualified for the Olympics in 1992, 1996 (qualified as hosts), 2000 (fourth place), and 2008. Missing an Olympics is a wasted opportunity to give U-23 players experience in a competitive tournament environment that is difficult to replicate. In fairness, Italy last qualified for the Olympics in 2008. While France qualified for the 2020 Olympics, they last qualified in 1996. However, some of the best young players in other countries elect not to play in U-21 or U-23 tournaments because they are already playing for their men's national teams. In addition, players' countries in competitive regions already get more similar experiences to the Olympics with regional and youth tournament competitions, such as the U-19 European Championships and UEFA Youth League Club titles.

147. See Diane Vaughan's book titled *The Challenger Disaster Launch Decision*, Scott Snook's book titled *The Accidental Shootdown of U.S. Black Hawks*, or Steven Mandis' book titled *What Happened to Goldman Sachs*.

Keep in mind this book is primarily focused on the USMNT. In our investigation of what happened to the USMNT, we learned the importance of such factors as culture, style of play, familiarity, team chemistry, skill level as defined by players and minutes in the Top Five Leagues, the too-tired-and-old effect, luck, red cards, home-field advantage, and mental and physical conditioning for a knockout tournament with games every few days. These factors impact the USMNT's performance on the field.

We turn our attention to the identification and development of elite male soccer players even before they are selected for the USMNT. We chose to focus on pay-to-play, Hispanic origin and Black American players, dual nationals, MLS, college soccer, and soccer culture in the U.S. Each of these topics could be a book in and of itself. Below, we provide some background, context, and ideas. We make some suggestions as outsiders, but we are smart enough to know that we don't know everything and that there are no simple solutions.

Pay-to-Play and Economic Incentives

Earlier, we mentioned the power of economic incentives in the 1980s and 1990s created by Italian industrialists and Colombian drug lords for the identification and development of soccer players. Today, around most of the world, the economic incentives are driven by professional soccer clubs. The clubs are willing to pay transfer fees and other compensation for, or pay to develop themselves, valuable players from whom they expect to generate an economic return on their investment. The very top clubs in the Top Five Leagues pay a lot of money to an entire global system to identify and develop players. In order to help explain and provide context, we use Brazilian forward Vinícius Júnior, who started playing for Real Madrid in 2018.

Economic Incentive in Brazil: Vinícius Júnior

Vinícius was born in the outskirts of Rio de Janeiro, Brazil, on July 12, 2000. In 2006, his father took him to a local soccer school affiliated with Clube de Regatas do Flamengo, commonly referred to as Flamengo, a Brazilian soccer club based in Rio de Janeiro, because they were passionate fans. There are over 50 schools affiliated with Flamengo around the area of Rio de Janeiro. The local school was run by Carlos Eduardo Abrantes, known as Cacau. To develop Vinícius, Cacau had him play both futsal and soccer.[148]

At seven years old, Cacau saw Vinícius was talented, so he had him play soccer against the best nine-year-olds to develop faster. Vinícius' family often could not afford to pay the monthly fees to attend the school, and often did not have enough to eat. So Cacau would allow the family to skip payments and gave Vinícius soccer shoes and a backpack to bring to training. Also, his wife would sometimes give Vinícius some extra food. In 2010, Vinícius was selected by Flamengo to start training for free at their youth academy, Ninho do Urubu (the "Vultures' Nest"), on the other side of Rio de Janeiro. His father worked as a building manager and already had a long commute. His mother could no longer take him to training. Vinícius had to live with his uncle to be closer to the training center, avoiding a commute that sometimes took three hours. By the time he was 14 years old, Vinícius' skills were clear, and TFM, one of Brazil's soccer agencies, started to manage his career, taking the place of a previous agent and providing financial support to Vinícius' family. The informal arrangement carried risks because in Brazil players cannot sign with an agent until they are 18. While Vinícius' family did not have to pay for his training at Flamengo's academy, his family had expenses. TFM helped Vinícius' family rent an apartment closer to Flamengo's training center, gave money to his father to leave his job to be close to his son and provide him with support, and paid for Vinícius to attend two high-performance facilities in the U.S. that are used by professional sports franchises.

Scouts working for Real Madrid noticed Vinícius' talent and potential while he was playing for Flamengo's youth teams. In 2015, Vinícius was called up for Brazil for the South American U-15 Championship, which Brazil won, and he was the second-highest goal scorer of the tournament.

---

148. Futsal is an indoor/hard court version of the sport of soccer. It's 5-on-5 with one goalkeeper and four outfield players. The game is played on what looks a lot like a basketball court. It is not "indoor soccer" of the American variety. That game involves hockey-style boards and artificial grass. The name futsal is an abbreviation of *futebol de salão*, which literally translates as "ballroom football," because it was meant to be classy with neat touches, pretty dribbles, and no heavy fouls.

After leading Brazil in winning the South American U-17 Championship, Vinícius Júnior was named the tournament's best player and was the top goal scorer with seven goals. On May 13, 2017, Vinícius debuted for Flamengo's first team.

On May 23, 2017, Real Madrid signed a contract to acquire Vinícius (who was still only 16), effective after his 18th birthday on July 12, 2018.[149] His transfer fee reportedly was $50 million, which was, at the time, the second-most-expensive sale of a player in the history of Brazilian soccer (behind only Neymar). Keep in mind the transfer fee is not his salary, which was reportedly close to $6 million per year.

The transfer fee for Vinícius goes to many people and organizations. Professional club youth academies can get a return on their investment through two types of compensation mechanisms described in FIFA's Regulations on the Status and Transfer of Players (RSTP): training compensation and solidarity mechanism payments. FIFA mandates that whenever a player is transferred to another club prior to the end of their contract, and that transfer involves moving to another country—an "international transfer," or a "national transfer with international dimension"—5 percent of the transfer fee is set aside for payment to the youth clubs responsible for the player's development from 12 to 23 years old in what is called a "solidarity payment." The rules also stipulate that when a player signs his first professional contract, and that contract involves a change of international association, the pro club is obligated to pay "training and development compensation" to the youth clubs that "trained and educated" the player between the ages of 12 and 21. Training compensation is a flat fee paid by a club when (1) a male player is registered for the first time as a professional (i.e., signs his first professional contract); or (2) a professional player is transferred between clubs of two different associations (whether during or at the end of his contract) before the end of the year of his 23rd birthday. Training compensation is paid to the clubs that trained the player but ultimately did not sign him to his first professional contract. The intent of training compensation is to mitigate the

---

149. Age 18 is the minimum age for international transfer—within Europe it is 16 and there are a few exceptions for various reasons.

poaching of talented players from poorer clubs without compensation for the investment in training the player. The intent of both solidarity payments and training compensation, as one can clearly see, is to give clubs that invest training resources some level of protection and return on their investment.

Cacau, TFM, and Flamengo all got paid some compensation for their training of Vinícius—a return on their investment. Around the world, scouts, agents, and professional clubs have an economic incentive to identify and develop talent. In the case of Vinícius, Real Madrid, one of the biggest European clubs, also had an economic incentive to sign him, and ultimately paid a premium to do so. Essentially, Real Madrid paid for the identification and development of a Brazilian national player.

The cost to Real Madrid is very high because the probability of successfully identifying and developing a player like Vinícius is so low. The scouts, agents, professional club youth academies, and others have all of the upfront costs and take all the risk of generating no return. An ugly truth is that *less than 1 percent* of the boys who enter Top Five League club youth academies at the age of nine make it as a professional soccer player *at any level*. For those who are at youth academies at age 16, five out of six (83 percent) are not playing professional soccer at any level at age 21.[150]

While the probabilities are low, around five out of six (83 percent) players in the Top Five Leagues played for a top-division club youth academy by age 13 or played for their country's U-15 or U-16 team. Around the world, generally most soccer players and their families accept that if they don't meet that criteria, they most likely will not have a professional career. The parents and players understand if a player's development is not being paid for by a professional soccer club with an economic incentive to produce professional players and generate a return, then they have to ask themselves what the incentive is for them to personally spend the money and make the tremendous sacrifices. Around the rest of world, generally,

---

150. USSF's IMG U-17 Residency Program had slightly better success than most Top Five League club youth academies —seven out of ten (70 percent) of IMGS Residency Program graduates are not playing professional soccer at any level at age 21.

athletics is not an activity that leads to acceptance to a more selective college and athletic scholarships don't exist.

Economic Incentive in USA: Before April 2019

For a lot of different reasons, prior to April 2019, the United States did not adhere to FIFA's RSTP. MLS youth academies did not receive training compensation and solidarity mechanism payments. Therefore, there was less economic incentive for MLS clubs to identify and develop players than other professional clubs around the world.[151] Compounding this is the fact that the clubs also didn't have the associated increase in revenues in the form of these payments to reinvest in their academy systems, which restricts investment.

Without a strong economic incentive for MLS clubs to pay for identification and development in the United States, there was a void. The parents who could afford to pay for the development of their sons filled that void. They essentially acted as Flamengo and agents. The economic incentive for the parents was the entrance to a more selective college or college scholarship for their sons—and the system of pay-to-play blossomed. Therefore, the identification and development of soccer players was generally geared toward college—that was the economic incentive or return on their investment. The parents were willing to pay the upfront costs and take on the risk. Obviously, the problem is pay-to-play restricts the available talent pool because not every family can afford to pay the fees.

Around the world, the same challenges exist. As mentioned, Vinícius' family had to pay for him to be able to attend soccer school until he was 10 years old and was selected for the Flamengo's youth academy. Typically, players selected at young ages to train at professional club youth academies must live within commuting distance of the facilities. Vinícius' family made sacrifices for him to not have to commute three hours each way to practice. If they were unwilling to or couldn't afford to do so, or weren't

---

151. MLS did establish incentives to develop homegrown players, and there was an economic benefit—it often was cheaper than paying a transfer fee for an international player. However, the revenue possibilities of RSTP made the economic incentives stronger.

willing to take the risks or have agents be willing to take the risks, Vinícius wouldn't be playing for Real Madrid or Brazil. The economic incentives encouraged it to happen.

Of course, talented boys can be missed or overlooked—but, more often than not, with economic incentives, they will be discovered. When we were with executives of top European clubs, it was not uncommon for parents to approach them and say that their son is super talented and they should give him a tryout. Most often the club executives would politely explain, "Don't worry; we pay a lot of experienced people a lot of money to find great soccer players with potential, and if your son is as good as you say, trust us; they will find him and bring him to us." As transfer fees rise for U.S. players and solidarity payments and training compensation increase (discussed below), eventually, this will become a more common answer in the United States.[152]

Economic Incentive in the USA: Since April 2019

Since April 2019, Major League Soccer requires foreign clubs that acquire players trained in all MLS academies to compensate them per FIFA's RSTP. The change brings MLS in line with the rest of the world, and will further drive the identification and development of future USMNT players. In the 2018–19 season, the estimated amount of the global RSTP payments was around $75 million. Solidarity payments totaled around $63 million: 23 clubs made at least $1.130 million in just solidarity payments (three apiece from Brazil, Portugal, and Spain; two apiece from Mexico and the Netherlands) and 117 clubs made at least $282,000. Training compensation payments totaled around $12 million. If MLS wanted to accelerate investment, it could also consider a domestic training compensation and solidarity fee system for professional signings

---

152. European clubs are figuring out USMNT stars have a lot of value to MLS, who themselves can afford to pay higher transfer fees. The New York/New Jersey Metro Stars received a $250,000 transfer fee (and a portion of any sell-on fee) when they sent Michael Bradley to Dutch club Heerenveen in 2006. According to transfermarkt, in 2012, Roma paid a base transfer fee of $4.1 million for Bradley. In 2014, Toronto FC paid Roma an $8.1 million base transfer fee. The value of USMNT stars can be higher in MLS than in Europe because of marketing. Besides his talent, it is possible this was one consideration for Chelsea signing Christian Pulisic.

and transfers within North America. The FIFA rules only apply between national federations.

Prior to the change, MLS did have a club youth academy system since 2007, and reportedly all the clubs combined invested around $70 million in the system in the 2019 season alone. The investments have produced more than 250 homegrown players who have become professional and national team players, including recent standout players such as Brenden Aaronson (Philadelphia Union), Reggie Cannon (FC Dallas), Jesùs Ferreira (FC Dallas), and Matt Miazga (New York Red Bulls). MLS academies still need to develop their own traditions, values, and heritage where the players feel they are playing for something much larger than themselves— that takes time. USMNT players used to get this feeling in college.

In May and August 2020, a total of 83 elite academy clubs that formerly participated in the U.S. Soccer Development Academy joined MLS' 30 existing youth club academies as part of a new elite player development platform. The 113 clubs include more than 11,000 players throughout the U.S. and Canada and will consist of elite year-round competition, as well as player identification initiatives, coaching education opportunities, and additional programming to create a premier player development environment. Member clubs will collaborate on the competition format and league structure for the year-round program aimed at developing elite players in the United States and Canada. The league is expected to include U-13, -14, -15, -17, and -19 age groups.

Outside of the U.S., typically professional club youth academies start their free training earlier, as was the case for Vinícius, who was 10 when he started the Flamengo youth academy. In Europe, Barcelona (La Masia) and Real Madrid's (La Fábrica) youth academies start with U-8 teams, and Bayern Munich, Borussia Dortmund, Juventus, and Manchester United's youth academies start at U-10. Most of their boarding options are from 14 to 18 years old. Therefore, if a boy doesn't live within driving distance to a top club, then he will have to wait until around 14 years old to board at the youth academy.

In 2019, 34 percent of the USMNT roster at the 2019 CONCACAF Gold Cup were developed in MLS youth academies. That is up from 8 percent in 2015 for the same Gold Cup tournament. According to the USSF, around 90 percent of their youth national team players have come from the 113 clubs in new elite player development, and about 70 to 80 percent of those players come from MLS club youth academies. Most of the rest are based internationally. One of the challenges to the development of the USMNT is that not all MLS clubs are intensely focused on their youth academies. The website Chasing a Cup rated FC Dallas as the gold standard of youth academies in MLS—and that helps, because they are in a state that naturally produces a high percentage of USMNT players. The best academies need to be in the areas where there are a lot of skilled boys with potential coming from communities that prioritize soccer—especially in Southern California. Currently, MLS youth academies are restricted to local territories, but perhaps they should be able to recruit players nationally after a certain age. Certain MLS clubs will develop reputations for developing players and playing young homegrown players on their first team, and that will force other MLS clubs not taking advantage of their territories or doing a poor job at identifying skilled players to invest and improve—which will help MLS and the USMNT.

While MLS youth academies are free, and most elite academy clubs offer some sort of need-based financial assistance, the change in April 2019 for MLS to adhere to FIFA's RSTP will not eliminate pay-to-play for male players. There will always be parents willing to pay the development costs and take the financial risks, and this is actually important. MLS clubs don't have enough resources to compete against the clubs in the Top Five Leagues. American parents who can afford pay-to-play are actually supplementing the cost of the development of soccer in America. It is economically inefficient, because the money isn't being spent on the best identified players with potential and often results in players from lower socioeconomic backgrounds being at a disadvantage or boxed out of the system entirely. Therefore, it isn't necessarily right, but it does help overall. We also found many instances of families and local organizations helping talented young players and their families. It didn't seem easy, but in many cases it seemed that if there was a will, there was a way.[153]

It is clear that if people want to reduce the costs of pay-to-play or improve identification and development for the USMNT, then they need to focus on economic incentives. For example, getting a coaching license in the U.S. is much more expensive than in France, Germany, and Spain, which restricts the number of coaches and therefore access to quality coaching in the U.S. The USSF could more heavily subsidize the cost for getting soccer coaching licenses and/or reimburse some of the licensing expenses if a graduating coach works at a program serving underprivileged or rural areas or U-10s and/or better utilize online learning to lower costs. Theoretically, the more licensed coaches there are looking for positions, the less programs will have to pay coaches. The less programs have to pay coaches, the less they have to charge to play. Also, more coaches available at younger ages and/or in rural or underprivileged areas makes soccer more accessible before reaching MLS youth academies.

Keep in mind, economic incentives can also have many unintended consequences. For example, the fees and expenses of AAU basketball are comparable to elite youth travel soccer programs. Most elite basketball players don't pay the fees and expenses. The basketball shoe companies have economic incentives—exposure to many potential consumers and brand affinity with potential NBA stars—to help financially support the identification and development of elite basketball players at the AAU and high school youth level. The basketball shoe companies sponsor teams and pay coaches in return for having the coaches require their team to play in their basketball shoes and apparel. The more the coach wins, the more attention and dollars he and his team attract—which has led to numerous scandals and emphasis on winning versus fundamentals.

As a comparison to Europe, at 13 years of age, Slovenian Luka Dončić signed a five-year contract with the youth academy of Real Madrid Basketball. He immediately stood out on the U-16 team. He lived in the youth academy with soccer and basketball prospects. He debuted for the

---

153. We want to make clear we are not "for" pay-to-play. We are for more economic incentives and community support to make the game more accessible, especially at younger ages.

Real Madrid senior team in 2015, at age 16, becoming the youngest in club history. He led Real Madrid to the 2018 EuroLeague title, winning the EuroLeague MVP. In 2018, Dončić declared for the NBA draft and joined the Dallas Mavericks. Real Madrid Basketball had an economic incentive to identify and develop Dončić. He had to buy out his contract with Real Madrid to play for Dallas, which was reportedly between $1 and $2 million and was partly paid by Dallas. This should be a warning to USA Basketball. The economic incentives for identification and development in European basketball, combined with having teenage boys play with men in professional leagues, will result in European basketball players potentially developing better and faster than those who develop through the AAU and college system, in part because, typically, AAU and college players practice and play against boys and young men their own age. Players can develop and improve faster by playing against older, bigger, quicker, stronger, and better players. More top basketball prospects will play overseas for this reason.[154]

Any economic incentives for soccer in the U.S. should be focused on developing fundamentals and reaching more players.

Hispanic Origin and Black American Players

Much has been written about the USMNT's recruiting efforts (or lack thereof) of Hispanic origin and Black American players. Soccer is highly popular in Hispanic origin communities, and the demographics show an increasing number of Hispanic origin players. Brad Rothenberg—the son of Alan Rothenberg, who headed U.S. Soccer in the 1990s—and his organization Alianza de Futbol have been strong advocates for more Hispanic origin player identification and development. The Allstate Sueno Alianza National Showcase has 50 finalists chosen out of around 5,000 candidates to compete in front of around 30 scouts from Europe, MLS, and Liga MX. He believes major talent pools from which USMNT recruits remain disproportionately white when it comes to homegrown talent. Critics claim the USMNT recruiters focus their efforts on pay-to-pay U.S. Soccer Development Academies and MLS youth club academies,

---

154. Dončić played soccer growing up but quit because he was too tall. His father is a basketball coach and former basketball player—family is important.

which are more likely to have white, higher-income players whose parents could afford the development costs to reach those academies. Soccer writer Derek Richey pointed out to us one important phenomenon we can't really explain with data: young Hispanic origin players from the U.S. are not having as much success as others in Europe.

We examined the breakdown of players who were of Hispanic origin. We divided the players between those born in the U.S. and those born outside the U.S. Generally, the number of players with Hispanic origin ties has increased. For context, in 2019, 33 percent and 25 percent of MLS players and coaches reported being of Hispanic origin, respectively.

Table: Breakdown of Origins of USMNT

Year	Hispanic Origin Ties	% Hispanic Origin Ties	Born Outside US	% Born Outside US
1990	2	9%	2	9%
1994	5	23%	7	32%
1998	3	14%	7	32%
2002	3	13%	5	22%
2006	3	13%	1	4%
2010	5	22%	2	9%
2014	4	17%	5	22%
2017	7	30%	2	9%

The chart below is a breakdown of USMNT players' ties to Europe. It is the same approach as Hispanic origin, just European origin (i.e., a player was born there, is a dual national, or is first-generation American, both of whose parents emigrated from Europe). As expected, a large percentage of players have ties to Europe.

Table: Breakdown of Origins of USMNT

Year	# Immigrant Ties	# European Ties	# Hispanic Origin Ties	# Native American	% European Ties	% Hispanic Origin Ties
1990	6	4	2	0	18%	9%
1994	12	7	5	0	32%	23%
1998	11	8	3	0	36%	14%
2002	12	8	3	0	35%	13%
2006	9	6	3	0	26%	13%
2010	16	8	5	0	35%	22%
2014	15	11	4	2	48%	17%
2017	15	6	7	2	26%	30%

*Note that in 2010 and 2017, there is one player who is double counted for both Europe and Latin America: Benny Feilhaber was born in Brazil but is a dual citizen of the U.S. and Austria.

We examined the breakdown of players who were Black Americans. For that group, the number has increased over time. (In 1984, Eddie Hawkins became the first native-born Black player to appear with the USMNT.

In 1990, Desmond Armstrong and Jimmy Banks [his son Jimmy " J.C." Banks Jr. played in MLS] were the first to play in a World Cup. Desmond Armstrong became the first American player ever to sign a contract to play in Brazil.) We divided the players between those raised in the U.S. and those raised outside the U.S. Generally, the number of Black Americans has increased. We also sub-divided those two groups into those with mixed-race parents and those with a family member in the military. The majority of Black American players have mixed-race parents, have a family member in the military, or grew up outside the U.S. For context, in 2019, around 25 percent of MLS players reported being Black—10 percent of MLS players identify as African American, and around 15 percent are Black but don't identify themselves as African American.

Table: Breakdown of Origins of USMNT

Year	# Black American	% Black American	Born Outside US	% Born Outside US
1990	2	9%	2	9%
1994	2	9%	7	32%
1998	2	9%	7	32%
2002	4	17%	5	22%
2006	5	22%	1	4%
2010	8	35%	2	9%
2014	9	39%	5	22%
2017	6	26%	2	9%

It would be unfair to say that the USMNT have not had diverse teams. The makeup of the team has evolved over the years to include players with many different backgrounds. The number of dual nationals, those with immigrant ties, and Hispanic origin and Black American players has increased over time. Generally, the number of players born outside the U.S. has declined, with the exception of 2014, when Klinsmann included four German American players born outside the U.S.[155]

Those players who have dual nationalities because of immigrant ties to Europe have had advantages over other players to play and develop in Europe because of visa and league restrictions there.

---

155. The only German American not born in Germany was Julian Green, who was born in Florida.

The demographic breakdown of the USMNT for each World Cup is in the table below.

Table: Demographic Breakdown of the USMNT: 1990–2017

Year	# Born Outside US	# Dual Nationals	# Immigrant Ties	% Immigrant Ties	# Black American
1990	2	1	6	27%	2
1994	7	9	12	55%	2
1998	7	9	11	50%	2
2002	5	11	12	52%	4
2006	1	9	9	39%	5
2010	2	16	16	70%	8
2014	5	15	15	65%	9
2017	2	14	15	65%	6

"Immigrant ties" is defined as players who were either born outside the U.S., are dual nationals, or are immigrants or children of immigrants. As expected, there is significant overlap between groups (e.g., a player with dual citizenship would also be considered to have immigrant ties, but could also have been born outside the U.S.).

Immigrant ties can impact development. If a player can use a passport that is accepted in the European Union, he can bypass stringent regulations, including work permit rules. Those with Hispanic origin ties, on the other hand, can be relatively closed off to Europe and have fewer good developmental opportunities in Latin America. The same can be said of American players without recent immigrant ties and access to a second passport.

Throughout the U.S. Soccer system there are not enough who understand Hispanic origin and Black American players' communities. There are biases and discrimination in player identification and development in the system, just like there are in many college and professional sports. However, one of the great things about sports is that eventually, competition and economic incentives break down many of these barriers. MLS youth academies now have a stronger economic incentive. Still, the USSF could probably improve in cultivating and raising awareness of Hispanic origin and Black American players. This would likely need to include more corporate sponsorship, which also raises a number of complex issues.

Biases and discrimination related to coaching and executive opportunities are much more difficult to break down. The USSF adopted a version of the NFL's Rooney Rule in 2014.[156,157] The Rooney Rule requires NFL teams to interview ethnic-minority candidates for head coaching and senior football operation jobs. The USSF should also include women along with ethnic minorities—which fits with the equal-opportunity, underdog values of the Spirit of '76.[158,159] The interview process and accompanying exposure as well as feedback are invaluable to those trying to overcome what can be perceived as a closed, inner circle. Diversity is important in soccer in the U.S. because soccer is viewed as a sport of equal opportunity. The USSF and MLS will need to keep this in mind as they continue to try to retain and attract more fans. The NBA, the NFL, and MLB have female assistant coaches. The NHL and MLS do not.

156. On December 7, 2014, U.S. Soccer passed the following resolution: "The Board of Directors for the United States Soccer Federation, Inc. has resolved that for each open senior executive, full-time head coach, and full-time assistant coach position, U.S. Soccer shall create a list of potential candidates which shall include minority candidates, and shall interview at least one minority candidate for each position."

157. There are no quick solutions. Research by the late economist CC DuBois showed that the Rooney Rule did actually have a positive effect on coaching diversity, compared with NCAA coaches and NFL coordinators, who did not have similar interview requirements. In 2016, Jason Reid of The Undefeated pointed out that the rule has two fatal flaws: the temptation to substitute "fake" interviews in place of a search for real diversity, and the fact that assistant coach positions, a crucial step to head-coaching jobs, are not under the umbrella. The NFL did recently expand the rule again to include women—for all executive openings in the commissioner's office, a woman must be interviewed. The San Francisco 49ers were the first team to formally adopt the practice, but the same flaws still apply.

158. We believe Bruce Arena has been the only coach who had discussions with a woman, Lauren Gregg, to be an assistant coach for the USMNT. Arena helped recruit Gregg to become the women's coach at the University of Virginia, where they became friends. Bob Bradley had Egyptian-born American Zak Abdel as a goalkeeping coach. Jürgen Klinsmann had Uruguayan-born American Tab Ramos as an assistant coach. The USSF created an employee-led Diversity, Equity, and Inclusion Council, and launched the Jill Ellis Scholarship Fund and SheChampions Mentorship Program, designed to encourage more women to enter coaching.

159. In 2019, the Institute for Diversity and Ethics in Sport (TIDES) at the University of Central Florida gave MLS an A for racial hiring, a C for gender hiring, and an overall grade of B. In 2019, 33 percent and 25 percent of MLS players and coaches, respectively, reported being of Hispanic origin. In 2019, 59 percent and 75 percent of NFL and NBA players, respectively, were Black Americans, but only 9 percent and 27 percent of the head coaches were. In 2018, 29 percent and only 10 percent of MLB players and head coaches, respectively, were of Hispanic origin. In 2019, around 25 percent of MLS players reported being Black, but only two head coaches did. As with most major leagues, many MLS clubs have male-dominated office environments.

Dual Nationals

The USMNT have had a history of dual nationals, including naturalized citizens, who have been well liked and respected. The 1994 World Cup squad had seven naturalized citizens or dual nationals—Fernando Clavijo (Uruguay), Thomas Dooley (Germany), Frank Klopas (Greece), Hugo Pérez (El Salvador), Tab Ramos (Uruguay), Earnie Stewart (the Netherlands), and Roy Wegerle (South Africa). The 2002 World Cup squad had five naturalized citizens—Jeff Agoos (Switzerland), Carlos Llamosa (Colombia), Pablo Mastroeni (Argentina), David Regis (Martinique), and Earnie Stewart (the Netherlands).

Dual nationals are very important to World Cup success. Of the top four teams in the 2014 World Cup, 42 percent of their players were dual nationals. Runner-up Argentina had a total of 18 players, with 17 of the 18 being European (10 Italy, six Spain, one France). Third-place finisher the Netherlands had nine dual nationals, with Suriname being the most commonly represented (four players). Fourth-place finisher Brazil had seven dual nationals, all of whom had European ties, particularly Spain. Germany, the winner, had four dual nationals—most players are in the Bundesliga. The USMNT had 15 dual nationals, as many players seek to play in Europe.

As demographics continue to shift over time, more and more players will be dual nationals and have choices about their international futures.[160] With regard to the U.S. and Mexico, stories like this have been happening for some time, and will only become increasingly common. In 2018, USMNT fans were rightfully concerned when Monterrey midfielder Jonathan Gonzalez, who had represented the U.S. at the youth level, filed his one-time switch in 2018 and became a Mexico international. While Gonzalez was a member of the U.S. U-14 program when he participated in Alianza, the showcase helped him secure a place in Monterrey's academy. He said he felt ignored by U.S. Soccer and the Mexican federation showed

---

160. In the 2016, nearly 50 foreign-born athletes proudly represented the U.S. as part of the Olympic team in Rio de Janeiro, and eight of them won medals.

more interest.[161] Nevertheless, the U.S. still seems to be "winning" the U.S.-Mexican dual nationals battle, at least when looking at World Cup rosters. From the 1990 to 2002 World Cups, the USMNT had no U.S.-Mexican dual nationals on the roster. In 2006, there was one player. In 2010, there were three, then only one in 2014, and then three again in 2017 for the World Cup qualifiers. Over that same time span, there was never a single player on the Mexico World Cup team who was eligible to play for the U.S. Even more recently, in the 2019 CONCACAF Gold Cup, the USMNT had 11 players total who were dual nationals, two of whom were Mexican American. (Jonathan Gonzalez, who was born in 1999, did not play for Mexico in the 2018 World Cup or 2019 Gold Cup.) This compares to three dual nationals on Mexico, all of whom had Spanish ties.

The USMNT will always have players not born or raised in the U.S. As the world becomes more global, the USMNT will not only have to identify eligible dual national players, they will have to actively recruit them—similar to college coaches. There are several key players in the past who could have helped the USMNT, such as Giuseppe Rossi (Italy) and Neven Subotić (Serbia). The 2022 World Cup cycle has several young dual national players who are undecided who could also help, such as 18-year old Yunus Musah (England, Ghana, and Italy). Musah was born in New York City to Ghanaian parents, moved to Italy as an infant, started his youth career in Italy, joined Arsenal's Academy in London at 10 years old, and then joined Valencia in Spain in 2019. It helps team chemistry if these players are identified and recruited earlier so they can become familiar with the system and meaningfully participate in World Cup qualification.

MLS

Overall, MLS has been very beneficial to the development of soccer in the U.S. MLS has helped drive the growth and popularity of soccer in the U.S. and given more American players the opportunity to play professional soccer. The league has invested significant amounts of money

---

161. In fairness, he was a regular part of the U.S. youth national team for years, during which time Mexico showed no interest.

in player identification and development as well. Most importantly, MLS (and three men in particular—Philip Anschutz, Lamar Hunt, and Robert Kraft) kept soccer alive and relevant in the United States, and all fans of soccer in the U.S. owe the three men and their families a great deal of gratitude.[162]

As background, MLS began playing with 10 teams in 1996 and grew to 12 teams in 1998. However, MLS had reportedly lost an estimated $250 million during its first five years. Following 9/11, the three principal owners had decided to shut down MLS and had spoken to bankruptcy lawyers. A couple of days later, they changed their minds and banded together to eliminate two teams and keep 10 clubs between the three of them, taking a big financial risk.

Compounding the league's challenges, as previously mentioned, the 1998 World Cup ratings were around 50 percent lower than 1994. The poor ratings had serious consequences. Street & Smith's *Sports Business Daily* reported that the 2002 and 2006 World Cups came very close to not being televised in English in the United States. No major networks bid on the rights. While the key MLS owners were facing stagnating attendance and staggering losses, they formed a subsidiary to buy the TV rights from FIFA, cover the production costs, and ensure the World Cups aired on ESPN to continue to promote soccer in America. Then they negotiated an agreement with ABC and ESPN to broadcast the tournament. This was the start of Soccer United Marketing (SUM), and the board of SUM was, and is, composed only of the owners from each MLS club.[163] The estimated cost of the rights was around $70 million. Although SUM recouped some of that cost from the sale of advertising, SUM incurred a loss. In addition, IMG represented U.S. Soccer's commercial rights from 1999 to 2004. IMG was losing money on the contract (which went through 2006) and wanted to terminate the relationship. SUM purchased the contract from IMG in 2004 and has represented U.S. Soccer since then. SUM took over

---

162. Almost everyone we interviewed also pointed to a few people who don't get enough recognition for their contributions to soccer in the U.S., including Sunil Gulati, Don Garber, Dan Flynn, Werner Fricker, Alan Rothenberg, and Hank Steinbrecher.

163. Providence Equity owned a minority stake from 2012 to 2017 and had a board seat.

U.S. Soccer's marketing out of necessity at a time when there appeared to be little money being made from the national teams.

Today, SUM has more than 150 full-time staff dedicated to generating revenue and promoting soccer. SUM holds the broadcast rights to the Mexico men's national team games in the U.S. and the Gold Cup. SUM bundles many of its MLS, U.S. Soccer (men's and women's), Mexico men's national games, and other rights into packages to make them more attractive to broadcasters.[164] Their entire bundle takes in $90 million per year through 2022 (including sponsorships). SUM pays U.S. Soccer an average annual guarantee of nearly $30 million per year with some possible upside. With the guaranteed payments, SUM, not USSF, takes economic risk—for example, not qualifying for the World Cup.[165] Since 2004, SUM has paid the USSF more than $190 million to help the USSF fund its operations and programs. The amount of SUM guaranteed payments through the term of the agreement in 2022 is estimated to be more than $300 million.

Around the world, most federations and domestic leagues are not economically aligned. The domestic leagues do what is in their best interest. They don't have any economic incentive, except having their respective country's stars playing in their home country increases their domestic league's popularity. In contrast, the U.S. have an advantage in that MLS has a direct economic interest in the success and popularity of the U.S. national soccer teams, especially because of the economic risk that it takes. MLS has an economic incentive to develop homegrown USMNT-eligible players to help the USMNT to improve and therefore improve TV ratings.[166] Rightly or wrongly, the perception of the legitimacy of MLS and the value of their players are highly correlated to the execution of the USMNT's mission—proving the legitimacy of soccer in the U.S. MLS should consider some more actions to help the USMNT because it directly economically benefits them. It's not an obligation—it's smart business.

---

164. In the beginning, MLS had difficulty getting a big broadcasting deal and bundling the U.S. national teams' games helped. This has changed over time.

165. The guarantees from SUM and Nike have allowed the USSF to better plan for the future.

166. Ironically, MLS/SUM hope Mexico do well too.

A 2015 academic study by Carsten Richter revealed a correlation between the number of foreign players and the performance of clubs and the national team. The results show that a higher number of foreign players have a positive influence on the clubs in the league and in European competitions. Furthermore, the results also highlight that a league with more foreign players has a negative influence on the performance of the national team (e.g., England and the Premier League).

In MLS, only up to eight foreign players are permitted on a 30-man roster, leaving 22 spots (73 percent) for a "domestic player" (i.e., U.S. citizen, green-card holder, refugee, or homegrown international).[167] The intention of this rule makes sense to help the development of U.S. Soccer and the USMNT. However, many MLS green-card holders are not USMNT-eligible (e.g., David Beckham was a green-card holder). There have been teams in MLS for which none of their starting XI in a game were USMNT-eligible.

Even with the MLS rule, the percentage of minutes for U.S.-born players (this does not necessarily mean USMNT-eligible) in MLS has fallen from 53 percent in 2012 to 42 percent in 2018. In comparison, in 2018, Spaniards claimed 59 percent of La Liga minutes, French 51 percent of Ligue 1, Germans 50 percent in the Bundesliga, Italians 43 percent in Serie A, and English 33 percent in the English Premier League.[168]

MLS is not alone in having an ineffective "domestic" rule. When Italy had a poor 2014 World Cup and recognized the number of spots in Serie A claimed by Italians was declining, Serie A was pressured to decree starting in 2016 that each club's 25-man squad has to include at least four homegrown players and at least four more club-trained players (the minimum eight players represent 33 percent of the squad; while most homegrown players and club-trained players are Italy-eligible, some are not). The change didn't have the intended impact—both the number of Italian players and minutes claimed by Italians in Serie A actually declined

---

167. International spots are actually tradeable, so a particular club could have more international players.

168. Of the countries with a Top Five League, England has gone the longest without winning the World Cup. However, the Premier League has the most revenues.

from 43 percent to 40 percent! And Italy didn't qualify for the 2018 World Cup.

**Table: Italian Players and Their Minutes
in Serie A from 2014–15 to 2018–19**

Season	# Italian Players	% of Total	Minutes	% of Total
2014–15	236	43%	330,518	43%
2015–16	224	43%	326,159	43%
2017–18	221	43%	337,273	43%
2018–19	206	41%	311,178	40%

Source: Centro Studi AIC

As mentioned previously, mandating the number of players doesn't necessarily change the number of minutes played—and it's the actual game minutes that matter. MLS could either reward or penalize clubs for the number of minutes of homegrown players.[169] The reward or penalty could relate to general allocation money (GAM). GAM is the money that is available to a club in addition to its salary budget. Each MLS club receives an annual allotment of GAM and that money can be used to pay down the cost of a player.

MLS could make other rule changes. MLS requires its clubs to not have more than eight foreign players, but during the season, if a player receives a green card, then the club has another spot for a foreign player. MLS could alter the rule so that if a change in status from foreign player to green-card holder is made during the season, it wouldn't free up a foreign player spot. MLS also could allow five substitutions, which could increase minutes of USMNT-eligible players. Rewarding the use of homegrown players will encourage more investment in youth academies. MLS would have to take many factors into consideration with any changes, including complex U.S. labor laws, impact to marketability of the league, impact to quality of the league's product, marketability of and interest in homegrown (and possible future USMNT) stars, and protecting stars (as they may not have to play as many minutes per season or play as many minutes at the end of games, when injuries most often occur).

---

169. Most homegrown players are USMNT-eligible. MLS can't mandate only U.S. citizens because of labor laws.

As for promotion and relegation, we understand many observers believe that promotion and relegation would encourage more intensity of competition, provide greater opportunities, and be more in line with soccer globally.[170] This argument makes sense. On the other hand, the economic risks of relegation can constrain experimentation, innovation, and, most importantly, investment.[171] In Europe, when the bottom-half-of-the-table clubs vote on league issues, they have a shorter-term perspective than the top clubs because of promotion and relegation. Typically, they make poor decisions that maximize revenues today or limit long-term investments because they lack confidence they will be in the top league the following year.

Observers can't discuss promotion and relegation in the U.S. without the context of where the U.S. is in the development of soccer as a sport. For context, while MLS has made strides, in 2019 the value of broadcasting rights for the English Premier League, Bundesliga, and MLS were $3.8 billion, $1.6 billion, and $105 million, respectively. In 2019, the average player earned $4.1 million, $2.1 million, and $412,000 in the EPL, Bundesliga, and MLS, respectively. If the U.S. had promotion and relegation, it is far less likely that MLS owners would invest in building stadiums and youth academies and importing talented players. Modern, fan-friendly stadiums are necessary for an attractive live experience as well as making the game attractive in a competitive and saturated TV market. Without a great experience in person and on TV, soccer would not have as much exposure and growth. In addition, if there were less certainty, MLS owners may not be willing to invest in youth academies. MLS clubs don't have the same resources as the big clubs in Europe to spend on academies. In order for America to improve, it needs MLS owners to spend as much money on identifying and developing players and having them play against more skilled players (like Italy 1980s–90s and Colombia 1990s).[172]

---

170. Liga MX is ending promotion and relegation. Reportedly, some believe that may be to make it easier to merge with MLS.

171. In some major North American leagues there is an issue of freeloaders because of large TV contracts. This wouldn't be as prevalent in MLS because MLS's TV contract is much smaller and MLS clubs rely much more on local sponsorship and stadium revenues.

172. We are not arguing that promotion and relegation should never exist in MLS in the future; we just believe further development and investment are needed before that can take place.

As for promotion and relegation creating players with a more competitive spirit, the top clubs that identify and develop (and purchase) players and drive the entire global system are not motivated by promotion and relegation. Generally, these top clubs are already established. An ugly truth: over the last 15 seasons ending in 2019, just six clubs have claimed 58 of the 60 Champions League berths in the EPL—Arsenal, Chelsea, Liverpool, Man United, Man City, and Tottenham (the "Big Six"). Everton in 2005 and Leicester in 2016 are the only exceptions.[173] In addition, 18 players and all of the starting XI on the 23-man England squad in the 2018 World Cup were from the Big Six (the exceptions: three goalkeepers, two from Leicester City and one from Stoke City). The majority of the players played in the Big Six youth academies. Generally, this concentration is true among all the Top Five Leagues, which is why their countries have a familiarity advantage over other countries—which is a much bigger issue than promotion and relegation. The top clubs (and their players) are focused on qualifying for European competitions—a big economic incentive—not promotion and relegation. This is what drives them to build a culture of success—a brand fans identify and attract with to build commercial revenues and develop talent. The top clubs have the money and every incentive (more money, prestige, and exposure from

173. While critics predicted the lack of parity would be boring, the English Premier League has thrived.

European competition) to identify and attract talent and bring them to their clubs or their youth academies.[174]

MLS clubs are trying to catch up to the history, traditions, brands, cultures, fan bases, youth academies, and financial clout of the big clubs in Europe. Fans of the USMNT should be hoping MLS clubs make more money faster. In general, the more money a soccer club makes, the more money will be invested—which in the case of MLS will improve the USMNT (as well as other CONCACAF countries, just like the Top Five Leagues are improving the USMNT and other countries).

Assuming MLS club owners won't adopt promotion and relegation—for a variety of reasons—MLS should exploit the protection of no relegation to encourage more experimentation, innovation, and investment, including providing more minutes to homegrown players. As for achieving more competition, the regular season could be much more important than postseason with the MLS champion coming out of the regular season, with much larger bonuses for regular season performances.

---

174. In 1992 the top 22 clubs in England broke away from 70 other professional English clubs to create the English Premier League to not share broadcasting rights with so many clubs. Many critics predicted the demise of English soccer as smaller clubs would lack funding. Instead, there is more money in English soccer than any other country, and the league under the Premier League has more revenues than most European first-division leagues. At the time, the reason England's federation supported such a move to happen—to help the England national team. They wanted their top players who were on the top clubs anyway to play fewer matches because they thought they were too tired going into international tournaments. In addition, they thought that if the top clubs would make more money, they would invest more money into the academies. Many of the clubs, such as Manchester United, invested the additional money into youth academies and infrastructure. Manchester United youth academy graduates from the 1990s who played for England included David Beckham, Wes Brown, Nicky Butt, Phil Neville, Gary Neville, and Paul Scholes. USMNT member and LAFC executive vice president and general manager John Thorrington also was at the Manchester United youth academy at the time. Liverpool's youth academy developed Jamie Carragher, Robbie Fowler, Steven Gerrard, and Michael Owen. Arsenal developed Ashley Cole and Martin Keown. With this core group of youth academy graduates from just three clubs, England lost to eventual champion Brazil in the quarterfinals in 2002 and in the quarterfinals in 2006 to Portugal on penalty kicks. The majority of players on England played at youth academies of established England Premier clubs. Typically, they did not develop at recently promoted English Football League Championship club youth academies. The unintended consequence for England was that the revenues of the English Premier League eventually became so large, more than twice La Liga's, that the English clubs could buy the rights to the best players in the world, and the number of minutes for England-eligible players declined, which has negatively impacted England.

As it relates to the development of national team players, a salary cap for competitive balance is one of the biggest disadvantages of the structure of MLS. In 2011, UEFA implemented Financial Fair Play (FFP), which prevents European professional clubs from spending more than they earn. The higher the revenues of a European club, the more it can spend on players—there is no "cap," per se. This has led to a few dominant clubs in each country (e.g., Bayern, Barcelona, Juventus, Milan, PSG, Real Madrid) with global brands and marketing machines that can afford the best young talent from their country and around the world. The result is their national team players gain an advantage of familiarity. In contrast, MLS has a salary cap to encourage competitive balance, which it hopes causes fan interest to rise. Some form of salary cap exists in the major North American sports. The empirical evidence of competitive balance in a sports league stimulating more fan interest is mixed. A consequence of the salary cap for competitive balance is there are no dominant clubs that hoard USMNT talent and build familiarity, and IMG U-17 was closed.

It's in the best economic interest of MLS to change rules to encourage clubs to have more USMNT-eligible talent playing more minutes and together at a few clubs. Familiarity has a powerful effect. The USMNT no longer has players gaining familiarity at a few dominant college teams, training in Mission Viejo or at the IMG Bradenton Residency Program. Perhaps a few MLS club youth academies will emerge as primary pipelines to the USMNT. Changes that help improve the USMNT are good for the value of SUM's USMNT TV rights.

As for the MLS calendar, MLS schedules its season so that it doesn't compete head-to-head with the more popular NFL. The advantage of the MLS calendar is that generally players finish the season by the end of December and have time to rest and prepare for a World Cup that usually starts in June. Players on top European clubs that go far into European club tournaments finish their season in May, just weeks before the start of the World Cup. They are more tired and run-down.

One issue with MLS is not always respecting the FIFA international windows to play matches. Some MLS clubs and coaches try to be somewhat accommodating and work through schedule conflicts.[175] If MLS believes the best thing that could happen to its league is that the USMNT is a consistent contender at World Cups, and they economically benefit with the SUM contract, then sometimes there's not a perfect solution, and it should actually prioritize the USMNT. National teams already have very limited time together and MLS shouldn't limit it further. USMNT players need to play more together for familiarity, especially as there is not a core group playing together and so many players play in different leagues. USMNT coaches try to squeeze in practices between double fixtures and during tournaments. Typically, the USMNT hosts a month-long camp in January, but most European players can't attend. Most of the real work is done surrounding summer tournaments—right in the middle of the MLS season. MLS clubs can be stretched during national team tournaments—USMNT and U-X qualification matches and tournaments. There aren't any good answers. Casual fans are more likely to watch a USMNT match and become familiar with players, and that may be the gateway to them watching MLS. Those weeks may also provide more opportunities for homegrown players to play MLS games.

Lastly, as for the MLS calendar, under FIFA guidelines, every domestic club competition has to have two transfer windows—the offseason window and a midseason period when teams can sign players from outside of the league. Many top-level leagues around the world follow the fall-to-spring calendar, as opposed to MLS' spring-to-fall calendar. This puts MLS' midseason transfer window in the European offseason and impacts the willingness and ability of MLS clubs to buy and sell players—it is more difficult to get maximum transfer values midseason. For MLS to continue its rise at this stage, MLS needs to be a "selling league" to generate

---

175. Globally, there is a tremendous amount of gamesmanship among players, clubs, and national teams. Clubs that made large investments in players in terms of salaries and transfer fees are understandably worried that their player will get injured or tired in a friendly or qualification game. Some clubs and players negotiate for the maximum number of minutes to be played in a match. Some players will show up for national team duty and claim an injury. In selecting players, some clubs now consider the player's travel distance to home national matches, obligations expected by the national team, and relationship with their national team coach. South American players in Europe have a reputation for playing poorly immediately after returning from home matches because of the long travel, jet lag, and time-zone differences.

revenues and then eventually evolve into a buying league. As transfer prices rise, the players will bring more revenues to their MLS clubs and training academies (if they are homegrown players). The clubs will invest the additional revenues into infrastructure and player development.

MLS should consider a summer break of a few weeks to coincide with the European leagues' break. This would help maximize transfer fees. The Bundesliga takes a several-week-long "winter break." Today, for a variety of reasons, MLS clubs are hesitant to buy and sell players in the middle of the season. If it had a several-week-long break in July, for example, it would be able to buy and sell players at the same time as Europe—helping maximize transfer values. The headline transfer values capture attention and raise the stature of the league. MLS should actually consider hosting the Lamar Hunt U.S. Open Cup Tournament as a standalone event during this break, similar to the "MLS is Back Tournament."[176] The issue is it would extend the season, pitting MLS games against NCAA and NFL football games. The spotlight of the tournament and opportunity to maximize transfer values may actually be worth it. Lastly, in order to increase transfer values, MLS should consider MLS clubs being able to buy/pay transfer fees to other clubs.[177] This would help set a floor for players in the overall transfer market and increase fees to MLS clubs.

College Soccer

The Philadelphia Union traded away all of their draft picks at the 2019 MLS SuperDraft to FC Cincinnati for up to $200,000 in General Allocation Money. The Union owned the No. 13 pick overall but reportedly felt they would have only wanted one of the top eight players. With one of the top academies in MLS, Philadelphia believes there are better prospects within their youth academy than in college. Of the 76 players who were selected in the 2019 draft, 24 were active on an MLS

---

176. The tournament would provide USMNT-eligible players an experience similar to the World Cup where they live away from home and with teammates and have games every few days.

177. As previously mentioned, MLS could also consider a domestic training compensation and solidarity fee system for professional signings and transfers within North America. This, combined with MLS clubs being able to buy/pay transfer fees for other clubs, would provide even more economic incentives for identification and development.

roster in 2020. For various reasons, it's going to be less likely over time that the elite American players who will compete for one of 23 spots on the USMNT squad will have played college soccer. The chances of the around 450,000 high school male soccer players making one of the 24,000 spots on NCAA Division I squads is around 0.5 percent.[178] The percentage of foreign players playing college soccer grew from 12 percent in in 2012 to 34 percent in 2018. The dramatic increase is due to a combination of more elite U.S. prospects signing pro contracts and forgoing college, and competitive NCAA coaches looking for an edge and replacing that skill gap with foreigners who didn't progress through their home youth academies. Around 1.5 percent of eligible college soccer players will be drafted by MLS. The corresponding percentages for other sports are: basketball (1.2 percent), football (1.6 percent), hockey (6.8 percent), and baseball (6.8 percent). Typically, elite U.S. players will focus on playing at professional club youth academies and in Europe, which will benefit the USMNT. On the 2017 U.S. U-17 World Cup squad of 21 players, which reached the quarterfinals and finished in seventh place, only one player played college soccer.[179] College soccer will play an increasingly important role in the development of USMNT—but not in the way many think.

---

178. It's one of the lowest odds of major sports (baseball, basketball, and football are 2 percent, 1 percent, and 3 percent, respectively), and this is, in part, because around 34 percent of NCAA Division I soccer players are foreigners (baseball, basketball, and football are 2 percent, 15 percent, and less than 1 percent, respectively).

179. Regardless, college soccer should make some changes around scheduling to make college a more attractive option. The physical demands of the sport have increased, while the schedule has stayed the same, squeezing in two games per week—dramatically increasing the risk of injury. Fortunately, there has been a strong movement within the Division I coaching community to rectify the archaic schedule. Led by Sasho Cirovski, the longtime University of Maryland coach who has won three NCAA Men's Soccer Championships, a transformative two-semester soccer proposal dubbed "The 21st Century Model" gained enough support to be on the docket for a vote by the Division I Council in April 2020 before being delayed because of the global health pandemic. The proposal aims to change the current 25-game schedule, where players play one game every 3.4 days in the fall, to spread the games out over two semesters, with one game per 6.2 days—essentially going from two games per week to one game per week. Having games spread out allows for more time to balance rest and recovery with training and development—along with schoolwork and classes. It's supported by over 90 percent of the coaches and 80 percent of the players. Having a spring season also allows more broadcasting time for college soccer. Similar to the College World Series, in the spring there is an opportunity for something similar for college soccer.

Michael Bradley, Christian Pulisic, Gio Reyna, and Josh Sargent are all actually products of the college game—learning the game from at least one parent who played college soccer.[180] Similarly, John Harkes, Tony Meola, Tab Ramos, and Claudio Reyna are the products of learning the game from their immigrant fathers. The two high scorers on the 2017 U.S. U-17 World Cup squad were Sargent and Timothy Weah. Both of Sargent's parents played college soccer and Weah's father, George, from Liberia, won the Ballon d'Or playing for PSG and AC Milan. Three other notable players on the team were Taylor Booth, who plays for Bayern Munich II; Sergiño Dest, who plays for Barcelona; and Indiana Vassilev, who played for Aston Villa. Both of Booth's parents played college soccer. Dest grew up in the Netherlands. Vassilev's father, grandfather, and great-grandfather all played soccer in their native Bulgaria. The two high scorers on the 2015 U.S. U-17 World Cup squad were Brandon Vazquez and Pulisic. Both of Pulisic's parents played college soccer and Vazquez is a dual national whose parents drove him from San Diego to Tijuana to practice with Liga MX Club Tijuana's youth academy. MLS and the USSF should want college soccer alums to continue to have a connection to the sport. They are most likely going to produce the next generation of Christian Pulisics. If soccer in the U.S. loses that connection, it will lose a very valuable pool—family matters. One of the biggest differences between soccer in the U.S. and soccer powers is that soccer powers have many more generations who have played soccer at a very high level.

MLS and USSF should have a strong partnership with college soccer.[181] College players will most likely be eventual season-ticket holders and superfans of MLS clubs, but more importantly, many will encourage

---

180. Sebastian Berhalter attended the Columbus Crew SC Academy and the University of North Carolina for one year before becoming a homegrown player signing by the Columbus Crew. Both his parents, Gregg (the USMNT player and coach) and Rosalind, played soccer at the University of North Carolina. While Gregg is a two-time World Cup USMNT player, Rosalind is a two-time national champion. Rosalind's best friend Danielle Egan married Claudio Reyna.

181. The MLS draft could consider colleges in certain regions to be homegrown players, which would encourage more cooperation.

their children or children in their communities to play soccer.[182] The U.S. needs a larger pool of college soccer alumni who bring soccer culture and expertise to their children and their communities. In addition, college soccer alumni should be provided incentives and subsidies to get coaching licenses to help continue to grow the sport.[183,184] Pulisic's and Bradley's development demonstrates that fathers who played college soccer and then coach can uniquely provide opportunities for informal pickup games for their sons with more experienced, stronger, faster, and better players.

Soccer Culture in the U.S.

Conventional wisdom is that the USMNT won't or can't be as good at soccer as a country like Spain, for example, because the U.S. doesn't have a soccer culture (the argument continues that the U.S. is a football, basketball, and baseball country). Well, the No. 1 sport in Spain, by far, is soccer, but Spain have become a global basketball power, winning the Basketball World Cup in 2006 and 2019 (which is one more than the number of soccer World Cups Spain has won) and Olympic medals in 2008, 2012, and 2016. Spain have only won one Olympic gold medal in soccer in 1992 as the hosts. Spain did not become great by hiring American coaches and asking them to teach their athletes basketball. Generally, there wasn't a feeling in Spain that the best teachers had to be American or that their players had to be sent to the U.S. Spain have become great at basketball by having their own unique style and development of players. No top EuroLeague Basketball team is named after the "Bulls," "Celtics," or "Lakers." In the last 63 years, one American coach (Dan Peterson for Olimpia Milano in 1987) won a EuroLeague championship. Peterson is

---

182. Somehow the USSF also needs to consider how to get retired USMNT players to make a commitment to growing the game in like communities like Tony Sanneh and his Sanneh Foundation in the Twin Cities, Minnesota, metro area.

183. At one time there was a National Soccer Coaches Association (NSCAA, now United Soccer Coaches) waiver program for former college players.

184. In many ways the idea of or use of the word *coach* for players U-13 implies something different from what it should be. The term or idea of a coach is also associated with a win-loss record for children, which shifts the emphasis from teaching fundamentals to winning. They should not be "soccer coaches" but "soccer teachers."

also the only American coach to be named to the 50 Greatest EuroLeague Contributors list.

Dan Grunfield, whose father was a general manager in the NBA, played at Stanford from 2002 to 2006 and then played basketball in Spain after graduation. In 2011, he wrote an article for SBNation titled "Why Spain Serves up Best Basketball in Europe." Grunfeld explained the country's basketball success: "If you're looking at Spain's success on the basketball court, you have to start with their player development. How they teach the game, starting at a very early age, is pretty remarkable. It's definitely different than my experiences growing up, when I played a lot of games on travel teams, school teams and AAU teams, without much organized time devoted to my individual development as a player. In Spain, young players don't just play basketball, they learn basketball. It starts with the coaches, who need to be certified by the Spanish Basketball Federation. Even coaches who work with young players need to be knowledgeable and dedicated enough to get certification, and I think that helps, because players obviously benefit from experienced instruction."

He went into detail about player development:

> I used to see these Spanish youngsters, anywhere from eight-to-14 years old, working out in my team's gym, especially if I'd go in at night to get treatment from our crotchety old Spanish trainer. Once in a while, if our trainer needed a smoke break, I'd peek my head into the gym to watch them for a bit, and I was always kind of amazed. There would regularly be a whole team of players working with one coach. Their drills were serious and disciplined, without yelling or screaming or anything like that. Instead, the coaches would instruct and the players would listen, working on things like footwork, ball handling and shooting with the proper mechanics. These kids were learning and practicing key basketball basics, but they were also being taught important social lessons about the game. Without even knowing it, they were learning how to take direction. They were following instructions. They were listening. They were trusting their coach and applying his advice. Also, because there were multiple players working with the same coach, they were all learning how to function in a group dynamic. Now don't get me wrong, they weren't singing "Kumbaya" or

doing a team-building ropes course or anything like that. But they were definitely getting practical experience cooperating with other people, and I think this translates into better basketball.... If you look at the statistics in Spain's top league, the ACB, you'll see that on many teams, there are nine or 10 guys who each play around 20 minutes a game. That is very common there. When I played in the ACB, my team was like that, and no one complained about it. I think this winning spirit helps make their leagues extremely competitive, their national team ultra-cohesive, and, maybe to a lesser extent, their players successful in the NBA.

Grunfield is describing how Spain developed their own system and style based on their own culture, history with the sport, and skill level. In Spain, typically youth basketball is a more organized activity and played in indoor gyms.[185] Their culture of teamwork and passing was inspired by soccer. Spain developed in a different way in a different environment and culture—without basketball shoe sponsors and a culture of individual play. Their basketball also developed differently without a college system. Players could sign professional contracts at a young age, so there is an economic incentive to find and develop talent. The young players get lots of minutes against bigger and more experienced players because the coaches utilize all the players—this enhances development. Players also play with maximum effort and aggressiveness because there is less concern of fouling out when only playing 20 minutes.

There are also slight differences between the NBA and the International Basketball Federation (FIBA) that impact how the game is played and taught. For example, until 2010, the FIBA three-point line distance was 20'6" and in the NBA the distance is 23'9", which impacted the style of FIBA basketball development to emphasize shooting.[186]

---

185. In contrast in the U.S., typically youth players play informal pickup basketball games using in-ground and wall-mounted basketball hoops at playgrounds or residences. Spain's basketball coaches have licenses and have a common approach and style. (In contrast, in the U.S., most youth basketball coaches don't need licenses and the process for getting one is very simple and inexpensive. In many ways, young players in Spain learning basketball as an organized activity is similar to young players in the U.S. learning soccer. Young players in the U.S. learning basketball in informal pickup games is similar to young Brazilians.)

186. Today, the FIBA three-point line distance is 22'2".

We are not arguing that Spain's basketball system is better or worse. We are simply trying to point out that a style of play comes from an environment and culture. And if a soccer-loving country like Spain can be highly competitive in basketball, it challenges conventional wisdom that the USMNT can't be competitive in soccer. This also challenges the conventional wisdom that the USMNT don't win because America's best athletes play basketball, football, or baseball. Using the same line of thinking, Spain's best athletes would be playing soccer.

It is worth noting that it is easier to identify potential elite basketball players because of unique body-type standards and characteristics, such as height.[187]

---

187. The shortest player in the NBA from Spain is Ricky Rubio, at 6'4". The average NBA player from Spain is 6'9".

Chapter 14

Making a USMNT Player

Height, Weight, and Zig-Zag Shuttle Speed

Generally, every sport at an elite level favors specific body-type standards and characteristics for its players because of the basic differences in athletic abilities needed for various sports. Obviously, there are always exceptions. The average male professional soccer player is 5'9" and weighs 154 pounds. Great male soccer players' heights have ranged from 5'5" to 6'2". Soccer requires endurance running. A taller or heavier soccer player's body cannot dissipate heat as efficiently. Heat dissipation is critical for endurance running, as the central nervous system forces a slowing of effort as core body temperature rises. (This helps explain why almost all relatively tall players for both the USMNT and USWNT are from northern parts of the U.S. or countries, especially the goalkeepers—who are often among the tallest players and typically start playing soccer in other positions. Examples of tall players include Michelle Akers (Northern California), Jozy Altidore (New Jersey), John Brooks (Berlin, Germany), Geoff Cameron (Massachusetts), Brad Friedel (Ohio), Tim Howard (New Jersey), Kasey Keller (Washington), Alexi Lalas (Michigan), Samantha Mewis (Massachusetts), Alyssa Naeher (Connecticut), Oguchi Onyewu (Maryland), Toney Sanneh (Minnesota), Hope Solo (Washington), and Briana Scurry (Minnesota). Omar Gonzalez (Texas) is the one major exception. At 6'5", he is smart to play for Toronto FC. Goalkeeper Nick Rimando (5'9") is from Southern California.

We asked coaches at professional club youth academies in Europe what was the most common distinctive factor in predicting success at the next level. The most common answer was extraordinarily fast times, relative to their peers, in zig-zag shuttle sprints. The tests measure explosive acceleration in the first three or four strides and the ability to keep muscles working at optimum levels while changing directions. Zig-zag shuttle sprints require short strides with a low center of gravity. Therefore, typically professional soccer players have a low center of gravity and better heat dissipation for endurance running.[188]

It's highly unlikely that great NBA or NFL or MLB players would have become professional soccer players or vice versa. The average NBA player is 6'7" with an extraordinary wingspan for a human relative to his height. Height and wingspan allow a player to more easily grab rebounds, block shots, steal passes, and shoot over defenders. The average NFL player is 6'2" and weighs 247 pounds (nearly 25 pounds more than the average NBA player), and has exceptional explosiveness and speed for his size (an average NFL player can run 40 yards in 4.8 seconds). Among other things, body mass, explosiveness, and speed allow a player to exert more force. The average MLB player is 6'2"and weighs 207 pounds, and reportedly more than 80 percent of major league baseball players have visual acuity of 20/15 or better. Body mass increases the kinetic energy that can be transferred through a bat to the ball, and extraordinary vision allows the player to more quickly judge the speed, direction, and spin of a ball.

Tom Brady (6'4" and 225 pounds), LeBron James (6'9" and 250 pounds), and Mike Trout (6'2" and 235 pounds) are incredible American athletes and competitors. However, even if they had grown up wanting to be elite soccer players, they probably would have eventually opted out of soccer. They are too big and have too high of a center of gravity. Of course, there are always exceptions. It's fun to wonder: Could Russell Wilson, at

---

188. This helps explain why midfielders, who run the most and have to maneuver in tight spaces, are on average the shortest and lightest of all playing positions. In the 2018 World Cup, a few midfielders were 5'5" tall and weighed 130 pounds.

5'11" and 215 pounds, have played elite soccer?[189] Some elite athletes play a position (e.g., wide receiver or running back) or sport (e.g., track & field) where their body type and characteristics could fit soccer.[190] In those cases, typically the sport they pursue is heavily influenced by family and community (zip code), which are discussed later.[191] However, most elite athletes also have distinctive characteristics that help make them elite— elite hand-eye coordination for a wide receiver (not necessary in soccer) and elite stride frequency and length for a sprinter (as compared to elite zig-zag shuttle sprint speed and endurance). In addition, the great physical strength, speed, and explosiveness of a wide receiver or running back or sprinter are not required to be an elite soccer player—many are not (e.g., Messi, Neymar, etc.). Lastly, even if an athlete meets the distinctive characteristics of a soccer player and lives in a community that values soccer, the athlete just might not like endurance sports or might prefer the physical contact of football or the individual nature of sprinting.

Family

Family is an important factor in the identification and development of national team players. We estimate that at least 25 percent of all USMNT players had a family member who played or worked in collegiate or professional sports, and the majority of those were in soccer. It's unclear how much is related to genetics versus the environment in which they were raised.

Globally, a total of 319 father-son pairs have played for their respective national teams (and not always for the same country), with 41 of those pairs having 100 or more caps between them. Many father-son pairs are well known, including the Lampards of England, the Cruyffs of the

---

189. He was selected in the fourth round of the MLB draft. He and his wife, Ciara, own a minority stake in MLS' Seattle Sounders. Soccer was the first sport he ever played, before he started baseball and then football. He played goalkeeper and attacker.

190. The average NFL wide receiver is 6'0" and weighs 200 pounds. The average NFL running back is 6'0" and weighs 215 pounds. Sprinter Justin Gatlin is 6'1" and 175 pounds. Jozy Altidore is 6'1" and 175 pounds.

191. Odell Beckham Jr., who is 5'11" and 198 pounds, claims he was invited to join the U.S. national soccer team program as a 14-year-old but didn't pursue it because he grew up in New Orleans and there wasn't a MLS team.

Netherlands, the Maldinis of Italy, the Aubameyangs of Gabon, and the Hernandezes of Mexico. In USMNT history, there have been a few national team father-son pairs, including George (Liberia) and Timothy Weah (USMNT), Joe (Liberia) and Darlington Nagbe (USMNT), and Claudio (USMNT) and Giovanni Reyna (USMNT). There are also a few aspiring father-son pairs, including John (USMNT) and Ian Harkes (U-20), Jürgen (Germany) and Jonathan Klinsmann (U-23), and Gregg (USMNT) and Sebastian (U-17) Berhalter. When experts claim the USMNT aren't successful in the World Cup because the U.S. doesn't have a soccer culture or soccer tradition, they are missing that the U.S. doesn't have as many parents as traditional soccer powers who played at a competitive level. This is why college player alumni are so important to the development of soccer in the U.S.

And family is not just fathers. According to the website transfermarkt, there have been a staggering 722 sets of brothers on various national teams over the years, with 73 of those pairs having 100 or more caps between them. Many brother pairs are well-known, including Gary and Phil Neville of England; Paul Pogba of France and his twin brothers, Florentin and Mathias, of Guinea; Romelu and Jordan Lukaku of Belgium; Jérôme Boateng of Germany and Kevin-Prince Boateng of Ghana; and Rai and Socrates of Brazil. There have not been any notable USMNT brothers.

There are lots of examples of USMNT players whose fathers played college or professional soccer. Michael Bradley's father, Bob Bradley, played at Princeton. Christian Pulisic is a good example of having a father— and mother—with soccer pedigree. His parents, Kelley and Mark, both played collegiate soccer at George Mason University, and his father played professional indoor soccer for the Harrisburg Heat in the 1990s and later became a coach at both youth and professional levels.[192]

Claudio Reyna and his son, Giovanni, are a good USMNT father-son example. Claudio's father, who moved to the United States in 1968

---

192. Kelley was a teammate of Mia Hamm on the Shooting Stars Club Team and Lake Braddock High School. Her older brother also played soccer for George Mason. Mark's father, Mate, was from Croatia and passed his love of soccer on to his son. Mark's coach at George Mason was Gordon Bradley, who had coached the New York Cosmos in the 1970s. Christian also lived in England when he was seven years old, as his mother received a grant to teach there for a year.

from Argentina, grew up playing in the youth system of Independiente and played professionally with Los Andes, a professional team on the outskirts of Buenos Aires. Claudio, having played in four World Cups (and captain of the team in 2002 and 2006) and in the Bundesliga and Premier League for 13 years, was one of the most influential players of his generation and his 112 caps ranks 10th highest amongst all U.S. national team players. Claudio also married another fellow soccer player, Danielle Egan, who played in college at the University of North Carolina under Anson Dorrance, alongside Mia Hamm, Tisha Venturini, and Kristine Lilly, and was a member of the USWNT as well.[193]

Many people point to genetics as the reason family is important. However, that discounts player development related to family connections. For example, when Marcelo Balboa, Michael Bradley, Christian Pulisic, and Mike Sorber were in their early teens, their fathers, who coached soccer teams, utilized them in practices against older, bigger, stronger, faster, and more skilled players. This is exceptionally differentiated training and development. For them, soccer was a part of their lives, and their fathers' practices were like pickup games against better competition.[194]

Community (Zip Code), Pickup Games, and Futsal

Soccer was a part of the daily fabric of Kearny, New Jersey ("Soccer Town, USA"), which had an immigrant pool and strong soccer culture. A town of 36,000 residents on the outskirts of New York City produced three starting players (John Harkes, Tony Meola, and Tab Ramos) on the USMNT. It sounds remarkable, until one learns about Paris and Lyon. Around half of the starters of the 2018 World Cup–winning French squad grew up in poor, *banlieues* (literally translates to "suburbs" but can also be used to refer to poor, immigrant-dominated neighborhoods) of Paris and Lyon. Actually, of the 15 Paris-born players in the 2018 World Cup, only

---

193. Also, Gio was born in Sunderland, England, where his father played at the time.

194. The vast majority of the USWNT had a father or older brother who was/is active in sports and included them in their sports activities.

seven were on the French squad. The others played for Morocco, Portugal, Senegal, and Tunisia, home countries of their immigrant parents.

Every *banlieue* has state-subsidized soccer clubs with licensed coaches. Each *banlieue* holds open tryouts for boys at least 13 years old to be selected to go to another tryout at what is commonly referred to as "Clairefontaine," 30 miles southwest of Paris, which is France's central academy. The tryout at Clairefontaine is held over a three-day period, which is also attended by scouts from professional clubs around Europe. After the three days, the academy selects 22 players, with three or four of the 22 being goalkeepers. Players who are selected to attend Clairefontaine stay and train at the facilities from Monday through Friday. Players are given the weekend off to visit family and train and play with their parent professional club youth academies. Players are also required to meet educational criteria. All costs required to attend an academy are borne by the federation and the Ligue Nationale de Football. Graduates include Nicolas Anelka, Kylian Mbappé, Olivier Giroud, and Thierry Henry.

Prior to the establishment of Clairefontaine in 1988, France hadn't won a World Cup. Ten years later, with the combination of the central academy and rising immigration, France won their first World Cup in 1998, lost in the Final to Italy on penalty kicks in 2006, and won their second World Cup in 2018. France combines an established academy system with an immigrant pool that has soccer as a part of their daily lives. In addition, it is worth mentioning that 50 players born or raised in France were members of squads in the 2018 World Cup.[195]

Many of France's players grow up in urban environments with constrained space. This also impacts the style of play they grow up practicing. In the *banlieues*, they primarily play pickup, small-sided soccer games (sometimes futsal or a variant of it), with a mix of ages, in the small space of a concrete ball court. It's ideal for training skills at a micro level before moving to larger fields. The small space requires players to not only play quicker but also to make faster decisions. It inherently improves a player's spatial intelligence and the development of ball skills and control,

---

195. Brazil's 28 was the next highest total.

and encourages creativity. According to Dr. Emilio Miranda of São Paulo University, a futsal player will have 600 percent more touches on a ball than a traditional soccer player. With more touches on the ball, players try things they would not risk while playing a full-sided soccer game, where they have many fewer touches. As they get older and progress, they often play on primarily uneven dirt fields. The ball bounces unpredictably, which also hones ball control skills and reaction time.

USMNT players who were accomplished futsal players include Fernando Clavijo, Jim Gabarra, Hugo Pérez, Tab Ramos, Peter Vermes, and Mike Windischmann.[196] Mark Pulisic believed that for his son to become an elite technical player, he needed to play futsal as a child, and he founded the first futsal league in the Detroit area (where they lived at the time), running it on three basketball courts at an indoor facility. In an email to B/R Mag, Christian Pulisic wrote, "Futsal really improved my technical ability and my ability to work in tight spaces." Perhaps more soccer in the U.S. should be played in gyms or courts instead of large soccer fields.

The amount of pickup, informal soccer kids played between the ages of six and 12 also has a dramatic effect on skill level. In *The Away Game: The Epic Search for Soccer's Net Superstars*, Sebastian Abbott explains, "Not all play is equal.... Researchers have found that the key ingredient is not how much formal practice or how many official games players had as kids, but how much pickup soccer they played in informal settings like the street or schoolyard. One study published in 2012 looked at two different groups of elite players from English Premier League academies who were about 18 years old. One group scored higher than the other for game intelligence based on a series of tests using match footage. They found that the two groups accumulated about the same number of hours of formal practice and official competition during the previous six years. But the players with better game intelligence engaged in almost one and a half times as much pickup soccer than the other group. A similar study

---

196. The U.S. finished in third and second place in the 1989 and 1992 FIFA Futsal World Cups, respectively. Brazil won both tournaments. In 1989 Peter Vermes had six goals, one fewer than the Golden Boot winner. The U.S. have not qualified or gotten past the second round since.

published the same year found that more than 20 percent of the difference in game intelligence was accounted for by the amount of pickup soccer kids played between the ages of six and 12."

Today, technical skills developed from informal play and futsal are even important for goalkeepers. As more managers are playing soccer from the back, more goalkeepers are tasked with playing with their feet and starting attacks. Until recently, the USMNT had a long list of goalkeepers who played in the English Premier League (Kasey Keller, Brad Friedel, Tim Howard, Brad Guzan, Marcus Hahnemann, and Jurgen Sommer). Athleticism, quickness, and hand-eye coordination aren't enough anymore. Today, Zack Steffen is the only USMNT goalkeeper on a top Five League team (Manchester City), but Steffen is the backup option to Brazil's Ederson (who competes with Liverpool's Allison to start for Brazil).

When observers argue that great players develop in favelas in Rio de Janeiro or alleyways in Buenos Aires because of their drive to escape poverty, they are missing an important element. They are great, in part, because soccer is a part of the fabric of communities' daily lives, so they regularly play informal pickup games—and because they live in an urban environment they typically play soccer in the streets, which also helps develop their technical skills. The country is not the primary driver—it is the local community that is the primary driver behind the sport being played. Their informal pickup games are "free practices." And scouts and agents are economically incentivized to find them and bring them to professional club academies. No matter how popular soccer is in Brazil, if a Brazilian boy lives in an area with few other Brazilian boys around to play informal games, and another family member isn't passionate about or knowledgeable about the sport, and his parents have to drive him to practices with fields, it will be a challenge for the Brazilian boy to have many practice hours and touches. It wouldn't even matter if that Brazilian boy had free instruction—other challenges still exist. And even if a boy in a remote area and boy in a favela were from Brazil, they would most likely have different styles and approaches because they learned the games in different environments.

The best current example of different styles within Brazil is Manchester City's Gabriel Jesus, who developed his skills playing soccer in the north zone of São Paulo, which has more of a physical style of play than futsal/street soccer than even Southern São Paulo, where Neymar grew up, or Rio de Janeiro. Dunga, captain of the 1994 World Cup Brazil champion team, is from Rio Grande do Sul, which had many German and Lithuanian immigrants who played a different style from Rio de Janeiro, for example. They play a more Argentine or Uruguayan way—tough and without restraint.[197]

Sadly, kids in Kearny, New Jersey, just don't meet up at the outdoor courts and play pickup games as frequently anymore.

Month of Birth

Academic studies have shown that two sports in particular suffer from the relative age effect—soccer and hockey. The relative age effect (RAE) in sport refers to the lower presence of athletes born in the months furthest from the cutoff date established by the competitive system, which normally coincides with the last months of the year. Those who are born in the last months of the year leave the sport at an earlier age as a result of not being selected. Historically, around half of the players on the U.S. U-17 national team squad who qualify for the U-17 World Cup (for players born on or after January 1) were born in the first quarter of their respective qualifying year, and 75 percent are born in the first half of the year. The two primary factors that reduced the impact of RAE on the U.S. U-17 national team squad are (1) if the player was a dual national and/or primarily grew up outside the U.S. and (2) if the player had a family member who played or plays soccer.[198] Around 40 percent of the senior USMNT players are

---

197. As for the perception of poor children from favelas, none of the top five players of the 1982 Brazil World Cup squad, Zico, Sócrates, Falcão, Cerezo, and Éder, were from favelas. But they played street socer/futsal. Zico and Falcão's fathers played professional soccer. Sócrates went to one of the best schools in Brazil and became a medical doctor after retiring from soccer.

198. Sergiño Dest grew up in the Netherlands, Jacobo Reyes grew up in Mexico, and Brandon Vazquez lived in the U.S. but trained in Mexico. Blaine Ferri's father played college and professional indoor soccer, Christian Pulisic's parents played college soccer, James Sands' twin brother Will Sands plays college soccer, and Auston Trusty's sister Onnie Trusty played college soccer.

born in the second six months of the year, which is consistent with other national teams around the world. However, eliminating players who had a family member who played soccer or were dual nationals, less than 25 percent of USMNT players are born in the second six months.

California and Hotbeds

Breaking down the USMNT by geography, the runaway leader is California, with more than 20 percent of all USMNT players. California has a population of around 40 million, which is about 12 percent of the United States. Removing goalkeepers, the percentages from California are higher. Removing players whose parents played soccer in college or professionally, the percentages go even higher. California is the most populous state in the country, and much of it has mild weather, allowing for year-round play.[199] After California are Texas (9 percent of players), New York/New Jersey (8 percent), and the Washington, D.C./Maryland area (6 percent). More than half of the immigrants in the U.S. live in these four areas, and the majority of them come from countries where soccer is the most popular sport. Of course, there are a few other hotbeds for various reasons, such as St. Louis and Seattle/Washington.[200]

The high percentage from California (and Southern California) doesn't surprise us. We discovered that, like France, many soccer powers get most of their players from a few areas in their countries that are close to or have many professional soccer clubs. Another example is Germany. More than *50 percent* of the players on the 2014 World Cup–winning Germany squad *are from two states*, North Rhine-Westphalia, which has seven Bundesliga clubs (including Bayern Leverkusen, Borussia Dortmund, Borussia Mönchengladbach, and Schalke) and Bavaria, which has six Bundesliga clubs (including Bayern Munich). It's a six-hour drive from Dortmund in North Rhine-Westphalia to Munich in Bavaria, about the same as Los Angeles to San Francisco. The two states combined have a

---

199. California has a larger population than Canada or Australia.

200. A breakdown of the 113 youth clubs in the new elite player development system are 26 in California, 12 in Florida, 14 in New York/New Jersey. However, there are only nine in Texas, which, after California, produces the most players, and only five in the Washington, D.C./Maryland area. Two are in St. Louis, but only one is in Seattle/Washington.

lower population than California, but they have 13 Bundesliga clubs with youth academies (California has three MLS clubs). Investigating even further, we discovered seven of the starting XI for Germany came from just two youth academies—Bayern Munich (four) and Schalke (three). The majority of the 23-man squad came from just four youth academies: Bayern (five), Schalke (four), Borussia Dortmund (two), and Mainz (two).

As to relegation and promotion creating players with a more competitive spirit, the last times Bayern Munich, Borussia Dortmund, and Mainz were relegated were 1955, 1986, and 2006, respectively. The top clubs that identify and develop (and purchase) players are not developing talent because of the threat of promotion and relegation. They are focused on revenues from European competitions.

Just like most countries around the world, Germany could be overlooking lots of talent. The two states that the majority of the players come from only represent around 35 percent of the country's population. Only one player on the 2014 German team, Toni Kroos, was from East Germany, even though the region represents over 15 percent of the country's population. There are few East German clubs in the Bundesliga. However, we discovered family matters and can create exceptions. Kroos' mother was a former German badminton player and his father was a former professional wrestler and soccer coach. Kroos' younger brother also plays professional soccer. Eventually, Toni Kroos was discovered by Bayern Munich and he joined their youth academy at 16. Only one German player was from Berlin, the largest city in Germany—Jérôme Boateng. He was the only Black German (who make up less than 1 percent of the population) player on the team. He also meets the exception rules. He is a dual national and his paternal half-brother Kevin-Prince Boateng plays for Ghana. At 14 he was playing Hertha BSC's youth academy.

The data about the 2018 World Cup–winning France squad and the 2014 World Cup–winning German squad challenge a regular notion—that the USMNT are at a disadvantage because the U.S. is too geographically large. Community (zip code) matters. Most national team players come from a few places in a country where soccer is an important part of the fabric of the community, and they have access to the youth academy of a professional club. If they don't, family matters even more—this is an ugly truth in the U.S. as well as around the world.

Youth Academies

Youth academies run by professional clubs are critical for national team success. In February of 2001 the Bundesliga made it mandatory for all 18 top-flight professional teams to run a youth academy—essentially a school for promising soccer players, with teams and coaches going all the way down to the U-12 level. Later, academies became mandatory for all 36 professional teams in the top two German divisions. Economic necessity was a part of the reason for this focus on youth academies. The Kirch media conglomerate, which was the cash cow for the country's national soccer league, the Bundesliga, collapsed, forcing clubs to rely on cheaper homegrown players versus more expensive imports.

The Bundesliga also provided economic incentives—the better the youth academy is, the more funding it gets. Under Bundesliga rules, a club with a top-rated three-star academy gets an additional $400,000 in funding every year—which is significant for smaller teams. Between 2001 and 2011, professional teams in Germany spent $681 million on the development of youth soccer. At the same time, the German Football Association, the body that controls the national team itself, started its own $13 million-per-year youth initiative. According to the *New York Times*, in 2014 there were 366 German federation-operated youth centers in the country, which serve 25,000 players.

In 2015, Bettina Grossmann and Martin Lames wrote an academic paper, "From Talent to Professional Football—Youthism in German Football." They examined 821 U-17 Bundesliga players born in 1993 and tracked their career development until the 2012–13 season. They found that less than 10 percent were able to sign a contract for a professional team in Germany (first-, second-, and third-league) and more than 45 percent quit playing soccer before advancing to the senior level. Twenty-nine out of 36 (81 percent) first-league Bundesliga players born in 1993 (season 2012–13) were trained in a professional youth academy, two players were educated in a fourth-league club, and five players were transfers from a foreign country.

They concluded the implementation of mandatory youth academies was a positive for the development of a great number of very well-educated soccer players, so that the most talented players can reach higher individual levels due to an intensive soccer education and better competition. However, they also had some concerns about the physical, mental, and emotional overloads in youth players due to the daily demands of coaches, parents, and peers that might result in exhaustion and might lead to an earlier end of careers. They recommended that club coaches limit the number of games per week, balance physical loads in practice and regeneration, and develop individual plans for every player to reduce the risk of injury and burnout.

Sports Specialization in Young Athletes

It is impossible to fully analyze the USMNT without some questions regarding whether or not soccer players should specialize at earlier ages or play multiple sports. Specialization in early to middle childhood has become increasingly common for soccer players. For example, there are a growing number of soccer travel leagues that begin at eight years of age and an increase in the number of players younger than 20 years old in soccer in the Olympics. There is some academic debate as to whether sports specialization and intense practice time must begin during early childhood and to the exclusion of other sports to achieve elite levels. While most experts agree that some degree of specialization is necessary to achieve elite levels and maximize potential for success, there is a concern that sports specialization before adolescence may be detrimental to a young athlete. For most sports, there is no evidence that intense training and specialization before puberty are necessary to achieve elite status. Risks of early sports specialization include higher rates of injury, increased psychological stress, and quitting sports at a young age. For example, a study of swimmers demonstrated that athletes who began specialized training in swimming around age 12 to 13 spent a longer time on the national team and ended their careers later than swimmers who specialized around age nine to 10.

The amount of training necessary to develop elite-level sports skills has long been debated. Malcolm Gladwell's book *Outliers: The Story of Success* describes the "10,000-hour rule" of academic Anders Ericsson and several colleagues, which states that, to achieve expertise, musicians must practice 10,000 hours over 10 years. This intensive practice is more likely to be successful if begun during the early years of development. Lesser practice and a delayed start resulted in less expertise. These concepts have been extrapolated to sports.

Further studies have demonstrated that what is important is the feedback and the reinforcement for improvement associated with the repetitions that make the difference. Under these conditions, students become addicted to information that helps them improve. The biggest issue is that every student matures differently, and if and when he or she is willing to accept and seek reinforcement will help dictate when he or she should specialize. This is why it is impossible to have a standard answer on when an athlete should specialize.

Academic Jean Côté and colleagues examined the development activities of elite ice hockey players and other athletes and found that there were three stages of development—sampling (ages six to 12), specializing (ages 13 to 15), and investment (age 16-plus). Some studies discovered that children who become involved in deliberate play because of their own interest in the activity, as opposed to external reasons such as adult direction or winning trophies, seek feedback, and even stay in the sport longer. Since every child may develop this interest at different times and for different reasons, it is impossible to have a standard answer on when an athlete should specialize.

In 2014, Manuel Horning and colleagues wrote an academic paper titled "Practice and Play in the Development of German Top-Level Professional Football Players." They examined the developmental sporting activities of 52 German players in the Bundesliga (including 18 senior national team members). They reported their hours of organized soccer practice/training, including its "microstructure" (proportions of physical conditioning, skill exercises, and playing forms), informal pick-up play, and engagement in other sports through their career, respectively.

Analyses revealed that the players in the Bundesliga performed moderate amounts of organized soccer practice/training throughout their career. They accumulated on average 4,264 hours over around 16 years before debuting in the Bundesliga. Those who were selected for the senior German national team averaged 4,532 hours over around 17 years before their first cap. The percentage of time of organized practice/training was 52 percent of their time during childhood, 45 percent during adolescence, and 40 percent during adulthood. Physical conditioning time increased as they got older from 13 percent, 14 percent, and 23 percent, respectively. The Bundesliga players in the study engaged in extensive informal pickup soccer consisting of 68 percent during childhood, 54 percent during adolescence, and 9 percent during adulthood. National team players had more informal pickup soccer in childhood, more engagement in other sports in adolescence, and later specialization than other German players.

In conclusion, any great athlete, no matter his or her sport, has a view on specialization, and oftentimes that view is greatly influenced by his or her own personal experiences or biases. For example, Roger Federer was an all-around great athlete who chose to focus on tennis much later than many top players. Tiger Woods specialized in golf very early. Both athletes eventually became the best in the world at their respective sport, and both took very different approaches to getting there.

Chapter 15

Why Do the USWNT Win?

The comparisons between the USWNT and USMNT are not always fair, as the two teams developed so differently and have their own unique histories, economic and professional opportunities, systems, environments, and challenges. However, since the teams are so often associated and compared, it would seem incomplete to analyze the USMNT without trying to answer some questions about the USWNT. The most obvious is: Why do the USWNT win?

Most soccer fans believe the USWNT have always dominated. The reality is that the USWNT *have not* always dominated, and other countries have had a longer history of a women's national soccer team than the United States. To provide context, the Women's Nordic Football Champions between Denmark, Finland, Norway, and Sweden started in 1974. The UEFA Women's European Championships began in 1984 with 16 teams. Sweden beat England on penalties in the Final. Pia Sundhage, who would later coach the USWNT from 2008 to 2012, converted the final penalty kick for Sweden to win.

Only 80 NCAA schools sponsored women's soccer in 1981–82, the first year of the NCAA women's championships, making it at the time about as widespread as women's fencing.[201] The first year the United States

---

201. St. Louis University won the first men's NCAA soccer championship in 1959.

women's national soccer team played an international match was 1985. Coached by Mike Ryan, the USWNT played four matches in Italy at the Mundialito (Spanish for "little World Cup") tournament, losing three and drawing one. In their first match, on August 18, 1985, the USWNT, accustomed to a polite women's game as it was then in the United States, were outplayed by a more experienced and physical Italy team and lost 1–0. Italy had lost to Sweden in the semifinals in the 1984 Women's Euros. The Italian fans greeted the American team enthusiastically and chanted "Ooosa!" ("USA!"), a pregame chant that the USWNT team adopted for itself. The USWNT then tied Denmark 2–2, lost to England 1–3, and lost to Denmark 0–1 the second time they played them. Michelle Akers scored the first USWNT international goal. With several new players and a new coach, Anson Dorrance, the team returned to play the tournament again in 1986. The team's record was better. They beat China 2–1, Brazil 2–1, and Japan 3–1 and lost to Italy 0–1. At the time, the USWNT most likely couldn't beat one of the top four European teams—England, Italy, Norway, and Sweden.

The article in the *New York Times* about the USWNT beating Norway 2–1 in the 1991 Women's World Cup Final in China was on page eight of the sports section—it certainly wasn't national news. The only people to greet the USWNT at the airport were their families and close friends. In contrast, when Norway won the 1995 Women's World Cup (having beaten the USWNT in the semifinals), one of every four Norwegians watched the championship match on television. When the players returned from the tournament in Sweden, their plane was escorted into Oslo by two F-16 fighter jets.

In July 2019, the USWNT beat the Netherlands in the 2019 Women's World Cup Final 2–0, following a month-long tournament in France that attracted more attention than ever before. The USWNT rolled through the opening round with statement wins over Thailand (13–0), Chile (3–0), and Sweden (2–0). Brushing aside criticism about perceived arrogance and excessive goal celebrations, the USWNT then powered through the heart of European soccer with victories over Spain (2–1), France (2–1), and England (2–1) to dominate the reigning European champions, the

Netherlands (2–0). It was the fifth time the USWNT had played a World Cup Final out of only eight tournaments ever. The USWNT is the first team to reach three consecutive Finals and joined Germany as a repeat champion (2003 and 2007). With the 2019 win in France, the USWNT has a record four Women's World Cup trophies. Similar to the USWNT winning the World Cup in 1999 after a dismal USMNT World Cup, the USWNT won the World Cup in 2019 after the USMNT failed to qualify.

Table: Women's FIFA World Cup Winners

National Team	WC Wins	WC Runners-up	WC Total Finals	WC Years Won	WC Years Runners-up
United States	4	1	5	1991, 1999, 2015, 2019	2011
Germany	2	.1	3	2003, 2007	1995
Japan	1	1	2	2011	2015
Norway	1	1	2	1995	1991
Brazil	0	1	1	--	2007
China PR	0	1	1	--	1999
Netherlands	0	1	1	--	2019
Sweden	0	1	1	--	2003

There is no doubt that the USWNT are currently the best women's *team* in the world.

What changed from the 1980s? Why do the UWSNT win? We previously discussed the USWNT's *why, how,* and *who,* as well as their team chemistry. We also discovered a few other reasons why the USWNT win.

Talent/Skill

While having great players does not necessarily guarantee success, especially if those players don't work well together, it certainly helps. Since 2001, FIFA has annually awarded a Women's World Player of the Year (from 2001 to 2015, the award was called "FIFA Women's World Player of the Year" and since 2016, the award has been called "The Best FIFA Women's Player"). With six wins since the award's inception (Mia Hamm in 2001 and 2002, Abby Wambach in 2012, Carli Lloyd in 2015 and 2016, and Megan Rapinoe in 2019), the USWNT are tied for most wins with Brazil, followed by five for Germany, and one each for the Netherlands and Japan. The Ballon d'Or award also has a female equivalent, but it has only been in existence for two years. In the first year of the award, 2018,

Ada Hegerberg of Norway became the inaugural recipient, and in 2019, Megan Rapinoe became the second.

Title IX

In 1971, there were only 700 high school female soccer players. In 1972, legislators passed Title IX, a federal civil rights law that protects people from discrimination based on sex in education programs or activities that receive federal financial assistance. Essentially, if high schools and colleges wanted men's soccer teams, then they had to offer women's teams. The result was that by 2006, there were about three million registered youth female players worldwide, and more than *half* of them were in the U.S. In 2014, there were nearly 376,000 high school female soccer players. And more young players mean greater competition and a bigger player pool. Because of Title IX, in high schools, girls make up 47 percent of all soccer players. In the NCAA, 53 percent of soccer players are female, and 61 percent specifically in Division I. So, the USWNT has a built-in development system provided by high schools and colleges around the country.

Winning Created a Platform

But it wasn't just Title IX that pushed women's soccer into the American mainstream and onto the world stage. It was also World Cup and Olympic victories. While the USWNT winning the first women's World Cup in history in 1991 didn't get much attention, the USWNT winning the 1996 Olympic gold medal on home soil did. The gold medal match captured more attention than expected. And shortly after, major brands sponsored some of the USWNT players and promoted them, cementing them as American icons.

Then there was the World Cup of 1999 in the United States, when women's soccer exploded.[202] The Final versus China is widely considered

---

202. Originally FIFA requested that the Women's World Cup games be held in large high school or small college stadiums with around 10,000 seats. Alan Rothenberg said no. He said that the team is bigger than that, greater than that, and that the USSF would sell out the biggest stadiums in the country. The players contributed by selling themselves to the public with the support of the coaching staff. After practices, players would spend hours a day selling their story and the game.

the biggest moment in U.S. women's sports. Ever. The game set a world attendance record for a women's sporting event of 90,185 in a sellout at the Rose Bowl in Southern California, and it set a record for the largest U.S. television audience for *any* (men's or women's) soccer match with 18 million viewers.

After the 1999 World Cup in the United States, it seemed like *every American girl* wanted to play soccer—which only increased the pool of talent. It had the same impact on the next generation as Pelé did with the New York Cosmos and the 1994 World Cup. But the team's success isn't just about the popularity of women's soccer in America. The popularity also coincided with an American cultural movement for women to have equal opportunity and that girls and women should embrace their athleticism.

The 2015 Women's World Cup Final between the USWNT and Japan set a new television audience record. The Final reached 23 million viewers and had higher ratings than the NBA Finals and the Stanley Cup Finals. The Final was also the most watched U.S. Spanish-language broadcast of a FIFA Women's World Cup match in history. The popularity gained by the USWNT after that World Cup was enormous as well, and led to Alex Morgan appearing on the U.S. cover of EA Sports' *FIFA 16* alongside Lionel Messi, who appeared on the global cover of the game.[203]

Every USWNT Final was a platform for a celebration of the team's mission and values. At the 2019 World Cup tournament, USWNT fans showed their support by chanting "equal pay" ahead of games, and they renewed the call when the FIFA president took to the field to congratulate the team following the Final. With regard to their fight for legitimacy, on a day that should have been all about the World Cup, the USWNT had to share the soccer spotlight. There were not one but two men's soccer championships scheduled on the same day: the Copa América and CONCACAF Gold Cup. FIFA said having all three tournament Finals on the same day would draw attention to the sport.

In the Final of the SheBelieves Cup in March 2020, the USWNT players wore their warm-up jerseys inside out in an apparent protest

---

203. Canada's Christine Sinclair and Australia's Stephanie Catley appeared on the Canadian and Australian covers, respectively.

about equal pay before their 3–1 victory over Japan (which extended the USWNT's unbeaten streak to 31 matches).

The celebration of values wasn't reserved for Finals—which many fans can't attend and celebrate in person. Most observers don't realize that recently, more fans have been turning out to watch the USWNT play than the USMNT. For example, in 2019, the USWNT had an average attendance 15 percent greater than the USMNT. During 2019, the USWNT averaged 25,122 spectators per match, while the USMNT averaged 21,738. Historically, this has not always been the case. Using the 2011–15 cycle as an example, average attendance for the USMNT was 33,200 per game compared to 15,499 for the women. For the 2015–19 cycle, average attendance for the men was 28,913 compared to 20,208 for the women—representing a large uptick for the women and a significant narrowing of the gap. The table below shows how the figures have changed over the years. World Cup qualifying and World Cup years can impact the data.

Table: Average Attendance for USMNT and USWNT Matches (2015–19)

Year	Men - Avg. Attendance	Women - Avg. Attendance	% Diff (Men v. Women)
2015	34,548	27,766	24%
2016	27,505	15,937	73%
2017	29,735	18,150	64%
2018	31,037	14,064	121%
2019	21,738	25,122	-13%

Each game, each Final, is a platform and draws more girls and young women into the sport—and serves to broaden the potential player pool.

Relative Suppression of Women's Soccer

The success of the USWNT is also about the relative *suppression* of the sport abroad. As recently as the 1980s, several of the 24 countries involved in the 2019 World Cup had imposed outright bans on or nonrecognition of women's soccer. England, for example, essentially banned women's soccer from 1921 to 1971. Germany did the same, from 1955 to 1970. And so did Brazil, from 1941 to 1981. Spain didn't recognize women's soccer until 1980. These countries claimed that soccer was simply not a woman's sport. So, for a long time, there were not as many teams abroad, although as mentioned, the NCAA didn't have a women's soccer championship until 1982 and the USWNT didn't start until 1985.

Other countries are now catching up. And that's largely thanks to a sharp increase in the number of players in Europe and increase in money. From 2012 to 2017, for example, European soccer associations have more than doubled their spending on women's teams, from about $50 million to over $125 million. And with more money, there will be better identification and development. This is a very real threat to the USWNT's dominance in the future, especially as more European clubs support and promote the women's game.

Leadership

Most Americans can quickly name some of the most important players in the history of the USWNT—Michelle Akers, Julie Foudy, Mia Hamm, Kristine Lilly, Carli Lloyd, Alex Morgan, Megan Rapinoe, Hope Solo, and Abby Wambach are just a few examples. Many would neglect to mention Carla Overbeck. However, she was captain of the USWNT that won Olympic gold in 1996 and the World Cup in 1999, a team that over four years of international play posted an 84–6–6 record. Her teammate, goalkeeper Briana Scurry, said, "Carla was the heartbeat of that team and the engine. Everything about the essence of the team—that was Carla."

Overbeck was arguably the key to their success. Although she played almost every minute of every game, few ever focused on her. Her skills were described by a former coach as "average at best." She played defense and seldom scored. To the outside world she was undistinguishable, but to her teammates she was essential. She would pass the ball forward as soon as she had the opportunity. She increased the amount of time it was at the feet of her teammates. This selfless instinct helped the team generate more scoring chances.

The same selfless mentality carried over off the field. When the USWNT team arrived at a hotel after some grueling international flight, Overbeck would carry everyone's bags to their hotel rooms. "I'm the captain," she explained, "but I'm no better than anybody else. I'm certainly not a better soccer player."

The story about Overbeck carrying the luggage appears in *The Captain Class: The Hidden Force That Creates the World's Greatest Teams*, a book that challenges some conventional ideas about leadership. The author, Sam Walker, is an editor at the *Wall Street Journal* and an avid sports fan. He studied 1,200 teams in 37 sports, traveling around the world to conduct interviews to find the one thing that extraordinary teams had in common. It was not the coach. It was not a superstar player. The key to success was that each had an extraordinary captain—like Carla Overbeck.

These captains had shared traits, including a near-hostility to fame and celebrity, a ceaseless work ethic, and a willingness to do anything to further the team. They were rarely the best players and seldom gave big emotional speeches, but talked constantly during games. Most importantly, Walker demonstrates how the superstars were often reliant on the captains who facilitated in ways that were invisible. Great captains lowered themselves in relation to the group whenever possible in order to earn the moral authority to drive the team. Overbeck explained after some brutal conditioning drill, "They'd be dying, and I'd be like, 'F--king Norway is doing sh-t like this.' I'm sure they hated me." But her teammates didn't hate her. They respected her and point to her as having helped define the team's culture, which led to success both on and off the field.

There are many examples of leadership beyond a coach or captain or famous player. For example, 1991 Women's World Cup Gold Ball Award winner Carin Jennings-Gabarra epitomized the speed, fitness, and mental strength coach Anson Dorrance demanded of his players. She said, "Before every game, Anson would challenge us, asking us which of us was going to make the difference. I always wanted to be that player." Even though she wasn't the captain, teammates saw Jennings-Gabarra as setting the standard for the group.

Competition

As it has been since the early 1980s, University of North Carolina women's soccer is one of the preeminent programs of the college ranks. There are dozens of Tar Heel alumni playing professionally around the world, and the pipeline will undoubtedly continue as long as Anson Dorrance is putting together excellent teams. Dorrance has one of the most successful coaching records in the history of athletics. Under his leadership, the Tar Heels have won 21 of the 31 NCAA Women's Soccer Championships. As of the end of the 2019 season, their record under Dorrance stood at 871–75–42 (a greater than 90 percent winning percentage) over 40 seasons.

His success at North Carolina led to the USSF hiring Dorrance as the coach of the USWNT in 1986. After taking the job, Dorrance sent a letter to the players he had inherited containing a stark warning: "If you don't come in fit, I will cut you!" He successfully juggled his duties with both the national team and UNC. In one extreme case, Dorrance left assistant coach Bill Palladino to lead UNC to a championship victory in the 1991 NCAA tournament while he coached the USWNT at the first Women's World Cup, held in China, which they won.

When Dorrance ended his tenure in 1994 with the national team, he had accumulated a record of 66–22–5 (.737). While with UNC and the USWNT, he has coached some of the finest players in women's soccer history, from Michelle Akers to Joy Fawcett to Mia Hamm to Kristine Lilly.

One cold, early morning in the second semester of Mia Hamm's senior year, out of the corner of his eye, Dorrance saw a figure going five yards forward and back, 10 and back, 15 and back. It's a grueling exercise he calls "cones." When the figure stopped and he could better focus, he saw it was Hamm. She was taking a break and was hunched over from exhaustion. Later he scribbled a note to her, dropped it in the mail, and forgot about it. Ten years later, after she had become world famous, she sent him a copy of her book called *Go for the Goal*. In the book was the note he had written her: "The vision of a champion is someone bent over drenched in sweat at the point of exhaustion when no one is watching."

In a *Sports Illustrated* article, Hamm said, "I grew up always good at sports, but being a girl I was never allowed to feel as good about it as the guys were. My toughness wasn't celebrated, but when I came here (to the University of North Carolina) it was okay to want to be the best." Dorrance fostered that sort of competitive environment back then at UNC and the USWNT that still exists now—when it's not as common for women to be encouraged to be that way. He wanted to establish a culture that embraced competitive women and supported them. The way he does that is through a tool he calls the competitive cauldron. It's basically an exercise where every element of practice is a competition, and it's evaluated and recorded to demonstrate where everyone is in 28 different categories. If a player does relatively worse, that player is going to see her name at the bottom of a list. He believes what that did was give his women athletes permission to compete. He believes one develops best when someone else is pushing them; one develops psychological strength when one competes, and one develops a standard for excellence if someone else is trying to compete against them. That's the environment he wanted to create, and what he thinks separates the UNC culture that he brought at the formation of the USWNT.

He believes there are competitive women athletes, and so for a lot of them, like what Hamm's quote is all about, they are looking for opportunity. *At last, someone is encouraging me to compete!* So now, when these athletes finally get to UNC, it's like, *Oh my gosh, this place exists? Where you're patting me on the back for beating everyone to death?* He created it at UNC and it lives on in the USWNT. It's the identity of both. He thinks that's what separated UNC and the USWNT. He believes it is what took the USWNT that couldn't beat the top women's teams in Europe in 1986 to World Cup champions in 1991.

Kristine Lilly believes the core of the team's mentality was a result of endless competition and discipline through intense practice and coaching. Lilly added, "The culture was continued through the years. I think what we all realized when you play for the U.S. team is that when you step into that environment, it's competitive. It's not like you come into it and you're just there. You have to earn it. You have to work at it. And when you realize what it takes, then it becomes bigger than yourself. That's powerful." Fellow '99er Michelle Akers added, "It was for-real every single game, and every practice, same thing. That's the mentality I love, and we even called it 'USA mentality.'"

Another part of competition is a sense of competitiveness between World Cup squads. Each group wants to accomplish more than their predecessors. They are very concerned about their legacy and setting the bar higher for the next squad.

Familiarity

Similar to how the youth academies of major European clubs are a critical factor behind World Cup championships, the University of North Carolina is a critical factor behind the USWNT World Cup championships—it represents 33 percent of the USWNT players who have won the Women's World Cup.

Table: Breakdown of Colleges Attended by the USWNT That Won the World Cup

World Cup Team	1991	1999	2015	2019	Totals
Coach	Anson Dorrance	Tony DiCicco	Jill Ellis	Jill Ellis	
UNC (#)	9	8	6	5	28
UNC (%)	50%	40%	26%	22%	33%
UC Berkley	2	2	1	1	6
Penn State	–	–	2	2	4
Stanford	1	1	2	3	7
UCF	2	–	–	–	2
Portland	–	2	1	1	4
UVA	–	–	2	3	5
Other	4	7	9	8	28
Total	18	20	23	23	84

Fifty percent of the 1991 Women's World Cup team played at UNC for Anson Dorrance, similar to how 45 percent of the 1980 U.S. Men's Olympic Hockey Team played at the University of Minnesota for Herb Brooks. It is important to note that in our interviews with the players from both teams, there was a feeling that their respective coaches selected and played the right players (not necessarily the best players) to help the team, regardless of which college they played for.

Familiarity with each other and systems are important factors in winning a World Cup. What also stands out is that almost every player on the USWNT, going all the way back to the inaugural 1991 World Cup, grew up playing in the United States and played on college teams. However, the U.S. college system is also training the women of other countries. For example, 22 of the 23 players on the Canada team for the 2019 Women's World Cup played on U.S. college teams.

Style of Play: Unconventional and Authentically American

In the 1991 World Cup, the first women's World Cup in FIFA history, the USWNT won all six of their games, outscoring opponents 25–5 and beating world powers Sweden, Germany, and Norway in the process. The foundation Dorrance laid with the 1991 squad with an emphasis on an "American style" also became the backbone for the USWNT's future success. Dorrance later said, "I think the key element was that we were different. We played a different style. We were very American in the way we approached the game and in our confidence going in to matches. We built our foundation on things like the individual duel. We were going to win every head ball, we were going to win every tackle, and we were going to win every one versus one contest when we were running at defenses."

In 1991 Dorrance used a 3-4-3, which was unheard of in European women's soccer at the time. He said, "People thought, 'You're not playing a 4-4-2, what kind of tactical midgets are you? You're going to high pressure? You can't high pressure in an event where you have a game every three days....' We were great duelers. We were gritty. We were to some extent irreverent because we didn't worship at the altar of the 4-4-2 and we didn't play the ball around in the back for half an hour to show we could possess it. We were different and we scared teams because we were different." He used a different style and didn't try to follow a conventional European system. He also used physical conditioning and American grittiness and competitiveness to overcome the other teams' strengths.[204] The pressing and emphasis on athleticism were to compensate for less technical skill and less tactical sophistication—by disrupting their superior opponents' play in their half of the field and utilizing set pieces, the USWNT could find opportunities to score.

Pay-to-Play

People may not want to read this, but it's an ugly truth—pay-to-play actually helped the USWNT win. Title IX led to many colleges starting

---

204. As a side note on player development, Dorrance believes that futsal is one of the best player development platforms. It amazes us how often futsal came up with elite players and coaches.

women's soccer teams. The economic incentive of entrance to a more selective college or an athletic scholarship motivated parents who had the financial means to pay for their daughters' player development. Contrast that to most of the rest of the world, where there was little to no economic incentive to pay for women's player development. Professional clubs were not focused on women's transfer fees, solidary payments, and training and development compensation because the financial upside wasn't deemed large enough. The limited funding that women's national teams did receive primarily came from the federations. Therefore, the parents of the United States were outspending the rest of the world on women's soccer player development. Then colleges, which are free for elite players on athletic scholarships, were playing the role of professional club youth academies to prepare women's players for the USWNT. Even better, the dominant college teams where essentially playing the role of Barcelona or Bayern Munich's youth academy—adding familiarity.

There is an unintended consequence. Pay-to-play doesn't necessarily favor the most talented children, but the children of parents who can afford player development. Pay-to-play acts as a filter to higher levels of development. For example, only 8 percent of female college soccer players are of Hispanic origin. Since the 1991 World Cup, there have only been 12 Black American or Hispanic origin women on the World Cup or Olympic USWNT. Five players on the 2019 squad (one was in the starting XI) were Black Americans, and none were of Hispanic origin.

Recently, women's soccer has changed dramatically, and this will alter the competitive landscape. Most European professional clubs have added women's professional teams with full-time professional contracts. Standing alone, most European club women's teams lose money. Today, the primary economic incentives of their parent clubs are cross-marketing to an installed base of fans and attracting women's soccer fans to their brands. Seven of the eight quarterfinalists (the USWNT being the exception) at the 2019 Women's World Cup were from Europe. In order to provide economic incentives for the elite women's players to stay in the U.S., MLS clubs will most likely have to match their European counterparts—and it may not be enough, because the top European clubs have more financial resources. Otherwise, more elite U.S. women will have more economic incentives to play in Europe. MLS should be following European clubs and at least have closer relationships with the professional women's teams and cross-market them with the same branding. Regardless, European national teams will become increasingly more competitive.

WARNING to the USWNT

The U.S. Women's U-20 team won their World Cup in 2012 but then were knocked out in the quarterfinals in 2014 by North Korea, semifinals in 2016 by North Korea (and lost to Japan in the match for third place), and group stage in 2018 (Spain and Japan advanced in their group).[205] Ignore the U-20 warning signs at your own peril.

In addition, women in Europe now have access to better coaching and facilities as a part of large European clubs. The women's teams are starting to recruit and play teenagers. These young players will face women who are bigger, faster, stronger, and better professional players, which accelerates development. Eventually, the pay-to-play model for college and women's soccer in the U.S. will be challenged by women's youth academies at clubs in Europe and an opportunity to play professionally there. Over time, the USWNT will have fewer players who attended college and have less familiarity, which may change team dynamics. More recently, USWNT players have signed with European club teams (including Sam Mewis, Rose Lavelle, Emily Sonnett, Tobin Heath, Christen Press, and Alex Morgan) and as more investment gets made in Europe, we only see that trend accelerating.

Historically, the USWNT players have not had large club salaries and have not had to worry as much about club obligations as their national team obligations, as the national team is the clear priority. These are very big differences from the USMNT players. The USWNT players depend more on a national team salary and benefits. In many ways, the USWNT players economically rely more on each other and the sponsorships that

---

205. North Korea had several players test positive for performance-enhancing drugs during the 2011 Women's World Cup and were banned from the 2015 tournament.

they get because of their association with the national team.[206] This fosters an environment of everyone needing to work together and promote the sport. As salaries increase in Europe and the clubs expect players to balance club and national team obligations, team dynamics may change. In addition, international competition, World Cups and Olympics, have been the primary ways for women to have a platform. As more of the best women's players go to Europe, the Women's Champions League will become an increasingly important part of their legacy and identity.

Lastly, after equal pay, diversity will become an increasingly important topic for the USWNT because they are viewed as leaders in social equality—it's an important part of their powerful and inspirational *why*.

Off the Field

The USWNT's mission and identity attracts lots of followers. As of November 28, 2020, @USWNT had 2.4 million Twitter followers, compared to 2.1 million for @USMNT. USWNT players such as Alex Morgan (3.9M), Megan Rapinoe (915k), Carli Lloyd (910k), and Kelley O'Hara (608k) have more followers than Christian Pulisic (548k). Christen Press (539k) and Tobin Heath (504k) are not far behind him. Julie Ertz (348k), Rose Lavelle (179k), and Sam Mewis (89k) have more followers than Weston McKennie (51k), Jordan Morris (44k), Tyler Adams (20k), and Josh Sargent (17k).

---

206. This was generally true for the men in the 1990s.

Conclusion

Rituals. A USMNT player kissed the USA patch on his jersey before he put it on for the game. Another secretly placed a picture of loved ones between his shin pad and sock. Several wouldn't step on the white sideline as they walked onto the field or had to sit in the same seat on the bus to the game. One USMNT fan has to kiss her husband's bald head for good luck before matches. Another fan paints his face with red, white, and blue stripes for games, even if he watches alone at home. Several wear a lucky USA player's jersey, a Stars-and-Stripes bandana—or even underwear. Rituals connect a community. Everyone plays their part.

I believe. What started out as a chant at a Naval Academy Prep School that carried to the thousands of Midshipmen in the student section of a football game jumping up and down in the bleachers performing the chant became a rallying cry for U.S. Soccer fans.[207] Fans not just at the games but at homes, at viewing parties, and at bars, all optimistically jumping up and down and chanting, "I believe that we will win!" united with one voice—connected. Authentically American.

A USMNT goal is scored. Bedlam on the field as players raise their hands, hug, and jump on each other to celebrate. In living rooms and bars

---

207. In 1998, Naval Academy Preparatory School (NAPS) student Jay Rodriguez was assigned to create a chant to be used by his platoon and came up with "I believe that we will win!" Rodriguez passed along the chant to Corey Strong (Naval Academy, 2003), who was a cheerleader for the Naval Academy. Strong led fans in the chant during a 1999 Army-Navy football game. The chant spread and became most widely associated with the USMNT.

across the country, fans are doing the same, celebrating together as if they were on the team and had just scored the goal themselves. The connection is so real that those watching use the terms "we" and "us" and "our team," as opposed to "them" or "they." It's not just about the goals and winning, either. It's not all ups. The near-misses and the downs are just as important for building these moments that give fans so much emotion and joy—tears, chills, and goosebumps. If you don't believe us, watch the YouTube video of scenes of people's reaction to Landon Donovan's game-winning goal against Algeria, which, of course, has the soundtrack from the movie *Rudy*, a story about an underdog.[208] There isn't a comparable video of people's reaction to the Dream Team winning Olympic gold.

The USMNT play soccer—that is what they do. What matters is *why* they do it, *how* they do it, and *who* does it. They bring Americans together to believe in something greater than themselves and an American spirit—to be inspired and reassured that they too can win. The U.S. national soccer teams (and the women's ice hockey team) are the only national teams of major sports with that distinction. Unlike the movies *Rudy* or *Rocky* or *Miracle*, when the viewer knows the outcome when he or she watches, a USMNT fan never knows—that adds to the emotions when the team wins and provides moments to remember and share.

The USMNT played with grit and with something to prove. While they didn't have world-class talent, they had better skills than most observers gave them credit for. Not only did they defend all over the field, they did so with an "all for one and one for all" attitude. They could also break out on quick counter-attacks. We labeled the style the Spirit of '76. On the team's best days, the USMNT performed at a level that exceeded the sum of their parts.

Over the past few years, however, some of that identity has faded from the USMNT, and it's part of the problem of what happened to the USMNT. When the USMNT didn't qualify for the 2018 World Cup, initially, it led to anger because of what the USMNT means to many Americans. The

---

208. The USMNT watched it when they got back to their hotel after the game. The players were blown away and got re-energized. U.S. Soccer wanted to make a similar video, but fans beat them to it. The video is by YouTube user kitchel22130. It has more than 5 million views.

anger reflected the loss of what the fans originally identified with. The anger is actually an indication of the intensity of the original connection. Being apathetic about the results helps USMNT fans deal with the loss of what the USMNT meant. In a 2018 article for *The New Republic* titled "The Joy of Watching a World Cup Without the U.S.," Andrew Helms wrote, "Why I'm relieved the men's national team didn't qualify for Russia this year." He raised many of the themes of this book and helped inspire our conclusions.

In the early days of the Jürgen Klinsmann era, it would have seemed unbelievable that the USMNT would not play in the 2018 World Cup. Klinsmann promised to raise the team from underdogs to the global elite. He said, "We're working on a different style of play.... A system, a style, that hopefully entertains you and hopefully shows the best teams in the world that we're able to play this game with them and not only to react to them."

It was an indictment of the USMNT's *how*—the Spirit of '76. The comments were enthusiastically welcomed at the time because over time, more and more of the USSF, USMNT, fans, and media progressively started to assume and believe if the USMNT didn't act and play like Europeans, then they were less legitimate and couldn't progress and win the World Cup. This change was not deliberate. It was based on false comparisons and unrealistic expectations.

Over his five and a half years leading the team, there were some bright spots and the wins and near-wins drowned out the warning signs of drift. But during the 2014 World Cup, when the USMNT advanced out of the Group of Death and almost beat Belgium, the underlying statistics revealed the reality. Among the seven USMNTs that have qualified for the World Cup in American soccer's modern era, Klinsmann's side took the fewest shots per 90 minutes, yielded the most, and eclipsed only the 1994 squad in possession. The team lost 2–1 against Belgium in extra time in the Round of 16—but it required Tim Howard to make a World Cup–record 16 saves to keep the game close.

In the 2014 World Cup there were moments of joy, like John Brooks' game-winning header against Ghana, but there were more moments of frustration as a team without an identity fumbled for one. There was no clear system of play (*how*), and in desperation the players tried to revert to the "Spirit of '76"—the USMNT ran more than any other team in Brazil on average and Michael Bradley ran more than any other player in the entire tournament on average.

After the 2014 World Cup, the situation deteriorated even further for the USMNT. Regardless of the wins or losses, fans didn't identify with the team—who were no longer fun to root for. If the U.S. team used to exceed the sum of its parts, by 2016 the inverse had become true. The USSF, media, and fans thought the USMNT needed to be European, when in reality, the solutions had to ultimately come from the U.S.

Although the USMNT managed a brief rebound under Bruce Arena once Klinsmann was fired, it was a patch job and kick-the-can-down-the-road strategy—just qualify for the World Cup and then try to figure things out. Maybe it could have worked, but it was too little, too late.

On paper the USMNT were better than most of the teams they lost to during qualification. The primary problem was not player identification and development—pay-to-play, minutes of USMNT-eligible players in MLS, neglecting Hispanic origin or Black American players, or relegation and promotion. The primary problem was not bad luck, which of course can impact a game, but over the course of many games in qualification, luck should even itself out. If the too-tired-and-old effect and third-cycle trap of using too many established players was a problem, it was related to *why*. The *why* was *just qualify and we will figure it out*—and that just wasn't compelling or inspirational enough.

Against Trinidad & Tobago, the USMNT played without a *why*, leaving viewers angry and confused as to when their team had lost its grit. The identity and style coming out of the 1994 World Cup as the Spirit of '76, embracing an underdog status or mentality similar to the American Patriots in 1776, was no more. In the final minutes, down 2–1, no one on the USMNT would score a last-minute goal and save the day. To be honest, the team didn't deserve that kind of fairytale ending—they neither acted like nor considered themselves underdogs.

In contrast, in the final minutes of extra time at the 2010 World Cup, USMNT fans held out hope that, although the USMNT were down a goal to Ghana, Donovan could summon one final heroic moment like he had against Algeria. With *why* and *how*, no one was screaming at their TVs wondering where the team's famous grit had gone.

The USMNT lost that day against Ghana. Those who think the USMNT just play soccer and their progress is only measured by wins and comparisons to previous results are missing something very important. There's a beautiful irrationality about the USMNT. Fans knew that the USMNT weren't going to win the World Cup, but nurturing the hope for one more game was enough to unite and inspire a country. The players and their identity represented them—the underdog in them. They were connected.

The USMNT have to regain the Spirit of '76 that they lost—or, better yet, adapt and evolve it with young talented players. What matters more than winning the World Cup (although of course that would bring tremendous joy) is the players and fans being connected and believing again that the USMNT represent the underdog and grit in them.

The USMNT can be both a legitimate World Cup contender and overachieving underdog. The USWNT have balanced this perfectly. The USMNT need to do the same.

The USMNT are fortunate to have a great group of young rising stars coming through the system. From Tyler Adams (RB Leipzig) to Weston McKennie (on loan to Juventus) to Christian Pulisic (Chelsea) to Gio Reyna (Borussia Dortmund) to Chris Richards (Bayern Munich) to Josh Sargent (Werder Bremen) to Zack Steffen (Manchester City), the future has never looked brighter. To manage expectations, even with all of the American talent in Europe, our Imaginary 2020 World Cup USMNT's number of players and minutes in the Top Five Leagues would be less than 2010 and 2014. The numbers are more comparable to 1998–2006. However, the average age for our Imaginary 2020 USMNT is dramatically lower than any other World Cup team, and it's possible that by 2022 the entire USMNT starting XI play in the Top Five Leagues.

These young stars have chosen to develop their talents in Europe, but are also keenly aware of the original meaning of *why*. As Gio Reyna said in an interview, "From Christian all the way to myself, we have a lot of really good talent in between us. *We all have this hunger inside us to prove that Americans can play too*, and that we are there looking to win some trophies." (Our italics for emphasis.)

The next generation are ambitious and competitive. They are unafraid to leave the U.S. and go up against the best players in the world. They are the American underdogs in Europe who capture the imagination of fans in the U.S. Tyler Adams, a homegrown player of the New York Red Bulls youth academy, was the first American to score in a Champions League quarterfinal in 2020. A New York state native, Adams joined the Red Bulls youth academy after impressing at U-13 tryouts. He had a brief stint at the Bradenton U-17 Residency Program before it closed and became the first signing for the Red Bulls II (USL) in 2015. He made his MLS debut in 2016. Adams joined the Red Bulls' sister club RB Leipzig at age 19 after the 2018 season with 59 MLS games. Reportedly, RB Leipzig paid $3 million up front and granted the Red Bulls a 33 percent share of any future sale. Around the same time, Bayern Munich paid a reported fee of $1.25 million for U-20 defender Chris Richards from FC Dallas for Bayern Munich II. Philadelphia Union homegrown player Brenden Aaronson, 20 years old, moved to RB Salzburg in January 2021, after the MLS season ended. Philadelphia announced it would be the highest transfer fee paid for an American homegrown player from MLS. Early news reports indicated the fee was $6 million, with $3 million in possible incentives. With so many young American players now playing (or having played) in the Bundesliga, the league's emphasis on movement, team spirit, and efficiency, not to mention *kampfgeist* (will to win), is likely to influence the USMNT's style of play.[209] The USMNT benefits from players going to the same Top Five League so they have more familiarity.

---

209. Under Löw, Germany has predominantly played 4-2-3-1. Löw's default tactics still favor a reactive counter-attacking system—relying on bursts out of defense at breakneck speed. In the blink of an eye, it becomes a 4-3-3 with attacking midfielders pushing on.

One of the biggest challenges for any USMNT coach will be how to create familiarity and personal bonds and foster a culture and identity amongst players spread across several leagues and clubs so that they are willing to sacrifice themselves for the team and mission. Unlike Germany, for example, the USMNT don't have a core group of players from a few states and few club youth academies. And unlike France, for example, the USMNT don't have a core group of players from a few suburbs that played informal street soccer together and also trained at a few elite youth academies supervised by a federation. Technology (e.g., Zoom, WhatsApp group chats) can help a coach and team, but the USMNT have limited in-person time together and the MLS and European leagues have different calendars.

While USMNT players in Europe is very exciting, the fans, media, and USMNT can't overlook or neglect or disrespect the great USMNT talents who are in MLS for personal reasons or because it took more time for them to develop. For example, Jordan Morris wanted to attend Stanford and play in his hometown—people should respect and understand his personal decisions.[210,211] Also don't forget the USMNT have found great contributors on Liga MX clubs like Cle Kooiman and Hércules Gómez. Many fans and media often overlook MLS or Liga MX when they discuss the potential talent of the USMNT. The players also need to respect that their decisions have consequences, and they may not make the USMNT by not challenging themselves against the best competition.

---

210. Landon Donovan unfairly received criticism for not playing more in Europe, among other things. Similarly, Jordan Morris unfairly received criticism for not going to Europe. Donovan and Morris have made tremendous sacrifices for and contributions to the USMNT. Fans sometimes forget that players are human beings. They have the right to make personal choices, and people should respect their decisions. The media and fans may not agree with their decisions or think their decisions are not in the best interests of the USMNT, but the media and fans should respect and understand their decisions. And the players have to accept responsibility and understand the potential consequences for their decisions.

211. Versatile center back Aaron Long didn't have a natural progression. Long made the Cal South state team once. He only had one college soccer scholarship offer. He never played on the youth national team. He wasn't invited to the 2014 MLS combine. He chose to leave the West Coast to play for the Red Bulls on the East Coast to develop and get opportunities. In 2018, at 26 years old, he received his first call up to the USMNT. The following year he captained the national team in a friendly against Panama.

Perceptions are changing in all circles that it is a source of pride to send American teenagers to play in the Top Five Leagues. The change is, in part, driven by changing economic incentives—MLS clubs get training compensation and solidarity payments and Top Five Leagues get young, marketable American stars who attract attention in a large U.S. market. There is a goldmine of talent in the U.S., and the learning environments are rapidly improving. MLS academies and local amateur soccer clubs are also getting better and better. MLS continues to increase its investment in development.

The USMNT also has talented dual nationals such as Sergiño Dest, who was born in the Netherlands to a Dutch mother and Surinamese American father and plays right back for Barcelona.[212] He joins a long line of players who have moved from Ajax to Barcelona, including Johan Cruyff. In addition, Konrad de la Fuente, who was born to Haitian parents of Dominican descent and moved to Spain at the age of 10 when his father took a job at the Haitian consulate in Barcelona, plays at the Barcelona youth academy (FC Barcelona B). On December 5, 2020, Christian Pulisic, Weston McKennie, and Gio Reyna all scored for their respective Top Five League clubs. It was the first time in 15 years that three different Americans scored in one of the five major European leagues on the same day. The last time, on August 27, 2005, it was Brian McBride, Jermaine Jones, and Claudio Reyna.

Remember, the USWNT's *why* evolved, rather than drifted or changed, and now has extended from fighting for the legitimacy of women's soccer in the U.S. to proving women's sports deserve equal pay. Their mission is starting to evolve to include social justice and equality for everyone. As the USWNT's mission has gained a higher purpose and evolved in such a positive way, they have maintained their *why* and underdog status as well

---

212. USMNT coach Gregg Berhalter and sporting director Earnie Stewart went to Amsterdam in October 2019 and met with Dest and his father the day after Ajax's UEFA Champions League match against USMNT teammate Christian Pulisic and Chelsea before Dest made his final decision to play for the USMNT. Dest's story is similar to Stewart's, who was born in the Netherlands to a Dutch mother and American serviceman and spent most of his life in the Netherlands.

as grown their fan base. Similar to the USWNT, the USMNT's mission needs to evolve.

The biggest step in the development of the USMNT in almost a decade has gone largely unnoticed—and it's not on the field. The young Americans in Europe are not only embracing the mission (or *why*) of fighting for the legitimacy of soccer in the U.S. (as Gio Reyna said above), they are extending it to fighting for equality and social justice. Then Schalke, and now Juventus, midfielder Weston McKennie and other USMNT players are using their platform to push for change.[213] Weston McKennie wore a JUSTICE FOR GEORGE armband in his side's Bundesliga game in memory of George Floyd, an American Black man who died as a police offer knelt on his neck despite pleading to officers that he could not breathe. The referee asked him to remove the armband, as the league has a rule that a player can't wear anything making a political statement. He refused. Afterward, McKennie said, "The league and everyone in soccer always preaches 'say no to racism.' So, I didn't think that there would be a problem. If I have to take the consequences to express my opinion, to express my feelings, to stand up for what I believe in, then that's something I have to do." The 21-year-old received huge praise on social media for fighting for equality. Tyler Adams posted a picture of cleats he wore in a game showing he had BLACK LIVES MATTER written on his left shoe and JUSTICE 4 GEORGE on the right. Zach Steffen, who played for the University of Maryland and Columbus Crew before signing with Manchester City, said, "We have a big role to play…change is really only going to come through actions." Steffen has a foundation that supplies computer equipment to children from disadvantaged communities. During their November 2020 friendlies, the USMNT players wore jackets over their jerseys that read BE THE CHANGE on the front and had varying messages of the players' choice across the back.

---

213. Very rugged and hardworking, Schalke 04 are known as the working-class team due to their location in the very industrial working town of Gelsenkirchen. The tunnel in their stadium to the field is made to resemble a mine shaft to remind the players of their heritage! The club's identity makes them incredibly popular within Germany—just not in Dortmund. McKennie is the first American to play for Juventus.

When players such as Adams, Dest, McKennie, Pulisic, Reyna, Sargent, and Steffen play for the USMNT the U.S. fans will care—not just because of their skill level or that they play in Europe, but because of *who* they are and *why* they play.[214] If they want to effectively use their platform as USMNT players, they will have to make sure the fans identify with them. The identity of the USMNT includes grit and underdog mentality as well as the belief in and hope of equal opportunity.[215] It doesn't matter if the USMNT play CONCACAF nations against whom on paper the USMNT are favorites or if they play soccer powers and are underdogs, each and every time the USMNT need to live up to their identity and values—that is an outcome and expectations they can control. For example, Atlético Madrid, with very talented players, play with the same style and identity against Real Madrid and Barcelona as they do other La Liga clubs. They believe if they don't, they will lose their identity, and that the players, as well as fans, will be confused. This should challenge the idea that the USMNT can play one way versus lower-ranked teams and another way against soccer powers. This young talented USMNT will need to prove they have the right kind of team spirit, mentality, and grit to never give up and fight to win regardless of the circumstances. The captains and leaders need to be respected for having a willingness to do anything to further the team—even if that means not playing in their traditional position or not playing at all. The coaches will have to select a team of the right players (not necessarily the best players) who want to sacrifice for each other for

---

214. International soccer is very particular. At an international level, players like Cobi Jones and Alexi Lalas were able to compete without having ever played professional club soccer. The USMNT should not necessarily be looking for the best players, they should be looking for the right ones. In addition, the coach and captain will have the responsibility of making sure that players not playing in Europe don't feel slighted in any way—that there is an equal opportunity. The players themselves will have to be accountable for this attitude. Players can't be talking about equality and equal opportunity and not take that attitude to USMNT camps. There needs to be mutual respect and understanding. We also believe a captain and leadership will be very important to unite a mix of different players and experiences.

215. We do believe the *how*—Spirit of '76—needs to be emphasized, which does not mean it can't evolve or be adapted over time, especially with skill level. For example, the USMNT are taking advantage of their athleticism and utilizing a compact, high press to be aggressive in defense (e.g., "modernizing and evolving the counter-attack"). We also believe the USMNT should be much closer to and supportive publicly of the USWNT. They can't claim to be "for social justice" or "all equal" and not be publicly supportive of equal pay, conditions, and opportunities for women.

the team to succeed and make sure the players have a good understanding of what they need to do through consistency. The dialogue about the USMNT needs to be centered on who they are, not who they aren't or the result that could have been.

What the fans want—win or lose—is to watch is a group of remarkable young men, loveable characters, give them what no other major U.S. men's national sports team can give them—a chance not only to dream, but a chance to believe that equal opportunity exits, an underdog has a chance, and the American Dream and spirit are alive and well. *What happened to the USMNT matters because the USMNT (and USWNT) represent much more than a national sports team.*

The Ugly Truth about How Spain Won the 2010 World Cup (*...Continued from the Introduction*)

Spain has many different regional cultures, including Basque and Catalan.[216] Obviously, there is a rivalry between Barcelona and Real Madrid ("El Clásico"). The coach, Vincente Del Bosque, a former Real Madrid player and coach, adopted Barcelona's *tiki-taka* system for the team and got everyone to buy into the system (*how*). In a 2012 interview with Jimmy Burns of *The Guardian*, Del Bosque said, "Spain is not Barcelona, nor is it Real Madrid. Any victory belongs to Spanish soccer." Del Bosque explained, "I think there were two players in particular, Xavi Hernández [vice-captain of Barcelona] and Iker Casillas [captain of Real Madrid] [Spain's two captains] who knew that the national squad was worth defending." Del Bosque made statements that the team were playing *to prove* Spanish soccer and La Liga, where many of the players played, are the best in the world (the *why*). Del Bosque had masterfully managed to get the players of reigning European Champions Spain to embrace an "underdogs status" with something to prove. In addition, at a time when the Spanish economy was in crisis, with among the highest

---

216. In 2010, the Catalan national soccer team, which are not recognized by FIFA or UEFA, were coached by Johan Cruyff. Athletic Bilbao have a policy where only players native to the Basque region are eligible to play for them.

unemployment rates in Europe, the country needed a good news story. The players' mission or *why* took on additional emotional significance.

Reportedly, some of the coach's decisions on squad selection were to improve team chemistry and have the fans and media view the team as theirs (*who* and *identity*). Del Bosque said, "I wanted, as a national coach...to make Catalans and Basques feel good about supporting a Spanish side.... The thought of using football to help unite [Spaniards] is something that makes me feel happy." Two players from Athletic Bilbao (the Basque region) were on the 23-man roster and played a total of 50 minutes in the group stage in the 2010 World Cup. Del Bosque didn't just try to make the team theirs by geographic location, but by having players that Spain were proud of. He concluded, "Football has an important role to play in society, players should have a sense of social responsibility, have a moral dimension."

Like we were guilty of in the introduction, while soccer experts were busy analyzing *tiki-taka—how* Spain won the 2010 World Cup—*the ugly truth is* we and they missed the *why* and *who. And when the why, how, and who come together—win or lose—soccer is the beautiful game.*

Afterword

Why Us to Try to Answer the Question

In 2014, Real Madrid gave me unprecedented access to write a book about how the club is managed both on and off the field, which was published in 2016 and titled *The Real Madrid Way* (BenBella Books). To be honest, I was very surprised. Real Madrid have the most European UEFA Champions League/European trophies and one of the highest revenues, if not the highest, largest player payrolls, and most social media followers in any sport worldwide. While I taught in the finance and economics department at Columbia Business School, I didn't follow European soccer, didn't have any expertise in sports or soccer or Real Madrid, and, even worse, didn't even speak Spanish. I learned, and then I explained in my book why Real Madrid are successful and how they select players and coaches, manage their business and brand, and make money. After cold-calling Billy Beane, the executive vice president of baseball operations of Major League Baseball's Oakland Athletics and the central character of the book and movie *Moneyball,* and requesting that he read a prepublication draft of my book to provide feedback, he asked me, "Why would Real Madrid give an outsider so much access and information? And why would Real Madrid let someone make the information public, because competitors could copy them?" I asked Floretino Pérez, president of Real Madrid, and Carlos Martínez de Albornoz, a key member of the Real Madrid executive team, that same question. They explained to me that behind every great brand is trust, and transparency supports trust. And transparency is something

375

their fans expect and value. At the center of everything the club did both on and off the field are a unique culture, an underlying set of beliefs, and expectations and values that contribute to the social environment—that took decades to develop, nurture, and support. Their culture and values led to an authentic identity. They explained that, unlike data analytics or marketing strategies, their culture can't be simply copied in just a few years, and is therefore a unique and protected asset.

The Real Madrid Way (*La Formula Real Madrid* in Spanish) has been published in many languages around the world. The BBC World Service produced *The Documentary, Inside Real Madrid* based on the book. Because of the book's success (which I attribute to people's interest in sports and the hundreds of millions of global, loyal, and passionate Real Madrid fans) and the fact that I make my email publicly available (sgm2130@ columbia.edu), I have been contacted by senior executives from leagues and teams all over the world for advice. I think many of the executives feel comfortable talking with me because I don't charge them for my advice or time (so I am not selling any services or products), and I have previously worked at Goldman Sachs and Citigroup and as a senior advisor to McKinsey (so I understand complex business and management issues). As I have helped them, I have learned even more about what helps make organizations successful.

Admittedly, I am not a sports or soccer expert. Like most people, I have been a fan of my local professional sports teams since I was a child. I played two varsity sports (fencing and tennis) in college and twice finished the Ironman World Championships in Kona, Hawaii. However, I have never coached or managed a college or professional sports team or been a front office executive. While that may have disadvantages, it also has some advantages. I don't take things for granted. I have to ask a lot of questions about why and how things are the way they are. I question basic assumptions, and this allows me to challenge conventional wisdom. I have to utilize research, data, and analysis versus primarily relying on anecdotes or personal experiences, which can have biases.

How the Book Came to Be

Because of my Real Madrid book, soccer fans ask me a lot of questions. For example, fans of Italian soccer would ask me why Italy's Serie A League was so dominant in the 1980s and 1990s and then fell behind other European leagues. (Also, Italy, a four-time World Cup winner, failed to qualify for the 2018 World Cup). It seemed like an interesting question, and I couldn't resist the opportunity to do research in Italy and be able to better connect with my many Italian friends, so I co-authored a book titled *What Happened to Serie A* (Arena Sport, 2018).

While working on the Serie A book, in 2018 I met an Under-X (X to protect his confidentiality) Men's U.S. Soccer Team coach. He told me that because of my unique background and contacts that I had built over the years writing about soccer, I should research what happened to the U.S. men's national soccer team. They had just failed to qualify for the 2018 World Cup for the first time since 1990. I guess, like many Americans, I was curious what happened with the results and enthusiasm.

I use the word *we* because this project was so complex I enlisted the help of a co-author, Sarah Parsons Wolter. She played women's varsity hockey at Dartmouth and won the school's Best All-Around Athlete award. Sarah works in finance, graduated in the top 5 percent of her Columbia University Business School class, and co-authored the book on Serie A with me. Also, she has finished several of the seven major marathons. Most importantly for this project, she was the youngest member of the U.S. Women's Hockey Team in the 2006 Olympics in Turin, Italy. She has unique insights into national team and tournament dynamics.

Many people helped us by making introductions or reading drafts of the book or being interviewed. We are incredibly grateful for their time, and will not mention them by name to protect their privacy. A few people went well above and beyond to help (they know who they are because they are still exhausted by our texts, emails, and follow-up calls)—and we can't thank you enough. In addition, a few enthusiastic students (or former students) helped tremendously: Lyle Adams (Columbia), Tobi Bello (Columbia), Ignacio Mochales Cuesta (Real Madrid Graduate School), and Joao Paulo Murray (Syracuse).

We also want to thank Michelle Bruton, Adam Motin, Clarissa Young, Sam Ofman, Stefani Szenda, and the many people at Triumph Books, a division of Independent Publishers Group, who believed in us and the importance of the project.

Please Note

In addition to gathering and analyzing publicly available information and data from news sources and data sources such as FIFA and Opta, we interviewed more than 70 people for the book, including current and former USMNT and other countries' national teams' players, coaches, and staff. We appreciate their help. To make people comfortable speaking with us, we promised to maintain confidentiality and protect their privacy. We never mention who we spoke to or quote anyone from our interviews.

In full disclosure, and because this is publicly available information, Sunil Gulati, former president of the USSF, is a colleague of mine at Columbia University, and Carlos Cordeiro, former president of the USSF, and I were colleagues at Goldman Sachs.

The analysis and conclusions are our own views, and we are humble enough to recognize we are not always right and don't have all of the information. We are always looking to improve and gather more information, so please feel free to contact us at sgm2130@columbia.edu.

Appendix

Table: Breakdown of USMNT Players in 1994 to 2017 World Cups

	1994	1998	2002	2006	2010	2014	2017
World Cup Finish	Round of 16	Group Stage	Quarterfinals	Group Stage	Round of 16	Round of 16	DNQ
World Cup Place (#)	14	32	8	25	12	15	NA
Coach	Bora Milutinović	Steve Sampson	Bruce Arena	Bruce Arena	Bob Bradley	Jürgen Klinsmann	Bruce Arena
Total Team Caps	425	1,156	1,153	1,030	813	820	1,245
Avg. Age Team	26.4	28.3	28.3	28.3	26.9	27.3	20.6
Avg. Age Starters	28.1	26.7	27.4	28.7	27.2	29.1	27.2
# US Players (MLS)	15	16	11	11	4	10	16
% US Players (MLS)	68%	73%	48%	48%	17%	43%	70%
# US Starters (MLS)	6	6	6	3	2	4	6
% US Starters (MLS)	55%	55%	55%	27%	18%	36%	55%
# Players Top 5 Leagues	1	5	8	6	12	10	4
% Players Top 5 Leagues	5%	23%	35%	26%	52%	43%	17%
Total Minutes Top 5 Leagues	1,857	11,025	12,652	12,312	23,265	23,042	9,156
Total Minutes Top 5 Leagues (ex. Goalies)	1,857	6,975	7,972	8,668	15,285	16,359	9,156
Avg. Minutes/Player Top 5 League	1,857	2,205	15,81.5	2,052	1,939	2,304	2,289
# Players Europe	6	6	12	12	17	12	5
Total Minutes Europe	7,484	13,674	21,548	31,875	32,140	27,457	13,476
% Players Europe	27%	26%	52%	52%	74%	52%	22%
# Players College	17	18	17	17	15	11	14
% Players College	77%	82%	74%	74%	65%	48%	61%
# Players who left US	22	20	21	18	23	17	16
% Players who left US	100%	91%	91%	78%	100%	74%	70%

Table: Breakdown of Where Mexico National Team Players Play

Year	WC Finish	# in Mexico	# in MLS	# in Europe	# Top 5 League
1994	13	20	0	2	2
1998	13	21	1	0	0
2002	11	19	0	4	4
2006	15	19	1	3	3
2010	14	14	0	9	5
2014	10	15	0	8	6
2018	12	9	3	11	6

Table: World Cup Group Stage Relative Level of Difficulty for USMNT (1994–2014)

Year	Group Total Seeds	Group Total Seeds (w/ US)	Players Top 5 League (ex. US)	Players Top 5 League (w/ US)	Minutes Top 5 League (ex. US)	Minutes Top 5 League (w/ US)
1994	47	73	10	11	26,812	28,669
1998	88	123	42	47	114,327	125,352
2002	76	95	17	25	41,081	53,733
2006	66	73	42	48	124,856	137,168
2010	85	96	43	55	110,025	133,290
2014	39	52	44	54	121,045	144,087

Table: Arena, Bradley, and Klinsmann World Cup Records

World Cup	Bruce Arena—2002	Bruce Arena—2006	Bob Bradley	Jürgen Klinsmann
WC Year	2002	2006	2010	2014
WC Finish	Quarterfinals	Group Stage	Round of 16	Round of 16
WC Place (#)	8	25	12	15
WC Record (W-L-T)	2–2–1	0–2–1	1–1–2	1–2–1
WC Avg. GFPG	1.4	0.7	1.3	1.3
WC Avg. GAPG	1.4	2	1.3	1.5
Group Stage Finish	2	4	1	2
Qualification Record	8–4–4	12–2–4	13–3–2	11–3–2

Table: Arena, Bradley, and Klinsmann Win/Loss Records

Excluding Friendlies	Bruce Arena—2002	Bruce Arena—2006	Bruce Arena 1998–2006	Bruce Arena Total	Bob Bradley	Jürgen Klinsmann
Tenure	October 26, 1998 –June 21, 2002	June 23, 2002 –July 14, 2006	October 26, 1998 –July 14, 2006	October 26, 1998 –July 14, 2006; November 22, 2016 –October 13, 20017	December 8, 2006 –July 28, 2011	July 29, 2011 –November 21, 2016
Total Matches	35	35	70	84	48	47
Total Wins	20	21	41	49	30	28
Total Losses	10	7	17	19	13	14
Total Ties	5	7	12	16	5	5
Winning Percentage Total	64.3%	70.0%	67.1%	67.9%	67.7%	64.9%
Avg. Goals For	1.71	1.83	1.77	1.82	1.90	2.02
Avg. Goals Against	0.89	0.8	0.84	0.83	1.15	1.11
Goal Differential (GF - GA)	29	36	65	83	36	43
Goal Differential (Avg.)	0.8	1.0	0.93	0.99	0.75	0.91
Wins Home	13	14	27	33	19	21
Wins Away	7	7	14	16	11	7
Losses Home	3	2	5	6	8	7
Losses Away	7	5	12	13	5	7
Ties Home	1	3	4	5	2	1
Ties Away	4	4	8	11	3	4
Record Home	13–3–1	14–2–3	27–5–4	33–6–5	19–8–2	21–7–1
Record Away	7–7–4	7–5–4	14–12–8	16–13–11	11–5–3	7–7–4
Winning Percentage Home	79.4%	81.6%	80.6%	80.7%	69.0%	74.1%
Winning Percentage Away	50.0%	56.3%	52.9%	53.8%	65.8%	50.0%

Table: Arena, Bradley, and Klinsmann Player Pools

Bruce Arena		Bob Bradley		Jürgen Klinsmann	
2004–2005		**2008–2009**		**2012–2013**	
Total Player Pool	59	Total Player Pool	57	Total Player Pool	49
Total Play in Match	54	Total Play in Match	54	Total Play in Match	45
Avg. Age	26.1	Avg. Age	25.3	Avg. Age	25.7
20 and under # players	6	20 and under # players	3	20 and under # players	3
20 and under # games played	26	20 and under # games played	45	20 and under # games played	4
20 and under # minutes played	1,498	20 and under # minutes played	3,294	20 and under # minutes played	160
2005–2006		**2009–2010**		**2013–2014**	
Total Player Pool	49	Total Player Pool	56	Total Player Pool	52
Total Play in Match	47	Total Play in Match	43	Total Play in Match	44
Avg. Age	25.6	Avg. Age	25.8	Avg. Age	25.8
20 and under # players	8	20 and under # players	2	20 and under # players	8
20 and under # games played	13	20 and under # games played	8	20 and under # games played	18
20 and under # minutes played	521	20 and under # minutes played	689	20 and under # minutes played	654

Table: U.S. Men's Olympic Soccer Tournament History

Year	Round	Position
1992	Group Stage	9th
1996	Group Stage	10th
2000	Semifinals	11th
2004	**Did Not Qualify**	
2008	Group Stage	9th
2012	**Did Not Qualify**	
2016	**Did Not Qualify**	
2020	TBD	

Table: U.S. Men's FIFA U-17 World Cup Record

Year	Round	Position
1985	Group Stage	12th
1987	Group Stage	13th
1989	Group Stage	9th
1991	Quarterfinals	5th
1993	Quarterfinals	7th
1995	Group Stage	15th
1997	Group Stage	11th
1999	Semifinals	4th
2001	Group Stage	15th
2003	Quarterfinals	5th
2005	Quarterfinals	5th
2007	Round of 16	16th
2009	Round of 16	12th
2011	Round of 16	12th
2013	**Did Not Qualify**	
2015	**Group Stage**	**21st**
2017	Quarterfinals	7th
2019	**Group Stage**	**20th**
2021	TBD	

Table: ESPN's Big Board by Austin Lindberg (November 14, 2020)
— Selected Information

Player	Youth	Age @ '22 WC	Club	League	MLS Academy	Family Play	Dual National	Trained / Lived Abroad
Christian Pulisic	Pennsylvania	24	Chelsea	Premier League		Both Parents	Yes	
Sergiño Dest	Netherlands	22	Barcelona	La Liga			Yes	Yes
Gio Reyna	New York/New Jersey	20	Borussia Dortmund	Bundesliga	NYCFC	Both Parents	Yes	Yes
Tyler Adams	New York	23	RB Leipzig	Bundesliga	NY Red Bulls	Brother		
**Yunus Musah	London	19	Valencia	La Liga			Yes	Yes
Zach Steffen	Pennsylvania	27	Manchester City	Premier League	Philadelphia Union	Sister		Yes
Antonee Robinson	England	25	Fulham	Premier League		Father		Yes
Weston McKennie	Texas	24	Juventus (from Schalke)	Serie A	FC Dallas			Yes
Chris Richards	Alabama/Texas	22	Hoffenheim (from Bayern Munich)	Bundesliga	FC Dallas			
Brenden Aaronson	Pennsylvania/New Jersey	22	Philadelphia Union	MLS	Philadelphia Union	Father/Brothers		
John Brooks	Germany	29	Wolfsburg	Bundesliga				Yes
Josh Sargent	Missouri	22	Werder Bremen	Bundesliga				
Reggie Cannon	Texas	24	Boavista	Primeira (Portugal)	FC Dallas			
Matt Miazga	New Jersey	27	Anderlecht (from Chelsea)	Belgian First	NY Red Bulls		Yes	
Sebastian Lletget	California	30	LA Galaxy	MLS			Yes	Yes
Jozy Altidore	New Jersey	33	Toronto FC	MLS			Yes	
Tim Weah	Florida/New York	22	Lille	Ligue 1	NY Red Bulls	Father/Uncle/Cousin		
Jordan Morris	Washington	28	Seattle Sounders	MLS	Seattle	Brother		
Walker Zimmerman	Georgia	29	Nashville SC	MLS				
Richard Ledezma	Arizona	22	PSV Eindhoven	Eredivisie (Dutch 1)	Real Salt Lake		Yes	
Michael Bradley	New Jersey/Illinois	35	Toronto FC	MLS		Father		
Sean Johnson	Georgia	33	NYCFC	MLS			Yes	
Ethan Horvath	Colorado	27	Club Brugge	Belgian First	Real Colorado	Father	Yes	
Missing Out								
Mark McKenzie	Delaware/New York	23	Philadelphia Union	MLS	Philadelphia Union	Father	Yes	
Cristian Roldan	California	27	Seattle Sounders	MLS		Brothers	Yes	
Paul Arriola	California	27	DC United	MLS	LA Galaxy		Yes	Yes
Paxton Pomykal	Texas	22	FC Dallas	MLS	FC Dallas	Father/Brothers		
Konrad de la Fuente	Spain/FL	21	Barcelona B	La Liga B			Yes	Yes
Ulysses Llanez	California	21	Heerenveen (from Wolfsburg)	Eredivisie (Dutch 1)	LA Galaxy		Yes	Yes
Sebastian Soto	California/Arizona	22	Telstar (from Norwich City)	Eerste (Dutch 2)	Real Salt Lake		Yes	Yes

Table: Summary of ESPN's Big Board by Austin Lindberg (November 14, 2020)
— Selected Information

	Of 23	Of 30
# Players Top 5 Leagues	12	12
Total Minutes Top 5 Leagues (as of February 6, 2021)	15,569	15,569
Total Minutes Top 5 Leagues (grossed up)	29,007	29,007
# Players Champions/Europa League Play	10	10
# Minutes Champions/Europa League Play*	1,874	1,874
Avg. Age Top 5 Leagues @ '22 World Cup	23.3	23.3
Avg. Age All Players	25.6	25.1
# Different Leagues Represented	10	14
Highest # Players On Same Team	1	2
Attended MLS Academy	12	17
Attended IMG Academy	7	8
Played College	5	9
# Dual Nationals (Dual National)	10	16
# Lived/Trained Abroad in Youth	12	16
# Family Played (Parent or Sibling) at Least College/MLS Academy	10	13
# Family Played, Youth Abroad, or Dual National	19	26
# Born in 2H of Year w/o Family, Abroad, or Dual National	0	0
Shortest Height	5'8"	5'6"
# Taller than 6'1" (ex. Goalies)	3	3
# Black or Hispanic Origin	12	18
# Hispanic Origin	1	5

*Through Group Stage matches

Table: # of Players, Minutes, and Average Age of USMNT in Europe
(2020=Imaginary Team Only; 2021=ESPN Squad)

	1994	1998	2002	2006	2010	2014	2017	2020	2021
# Players Top 5 Leagues	1	5	8	6	12	10	4	8	12
Total Minutes Top 5 Leagues	1,857	11,025	12,652	12,312	23,265	23,042	9,156	13,507	29,007*
Avg. Age Top 5 League Players	30.0	27.0	30.0	30.3	27.3	26.5	26.0	22.5	23.3
# Players Europe	6	6	12	12	17	12	5	12	16
Total Minutes Europe	7,484	13,674	21,548	31,875	32,140	27,457	13,476	23,269	37,311*
Avg. Age Europe Players	26.5	27.3	29.0	29.2	27.2	25.9	27.0	22.2	23.7
# Players Champions/Europa League Play	0	2	0	1	3	2	1	5	10
Total Minutes Champions/Europa League Play	0	750	0	0	1,152	253	546	23	1,874
Avg. Age Champions/Europa Players	N/A	28.5	N/A	27	28.7	25.5	19.0	21.0	22.9

2020 is from Imaginary Team List. 2021 is from ESPN Big Board List and does not capture all players

*Total Minutes Top 5 Leagues and Europe for 2021 is grossed up to reflect the season is only partially completed

This is calculated by taking the number of minutes played by each player as of February 6, 2021, and adding the number of games left for each player multiplied by the average minutes per game each player has played thus far

Average age for 2021 reflects figures at the time of the 2022 World Cup